Requests for permission should be addressed to: Ascend Books, LLC, Attn: Rights and Permissions Department, 12710 Pflumm Road, Suite 200, Olathe, KS. 66062

10 9 8 7 6 5 4 3 2 1

ISBN: print book 978-0-9912756-4-9
ISBN: e-book 978-0-9912756-5-6

Library of Congress Cataloging-in-Publications Data Available Upon Request
Publisher: Bob Snodgrass
Editor: Jim Bradford
Publication Coordinator: Christine Drummond
Sales and Marketing: Lenny Cohen and Dylan Tucker
Dust Jacket and Book Design: Rob Peters

All photos courtesy of Art Davie unless otherwise indicated.

Printed in the United States of America

www.ascendbooks.com

TABLE OF CONTENTS

DEDICATION

**Dedicated to the 10 men who competed in the first
Ultimate Fighting Championship:**

Royce Gracie
Gerard Gordeau
Ken Shamrock
Kevin Rosier
Teila Tuli
Zane Frazier
Art Jimmerson
Pat Smith
Jason DeLucia
Trent Jenkins

FOREWORD
"BIG" JOHN McCARTHY

THIS has taken me 20 years, so this is no doubt coming later than it should have. But there is something that I need to say. Art Davie—thank you for providing me a chance at a life I only dreamed of. I have had such a rich life, seen so many things, gone to so many places and been part of the growth of the sport that I love, all made possible because of a dream you fought for. You took big chances, rolled the dice and created a legacy not only for you, but also for others. Some from the past, some from our present and many more who will be part of the future of MMA.

What is it about people who change the world, push evolution forward and make an impact that positively affects millions of people's lives? The real question is how do you even realize when you cross paths with one of those special few? I have always said I needed a crystal ball. Not just one that sits on your desk at work or a mantel at home. But one that is true to life, gets all cloudy, dark and scary, and then blazes out beams of light showing the future. At least the crystal ball would have been able to answer the questions of my future. It would have told me about a family from Brazil that would have a great impact in my life. And it would have also told me that the loud, smartass ad man who I first met at the Gracie Jiu-Jitsu Academy would be someone who was going to help change my life in ways I never thought possible!

Simply put, Art Davie changed my life. That's a bold statement to make, and one that over 20 years ago I never would have made. But he absolutely did, and I have always known I needed to thank him for it. Not that my life before the Ultimate Fighting Championship was bad; it absolutely was not. However, as you get older and have the ability to look back at the road traveled, you can see where the road forked, and get a very good indication of who and what helped make those changes possible.

The first time I met Art, I really didn't know what to think of the Brooklyn raised salesman who seemed like he could out talk everyone in the place, and probably sell ice to Eskimos. Art is a fast talker who can capture your attention with bold statements and slick lines, but there is no denying that he is smart. Maybe not MIT smart, but definitely smart at what he does, and street smart as hell. He can read people well, and knows how to use what I call "Verbal Jiu-jitsu" as well as anyone. He is a black belt with words. He possesses the qualities that you find in very successful people. Art doesn't take "no" for an answer, and works tirelessly to get to where he wants to go before anyone else can get there.

Over the years I came to know Art well. In one way or another we worked together debating about fighters, writing rules, giving nicknames or just kicking back in his office talking about fights. Art gave me the nickname "Big John." He wasn't the first to say it—that would be my mom. But he was the first to push it in every introduction he made, and eventually had announcers following his lead.

Many people take credit for starting the Ultimate Fighting Championship, or are given credit for it by other misinformed individuals. Even more say they were there, or were part of the circus that finally came to fruition on November 12, 1993. Well I can tell you that I was there, I was part of that circus and I can emphatically state that I had nothing to do with the beginning of the UFC. But I know who did, and the man at the top of that list is Art Davie.

The story you are about to read is true. None of the names were changed to protect the innocent, and fortunately none of the names were changed to protect the clueless. You will learn the exact involvement of key players, because Art needed them all to pull off one of the most amazing feats in modern day sports. Though a dream by any standard, Art was able to create a sport that in 20 years has become common around the world. And the very company that he created is now worth approximately $3.5 billion! Think about every other major sport on the planet, and they all have a long history dating back decades and even centuries.

Twenty years ago I was listening to Art talk about the fighters who were going to be part of the very first UFC. He compared them to guys like Chuck Yeager, stepping into the X-15 rocket plane, and attempting to break the speed of sound. Art dramatically labeled them as guys testing the outer boundaries of the martial arts, and said that they would someday be remembered for changing the martial arts in a way that was never seen before. Art was right. If not for guys like Teila Tuli, Gerard Gordeau, Kevin Rosier, Zane Frazier, Trent Jenkins, Jason DeLucia, Ken Shamrock, Pat Smith, Art Jimmerson and Royce Gracie taking that first step, we never would have heard of Georges St-Pierre, Randy Couture, Anderson Silva, BJ Penn and Chuck Liddell.

As we get older, we hopefully get wiser. And we probably get a little more sentimental about life, and what part we have taken in the grand scheme of things. I know that in the end, my hope is that I did enough to make my children proud. I hope that I went about doing things the right way, even if that meant that there was going to be a lot of hard work involved in getting things to their rightful place. One of the best and truest statements I have ever heard spoken about Art and the UFC was actually said by Art himself. When he was interviewed about the 20th anniversary of the UFC, he said, "Long after I'm gone, MMA will still be around."

Yes it will, Art. Oh, yes, it will!

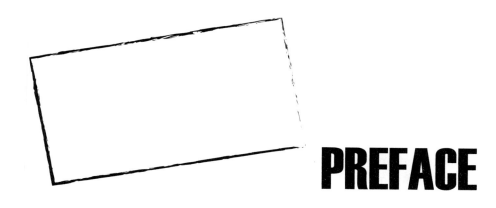

PREFACE

THERE IS A TIDE IN THE AFFAIRS OF MEN, WHICH, WHEN TAKEN AT THE FLOOD, LEADS ON TO FORTUNE...
— WILLIAM SHAKESPEARE

THIS is the inside, behind-the-scenes, no bullshit story of the most important Ultimate Fighting Championship event in history: the first UFC. Yes, the very first one—held in Denver, on November 12, 1993. When finally unleashed on an unsuspecting public, it gave birth to the sport that became known as mixed martial arts (MMA). It was of course the most significant event in UFC and MMA history because it was the first. If it had failed, there would be no UFC today. Moreover, having been the first, it still stands as the most difficult and unlikely to have ever been staged. Without a doubt, if it had flopped, the entire genre would never have been born, not as we know it anyway.

Despite being just a loose cannon advertising executive, I truly believed that I could pull this off. As you'll discover in this book, I enlisted those who gave me the credibility and the money that I knew I lacked, and so desperately needed, to make my dream a reality.

Now I'm not going to tell you that I invented mixed match fighting— taking different styles from the various martial arts and combat sports and throwing them together. Far from it.

I was simply the guy who knew that it would consistently work on a major scale, and then went about trying to prove it.

How the UFC was created, and who really built it will be disclosed in this book; nothing will be held back. You will see what part I played, and what parts were played by the talented people who joined this circus.

As I said, all true.

The creation of the first Ultimate Fighting Championship evolved over four years, from a modest idea that I had for an advertising client, into a quest that consumed my entire life. The UFC was not pre-destined to be a success, nor even happen, and the rejections and roadblocks seemed endless. I knew where I wanted to go—I just had no road map on how to get there, or even if it was possible to reach my destination.

Now, when anyone writes history, either from a personal viewpoint— or more objectively as a journalist or historian—they write through the prism of their perspective. This may include any number of small biases, as well as major axes they want to grind (certainly journalists and historians can be accused of this as well). So, it's important for you as the reader to get a handle on this writer's angle—my perspective. In this case, who am I, and where am I coming from in writing this account of the creation of the Ultimate Fighting Championship?

I can answer this by stating at the outset that, first and foremost, I was a true believer. There was no doubt in my mind that people wanted to have the eternal question answered: Who was really the world's greatest fighter? Making money was very important to me, but secondary. I felt that the UFC would become a hugely successful franchise, but only if we followed this vision, and kept in search of this answer. Some of the people simply saw the UFC as a means to an end, not as an end in itself—which it always was to me.

Also, let me again be clear that this is a tell-all book. That means I'm going to let you know what really happened, especially my fuck-ups and the fuck-ups of those who rode with me. When you go this route, you're bound to step on toes, and paint some of the major players in a less-than-favorable light. So be it.

I have done my best to give credit where credit is due, even in the case of those who I thought were jerks, thieves and assholes.

And as you read this book, you'll discover that some previously unknown people played a major role in contributing to and ultimately helping launch the UFC. It's my hope that their anonymity will now fade, just as the exaggerated and false claims of others will be exposed. But that is for you to decide. All that I can do is reveal the true story of what really happened—as I lived it.

But, let me say it again clearly: I did not do it alone. It took the sweat, labor and outright love of many people to make it all happen. I was the chef, who working without a recipe, combined all of the necessary ingredients to turn them into a finished meal. Without these ingredients, nothing would have happened. But without the chef, the ingredients never would have combined into something great.

This book is everything you wanted to know about how the first Ultimate Fighting Championship came to be, told by the only person who was there from the very beginning: Me.

— *Art Davie, 2014*

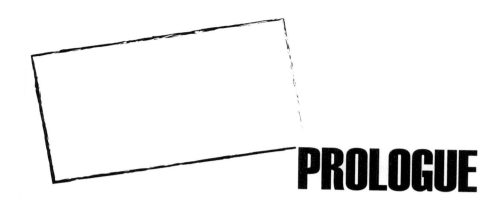

PROLOGUE

THE PEOPLE ARE A MANY-HEADED BEAST
— HORACE, Epistles, Bk I, epistle i, L, 76

A peroxide blonde with tits the size of grapefruits corrals me.

"Hey, honey," she says to me in a voice that sounds like she mail ordered it from Yazoo City, Mississippi, and seems jarringly out of place here in Colorado.

"Honey, are you with the show?"

I look over at her and her boyfriend, who is missing more than a few teeth, and say, "Uh...I'm...uh...just a salesman."

She looks confused by this. And the fact that I'm wearing a monkey suit flusters her big time—like I'm the ring announcer or something.

"Are we gonna see some ass kickin' tonight?"

She's now grabbing at the sleeve of my tuxedo jacket with her pudgy fingers, and continues on.

"I hope somebody gets fucked up."

Her joy-boy grins at me in a slack-jawed, dumb-ass sort of way.

I want to get as far away from these two as quickly possible. Without making eye contact, I say tersely, with pursed lips, "I just hope no one dies tonight."

This stops her cold, and the idiot grin evaporates from the boyfriend's face.

I keep moving—continually circling our specially constructed eight-sided fighting area, which is enclosed by chain-link fence, and elevated off the arena floor. I'm obsessively double- and triple-checking for exactly what, I'm not sure.

Everyone keeps calling it a "ring," but it's not a ring, it's a cage. I just don't want to refer to this thing as a cage, and make the brutality that I'm certain is about to unfold seem, well, even more brutal to the critics that no doubt will be coming our way. I still have no idea what to call this beautiful monstrosity, but that's the least of my concerns right now. I don't even know what to call the sport that we're about to unleash tonight.

Standing on the floor, in the center of McNichols Sports Arena in Denver, I can't believe that my four years of hard work and big dreams are about to become a reality. I also can't believe that I was able to rent the home of the Denver Nuggets for $4,000. Tonight's world premiere requires a big stage, and while this isn't Madison Square Garden or Caesar's Palace, it's a very respectable, if slightly worn, NBA building.

The first two fighters in the tournament are introduced, and the fans, mostly white, young and rowdy, immediately heat up. One of our Pay-Per-View TV commentators, football Hall of Famer Jim Brown, says, "I'm kind of worried about the crowd." No shit. They're on the verge of becoming the world's biggest mosh pit—minus the rhythm and civility. These people have come to see blood, as well as a few broken bones and major concussions for good measure.

Standing here, despite all of the worries and chaos, I feel like I've climbed to base camp on Mt. Everest. I'm juiced on adrenaline, but I know that I have another 9,000 feet to go. It's been a wild ride for my partners and me. We're a motley collection of heroes, villains, fools and crazies. And now all of us are poised and waiting.

Ravenous wolves eyeing a feast of meat and blood have nothing on this crowd. They're staring intently at these two monsters who are standing opposite each other, and waiting to be unleashed in our opening fight. Absolutely none of us—the fighters included—are exactly sure what is about to occur.

Depending on your vantage point Teila Tuli is either wearing a kilt, a plaid skirt or some kind of native costume from the Pacific Islands.

This big, fat Hawaiian is so massive at 420 pounds, that regular fighting shorts aren't an option. I should know, because we searched Denver in vain trying to find a pair.

"Excuse me, ma'am, do you have size 60 waist boxing trunks?"

He has a neck on him that rivals one of those Tosa fighting dogs from Japan. Tuli is so heavy, he walks bowlegged, and with his feet jutting outwards from carrying his massive girth.

I was told that he'd been kicked out of sumo in Japan for tossing a reporter through a glass wall or some such hooliganism. When I heard that, I immediately thought, "I like this guy already."

I had planned to open up this tournament to every single motherfucker who could fight, whether they had a black belt or a black record. Guys exactly like Tuli. One of my confidants in all of this craziness, the Academy Award nominated screenwriter John Milius, said it to me best, "This is the search for the real Superman."

Well, perhaps Superman can come in all shapes and sizes, and maybe wears a Polynesian-looking sarong around his enormous waist, instead of a red cape around his neck.

Before the fight, Tuli had asked me if he could pick up his opponents, and throw them over the top of the fence and onto the concrete arena floor. He claimed that he'd tossed loads of guys in street brawls back in Hawaii. If someone were stupid enough to get into it with him, Tuli would just pick the dude up, and lob him like a missile. Fight over. The traditional martial arts bozos would never have booked a sumo guy. But this isn't a traditional martial arts event, not even close. This is the Ultimate Fighting Championship.

As Tuli waits for the bell, I can see that he's licking his lips nervously, and sweating like a barnyard pig. Whatever confidence Tuli had, now seems to be leaking out of his pores under the hot, white lights overhead.

Opposite him, Gerard Gordeau is standing calmly, like a professional assassin. The only thing now missing from this stone-cold Dutchman is his trademark cigarette, dangling from the corner of his mouth. Reminiscent of classic Humphrey Bogart, but with a level of iciness and menace that Bogey could never hope to muster.

"No problem, Art Davie," is the emotionless mantra that I always get from him—no matter what I ask.

In scruffy, well-worn karate pants and no top, Gordeau is a lanky, skinhead-looking Savate champion with badly inked tats. He's rumored to carry a pistol in his belt, and a razor in his sock back home. I've been told by my contacts in the Netherlands that he's the King of the Streets in Amsterdam—a muscle man for the brothels and the porn show owners. At 6-foot-5 and 216 pounds, Gordeau is all bone and gristle. He's lean, with razor sharp elbows, and long, ropy muscles. When he enters the fighting area (ring, cage, whatever), Gordeau rapidly thrusts stiff-arm salutes to the four corners of the arena. Fuck! Bob Meyrowitz, the owner of my Pay-Per-View partner, Semaphore Entertainment Group, who is helping to finance this fun, is very proudly Jewish. What can Meyrowitz be thinking now as he watches from his home in New York, after seeing this seeming display of white power, Aryan superiority or whatever the fuck it is—and in our very first bout?

Our Brazilian referee, Joao Alberto Barreto, gives the two men the signal to fight, and the bell rings. Gordeau immediately claims the center, poised to strike, while Tuli circles to his left, cautiously and seemingly without a real plan. After about 15 seconds, Tuli finally rushes in, head down, like a bull. Gordeau backpedals and pumps jabs that graze Tuli's massive skull. Then in a flash, Gordeau catches Tuli with a short right uppercut that viciously snaps the Hawaiian's head back, throws him off balance, and sends him careening into the fence. The crowd noise is a solid wall of sound. I can't hear my own thoughts.

The hippo drops hard and awkwardly onto his humongous ass. Gordeau, lightning-quick, steps up and throws a masterful kick to Tuli's face. It lands flush on his mouth with the sickening sound of a melon being struck by a ball-peen hammer. The power of the blow forces Tuli's lips back into his teeth, and shears off one of his incisors at the gums, which goes flying past our commentators and into the crowd. Tuli turns his head involuntarily, having just been hit with the equivalent of a baseball bat swung at full force by someone connecting with a fastball. Gordeau, methodical and in full control, doesn't let his opponent get up. He re-sets his feet, waits for Tuli to turn back towards him, and at the perfectly timed moment, throws a crushing right hand with the knuckles extended, that lands smack on the Hawaiian's right eyeball. There's a crimson explosion, as blood streams down Tuli's chest, and sprays the ref. His face is now a grotesque mask, and his eye is beyond swollen.

Barreto jumps in with his hands flapping, and he's signaling time out. Time Out! What the fuck is this time out? This is supposed to be a fight to the finish. Tuli tries to get to his feet, but he moves like a man caught in molasses. Gordeau now smells the kill. He leans forward, and then tries to push the ref away to get at his target again. Barreto stands his ground and backs Gordeau off, but is not at all sure as to what to do next.

The crowd is on its feet, simultaneously bubbling with excitement and boiling with anger. Stray shrieks of horror and delight fill the sticky air. I yell for the ref to let the fight continue, but he speaks Portuguese, not English. Only the fighter or his corner can stop the fight, not the referee. My business partner Rorion Gracie and I made this perfectly clear in the rules meeting the night before. No exceptions! So what if Tuli's eye is leaking blood like a broken faucet? This is what the people paid to see—real fighting with real consequences.

Now all hell breaks loose, and a flood of bodies quickly surrounds the outside of the fence: members of the fighter's corners, medical personnel, Rorion, me and God knows who else. Barreto keeps talking to Tuli in Portuguese which, of course, draws no reply. I'm not sure that this fallen behemoth would understand English right now. His brains have to be scrambled. Then Rorion starts shouting at the Tuli camp, "Is he ready to go? Is he ready to go?" They all ignore him, avoiding eye contact and staying silent.

In this mad confusion, I find Tuli's slightly less enormous brother, and grab him firmly by the arm. "Can he go again?" I bark. "Does he want to keep fighting or not?"

"No man," he tells me flatly. "He's had enough."

It's all over in 26 seconds. Those two savage shots absolutely destroyed the 420-lb. sumo wrestler, and evaporated his will to fight.

Gordeau's right hand is broken, and hangs there limply, like a sack of nuts and bolts. The swelling is just starting to occur, and it's horrific in terms of speed and size. Trust me—hitting a man in the head with a bare fist is like punching a bowling ball. Fragments of Tuli's shattered tooth are lodged in the pale, white flesh of Gordeau's right foot. The rest of that displaced incisor is likely still out there, among the emptied beer cups and discarded hot dog wrappers on the McNichols Arena floor.

Gordeau is unbelievably tough, and he'd better be. His next fight starts in under an hour.

Everyone is blown away by the savagery of the moment, no one more so than me. Another one of our TV commentators, Bill Wallace, a former kickboxing world champion, goes all pale and stuttering on-air at the sight of Gordeau's vicious kick to Tuli's face. Judging from his behavior, he's never seen a real fight before.

The owners and execs of our main sponsor, Gold's Gym, had flown in to Denver from Los Angeles for the event, with their wives in tow. Dressed to the nines in evening clothes, they all looked like they were going to see a Mr. Universe bodybuilding show. I put them in the front row, as close to the action as possible. When Tuli got poleaxed, the shattered ruins of his tooth flew right over their heads. I saw that they were all sick to their stomachs—green at the gills.

Two of the wives got up and left, right then and there. The entire group was gone by the third fight. Goodbye Gold's Gym. I never saw them again. That was the end of our sponsorship. But I didn't even care.

After that first fight, I knew. We had just spawned something truly special, and unlike anything that anyone had ever seen before. Suddenly without a single doubt or worry, I tell myself right then and there, the Ultimate Fighting Championship is going to be a monster hit. I can smell the bloodlust of young guys all over the planet. This is fucking real, and I fucking love it. And we still have the rest of the tournament to go—the night has just begun. God forgive me!

CHAPTER 1
THE·VERY·BEGINNING

A GREAT FLAME FOLLOWS A LITTLE SPARK.
— DANTE, Paradiso, Canto I, L, 34

SOMETIMES I'm asked if I was ever a fighter.

The answer is a big "no."

I was never a great athlete, serious martial artist, or bad-ass of any kind.

I wasn't the sturdiest Marine on a 20-mile hike or the fastest man through the obstacle course. It took me two tries to get a Rifle Marksman's badge. And while I boxed a bit as a kid, I was no big deal. I didn't get a belt studying taekwondo with Jhoon Rhee when I was stationed in the service in Washington D.C., and I never could make any real headway with my Muay Thai classes in North Hollywood. But I did have a few experiences with fighting that really shaped my life.

A lot of guys put on the gloves where I grew up in Brooklyn, New York in the 1950s. If you were Italian, Jewish or Irish, then you had a father, brother or uncle who boxed. So that meant that you boxed. It was a fact of life. It was inevitable that you got into the ring at some point. My father always told the story of being a teenage 115-lb. bantamweight and thrust into a bout against a kid who weighed 150 lb.

My old man repeated the story a dozen times to my cousins and me that he took a shellacking in that bout. But he said that he was determined to land just one good punch and when he did, he felt vindicated. Something about stick-to-itiveness and persistence in the face of overwhelming odds was the lesson that he wanted to impart. Tenacity. The story was just the sort of thing that you'd hear from the lips of a movie character in the 1940s—played by the likes of John Garfield or Jimmy Cagney. Anyway, it must have made an impression, because it didn't take a lot to get me into the Catholic Youth Organization ring at St. Thomas Aquinas where I took my pugilistic lessons in the early 1960s.

Actually, I wasn't too bad. The coach said that while I wasn't particularly fast, I seemed to be a natural counter-puncher. I did feel that as soon as my opponent committed and threw a punch, in that split-second, I could see an opening that (to me) looked huge. In these situations in the gym, I could tag my guy as often as not. Where my skill fell short was if my opponent had very quick reflexes. Anyway, there I was weighing about 145 lb.—a natural welterweight or junior welterweight. My boxing hero was the great world champion Carmine Basilio. I was the same height and weight as the famous Italian-American onion farmer from Conestoga, New York, which gave me both confidence and inspiration.

As a small guy, I was susceptible to the allure of lifting weights, and I screwed it all up by making the decision to get bigger. I soon discovered a regimen of weight training, and drinking two quarts of

Photo courtesy of Davie family

milk a day. In *Iron Man* magazine I had read that I too could bulk up by utilizing only a few exercises done three times a week, like the 20 rep squat, bench press, the bent over row and the behind-the-neck press.

After four months on this routine, I gained 30 lb. and not all of it muscle. But I could

Here I'm bench pressing 235 lb. in an effort to get bigger. By working out and adding more protein and calories to my diet, I went from 145 lb. to 182 lb. in a few months.

bench press 245 lb., squat a single rep with 360 lb., and thought I was hot shit now that I had bulked up. I wasn't hot anything, and I had slowed down enough to become a stationary target. Now, I had to box with guys who were 6-feet tall with a 75-inch reach, who weighed 190 lb. before cutting down to 175. This was a formula for disaster, which wasn't long in coming.

I got in the ring with a tall, rangy guy who was as fast as a cobra. I couldn't have hit him if I had a government model .45 with me. I took a beating—a good one. The second disaster came in the gym with a heavyweight, about 6-foot and 210 lb., who invited me to spar with him wearing 16-ounce gloves and headgear. He hit me with a short uppercut to the solar plexus so hard that I didn't lose consciousness, but I wished I had. I became, for all intents and purposes, paralyzed.

I looked comic in there as I metamorphosed into a mummy, and then just toppled to the canvas, not to rise until my opponent and a trainer lifted me up and dragged my bulked-up carcass back to the corner. There was no stool, but they quickly realized that I couldn't bend to sit anyway. I had stiffened up like a dried mackerel, so they deposited me flat on my back onto a nearby bench. I had no business being in the ring with anyone who wasn't a lightweight. After that experience, I took a well-earned sabbatical, and didn't put the gloves on again until years later.

My most memorable experience with fighting took place in the summer of 1965, and there were no boxing gloves involved. My father and uncle had bought adjoining cottages on Peconic Bay, out on Long Island, New York in the late 1950s. The place was great, and I spent a lot of golden summers there. The cottages were modest knotty pine little houses, and most of the kids in that world were nice, middle-class morons like me. We fished, swam and ran around like little wild men.

I had a good pal there named Johnny Nichols, a tall, rangy Irish kid with a wicked sense of humor—a natural comedian. One day he showed up with a thick-necked moose whose name I don't remember, or perhaps have suppressed. The kid was a classmate of Johnny's in high school, and was the varsity wrestling stud. Johnny brought him around, and the three of us stood there shooting the shit close to the water's edge on a hot July afternoon.

Johnny said, "Hey, Art's a boxer. He's been training for the Golden Gloves."

It wasn't entirely true. I was a boxer, sort of, but kept putting off signing up for the Gloves.

The grappler looked at me from under his pronounced brow ridges and said, "Oh really?"

He didn't look too impressed. The guy said that he wrestled at 76 kilos, and that he came in second in the state championships or something. He was four or five inches taller than me, and I was smart enough to realize that his walking around weight, before wrestling season, was probably 185 lb. We got to talking about our respective sports, and then the conversation turned to "what could a wrestler do versus a boxer?" Or maybe it was me, with my big mouth, who said something first. Actually, it was definitely me.

"Yeah, you know if a boxer like "Hurricane" Carter got in the ring with a wrestler, he'd land a left hook before the wrestler could do anything."

I went on and on and on. I should have kept my pie hole shut, because before I knew it, the moose was suggesting that we "spar." Johnny, my buddy, was having a field day with this, and kept cracking with the jokes. But his thick-necked friend, whose trapezius began at the bottom of his ears and connected directly to his middle deltoids, lunged at me quickly, and said, "Well, what would you do if I went for your legs?"

I jumped back like I'd been jabbed with a lit cigar. But now my temper and my adrenaline were up.

"Well, this is what you'd be looking at, boss," I said as I flicked out three jabs as fast as I could get my fist, shoulder, left arm and chest to cooperate.

The gauntlet had been thrown. With Johnny the Comedian acting as our improv ref, the wrestler and I squared off. I got set and figured I'd smack him in the nose with a sharp jab—and make sure to twist my fist at the end of the punch for more power. And then I'd hook off the jab. I'd been practicing this move in the gym, and thought I had a potent little combo going for me.

Of course, the best-laid plans of mice, men and bulked-up silly welterweights are meant to go awry. I threw the left jab alright. The moose was quick and pulled his head just out of range. The next thing I felt was the sensation of my left hook just barely ruffling his crew cut pate as my fist sailed harmlessly over his head. He shot a quick double-leg takedown, and just like that, I was down on the hot sand with 76 plus kilos of muscle and bone on top of me.

Suddenly the wrestler was squeezing my head between his hard skull and his shoulder, and using the gorilla power of his overdeveloped trapezius muscle. Everything went fuzzy, and without realizing it, I was yelling, "Uncle!" It was all over but the post-fight analysis. Johnny dropped the jokes and was really nice about smoothing things over between us. He said we were both sportsmen, but I didn't feel like a sportsman. I felt like a fool. We shook hands, and there were a lot of, "No hard feelings," and, "Nah, you're good man," sort of bullshit babble.

I'd had my ass kicked, but it didn't hurt—my pride did though. The muscle-head grappler had clearly outmaneuvered me. I felt like a fish out of water. All of my hours in the gym throwing punches counted for nothing as soon as I was flat on my back. I had absolutely no idea how to defend myself once I was taken off of my feet, and out of my element. All I could do was ask myself, "What just happened?"

CHAPTER 2

THE WORLD'S BEST FIGHTER

ALL MEN DREAM: BUT NOT EQUALLY. THOSE WHO DREAM BY NIGHT IN THE DUSTY RECESSES OF THEIR MINDS WAKE IN THE DAY TO FIND THAT IT WAS VANITY: BUT THE DREAMERS OF THE DAY ARE DANGEROUS MEN, FOR THEY MAY ACT THEIR DREAM WITH OPEN EYES, TO MAKE IT POSSIBLE.
— T.E. LAWRENCE, Seven Pillars of Wisdom

FOR the record, I was born in Brooklyn, New York, went to Catholic grade school (Good Shepherd), bounced through three high schools in four years (including two years at New York Military Academy where, in the fall and winter of 1962, Donald Trump was my roommate) and bummed my way through one year at St. John's University and a year at Pace College. Not waiting for the draft, I enlisted in the Marine Corps in 1966 and spent three-and-a-half years on active duty, including 11 months and nine days in the Republic of Vietnam. In 1970, I was honorably discharged as a sergeant with the Navy Achievement Medal (with combat 'V').

After the service, I was a car salesman in the Georgetown section of Washington, D.C. The first car I ever sold was to the Vietnam anti-war Senator from Wisconsin, and founder of Earth Day, Gaylord Nelson. I worked as a field counselor with street gangs for the Youth Services Agency in New York City for two years and ended up owning a car dealership in San Diego (Toyack Motors), one of the first new car discount brokerages in the U.S. I became known in San Diego at that time for a series of commercials I did where I performed my own stunts: jumping from a 10 story building onto an air bag, dangling from a helicopter, being thrown over a parked car, getting set on fire and my big finale, getting shot for real with a .357 magnum while wearing a bulletproof vest. I was always a stubborn, independent individualist who went his own way. Like my father before me—tenacious and a bit of a loner.

By 1980, I was working for Dennis Webb Advertising in San Diego, who had handled my business when I owned my car dealership. A year later, I was co-owner of an ad agency, Fiocco/Davie Incorporated, which I started with my close friend Mark Fiocco. We were both salesmen who loved to pitch, and who loved the "big idea." Mark and I decided to part ways when I wanted to move to Los Angeles thinking I could make it big in a bigger market. Mark's roots and family were in San Diego and he couldn't see living in Hollywood. Fair enough.

Photo courtesy of Lawrence Liodice

New York Military Academy with my mother and sister on a visit in 1963. I'm in full dress uniform for a Sunday parade. Note that I have no chevrons on my arm; I'm just a private.

We dissolved the agency amicably, and I went to work for J&P Marketing, which was a promotion marketing agency. Jim Plumb, the owner and president, had developed package goods manufacturers and distributors as the foundation of his business. Companies like Star-Kist Tuna, New York Seltzer and Wisdom Imports were J&P's meat and potatoes.

Wisdom Imports was a liquor and beer distributor that specialized in imported Mexican beer for the U.S. market. Their three big brands were Tecate, Bohemia and Carta Blanca. Our big October promotion for Bohemia was a Halloween campaign called, "Boo-hemia," which sounded kind of goofy, but was a successful multi-year campaign.

But by the fall of 1989, Jim had maxed out what he was doing for Wisdom and was concerned he might lose their account. In an effort to inject a level of freshness into their promotion campaigns, Jim brought me along to a meeting with Wisdom and introduced me as his "idea guy."

"Art's a real creative type," Jim told the category manager on our arrival. "This is the man you want to meet."

The truth was that I had nothing.

Jim was taking a shot in the dark by bringing me along, but he figured what the hell, maybe I could spitball something they would like. The Tecate brand's appeal was focused on young guys in their 20s. After the meeting at Wisdom Imports, Jim told me to sketch out some ideas our agency had not developed before. "Get really creative. Go big," he instructed. Jim couldn't afford to lose their business.

I started thinking about sporting events where we could create some cross-promotional opportunities. I had a precedent in mind. In 1948, Bill Cayton (who later became a noted boxing historian as well as Mike Tyson's manager) was in the advertising business, and came up with a brilliant idea for a show to sell Vaseline brand hair tonic. It was called "Greatest Fights of the Century," and featured old boxing matches dating back to the 1890s, repackaged for the post World War II TV audience. The show scored huge ratings and Vaseline sales skyrocketed.

At the time of the meeting with Wisdom, I

Photo courtesy of Art Davie

Being interviewed right before filming a TV commercial for my car dealership. Performing my own stunts, I'm about to be shot with a .357 magnum wearing a bulletproof vest. The piece of tape on my tie was the shooter's target.

was taking weekly instruction at a Muay Thai gym in North Hollywood, having moved on from the ill-fated boxing venture of my youth. Working out there was more than enough to convince me that Thai leg kicks were fucking devastating, and that with my tight hamstrings, I would never be a great kicker.

It was an outstanding workout though, and it gave me a real appreciation for a sport that I had previously known very little about. During the month of November 1989, I kept obsessively thinking about Wisdom Imports, "The World's Greatest Fights," Vaseline, Tecate Beer and the question that I posed to Mr. Muscle-head Grappler 24 years earlier on Peconic Bay, "What would a wrestler do versus a boxer?" Perhaps being at a Muay Thai gym triggered another memory from the 1960s—about one of my fellow Marines and a story he told me that involved an R&R trip to Thailand.

In 1969, I was stationed at Red Beach in Danang, Vietnam. There, I became friends with Jimmy from Chicago, who had been a star football player in high school. Along with fellow jarhead Tommy from Los Angeles, we'd wander over to the Republic of Korea Marines (called "ROKs") encampment to watch them do their taekwondo workouts. All three of us loved boxing and thought it was amazing to see these tough little guys go through their highly regimented striking drills. How they would do against a quick boxer in a real fight was a constant topic of debate between the three of us.

Photo courtesy of Art Davie

Jimmy went to Bangkok on R&R without Tommy or me, and came back to regale us with wild tales of debauchery. Aside from all of his love 'em and leave 'em stories, Jimmy also told us about a nightclub in Bangkok he had gone to with a bunch of other Marines, and the mixed match fight he'd watched there between a Thai boxer

Sergeant Davie at Red Beach, Danang, Vietnam in October 1969.

and an Indian wrestler. To hear Jimmy tell it, the Indian wrestler outweighed the little Thai guy by at least 40 lb., and they all thought he was going to get slaughtered.

But with his finely tuned Muay Thai, the local kept using devastating thigh kicks to keep the Indian at bay, and slowly wore him down. Then, he unloaded with his fists and elbows to knock his opponent out. We could not stop talking about this for a month. So maybe a boxer couldn't beat a wrestler, but it now looked like a Muay Thai fighter could. What about a ROK marine versus a judo black belt from Japan? A karate guy against a huge sumo wrestler? It provoked endless discussions and arguments. Could Bruce Lee beat Muhammad Ali?

I now wondered if perhaps Wisdom Imports would be interested in answering this question. Maybe, just maybe, this was exactly the type of cross-promotional opportunity that they would love, and would in turn help them sell a lot more Tecate beer. I knew this was a long shot, as Wisdom would have to fund an entirely new sport, instead of just sponsoring an existing event. But Jim Plumb had instructed me to "go big," so I was doing just that. If pairing fighting with the right product sponsor had struck gold for Bill Cayton, then why not for me?

I put my secretary, Joy, to work pulling articles for me on fighting, martial arts, boxing, wrestling, kung fu, Sambo—anything at all that I might be able to use. I called on Joe Kaufenberg, known as "T-shirt Joe," a kickboxing promoter in Los Angeles, and Karyn Turner who promoted kickboxing in Denver, with Coors beer as her sponsor. What I was looking for was anyone who had promoted a mixed match fighting event. Joe and Karyn were very friendly, and both tried to be helpful, but neither had ever considered what I was talking about. What would be the rules? Who would fight? Would this even be allowed?

One of my main inspirations was Pankration from the Ancient Olympiad, a sport described by scholars as a combination of striking and grappling in which anything outside of eye gouging and biting was allowed. It was introduced into the Greek Olympic Games in 648 BC. Within four Olympics it became wildly successful and quickly joined horseracing as the most popular sport in the entire Ancient Olympiad, dominating the Decathlon, boxing and wrestling.

This was an epic event which had spawned legendary athletes like Polydamas, a Thessalian who was the victor in the 93rd Olympiad (408 BC), and whose statue graced the Altis, the sacred grove of Zeus. I really loved the idea of bringing the imagery of Antiquity to a present day fighting event.

I knew that there were a number of modern examples of mixed match fighting, such as Muhammad Ali vs. Antonio Inoki, Gene LeBell vs. Milo Savage, and Andre the Giant vs. Chuck Wepner. Regardless if those fights were real (shoots) or fake (works), they did establish a precedent I could study. However, they served as nothing more than oddball one-offs. I was attempting to create an event for Wisdom Imports, which could lead to a viable franchise.

In my research, I discovered that Japan was quickly gaining traction as the home of strong-style pro wrestling, which blurred the lines between fact and fiction. Fighters would beat the shit out of each other, but the winner was predetermined, except when it was not.

And, of course, I knew that there were countless backyard, backroom and back-alley, no-holds-barred fights, where literally anything and everything would often be allowed. But these fights were never intended for public consumption, instead staged quietly throughout history for a select few, usually with gambling as the motivating factor.

As a marine, I had been given some rudimentary hand-to-hand combat instruction at Camp Lejeune in 1967. My memories of this experience prompted me to unearth the survey that the Department of the United States Navy had undertaken in the 1950s to figure out which martial arts would be the most useful for infantry troops in unarmed combat. They hired Joe Begala, who in 1943 as a Lieutenant Commander in the Navy had authored *Hand-to-Hand Combat*, which both the Navy and Marine Corps used as a training manual. In addition to his military service in World War II, Begala was the legendary wrestling coach at Kent State University, who had first taken the job in 1929. In the 1950s survey, Begala looked at combining elements of judo, jiu-jitsu and karate, as well as boxing into a mixed fighting style, which could be used in real life and death situations. But as far as I could tell, no tournaments or events were ever organized using these fighting techniques.

Pressing on with my research, I found the story of the first great boxing champion, John L. Sullivan and his training with William Muldoon. Of course, I knew all about the Boston Strong Boy, one of pugilism's all-time greats, but this tale was new to me. In 1889, Sullivan hired Muldoon, a Greco-Roman wrestling champion, physical culturist, and later the first chairman of the New York State Athletic Commission, to get him ready for his upcoming London Prize Ring Rules bare-knuckle world title bout against Jake Kilrain. It was Muldoon's job to whip the drunken, overweight and seemingly washed-up 30-year-old back into championship shape, which at times seemed a near impossibility.

As part of the conditioning regimen, Muldoon often grappled with Sullivan, and to his shock and utter dismay, Sullivan, who famously claimed that he could "lick any man in the house," discovered that he was helpless in the clinch and on the ground against the wrestler. Ultimately, the hard work with Muldoon paid off, as Sullivan defeated Kilrain in 75 rounds. Muldoon had known exactly what he was doing all along, despite the naysayers—Sullivan at times included. And Muldoon had also known that to beat the world heavyweight champion of boxing, you have to tie him up, and take him down.

The man who defeated Sullivan for the heavyweight boxing championship in 1892 was James J. Corbett, known as "Gentleman Jim" for his dress and manners. On multiple occasions, Corbett trained with Ernest Roeber, who held both the European and United States Greco-Roman Wrestling Heavyweight Championship. Despite being known as one of the cleverest boxers of his era, Corbett found that before he could even land a punch, Roeber would easily take him down to the mat, apply a hold, and make him yell "Uncle." Later Corbett said, "In a mixed match between a boxer and a wrestler, the wrestler will win nine times out of 10."

No one that I could find, however, attempted to merge boxing and wrestling into a new hybrid sport, other than the occasional curiosity bout.

The year before I began developing my pitch for Wisdom Imports, in 1988, I saw the movie *Bloodsport*, in which Jean-Claude Van Damme fights in a secretive Hong Kong tournament known as the "Kumite." The film was supposedly based on the real-life experiences of American martial artist Frank Dux. But in digging around, I discovered that if Dux had a black belt in anything, it was self-promotion, and that this supposed "true story" was highly questionable. If there had been a "Kumite," it was either a full contact karate event, or an underground fighting syndicate held in a few Asian countries. It certainly wasn't what the movie portrayed: an organized tournament in which fighters from around the world competed while using a wide array of styles and disciplines, sometimes in a battle to the death.

The closest thing that I could find to ancient Olympic Pankration, and to what I aspired to create for Wisdom Imports, was vale tudo. Literally translated from Portuguese to English as "everything goes," vale tudo wasn't so much a fighting style as a meeting place for fighting styles. Popularized in the 1920s in Brazil, vale tudo often took place at circuses across the country, where two fighters would meet in a bout with no or very few rules. Sometimes the contests would be pre-arraigned and advertised, other times they came as the result of an open challenge to the audience by the travelling circus "champion." It was very similar conceptually to what was occurring in the same era at circuses throughout the U.S., although those bouts were often referred to as catch-as-catch-can or no-holds-barred, and were usually grappling based.

The thing about vale tudo though was that it was never organized on a larger scale. There was no set of rules universally agreed upon, no universally recognized champions. There was never an official vale tudo sanctioning body, governing agency, or wide scale promotion. Vale tudo could take place under a circus tent, in a boxing ring at a huge stadium, on a mat in a martial arts school or beneath the sun on a sandy Brazilian beach.

Sometimes vale tudo fights were massive events, with thousands of tickets sold, and millions watching on Brazilian television. Other times, they were held quietly in private, by invitation only. In essence, they were fights based upon the agreement and willingness of the two participants. My style against your style to see who is the better man.

Having just read up on vale tudo, and its place in Brazil, my secretary Joy gave me an article that she'd recently found, which was from the September 1989 issue of *Playboy* magazine. Written by Pat Jordan and entitled "Bad," it detailed the first family of jiu-jitsu, the Gracies, how they had perfected their own brand of martial arts in their native Brazil, and then brought it to Southern California. According to Jordan, they were absolutely unbeatable, or so the Gracies claimed.

What really caught my attention in the article was the open challenge that the Gracie family had issued to the entire martial arts community. Your style against our style, your $100,000 against ours—winner take all. A real fight and we'll kick your ass every time. Or, we'll choke you out or torque the hell out of your limbs until you quit. This challenge seemed to be rooted in vale tudo from their native Brazil, and I quickly discovered that family patriarch Hélio was a huge part of that history, having participated in a number of classic fights.

The focal point of the article was not Hélio though, but his oldest son, 37-year-old Rorion. He was the first of the family to come to the U.S. from Brazil, and the one who seemed the most responsible for advocating Gracie Jiu-Jitsu in his new country. Jordan wrote that "the toughest man in the United States" lived "in a modest ranch house on a tidy little street of similar homes in Torrance, California." I knew that South Bay LA suburb well, as it wasn't too terribly far from my office.

Now this Gracie Challenge vale tudo thing was exactly what I wanted to do, except instead of holding this type of fighting in private at a gym or dojo like the Gracies were apparently doing, I'd stage this as a public spectacle writ large, with Wisdom Imports footing the bill, on behalf of the Tecate beer brand. National television, big arena, huge crowd. And I didn't want many rules, other than some basic safety things like no groin strikes, no eye gouging–shit like that.

I had no trouble tracking down the Gracie Jiu-Jitsu phone number, as it was listed in the Yellow Pages. It turned out to be Rorion Gracie's home and I spoke to his wife, Suzanne. She said he wasn't in, but she would have him call me when he returned. Suzanne seemed to think that I was some sort of Hollywood producer, even though I told her I worked in marketing. But no return call ever came.

I decided on the "World's Best Fighter," for the working title, wrote a basic outline and executive summary, and submitted my pitch to Wisdom Imports in February 1990. My premise was simple: just let them fight, and see what happens. It absolutely couldn't miss.

But to my utter dismay, all of the hours and effort over the past three months that I'd put into creating this no-holds-barred, mixed match fighting event suddenly seemed like a colossal waste of time. Wisdom passed. It just wasn't right for them, was what they told Jim Plumb and me without further explanation. Maybe the idea of taking on this huge project was more than they had wanted. Perhaps it was just too violent for their tastes. Whatever, as it really didn't matter at that point. I was definitely disappointed. But in the ad game, I knew that rejection was standard operating procedure. It just wasn't their thing.

Soon after this, my headhunter came up with a job opportunity for me to go to work for a direct response advertising agency in Torrance. The position was director of client services for the Creative Direct Marketing Group, and it was a juicy offer. I took the gig, and rented a small apartment in Torrance's downtown section. It was above commercial stores and the city was re-building the entire area. A big urban renewal thing.

I became the manager of the apartments in return for reduced rent, and I took a second apartment, on the same floor, to serve as an office for any entrepreneurial projects that I might develop on my own. My apartment was on El Prado Avenue, but my office address was 1308 Sartori Avenue, as the building occupied the whole corner.

My new job at Creative Direct Marketing Group (CDMG) was great, but it was also all encompassing. Ten hours a day, and then I was in my little entrepreneurial office on evenings and weekends more often than not. But despite my workload, I kept thinking about the World's Best Fighter. I just couldn't let this go. Late one night, I re-read the *Playboy* article about the unbeatable Gracies of Brazil, and vowed to get in touch with Rorion this time around.

CHAPTER 3
THE BOYS FROM BRAZIL

A RARE BIRD ON EARTH, COMPARABLE TO A BLACK SWAN.
—— DECIMUS JUNIUS JUVENAL SATIRES 16. VI, 165

ON an uncharacteristically hot day in August 1990—uninvited and unannounced—I walked over to the Gracie Jiu-Jitsu Academy on Carson Street. It was located just a few blocks from my apartment and personal office, and I had already driven by it a number of times. I was on a fact-finding mission, to see if the Gracie family and their Brazilian jiu-jitsu could somehow factor into and revive my World's Best Fighter idea. The worst that could happen was that they'd tell me to get lost.

When I arrived, their school, the Gracie Academy looked pretty sharp. Inside a few workers were painting the trim. I recognized Hélio, the family patriarch from the article, but he didn't speak a word of English. There was a quiet dignity to him, and he seemed to be a man who always commanded respect.

I also observed a tall, lanky kid, who seemed very shy, and like he might still be a teen. He introduced himself to me as Royce, but didn't say two words after that. I wasn't sure from this meeting if he spoke much English, either. He too was quiet and unpretentious. My first venture into the den of the fearsome family of no-holds-barred fighters was pretty inconspicuous. Hélio and Royce were helping the construction workers put the finishing touches on the juice bar. I stayed a while and watched them work. Rorion wasn't there, so I left my card.

A couple of days later I finally got a call from the elusive Rorion Gracie. He was incredibly friendly on the phone. I pitched him very briefly about the event that I wanted to create—but something beyond the Gracie Challenge, the thing that I had read about in that *Playboy* article. Rorion was very non-committal, but invited me to come over and meet with him. We set an appointment and I trotted over there on my lunch break.

Rorion made an immediate and powerful impression on me. There was no sense of menace about him. Instead, Rorion came across as personable, magnetic and quietly self-confident. He was tall and lean with broad shoulders, flashing dark eyes and a big, thick moustache. The overall impression was movie actor handsome, with the charisma to match. He had a strong handshake and was gracious, polite and engaging. But to my dismay, Rorion showed no real interest on his part in discussing my proposal, as much as I tried. As soon as I started on about the World's Best Fighter, he would shut me down. Instead, Rorion wanted to regale me with stories about the legendary Gracie family history, traditions and fights. Rorion also told me about his experiences as an actor, extra and fight advisor on Hollywood TV shows and movies, such as *Lethal Weapon* with Mel Gibson.

Normally I'm a fast talker, and the one driving the conversation, but in that meeting, all I could do was listen.

"Arturo, Gracie Jiu-Jitsu, it's not a style of martial arts. It's a source of instruction for Brazilian jiu-jitsu. I trademarked the name. My father is the originator of all Brazilian jiu-jitsu, but not Gracie Jiu-Jitsu. Other people teach Brazilian jiu-jitsu or jiu-jitsu. I teach jiu-jitsu. I don't teach Gracie Jiu-Jitsu. Gracie Jiu-Jitsu is just a source of instruction, a location, and a business."

Grandmaster Hélio Gracie from Brazil and his eldest son, Rorion, who popularized his family's jiu-jitsu in the U.S.

I couldn't help but think that this carefully stated pronouncement had some legal issues attached to it.

Photo courtesy of Charlie Anzalone

Rorion then asked me if I'd ever grappled. And the answer, of course, was no. I didn't tell him about my one disastrous experience on the beach in Peconic Bay with the thick-necked wrestler. I said that I had done a little boxing when I was younger, and had taken some Muay Thai classes, but that was about it.

"Come over tomorrow night and I'll give you a free lesson. I'll show you how to roll."

How could I turn that down? The next night, about 7 p.m., I walked over from my apartment, wearing a jogging suit and T-shirt. This experience was a revelation. Rorion showed me a couple of moves, and then got on top of me in the "mount position." There was nothing, absolutely nothing that I could do to counter it. I was helpless on the mat, like a child. Or perhaps more appropriately, like one of the numerous victims of the Gracie Challenge.

I came out of the little workout room very impressed. Rorion then brought me into his office, and told me that he had been teaching in his garage in Redondo Beach for a number of years. This new academy was the first commercial location that he'd ever leased. He was very proud and excited. I was truly impressed by our time on the mat and we continued to talk. It struck me how gifted Rorion was as an instructor. He knew how to communicate, both verbally and physically. He was a natural in every way—great social skills to go along with his obviously great jiu-jitsu skills.

At one point, sitting behind his big, new desk like the guru/leader/teacher that he was, Rorion gestured at an array of blue cards.

"These are the new membership cards for the academy. I'm going to be transferring my students from these cards," he said pointing to a battered Rolodex on his desk, "to these new blue cards."

I nodded and said, "Well, sign me up!"

I became student number 1, at the Gracie Academy. Rorion took a blank blue card off his desk and entered my name on card number 1. It was an accident of timing, as Rorion and his brothers already had more than 150 students who were relocating from the garage in Redondo Beach to the new academy in Torrance.

As was the case previously, I never really got to discuss with Rorion why I had originally called him in the first place. When I mentioned my World's Best Fighter idea again, I could tell from how he changed the subject that Rorion wasn't too interested in discussing it. He had his "Gracie Challenge." I knew this from the *Playboy* article. But he didn't seem to want to discuss the challenge, my project or how the two might come together. With his brand-new academy, Rorion's head was clearly full, so for the time being I decided to leave it alone. I was sure that I'd have plenty of opportunities to talk to him as student number 1.

To understand Rorion, and to understand the Gracies, I was fully aware that I had to know their history. I dove in doing even more research, which seemed vital for me in recruiting Rorion and his family as my allies.

Rorion had been born in Brazil in 1952, and had earned a bachelor's degree in law from Federal University in Rio de Janeiro. But, he never practiced law. Instead, Rorion's life work became promoting the Gracie name, and the type of instruction created by his father and uncle back in Brazil. He moved to Southern California in 1978, fully intent on popularizing Gracie Jiu-Jitsu in the U.S. He then served as the catalyst for the eventual emigration from Brazil of a number of his family members.

I also realized that the key to really understanding Rorion was through Hélio, his father—the patriarch. Hélio was the heart and soul of the Gracies, and it didn't take me long to figure out that his philosophy of life was imprinted on every one of his sons.

Hélio was the youngest brother of Carlos, who had learned jiu-jitsu from Mitsuyo Maeda, a Japanese-born, naturalized Brazilian. Maeda had changed his name to Otávio Maeda in his new country. He was a judo expert with direct lineage to the sport's founder (Kanō Jigorō) who had become

a prizefighter in no-holds-barred competitions; he was sometimes known as Conde Koma (Count Combat), a nickname he picked up in Spain before World War I. Maeda pioneered judo in Brazil, as well as the United Kingdom and other Western countries; and supposedly won more

Photo courtesy of Charlie Anzalone

Here I am with the whole Gracie family. That's Royce Gracie on the far left. Rickson is obscured behind him and then Rorion, Hélio, me, Relson, Royler and Rolker.

than 2,000 professional fights in his career. His accomplishments led to him being called the "toughest man who ever lived" and being referred to as "the Father of Brazilian jiu-jitsu."

Now, the father of Carlos and Hélio Gracie was a man named Gastão Gracie. He was a business partner of the American Circus in Belém, Brazil. In 1917, 14-year-old Carlos watched a demonstration by Maeda at the Da Paz Theatre and decided that he wanted to learn from him. Maeda accepted Carlos as a student, and the youngster went on to become a great exponent of the art, and ultimately, with his younger brother, Hélio, founded Gracie Jiu-Jitsu. The naturalized Brazilian Maeda was fundamental to the development of Brazilian jiu-jitsu, through his teaching of Carlos Gracie.

In 1921, Gastão Gracie moved his family to Rio de Janeiro. Carlos, then 17, passed Maeda's teachings on to his brothers Osvaldo, Gastão and Jorge. Hélio was too young and sick at that time to really learn the art and, due to his medical condition, was prohibited from taking part in the training sessions. He instead learned by watching his brothers.

Hélio eventually overcame his health problems and the youngest, smallest and skinniest of the Gracie boys ultimately became the family's champion, even though he weighed only 140 lb. He also became the father of Rorion, Relson, Rickson, Rolker, Royler, Royce, and Robin; and daughters Rerika and Ricci. For his part, Hélio's brother, Carlos, fathered 21 children.

In addition to Maeda and Carlos Gracie, I read about Oswaldo Baptista Fadda. He was perhaps best known for teaching students from the poorer areas of Rio de Janeiro, where jiu-jitsu was regarded as an upper-class sport. Despite being regarded by the Gracie family as an outcast, Fadda opened his own academy on the outskirts of Rio in 1950. He and his students began specializing in the use of foot locks, an often ignored part of the Brazilian jiu-jitsu curriculum. The following year, Fadda apparently felt confident that his school was ready for the next step, and issued a challenge to the Gracies through the media.

"We wish to challenge the Gracies, we respect them as the formidable adversaries they are, but we do not fear them. We have 20 pupils ready for the challenge."

Hélio accepted the challenge and the two teams fought at Gracie's academy. Fadda's team emerged victorious, making good use of their knowledge of foot locks, in which the opposition was lacking. José Guimarães, one of Fadda's pupils, actually choked Hélio unconscious. After the challenge, Fadda gave an interview in the *Revista do Esporte*.

"We put an end to the Gracie taboo," he was quoted as saying.

The Gracies had previously derided foot locks as a "suburban technique," but afterwards Hélio graciously acknowledged that Fadda's win was a sign that jiu-jitsu was truly for everyone. In an interview with the newspaper, Hélio said, "All you need is one Fadda to show that jiu-jitsu is not the Gracie's privilege."

I thought that perhaps Rorion's formal-sounding proclamation to me about Gracie Jiu-Jitsu during our first meeting was rooted in all of the claims and counterclaims as to the true "Father of Brazilian jiu-jitsu," which were so important back in his native country. Mitsuyo Maeda had a valid claim that he created Brazilian jiu-jitsu. So too did Hélio's oldest brother, Carlos. And Fadda seemed to fit somewhere in that mix.

Regardless of who was first and who was best, it was undeniable that Hélio was a true pioneer, just not the only pioneer. But none of that mattered to me.

As I started my weekly private lessons with Rorion at the Gracie Academy, I began to learn some of the philosophy that Hélio had imparted on his oldest son. The specter of "the old man," as Rorion called him, was everywhere. Every time Hélio showed up at the academy, I was blown away. Though not a big man by any standard, he dominated the room. His voice was low, but when he raised it, the whole room got quiet. He carried himself with a dignity and a grace that belied his strength. I watched him on the mat, and was rendered speechless by how supple, fit and agile he was at age 77. When Rorion would bring me over to Hélio, the encounter was always a bit awkward, as neither of us could speak the other's language. But his grip was firm, and I knew I was in the presence of someone truly unique.

In addition to the jiu-jitsu, I quickly learned that Rorion, Hélio, and seemingly the entire Gracie family took tremendous pride in and fanatically followed the diet developed by Uncle Carlos back in Brazil. It was a food-combining regimen that emphasized which foods could be eaten with others, all done for health reasons. It became apparent to me that the Gracie Diet and Gracie Jiu-Jitsu were intrinsically linked, and you couldn't be a real devotee of one, without being a disciple of the other.

As much as I quickly came to respect and admire the Gracies, they struck me as a family of birds of prey—extremely protective of their territory, and ready to swoop down on their enemies at all times.

The old man Hélio was the great bald eagle of the family, the anchor. Rorion was the heir apparent, the eagle in waiting. Rickson was without question the raptor. When I first saw him at the academy, where he was one of the instructors, he stood out from all the other big, bad men on the mat. He looked like a Brazilian Marlon Brando. And while Rickson was several inches shorter than Rorion (who was 6-foot-2), he easily outweighed his older brother by twenty pounds. He was the biggest and fiercest predator of all the Gracie brothers, the golden raptor, in fact. Relson, who lived in Hawaii, and who I only saw occasionally, was the black hawk, unpredictable, dangerous and a bit of an outcast. Royler and Royce, who both taught at the academy, were the young falcons, quick and carefree.

I began to interact with the Gracies to varying degrees, but my principal relationship was with Rorion. As well as being my instructor, he quickly became my friend.

Every Tuesday night at 8 p.m., I had a private class with Rorion, undertaking the famous 36 introductory lessons of Gracie Jiu-Jitsu that Hélio had pioneered. The key principle of the Gracie system was that 90 percent of the time in a real fight, the battle goes to the ground. So Gracie Jiu-Jitsu was heavily geared towards ground fighting. Strike to close the distance, execute a take down, and then dominate on the ground with positions leading to submissions. No flashy head kicks or spinning back fists or flying knees. Instead, it was all about perfecting the fundamentals, which were very subtle, yet incredibly devastating. Gracie Jiu-Jitsu was the first form of fighting that I had ever seen, ever heard of, where being on your back with your opponent on top of you was an offensive position. This was incredible to me, as Rorion taught me submission holds from positions that at first glance seemed not only defensive, but disastrous.

If only I had known this stuff in my boxer vs. wrestler match back on Peconic Bay. Gracie Jiu-Jitsu could beat you anywhere on the ground: from the top, side, or bottom—it didn't matter. And if you were better on your feet—superior with striking—it didn't matter. They weren't going to let you play that game. Sooner or later, probably sooner, you were going to be on the ground, getting schooled the Gracie way.

Within a few weeks of taking my first class, Rorion held a grand opening party for the new academy. It was on a Saturday and the place was packed. Rorion looked resplendent and was having a ball showing everybody the new palace of jiu-jitsu. I brought a date, Leslie Vargas, a girl I had been close to when I lived in San Diego. We hung out and schmoozed along with everyone else, with Leslie not quite sure what to make of my new friends.

Then, in the crowd, I saw a familiar face that I couldn't place. I noticed that he was looking at me, seemingly trying to figure out why I looked familiar to him. Suddenly, I realized that it was Pat Strong, a guy who I hadn't seen in over a decade. Pat had a leading role in the 1979 direct-to-video martial arts flick *Kill the Golden Goose*, which also featured iconic Hapkido Master Bong-Soo Han, martial arts legend Ed Parker and body builder Ken Waller. He had come to me through a mutual friend, who thought I could help him raise money for a follow-up film. I liked Pat, but passed, as it wasn't my area of expertise.

As we were having our reunion at the academy, the talk turned to the Gracie Challenge. Pat off-handedly mentioned to me that in 1982 he had approached Rorion about taking part in an idea he had for a tournament featuring different styles of martial artists. He was going to call it the World Freestyle Fighting Championship, and it was intended for the burgeoning home video market. Rather than tell him about my similarly themed World's Best Fighter idea, I just listened intently.

After Pat left, I asked Rorion about all of this. He said that he had considered it, but there was never a business plan, and zero capital had been raised. Then Rorion told me that I wasn't the first, and he doubted that I'd be the last, to approach him about trying to make money off the Gracie Challenge. Sometimes they were ideas for big events, like Pat's and mine. Other times the pitch was a one-off fight, where either he or Rickson would fight a karate guy or a kickboxer on the beach or in a boxing ring. The concept always seemed to revolve around turning the fight or fights into a videotape, which could then be sold directly through mail order, or to a big chain like Blockbuster. Rorion was, of course, all about making a buck, but he had never figured out how to make the Gracie Challenge something that could be successfully monetized.

All through the rest of 1990 and into 1991 I diligently took my weekly private lesson with Rorion, never once talking business, and continuing to build our friendship. Always in the back of my mind was the World's Best Fighter, and how I could get it off the ground. I knew that I had to be patient, which was not a problem, since I was incredibly busy with my daytime gig at CDMG. I waited for the right opportunity, which I figured would eventually come. I just wasn't sure when or how.

I really started to love Gracie Jiu-Jitsu, as it was not only a great workout, it also gave me new-found confidence as someone who could actually handle himself if the shit went down for real. I didn't actually expect any shit to go down in my life as a 40-something ad man in Torrance, but it was a good feeling to have just the same. And the academy itself was a really interesting place filled with fascinating characters.

I began to notice the student, who took a private lesson with Rorion right after me, had a familiar face. But unlike Pat Strong at the grand opening party, there was no returned look of recognition.

It was driving me crazy that I couldn't place this guy, so I finally asked Rorion.

"Oh, that's John Milius," was his reply, like it was no big deal.

To me however—a lifelong movie lover—this was a very big deal.

Milius had studied film at the University of Southern California School of Cinema-Television where his classmates included George Lucas of *Star Wars* fame.

Photo courtesy of Ethan Milius

He had gone on to become a major player in the film business, working on a number of highly successful movies such as *Conan the Barbarian* (for which he made a star of Arnold Schwarzenegger), *Apocalypse Now* (for which he was nominated for an Academy Award), and *Red Dawn* (for which he sealed his reputation in Hollywood as a right-wing zealot). Milius was a

The great screenwriter, director and Academy Award nominee, John Milius. John was a jiu-jitsu student of Rorion Gracie's who became the creative director for the first UFC.

director, producer and screenwriter who would often get big paychecks to punch up completed scripts with amazing dialogue, which he had done for movies such as *Jaws*, *Dirty Harry* and *The Hunt for Red October*.

I was fascinated by Milius. He was about 6-feet tall and heavyset with a full beard and moustache. We were close to the same age, and shared a passion for military history, warfare, warriors and the fighting arts. Milius, like me, though was no great shakes as an athlete. He had attempted to join the Marine Corps and volunteer for Vietnam service in the late 1960s, but was rejected due to chronic asthma. And he was a gun nut like me too—famously serving on the Board of Directors for the National Rifle Association, and describing himself in interviews as "an anarchist." He had a theatrical way of talking that was mesmerizing. I began to hang around when Milius was done with his class, just to be near the guy. One night Rorion invited me to join them in his office, and I was absolutely thrilled.

What really sealed our bond was cigars, for which Milius and I again shared a passion.

"What do you smoke?" he asked me.

"Macanudos," was my reply.

Milius then cleared his throat and announced, "Hmmm... Let me tell you what John Huston told me about cigars."

Now, John Houston was a of course a huge legend in Hollywood as a director (*The Maltese Falcon*, *The African Queen*, and *Treasure of the Sierra Madre*), actor (*Chinatown* and *The Wind and the Lion*), raconteur, womanizer (five wives) and cigar smoker.

Milius said to me, with his finger pointing for emphasis, "Houston taught me about cigars when I was a second unit director on *The Bible*. He told me that there are only two kinds of cigars: Cubans and rope. And that Jamaican cigar you've been smoking—is rope!"

I loved it. Milius, John Huston, cigars, all of it.

"Now, come out to the car with me," Milius said. "Let me introduce you to some Cubans."

I followed him out to his Cadillac, and when he unlocked the trunk, there sat a huge, gorgeous lacquered humidor. Milius opened the humidor and extracted three cigars for me: two Montecristo figurados and a Romeo y Julieta Churchill.

"Try these," he said. "And let me know if you taste the difference."

I zeroed in on Milius, from our spur-of-the-moment bull sessions at the Gracie Academy, that he would be a perfect fit for my World's Best Fighter project. I had no idea what he would do, or even if he would agree to come on board, but Milius was a guy that I somehow had to get involved. Our friendship was just developing, and I didn't want to start hassling him with favors and requests. But I kept Milius in mind for the future.

As much as Milius was into Gracie Jiu-Jitsu, it was nothing compared to his teenage son, Ethan. The kid absolutely worshipped his primary instructor Royce, and there were good-natured jokes from those in the Gracie Academy that Ethan was always lying out in the sun so that he could darken his skin to look Brazilian. He was an outstanding jiu-jitsu student; smart and athletic.

Milius had started taking Ethan to Gracie Jiu-Jitsu, after being turned on to it himself by Reb Brown, an actor who played Captain America in two made-for-TV movies.

Reb had a role in *Uncommon Valor*, a film on which Milius was one of the producers.

Milius told me that on the set, Randall "Tex" Cobb (a pro boxer and kickboxer) used to terrorize the cast and crew. He had been hired for a small part as an actor, but "Tex" had become a big pain in the ass. Bullying everyone, generally fucking with people, that type of thing. Even a superstar like Gene Hackman, who was the lead in the film, was not immune to this physical intimidation.

Photo courtesy of Kathy Kidd

But the guy who "Tex" steered clear of was Reb, who undoubtedly would have fucked him up. Reb played football at USC, boxed professionally and worked as a Los Angeles Sheriff's Deputy. But above all, the man was a devoted and accomplished student of Gracie Jiu-Jitsu. This made a huge impression on Milius, and soon he was on the mat, rolling with Rorion. I got to know Reb at the Academy too. He was a big, tough guy, but as sweet as they come.

Clay McBride, a Gracie Jiu-Jitsu student, who was an excellent martial artist and accomplished combat sportswriter and photographer.

I also got to know Clay McBride at the Gracie Academy, and he instantly earned my respect. He was a lanky guy, maybe 6-foot-1 and 180 lb. who wore glasses, and seemed very studious. Clay had polio as a child, but he didn't let this hamper him in any way. He was a true martial artist who studied a number of different disciplines. He had gotten into the whole Bruce Lee thing and Lee's Jeet Kune Do movement.

Clay had already been a martial artist for 17 years when he met Rorion. He quickly decided that Gracie Jiu-Jitsu was the most efficient, practical and realistic fighting style he'd experienced, and joined the growing list of Gracie devotees. A literate and articulate guy, Clay had written articles about the Gracies for martial arts magazines, like *Inside Karate* and *Inside Kung Fu*. Rorion was pretty close with Clay, closer in fact than he was with most of his students. He and I hit it off quickly too.

There were a lot of cops who trained Gracie Jiu-Jitsu, and as I continued my private sessions with Rorion, I could see why. This was an amazing way to neutralize a suspect. One quick choke or arm bar, and the perp would go quietly into the back of the patrol car. I started noticing one very big and powerful looking student, who was extremely friendly, but seemed ready to flip the switch to all business, if needed. Rorion told me the guy's name was John McCarthy, an LAPD officer, whose dad, Ron, played a key role in the first SWAT (police high-risk and tactical operations) teams in LA.

I liked the people who trained at the Gracie Academy, and I truly liked the Gracies. Even though I didn't really speak that much to Hélio,

Photo courtesy of John McCarthy

or to the other Gracie brothers who worked there as instructors: Rickson, Royler, Royce, and occasionally Relson when he was in from Hawaii—they all knew me, and always made me feel welcome. And Rorion and I seemed to be growing closer every week.

John McCarthy, a Los Angeles police officer, who was a jiu-jitsu student I often saw around the Gracie Academy in the early 1990s.

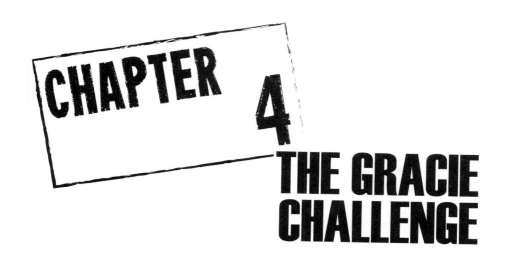

CHAPTER 4
THE GRACIE CHALLENGE

NO ONE CONQUERS WHO DOESN'T FIGHT.
— GABRIEL BIEL, Exposito Canonis Missae, lectio 78

I started to hang out a few times a week at the Gracie Academy, in addition to my regular Tuesday night lesson. The juice bar was the central meeting place after you finished your class. I would sometimes watch the big group classes, which were a lot different from the private lessons I was taking. There were a lot of blue belts rolling and tumbling, as they tried to gain the experience they needed to become purple belts. I soon figured out that if you wanted to become a purple belt you needed to roll with a lot of different guys. As I was now approaching 45, I also figured out that these classes were a fast ticket to the chiropractor for a guy like me. I got to watch Royce and he had the same approach to training students that he'd learned from Rorion, but without his social or verbal skills. It was always awesome to watch Rickson. He operated at another level entirely with his physicality and movement.

One Saturday afternoon, a young Hispanic guy came in asking for a fight. He wore an all-black gi, with a black belt and was apparently the stud at his karate school. This was going to be my first opportunity to witness in person the legendary Gracie Challenge, the backroom, vale tudo type fights I had read about in *Playboy*. I was beyond thrilled.

Finally, I was going to see a member of the Gracie Family go at it for real, and for $100,000. A key inspiration for my World's Best Fighter concept was about to occur right in front of me.

"How do you think this kid came up with $100,000?" I asked Rorion.

"What do you mean, Arturo?"

"$100,000. To put up for the Gracie Challenge."

Rorion laughed and said, "Arturo, he doesn't have $100,000."

"Well how much is he putting up then?"

Rorion explained to me that no one actually put up any money to take the Challenge. It was a test of styles and skills, not a contest for money. The Gracie Challenge at the Academy in Torrance was merely an extension of the long-standing Brazilian tradition of martial artists fighting each other informally to show the superiority of their discipline and its teachings. Just like vale tudo, but the kind of vale tudo that happened behind closed doors in Brazil, at jiu-jitsu academies and martial arts schools.

About once a month, some hot shot or tough guy would call the academy and make an appointment to come down to take the Gracie Challenge. He was usually a black belt from one martial art or another, and would drive in from Compton, Mira Loma, Anaheim or some other Southern California city. The guy would show up with his posse, and Rorion would do everything to make all of them feel incredibly welcome. But when they headed for the back room where the big mat was, Rorion made them all understand that this was going to be no holds-barred, a real fight. Afterwards, you shook hands—and that was it.

Well, all of these local "champions" went down to defeat the same way, including of course the Hispanic kid in the all black gi in the first Gracie Challenge I witnessed. The Gracies always prevailed. Usually, the Gracie brother would close the distance quickly, and immediately take down his opponent. Occasionally, the opposing fighter would come straight at the Gracie, with the result being the same. Before you knew it, "the grand master" would be squirming on his back, without a clue as to how to get his Brazilian opponent off of him. The submission would be inevitably locked on, and then the tap out would come. For those fighters who didn't know the etiquette of giving up by tapping with their own hand, the mat or their opponent, a cry of "I give!" or "That's enough!" or "Stop, stop, stop!" would end the fight.

The Gracies, in the long-standing family tradition, were all sportsmen. Once the Challenge was over and victory was obtained, the submission hold was released and there were no hard feelings. What fascinated me even more than the skill and speed at which the Gracie brothers dispatched their challengers—most of whom were highly accomplished martial artists—was how the losers almost always wanted to go again. It was as if they couldn't believe what had happened to them. Anyone can understand a knockout, but these guys simply couldn't figure out how they were caught in a choke that nearly put them to sleep, or why their shoulder felt as though it was going to pop. Watching these Gracie Challenges, and studying Gracie Jiu-Jitsu, I fully appreciated why the word art is in martial arts. These guys were master craftsmen of the highest order.

Afterwards, everybody shook hands and the loser left with his dignity, but not his self-confidence intact. As Rorion once said to me, "Imagine finding out that the fighting style to which you've dedicated your life is worthless."

All of the Gracie brothers who taught at the Academy were called upon to defend the family honor in the Challenge at one time or another. Often, though, it was Royler, all 5-foot-8 and 145 lb. of him, who would step up for the fight. I know that the family adored having this small, wiry guy destroy massive heavyweights, without absorbing any punishment. This is what Hélio had in mind when he worked to perfect his family's fighting system back in Brazil.

I absolutely loved watching the Gracies do their thing in the Challenges, but they were nothing like what Pat Jordan had colorfully described in his *Playboy* article. Although they were in fact real fights, I never saw so much as a bloodied nose or a split lip. The Gracies were so effective and so dominant with their jiu-jitsu, that these severe ass whippings were almost injury free. And there certainly wasn't $100,000 or even $1 at stake.

I asked Rorion why Jordan had written about the $100,000, and he told me that it had something to do with Benny "the Jet" Urquidez, but wouldn't expand.

My curiosity was too strong at this point to let this go, so I turned to Richard Bresler, who I figured might have the answer. Richard was a close friend and former roommate of Rorion's, who I knew at the academy. He was a long-time student of the Gracies, dating back to the days of training in the garage in Redondo Beach. When I asked Richard he was happy to tell me the story, in which it turned out, he figured prominently.

According to Richard, sometime in the early 1980s, his brother Daniel was training at a local kickboxing school. The two brothers got to arguing about which was more effective: kickboxing or jiu-jitsu. They considered a personal battle to decide the issue, but soon, one of them proposed that they get their respective teachers to settle the argument.

Daniel's kickboxing guru said that he'd never heard of Gracie Jiu-Jitsu and dismissed Richard as a full-of-shit blow-hard. But Richard persisted, so the head guy told him to bring his instructor over, and they would see about all of this. Rorion was a bit shocked that Richard had set up a match for him without his consent, but being a Gracie, he of course went anyway. So Rorion and the kickboxer moved around for a little bit, until Rorion eventually got his range, took the guy down, and choked him out.

The head guy of this kickboxing school turned out to be a disciple of Benny "the Jet" Urquidez, a champion kickboxer, occasional actor, and all-around bad ass who had supposedly studied a number of martial arts including judo, taekwondo, white crane kung fu and aikido. His reputation was highly regarded at the time by virtually everyone who read *Black Belt* magazine. Benny "the Jet" had some grappling experience, but was primarily known for his striking skills. When he heard about this fight in which one of his kickboxers lost to some Brazilian guy, he was determined to set things straight.

So they set up a match—Rorion vs. Benny "the Jet"—and as Richard told it, Rorion choked his opponent out 10 straight times.

A few years later, Rorion got a call from a producer who said he wanted to film a mixed match fight, and was looking for an opponent to face Benny "the Jet." The producer said, "I understand you are willing to fight other martial artists."

Rorion then responded to the producer, "Yeah, but you should tell Benny that you called Rorion Gracie."

But it looked as though Benny "the Jet" did in fact want a rematch, with the stakes now a lot higher, as this time it was going to be filmed. Rorion and Benny "the Jet" went around and around about money, and Benny "the Jet" eventually asked Rorion to put up $100,000 cash. In exchange, Benny "the Jet" was willing to put up his championship kickboxing belts, and nothing else. That killed the deal.

But even before they got to talking about money, there was a lot of wrangling about the rules and regulations. Benny "the Jet" apparently wanted time on the mat limited to 30 seconds. And there was the issue of where they would fight—in a boxing ring or on a mat? Would Rorion be allowed to wear his gi? Would they be bare-fisted, or would they wear gloves? What type of gloves? And what size would the gloves be? It went on and on and on.

As Richard told me this story, it rang incredibly true. Back in late 1989 and early 1990, when I was preparing my World's Best Fighter pitch for Wisdom Imports, I, of course, studied the few public mixed match fights that I could find. And what I discovered was that they always got hung up on the details.

In 1963, "Judo" Gene LeBell, who was a two-time AAU champion in the sport that gave rise to his nickname, fought Milo Savage, a pro boxer with 105 bouts to his credit. It was supposed to be "Judo vs. Boxing," but then the particulars started getting in the way.

LeBell wasn't allowed to throw kicks. In exchange, Savage had to wear a judo gi jacket in the ring. The reason for this wardrobe request was to give LeBell familiar hand holds for his clinches, throws and chokes. Savage agreed, but insisted that he would be allowed to wear speed bag gloves, which were smaller and lighter than regulation boxing gloves, giving him a lot more pop in his punches.

The fight ended in the fourth round, when LeBell used his opponent's gi jacket against him, gripping hard to execute a Harai goshi (sweeping hip throw), which dumped Savage on his ass. From there, LeBell applied a rear-naked choke, which put Savage into a very deep sleep.

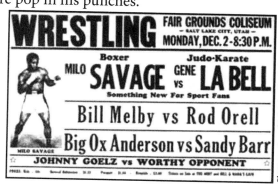

Here is an advertisement for the 1963 bout, held in Salt Lake City, between "Judo" Gene LeBell and boxer Milo Savage.

An even more egregious example of a mixed match fight being negotiated to death occurred 13 years after the LeBell vs. Savage fight—this time with "Judo" Gene as the referee. The bout was boxing's ruling World Heavyweight Boxing Champion Muhammad Ali taking on Japanese pro wrestling icon Antonio Inoki in Tokyo.

Depending on which version of history you believe, it was either the ultimate "Boxer vs. Wrestler" match-up, or a poorly-choreographed work. Regardless, what the bout unquestionably turned out to be was Inoki lying on the mat for the better part of 15 rounds, kicking away at the standing Ali's legs. Not even "Judo" Gene LeBell could save this debacle.

Under the agreed-upon rules, Inoki wasn't allowed to takedown Ali, nor was he allowed to grapple with him under any circumstances. Inoki was permitted to kick, but only when he was on the canvas, or sliding towards it. "The Greatest of All-Time" wound up landing just six punches total over 45 minutes of "fighting" against his constantly grounded opponent. If this was a work, then Ali vs. Inoki was the most boring work ever. In the end, a draw was declared, leaving the sold-out crowd at the Budokan and a worldwide television audience utterly disgusted.

As part of the trans-national undercard to the Ali vs. Inoki bout, another "Boxer vs. Wrestler" bout took place—this one at Shea Stadium in New York. The boxer in this match was Chuck Wepner, who was known as the "Bayonne Bleeder," and who claimed to be the inspiration for Sylvester Stallone's Rocky Balboa. Just like the cinematic Rocky, Wepner parlayed an undistinguished journeyman career into a fight for boxing's World Heavyweight Championship, with a highly surprising result. While Rocky lost a 15-round, split decision to

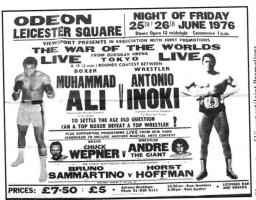

Here is a poster from the United Kingdom for the 1976 match held in Tokyo between heavyweight boxing champ, Muhammad Ali and Japanese wrestling star, Antonio Inoki. Note the undercard featured pro wrestler Andre the Giant vs. boxer Chuck Wepner.

Photo courtesy of Viewsport/Joint Promotions

Apollo Creed, Wepner made it to the 15th round of his title fight versus Muhammad Ali, where he was stopped via technical knockout. But it was a huge moral victory for Wepner, and he parlayed his new found celebrity into a mixed match fight versus one of the true superstars of pro wrestling. Billed as "the eighth wonder of the world," André René Roussimoff, better known as Andre the Giant, stood 7-foot-4, and weighed more than 450 lb.

The historical consensus is that this fight was an outright work. Regardless of the legitimacy of the bout, the reality was that Wepner vs. Andre the Giant was sloppy and painfully dull. Real or fake, it stands as yet another example of rules and regulations getting in the way. Andre the Giant had to break his hold every time Wepner grabbed or even touched the ring ropes—which happened continuously throughout the match, to the dismay of the vocal New York crowd. Not once did Wepner land a clean punch. So, virtually no punching, and no grappling, at least until the end, when Andre the Giant threw Wepner over the top rope in the least exciting way imaginable, and won via third round count out.

My takeaway from all of these mixed match bouts: Getting two fighters of different backgrounds to agree to anything is like asking two pit bulls to decide how a steak should to be divided. Even in worked fights, nobody could seem to agree on anything.

One of the many things I loved about the Gracie Challenges held in the backroom of the Academy, was that there was none of this negotiating bullshit. This was of course because fighters came to Torrance to fight the Gracies, not the other way around. If you wanted to haggle over the rules and the equipment and the dress code, then don't bother showing up. It was the Gracie Challenge after all.

But I knew that if you put this in a neutral venue, and more importantly, held it in public—with

Photo courtesy of Wrestling Monthly, November 1976

THE 'FARCICAL' ARTS CHAMPIONSHIP, FANS WERE BIGGEST LOSERS

The wrestling press in the U.S. was unanimous in their condemnation of the bout between Ali and Inoki in 1976. Note the referee: "Judo" Gene Lebell.

paying crowds, television cameras, and media—then people would start to get nervous. Likely not the Gracies, but certainly their opponents.

It's one thing to get your ass kicked with only a handful of people in attendance. It's something else entirely when the whole world is watching.

As much as the Gracie Challenge had been mythologized into a gladiatorial fight to death for big stakes, I still really respected what it actually was, and what it stood for. As I was finding out, almost no one was willing to throw down, "any time, any place." Be it Benny "the Jet" or Muhammad Ali, there were always stipulations and requests when a fighter was stepping out of his comfort zone. But not the Gracies. If you challenged them, no matter who you were, they'd fight you, and then see what happened. I felt that they deserved tremendous credit for this.

I knew that despite all of these potential and probable difficulties, there was something to the Gracie Challenge that could be taken to the next level. At its core, it was what I had envisioned all along for the World's Best Fighter: Practitioners from a vast array of martial arts and combat sports all coming together to see who was the best of the best, with very few rules, no time limits and the absence of a scoring system. Real fighting—just like my role models from Pankration in the ancient Olympic Games.

But Rorion seemed cautious if not closed off to the idea of lending his name—and his family's name—to such an event. It didn't seem to matter who was asking him.

A big reason for this was the money itself. Who would pay the appearance fees for all of the fighters to compete? Even if it was winner-take-all, where would that cash prize come from? Rorion knew first-hand in his dealings with Benny "the Jet" on their failed attempt at a re-match, that money was always a critical, if not the deciding factor. Sure you could get any two idiots to beat the shit out of each other for free, but if you wanted world-class martial artists and fighters competing, then someone would have to pony up.

And I knew that if the Gracie Challenge/World's Best Fighter was ever going to hit the big-time, the person who was going to have to pony up, or get an outside source to pony up, was going to have to be me.

CHAPTER 5

W.O.W. PROMOTIONS

**AN INVASION OF ARMIES CAN BE RESISTED, BUT
NOT AN IDEA WHOSE TIME HAS COME.**
— VICTOR HUGO, 'Histoire d'un crime,' 1852

I kept asking myself why I was so eager to get Rorion and his fighting family involved in my long-simmering World's Best Fighter idea. He wasn't a superstar in the sports world. Many hard-core martial arts enthusiasts hadn't even heard of him, let alone Gracie Jiu-Jitsu. And Rorion certainly wasn't a guy who could bankroll the project. Whatever money Rorion had seemed to be distributed amongst his family and poured back into the Academy.

But the answer that I kept coming back to was credibility—and in the fighting world, I had none. I was still a white belt in Gracie Jiu-Jitsu, despite all of my private sessions with Rorion, and I was a proverbial white belt in the world of combat sports. Outside of the Gracie Academy, nobody knew who I was. How would I be able to recruit fighters from across the spectrum of martial arts without any name recognition?

But if I had the Gracie moniker behind me, well, that was my foot in the door. And even if they hadn't heard of Rorion, or Hélio, or Gracie Jiu-Jitsu, I could quickly explain their credentials. That would be my initial lever. From there, I would know what to do from my business experience in advertising, marketing and promotions. I just had to get that first domino to fall.

In late 1991, Rorion mentioned to me that he was going to put together a second *Gracie Jiu-Jitsu in Action* videotape. He'd created the first one in 1988 with the help of Eric Sherman, one of his students who was in the movie business. Eric's dad was the noted motion picture director Vincent Sherman, who was a pretty big deal in post-World War II Hollywood, working with such major stars as Errol Flynn and Joan Crawford.

The first *Gracie Jiu-Jitsu in Action* was a one-hour grab bag of fights dating back to the 1950s. It included Hélio, Rickson, Rorion, and the legendary Rolls Gracie, who was actually the biological son of Hélio's brother Carlos, but who was raised by Hélio as his own. (Young, blond Rolls died tragically in a hang-gliding accident in 1982.) The tape was a bit amateurish, with choppy editing, stock music, and Rorion's accented monotone voice-over narration, but *Gracie Jiu-Jitsu in Action* was also mesmerizing. In essence, it was an infomercial for Gracie Jiu-Jitsu, showing the family kicking ass.

Rorion sold the videos at the Academy and through mail order ads placed in various martial arts magazines. He marketed them through his company Brajitsu, Inc., and never tried to sell it to a broadcaster or major video distribution company. That just wasn't his world.

"Do you have a database?" I asked Rorion.

"What's that?"

"You know, like the names and addresses of people who have taken your seminars."

"Oh yeah. Sure. Why Arturo?"

"Well, I know what to do with those names. How many names on that list?"

"Oh, about 25,000," Rorion said matter-of-factly.

"Twenty-five thousand! Really? Holy shit!" I yelled. "What if I could show you a way to turn that list into $100,000 cash?"

My heart leapt in my chest. With a decent video product and a list of 25,000 "warm" names, plus what I had learned about direct mail at CDMG, this was a match made in heaven.

It was also the way in that I had been looking for that, despite all of my time at the Gracie Academy, and my legitimate friendship with Rorion, I had never been able to find. I knew that I possessed the formula to turn those names and tapes into cold, hard cash. And I felt that if I could put real money in Rorion's pocket—which I had no doubt that I could—he'd in turn be open to lending the Gracie name and his personal credibility to the World's Best Fighter.

The second *Gracie Jiu-Jitsu in Action* video was well under way, and I didn't want Rorion to think that I was some Johnny-come-lately who would arrive at the last minute and take credit for all of the success. I knew he'd sell copies with his little ads in the martial arts magazines.

So instead I turned my attention towards a series of instructional tapes that Rorion was just completing called the *Basics of Gracie Jiu-Jitsu*. I offered to write the entire direct mail campaign (a service that I had been charging clients $10,000 to $20,000), and get the artwork done as well. All for free, well almost. I only asked that Rorion pay for the printing costs, which I would get for him at a discount. It took a fair amount of explanation on my part to get him up to speed on direct-response advertising. Soon though, he began to nod, and I could tell that he was seriously thinking about that $100,000 as a realistic goal.

It was at this time that I could see that Rorion was becoming more and more consumed with the business of Gracie Jiu-Jitsu, even above the jiu-jitsu itself. He was teaching fewer classes and spending less time on the mat, and he began with increasing frequency to pass me off to his younger brother, Royler, for my weekly private class.

Royler only spoke a handful of words in English, but it was enough for us to work out, and we quickly formed a friendly relationship. He was certainly a better communicator than Whitey Murphy from my boxing youth, who once smacked me on the back of the head and said, "Look wop, do it my way."

Royler was a really good and patient teacher, never rough or careless. But he remained a dangerous man nonetheless. I knew this from his dominating performances in the Gracie Challenge, and I found this out first-hand during one of our first sessions together. Royler gave me a "rib twister," as the cartilage between two of my ribs got torqued. It wasn't on purpose; there was nothing mean-spirited about it on Royler's part. It just happened as we grappled. And it hurt like hell.

A few weeks later, Royler was teaching me how to defend against punches using Gracie Jiu-Jitsu. Wearing boxing gloves, Royler caught me flush in the ribs with a solid right. The punch broke a rib on my left side, and I spent the next month taped up. Apart from the pain, it wasn't that big of a deal to me, but I could see immediately that Royler felt terrible. He couldn't have been nicer or more apologetic.

Be it Royler, Rorion or any of the Gracies, there were always constant little reminders that these guys really could hurt you very easily if they wanted to, and even if they didn't.

I knew that I was in no way a natural when it came to jiu-jitsu and even basic grappling, but I was growing increasingly restless that I hadn't progressed above white belt.

"Arturo be patient. All good things come in time," was Rorion's standard response to my questions about when my promotion to blue belt would finally come.

The Gracies were consummate professionals on absolutely everything when it came to their family's fighting art, belt ranks included. They just didn't give belt promotions because of a student's good attendance or money spent, like so many other martial arts instructors in the U.S.

I understood and really respected this integrity, and kept working out as hard as I could in pursuit of a blue belt. One night, about 15 minutes into my private one-hour class with Royler, Rorion came into our little padded workout room. He was smiling and didn't say a word. Rorion just gave a look to Royler, who nodded in reply, and then said to me, "Let's go. Understand?"

I knew that he was going to be seeking chokes and arm bars, and it was my responsibility to defend his submission attempts as best I could. We proceeded to then go at it non-stop for the next 15 or 20 minutes, with Royler going much harder than he'd ever gone against me before in all of our previous sessions. I knew, of course, that he was still nowhere near his top speed—not even close—but he had definitely turned up the intensity.

When we were done, I was sweat-soaked and absolutely exhausted. I had kept myself from getting choked out and arm barred, but I wasn't feeling proud, as much as relieved. Rorion had intently been watching my every move, and I saw now that he was grinning like a big cat.

He then approached me with one hand behind his back, and when Royler and I came over to where he was standing in that private workout room, Rorion said, "Arturo, you've earned this." With that he brought forward a blue belt.

I was in shock. Somehow, I didn't realize that this had been my test. I thought that Rorion had just stopped by to watch how I was progressing with his younger brother now working as my primary instructor. The moment kind of overwhelmed me, and I realized just how much Gracie Jiu-Jitsu had become part of my reality.

To get Rorion his $100,000, over Christmas 1991 at my kitchen table in Torrance, I wrote a killer direct mail piece, and had a friend of mine who was a graphic designer, do the layout at my direction as a favor. I delivered it to Rorion the next month; just as the *Basics of Gracie Jiu-Jitsu* tapes were being delivered.

I had told Rorion that we would wait until early February to give buyers a chance to pay their holiday bills, and then we dropped the campaign in the mail. It consisted of an eight page sales letter, an order form, a return envelope, a note of endorsement from John Milius, and a reprint of the *Playboy* article.

To say it was a huge hit would be a massive understatement. Rorion never would tell me the exact amount that the campaign generated, but I found out from his office manager, Helen, that the number was closer to $150,000 than it was to $100,000. Soon, he dumped his old beater Volvo station wagon and bought himself a new Chrysler sedan. The money was rolling in, so I asked Rorion for a meeting.

"Like what I did?" I asked him nonchalantly.

"Well, it was my money that paid for the printing," Rorion answered with a grin.

I decided not to respond, and quickly moved on.

"Now, do you want to make some real money? And make Gracie Jiu-Jitsu the most famous name in martial arts in the whole world?"

"Arturo, we're already famous."

I ignored this comment as well, and said, "Look, I'm going to show you how we can take this to the next level. But, no more freebies. I want 30 percent of the gross on all Gracie video sales we generate from direct marketing from now on."

You could have heard a pin drop. The shocked look on his face congealed like the yolk of a cold over-easy egg. Rorion said he would need time to think about it. This was a huge decision. I was his friend, and a loyal student, but he'd never partnered up with anybody in the U.S. I could see that this was a hurdle for him. The success of the direct mail campaign was no fluke though, and the cash that he was depositing was no mirage. But I knew that he needed time to think it over, so I backed off a bit.

Later that week, we met in his office at midday. Rorion told me that after much thought, he would like to offer me 20 percent. I countered with 25 percent, and we agreed on 22.5 percent. We signed the contract for me to do the company's direct marketing on April 13, 1992.

Without question, I could tell that this was a struggle for him. Rorion seemed like he was being asked to cut off a finger. One factor I understood very early on was that in Rorion's world, most of the people who he had any real contact with outside of his family, were his students. And when you're a martial arts guru, you became accustomed to having people fawn all over you.

If a student is a dentist, you're getting dental work done for free or at a deep discount. Ditto for a doctor, an attorney and an accountant. Virtually all of Rorion's students were happy to give him whatever he asked for, and he was well accustomed to being treated to, "I can get it for you wholesale," and, "Don't worry, you won't have to pay," kind of stuff.

When I proposed our deal on the Gracie videos, I wasn't doing what Rorion had come to expect from a student. And while I was his student as well as his friend, I was never really what could be called a "Gracie disciple." Rorion had plenty of students who had stars in their eyes. I was just too much of a realist.

Beyond all of this, I had come to know Rorion well enough to understand that he was a wannabe big thinker who was nervous about making a misstep in the United States, where the customs and rules were still unfamiliar to him after almost 15 years. He just didn't want to make any mistakes, certainly not when it had to do with Gracie Jiu-Jitsu. In Brazil, he knew the lay of the land, but in his adopted country, he was a naïf, a white belt, in fact. And as the oldest son of Grand Master Hélio Gracie, Rorion couldn't be a white belt in anything.

I understood this was what bothered and also limited him. He was the heir apparent, the favorite son, the chosen one, the future king. Or so he hoped. Giving away 22.5 percent of his business loomed like a potentially huge wrong turn to him. Rorion felt he couldn't afford to make a mistake that would open up his rightful destiny to one of his brothers or worse, to one of his cousins.

Rorion believed that it had to be him assuming the leadership of the family. After all, he had moved with almost nothing in his pockets to the U.S. in 1978, which paved the way for his family members to join him in Southern California. He made the biggest effort to be the most conversant in English. It was his vision and hard work that had created the Gracie Academy, which provided a place to propagate his father's martial art, diet and lifestyle. Rorion had lived his life putting forward to the world the accomplishments of Hélio Gracie, and the dominance of Gracie Jiu-Jitsu.

And yet there was Rickson. Always Rickson. The third son of Hélio, Rickson was born in 1958, six years after Rorion. He was the undisputed family champion, with a skill set, athleticism and ferocity that not even his brothers could match. His status in the family was sealed in 1980, when at just 21 years old, Rickson defeated Casimiro de Nascimento Martins, better known as Rei Zulu (King Zulu) in a vale tudo match, which was televised nationally in Brazil. The 32-year-old Rei Zulu had made his reputation by taking on all comers and claimed a 150 fight winning streak.

All that was left for him to do was publicly challenge Brazil's first family of fighting—the Gracies. Hélio of course accepted, and bypassed Rorion and second born son Relson in favor of Rickson to defend the family honor. Not only was Rickson 11 years younger and vastly less experienced than his fearsome opponent, he was also five inches shorter and almost 50 pounds lighter. But Rickson prevailed with a rear-naked choke submission, and then defeated Rei Zulu by the same method again four years later.

I found Rickson to be (paraphrasing Winston Churchill) a puzzle wrapped in an enigma. I never got to know him well, and I could never really get a read on the guy, despite seeing him constantly at the Gracie Academy. I knew his reputation as the baddest of the Gracies, and I'd seen his unbelievable talent on display in person at the academy.

I had kept hearing about Rickson's workout class, and how it was not designed for mere mortals. Having been a Marine, I decided that I had to see for myself just how hard it really was. It began at the ungodly hour of 6 a.m., and it was either scheduled for 60 or 90 minutes. I never found out because both times I took it, I dropped out after about 45 minutes. I wasn't alone. Two of the cops I was friendly with at the Academy took a powder about the same time I did, which made me feel somewhat better. Rickson was leading us with moves that were beyond anything that I'd ever been exposed to, even as a Marine. It would have taxed anyone, doing things like high repetition one-legged squats—well, taxed anyone but Rickson. It was mind-blowing and very advanced. I couldn't have kept up when I was 20. When I finally put my grand plan in motion, there was no doubt in my mind that Rickson would be my star fighter.

The money from the *Basics of Gracie Jiu-Jitsu* videotapes started rolling in. When my monthly commission check topped $21,000, I knew it was time to approach Rorion again about getting involved with me on the World's Best Fighter.

"What's your reluctance?" I asked him in his office at the Gracie Academy. "You know that I know how to make us money."

"But how would we make money on this Arturo? Would we sell this as another videotape?"

I laid out my full vision to Rorion, which had continued to evolve in my mind since I first started working on this as a pitch for Wisdom Imports almost three years earlier.

"We'd have 16 fighters in a tournament, all held in one night. The 16 guys will all represent a different form of fighting: karate, kickboxing, kung fu, boxing, sumo, wrestling. You get the idea. I figure that Rickson would represent Gracie Jiu-Jitsu."

"So my brother would have to fight all 15 guys in one night?"

"No, it'd be single elimination. The loser is out and the winner moves on to the next round. But to win the thing, you'd have to fight four times in one night. Could Rickson do that?"

"Of course," said Rorion. "We all could. We're Gracies." And with that, a wide smile creased his face.

I told him that I figured that we would have to bring in about $250,000 to get this thing up and running. We'd need that cash to form a new company, hire a secretary, and probably get an attorney on retainer. The bulk of the money, though, would be needed to book the arena and pay the fighters. If this was really going to be the World's Best Fighter, then we couldn't just find chumps for Rickson to choke out. We'd need legit names from the world of martial arts and combat sports. And I told Rorion that I envisioned this as a live Pay-Per-View (PPV) TV event, although cable TV was a possibility. What this wouldn't be was a straight-to-video production. The tournament and the live TV—ideally PPV—were the two key points that I felt certain would make this work.

Rorion took it all in, and then asked, "How much is this going to cost me?'"

"Right now, nothing. All I need is your support to get this thing going. I need to be able to use your name and the Gracie name."

To my delight and relief, Rorion agreed. He made it clear, though, that I was coming to him, not the other way around, and as such, this would not be his full-time job. He had his hands full with the burgeoning Gracie Jiu-Jitsu empire: running the Academy, teaching classes there, holding seminars across the region and overseeing the Brajitsu, Inc. videotape business. That was not only fine with me, it was fully expected. I never thought for a second that Rorion would pack it all in to focus full-time on the World's Best Fighter, nor did I want him to.

Rorion and I agreed that I'd work out of my entrepreneurial office down the hall from my apartment on the corner of El Prado and Satori, and he'd keep working out of his office at the Gracie Academy. We'd use the academy's address, 1951 West Carson Street in Torrance, for all business correspondence. Rorion knew, as did I, that this was going to be my top priority, with my work for Brajitsu, Inc. coming second. We shook hands, and that was that.

With Rorion finally in place, I was now ready to quit my day job. The pay was good and I genuinely liked the gig—but it required a 50-hour work week. I didn't have a wife or kids to support, and my expenses were pretty minimal. If I was ever going to get the World's Best Fighter off the ground, it had to be now.

I gave Craig Huey, the owner of Creative Direct Marketing Group, my resignation on June 12, 1992. I then shifted my energies full-time to my personal office. The money from the videotapes kept coming, and since my divorce a few years earlier, I had saved over fifty grand and shoved it into a bank account. I always planned for the next deal or a rainy day, which was a good habit I'd learned early on. Finally, I was now set to concentrate fully on the World's Best Fighter.

This was a familiar pattern for me, taking a chance in business. I had been self-employed more than half of my working life, so the prospect of going forward without the guarantee of success, was nothing new or daunting. It was also a familiar pattern for me to be without someone special. I was a multiple loser in the marriage sweepstakes, and there wasn't anyone in my life that seemed like a potential girlfriend at that point.

But there was a young woman who lived in my building who had drawn my attention. Her name was Maria, and she was a very attractive brunette, curvy and petite. She had an infant son, and during the time I'd been managing the building, I'd seen her every so often. It was just polite conversation in the hallway, always instigated by me. She seemed quiet, serious, and somewhat sad. Maria had been taking a course in massage therapy, and when she graduated, she rented one of the offices on the ground floor of our building for her place of business. Trying to break the ice with her, I booked a massage, which I hoped would spark a dialogue between us. She was very good and very professional, but neither of us said a word during the entire one-hour session. As I was about to leave, Maria paid me a nice compliment about the shape I was in. I told her I was taking jiu-jitsu lessons. Judging from her reaction, she had no idea what I was talking about, and more awkward silence followed.

After the massage, I kept toying with the idea of asking her out, but I never did. In truth, Maria just didn't seem attracted to me, her lone compliment aside. One Sunday morning I went to a café up the street for some breakfast, and when I returned, there was a hulk of a guy waiting by the security door downstairs. I approached and asked him if he was trying to buzz someone upstairs.

"Yeah, Maria in apartment five," he answered. "I'm her, um... I'm her... uh... boyfriend. She should be home, but she didn't answer. Maybe she's in the shower."

I was going up to my apartment, so I asked him his name, introduced myself as the manager, and we chatted a bit. At that point, I decided to let him in to the building, as he seemed harmless despite his massive frame. There was something familiar about the guy, and I kept thinking that perhaps I had seen him at the Gracie Academy. Then it hit me that he was one of the famous bodybuilders who had been featured in the film *Pumping Iron*.

I saw Maria the next night about 5 p.m. and asked her if it was all right that I had let her "boyfriend" in.

"Oh yeah. It was ok. Well, not really. We've broken up. In fact I have a court order against him."

Maria then told me that she had suspected him of sexually molesting her infant son. She also confirmed for me that he was indeed a famous bodybuilder. I could see that she was in the middle of a real-life soap opera. Clearly Maria had enough on her plate without me hassling her for a date, or even another massage. I needed to spend all of my energy on launching the World's Best Fighter, and figured that maybe being alone wasn't so bad.

When I had the opportunity, I asked Rorion what his dad thought of me. It was clear that everything that Hélio's children did—first and foremost Gracie Jiu-Jitsu—required his blessing.

Rorion laughed and replied, "The old man says that the only thing Art Davie knows about Gracie Jiu-Jitsu is how to make money with it."

While this could have been construed as a compliment, I suspected it was intended as the opposite. My personal relationship with Hélio was not much of a relationship at all. I saw him only at the Gracie Academy, and as he spoke Portuguese exclusively, my exchanges were pretty much limited to a respectful hello and goodbye.

The closest that I'd ever had to a real moment with him was when one of the students at the academy had brought along his girlfriend, who happened to be wearing very short shorts. Hélio looked at me, then moved his two fingers up and down vertically to indicate his appreciation of her slim-hipped physique. He then gave me a very rare smile, and I burst out laughing.

Regardless if Hélio actually liked me or not though, I really liked him. And I admired him even more. Hélio definitely made a lasting impression on me, as a man who was from another era—one that wasn't coming back. I saw him as a knight—a man for whom honor was everything.

Money wasn't Hélio's motivation in life. His creed, his values and his family were everything to him. And that put Hélio at the opposite end of the spectrum from so many people in the modern world. But Hélio didn't care. He lived by his code, and that was enough.

What can you say about a man who sired nine children, followed a strict food combining diet, helped create a new martial art, became a fighting champion, and put honor before cash? I guess you can say that such a man was a true legend.

Now focused full-time on the project, I immediately went to work, first on creating a brief executive summary, which would spell out my vision for the World's Best Fighter that I could take to potential investors and sponsors. From there, I would have to write our business plan, which is what would ultimately be needed to seal the multiple deals that would have to be made. But I knew from gigs in advertising, marketing and promotions that absolutely no one is going to read a comprehensive business plan without first becoming interested. And the way that you get people interested is through a tight executive summary.

There was going to be a hell of a lot of research involved on both documents, so I started spending as much time at the Torrance Public Library as I did at my office. Actually, the Torrance Public Library quickly became the de facto headquarters for the fledgling World's Best Fighter business.

It soon struck me, though, that the name that I had chosen for my pitch to Wisdom Imports back in 1989 wasn't quite right. This was going to be a true spectacle, and the World's Best Fighter just felt too generic. I needed something much bigger and imposing. As he was now on board, I knew that Rorion would have had no problem in us calling the event the Gracie Challenge, but I never even considered that name.

For starters, despite Rorion's claim to me that his family was "already famous," they were known in a few Western states. Namely California, Nevada, Utah, Arizona and maybe Colorado, Oregon and New Mexico. And even then, this was a subculture of a subculture of a subculture. The Gracie Jiu-Jitsu followers were fiercely loyal, incredibly proud and very vocal, but they were also few in number.

It was clear to me that Rorion and the entire family greatly over-valued the prominence of the Gracie name in the martial arts world. This was further evidenced by a story that I had heard at the academy about how a few years earlier, Rickson had flown to Japan on his own dime in search of a real fight. He called on promoters, television networks, martial arts organizations; anyone and everyone he could think of to make it happen. Apparently Rickson figured that because of his father's history with Japanese fighters, and the link of Gracie-Jiu-Jitsu back to Japanese jiu-jitsu, the big-money offers would come flooding in.

A huge part of Hélio's rise to prominence in Brazil involved three no-holds-barred fights that he had against Japanese opponents in the 1950s. The first two bouts were against Yukio Kato, who was touted as one of the top three judo players in the world. The results were a draw followed by a submission win for Hélio. The third fight, in 1951, took place against Kato's mentor, Masahiko Kimura, who was widely regarded as the greatest judoka of all time.

Kimura was so confident of victory, he announced to the press that if Hélio could last three minutes in the fight, then he should be considered the winner. Despite weighing 139 lb. to his Japanese opponent's 210 lb., Hélio surpassed the three-minute mark, reaching the 13th minute before being caught in a Gyaku ude-garami (an arm lock renamed, for obvious reasons, a Kimura). Hélio refused to submit, and with his arm looking in danger of being snapped, older brother Carlos jumped in to stop the fight. The referee then restored order, and attempted to resume the proceedings. But Hélio admitted defeat, giving the hard-earned victory to Kimura.

Even though he had lost, Hélio was hailed as a hero for his skill, determination and sportsmanship. What he had won was the full respect of Kimura, the Japanese fighting delegation and the nation of Brazil.

But three decades later, Rickson learned the hard way that the exploits of his father had either been forgotten by the people of Japan, or never known at all. The Gracie name meant nothing there. No one was interested in either fighting or promoting Rickson. Completely dejected, Rickson finally flew home, having struggled to find anyone in the Japanese fight game who would even talk to him.

The reality was that in the U.S., Japan, and around the world—even in California—there were serious lifelong martial artists who had no clue about Gracie Jiu-Jitsu. It just didn't register. So to a broad audience, the Gracie Challenge didn't have any name value.

Plus, I disliked the idea of having the name of the event be the name of one of the fighters in the event. As I was going to have to recruit the 15 guys that I needed to fill out the tournament, I knew that this surely would have reeked of a set up to them. I'm going to be fighting a guy named Gracie in something called the Gracie Challenge with another guy named Gracie as the co-owner of the promotion? No fucking way!

Right there was where Rorion and I differed philosophically. In addition to making lots of money, Rorion's goal was to publicize Gracie Jiu-Jitsu to the world. For him, my idea was a means to an end. For me, it was going to be the start of a franchise, where we would continually hold tournaments, scouring the earth for the next best of the best. I had been doing Gracie Jiu-Jitsu long enough, and had seen plenty of Gracie Challenges in the back room of the Academy to know that any Gracie brother would likely win—especially if that brother was Rickson.

But I really didn't care. For this to work, it was going to have to showcase both great fighting styles and great fighters. And now, thinking like a promoter, I knew that having a Gracie win every time out would eventually be bad for business, especially in the beginning. But first things first, we had to get this thing going before I started worrying about how many victories the Gracies would record.

In my mind, these tournaments were going to be a true collision of various martial arts and combat sports, all under one roof—the disparate worlds of fighting coming together. Just like vale tudo, except organized as a promotion—a franchise.

One weekend, I was over at my best friend Les Smith's place in Laguna Beach for a barbecue. I had taken him and his wife Prentice into my confidence. Even though I now knew that the name wasn't quite right, I was still calling my project the World's Best Fighter. As I'm telling them all about the proposed event, Prentice brightened up, looked at me and said, "The War of the Worlds. That's it Art. Call it the War of the Worlds." This was of course the title used by H.G. Wells for his classic science fiction novel, first published in 1898; and it struck me as a name that might actually work.

I knew though that there would be the matter of legally obtaining rights to the name. The book had been turned into a movie by Paramount in 1953, and if the film studio didn't have a legal claim, then the H.G.

Wells estate probably did. But I liked Prentice's idea. Licensing was a problem that I could only hope to deal with when everything else was ready to roll. For now, I decided that this would be my working title, which no one would have a problem with legally. To make things seem a bit more grandiose, I decided to subtitle the event the World Hand-to-Hand Combat Championship.

I also figured that legally it we would be OK to use the War of the Worlds name for the company that Rorion and I were going to need. No way were we doing this under Brajitsu, Inc. That was his company. This would be our company together, which to his credit, Rorion understood from the outset.

Just in case the copyright lawyers did come after us on the name, I decided to make an acronym out of War of the Worlds.

It was catchy and concise, and it obviously worked well as a pun, letting everyone know that we were going to dazzle them. In truth, I really liked it for a company name: W.O.W. Promotions.

I asked Rorion what he thought, and he said that it didn't matter to him in the least. Whatever name I picked was fine. Rorion was more than happy to leave the details to me. I wasn't sure if this was trust or disinterest. Either way, I kept moving forward.

Next up, I needed to figure out which fighting styles we should include. Obviously, Gracie Jiu-Jitsu was a given. I thought I would add boxing, kickboxing, judo, wrestling, some type of karate such as Kenpo or Shotokan and Muay Thai. I went to Rorion with my list, and asked him what else we should include. He told me that he didn't care, because they were all pretty much the same to him.

In others words, if it wasn't Gracie Jiu-Jitsu, it was shit. He truly believed this, as did Hélio, the rest of the brothers, and virtually every student at the academy. They all knew it from the Gracie Challenge—

Photo courtesy of Art Davie archives/W.O.W. Promotions

War of the Worlds—This became the second working title for my martial arts style vs. style event. I borrowed it temporarily from the title of the 19th century H.G. Wells novel.

stand-up fighters, whether they were from boxing, kung fu, or capoeira, didn't know what to do once they were taken off of their feet. And those with a clinch and grappling base, such as wrestlers, judo players and Sambo practitioners, couldn't adequately defend themselves from the myriad of submissions that would be coming their way.

I wondered to myself what Rorion would have said if I told him that I wanted someone from a rival Brazilian jiu-jitsu lineage in the field of 16 fighters. I didn't dare, but I had no doubt Rorion would have dismissed their style as worthless as well. Such was the self-confidence that surrounded the mystique of the unbeatable Gracies.

I then needed to figure out the prize money, not just how much, but how would we pay it out. The questions quickly mounted in my head. Would this be winner-take-all? Would we pay guarantees? Would the dollar amount escalate as a fighter progressed through the tournament, round-by-round?

I liked the idea of $100,000 for the total prize money. Not only was it an eye-catching amount, this dollar figure, of course, factored into the legend of the Gracies. In his 1989 *Playboy* article, Pat Jordan wrote: "Rorion Gracie has made a standing offer to fight anyone in the United States, winner take all, for $100,000. So far he has had no takers—for one simple reason. Rorion's fights are fights to the finish with no rules."

The origins of Rorion's Gracie Challenge dated back to Hélio and his older brother Carlos, initially announcing to Brazil, and to the wider world, that they wanted to test their style in a real fight. For them, it was a matter of honor, not money. Hélio, according to Rorion, once placed an ad in a Rio de Janeiro newspaper that translated to, "If you want a broken arm, call me."

Public fights in Brazil for money followed, sometimes in front of huge crowds, sometimes even on national television, but the original ethos never changed. And when Rorion and his brothers imported the Gracie Challenge to the backroom of the academy in Torrance, it was a revival of the earliest days of Hélio and Carlos taking on all comers. Tickets and television broadcast rights were never sold, nor even considered. You couldn't even get in to watch unless you had an inside connection. The closest that the Gracies ever came to directly making money off the Challenge was when a few of the fights were used as part of the two *Gracie Jiu-Jitsu in Action* tapes. The Gracies were really testing themselves, while simultaneously proving the point that their form of fighting reigned supreme.

I was designing War of the Worlds to be vastly different from the Gracie Challenge in terms of presentation and profit, but I wanted to keep its soul intact.

CHAPTER 6

THE ROAD TO MANDALAY

I'VE A NEATER, SWEETER MAIDEN IN A CLEANER, GREENER LAND! ON THE ROAD TO MANDALAY. . .
— RUDYARD KIPLING, Mandalay

LATE that summer, in August 1992, I convinced Rorion to purchase an exhibitor's booth for Brajitsu, Inc. at the Long Beach International Karate Championship—a huge martial arts tournament first held in 1964 by Kenpo Grandmaster Ed Parker. Many notable full-contact fighters earned their stripes at this event, including Chuck Norris, Billy Blanks, and Rorion's old nemesis, Benny "the Jet" Urquidez. It's also where Bruce Lee was originally introduced to the North American martial arts community. As a prelude to this annual tournament, a small martial arts trade show was held, which I knew would be perfect for us.

Rorion and I filled our little booth with Brajitsu, Inc. videos for sale, as well as a TV set and a VCR. We continuously ran the two *Gracie Jiu-Jitsu in Action* tapes, and they absolutely stopped the show. Huge crowds of people would keep forming in front of the TV, their mouths wide open.

"Look at that."

"Can you believe this shit?"

"This is unreal!"

Whatever lingering doubt that still remained for me about the potential success of War of the Worlds was put to rest right then and there in Long Beach. This was a fight crowd and they absolutely couldn't get enough. Those two tapes showing the Gracies whip ass in jiu-jitsu and vale tudo back in Brazil, and in the Gracie Challenges at the academy in Torrance, had completely mesmerized everyone who watched.

Rorion was thrilled that we sold all of the tapes that we brought with us to the booth. I was thrilled for what I was now sure was within my grasp.

After the triumph of Long Beach, I then turned to the business of where to hold our first-ever War of the Worlds. I was determined to make this big—big city, big arena, big crowds, and big-time feel. Holding the debut tournament in a hotel ballroom, National Guard Armory, high school gym or run down theater just wouldn't work. No matter how great the fights and fighters, it would still feel small-time and cheap.

The problem though was in finding a place that would actually allow us to hold a virtual no-holds-barred event. The big-time boxing states such as Nevada, New York, New Jersey and California had notoriously prickly athletic commissions. And with them came stringent regulations, and fat fees charged for the privilege of overseeing your event, and licensing everyone from the promoters to the fighters to the refs to the timekeepers.

Yet, you couldn't hold an event without their involvement. All of this bureaucracy and associated costs were why Vince McMahon, Jr., as head of the World Wrestling Federation, lobbied the state of New York for the reclassification of his "sport" to "sports entertainment." McMahon's efforts proved successful in 1989, and his wrestlers, refs and staff were suddenly free of governmental oversight, saving his WWF a significant amount of money.

I didn't have Vince McMahon's clout or his millions, and I knew that once I explained what War of the Worlds was about, most state athletic commissions would tell me to get lost. There were a lot of reasons for them to say no, with inherent liability and political fallout from a mixed matched fighting event with almost no rules being the primary ones.

From my new base of operations at the Torrance Public Library, I discovered that there were three states in the U.S. that actually allowed bare-knuckle boxing. One of the three was Colorado, which I figured must have been a holdover from its hardscrabble mining and agricultural past. For whatever reason, legally permitting this type of fighting had never gotten wiped off the books.

When I read this, my heart nearly leapt out of my chest. Just a few days before, I was researching Limited Liability Corporations (LLCs), and I found out that Colorado was in the tiny group of states that registered businesses in this category. The perfect match.

I had started a number of small companies in the past through my various entrepreneurial ventures, and from these experiences I had come to learn about the LLC form. Apparently the gas and oil drilling states were pioneers in LLCs, because you could protect investors with such a structure. If a well blew up, there were no doubt going to be scores of lawsuits. The attraction of the LLC was that an investor's exposure was limited to the size of his investment—and not a penny more. This was perfect for the War of the Worlds. If an investor contributed $10,000—that was the limit of his liability should the company be successfully sued.

Our version of a well blowing up was a fighter getting killed, paralyzed or severely injured. I didn't think the first two scenarios were likely, but I figured that the third was a given, especially if I matched up two strikers against each other, like a boxer versus a guy from Muay Thai. Someone was probably going to get knocked out in an unbelievably brutal fashion.

I quickly headed back to the Gracie Academy to tell Rorion that through my discoveries, Colorado was the perfect place to register W.O.W. Promotions, and hold our first event. Rorion was pretty well travelled through the U.S. from his Gracie Jiu-Jitsu seminars. But all he remembered about Colorado was that it snowed there, and he hated snow.

"Where would we hold the fights, Arturo?"

"I don't know, probably somewhere in Denver."

"I like the idea of the LLC, but I was thinking that maybe we could hold our first event in Brazil. In Rio."

The city of Rorion's birth actually made a lot of sense to me. Rio de Janeiro would certainly give War of the Worlds a big-time feel, as well as an exotic aura. As Brazil's second largest city, it was not only home to millions of potential ticket buyers, it was also a place that understood Gracie Jiu-Jitsu and vale tudo.

Rorion then told me that he knew the guy who would be perfect for us as our in-country promoter, Luiz Oscar Niemeyer.

Known to his friends as Lulu, of which Rorion was one, he was a close relative of the famed Oscar Niemeyer—one of the 20th century's leading architects who worked on the United Nations Headquarters in New York, as well as most of the government buildings in the city of Brasilia. The Niemeyers were a prominent family who knew the Gracies from when Rorion was still living in Brazil. Rorion had gotten close to Lulu when he was getting a degree at the University of Southern California's Annenberg School for Communication and Journalism.

Lulu was now an established and respected concert promoter in Brazil, serving as General Director/Partner of Mills & Niemeyer Promoções Ltda, which was based in Rio de Janeiro. The company had become known for staging massive concerts featuring American and British pop and rock stars throughout Brazil. Rorion called Lulu, who told him that he had an upcoming trip to Los Angeles, and that he'd love to sit down with us. It was all coming together now.

The three of us met at the Gracie Academy in October 1992, and I was instantly impressed. Lulu was a terrific guy, and didn't try to bullshit us about the hurdles that we would face if we held War of the Worlds in Rio, or any city in Brazil. He told Rorion and me, that in his experience, doing concerts in that country was an "adventure."

"Getting people to attend won't be a problem. Getting them to pay for tickets, now that will be a big problem. If your gate is 20,000 people, only 5,000 will pay," he said. "Thousands will be sneaking in by going over, under, or through the security fence. It's a way of life in Brazil. I always have to take this into account for everything that I promote."

It was the primary reason, Lulu said, why he was starting to shift his business to other South American countries, mainly Argentina. But I knew from my work in the marketing business that a raucous crowd of 20,000 with only 5,000 paid would look a lot better on TV than an arena with 5,000 paying customers, surrounded by 15,000 empty seats.

Rorion looked intently at his old friend, and kept nodding silently. War of the Worlds live from Rio de Janeiro certainly had a great ring to it. I immediately had visions of meeting a voluptuous, brown-skinned girl with a bubble butt. Despite his candid appraisal of what we'd be facing, Lulu seemed genuinely interested. He saw that there might be a real opportunity, given the Gracies' popularity in Rio, to stage the event there. We kicked around the idea of doing it in 12 months time: October 1993.

Rorion and I told Lulu that we'd seriously consider holding our first event in Rio, and if we did, he'd of course be our guy. We just weren't ready to commit to anything yet, including a tentative date. The reality was that we hadn't even raised a dollar of investment capital.

After Lulu left our meeting at the academy, I told Rorion that aside from whatever problems we would have with people sneaking in, there would be a lot of added costs and hassles with doing business in a far-away, non-English speaking country. It seemed pretty daunting for a first event. With that Rorion seemed to cool on a return to his hometown, and said that he really didn't care one way or the other. Just like our event name and the fighters that we'd recruit, it was pretty much my call. I didn't have a solid alternative in mind, other than Colorado. So for now, Rio de Janeiro would be my placeholder. It sounded a lot more glamorous than Denver or Colorado Springs.

With Rorion, and by way of association, his father and brothers in the fold, I had my credibility in the fight world that I so desperately needed to move War of the Worlds forward. What I lacked though was credibility in the show business world. Our fighting tournament wasn't just going to be a sporting event; it was also going to be pure entertainment. I envisioned it as being perpetually held in major arenas, and broadcast live on worldwide television. I, of course, didn't have a big name in Hollywood, but I knew someone who did.

Rorion and I had kept John Milius updated on what we were doing, but in a very conversational, and limited way. It was clear Milius loved Gracie Jiu-Jitsu, and that he was devoted to Rorion, with whom he was taking those private lessons every week. The guy had, of course, gotten his son Ethan involved, and the kid was now more hard-core than his dad. I figured that anyone who was willing to continually make that

God-forsaken drive through all of the traffic and construction from the pricey part of Los Angeles, down to the far less fashionable South Bay, must really be serious.

Milius and I had become friendly from chats in Rorion's office, but we weren't really friends. I truly liked and respected the guy, and I thought that he probably felt the same way about me, but our relationship hadn't progressed outside of the Gracie Academy.

It was different with Rorion and Milius, though. Being a serious player Academy Award nominee, Milius was used to having people look up to him. But since Rorion was his instructor, the dynamic of their relationship put Milius in the role of the admirer, rather than the one being admired. So I thought that it was Rorion, and not me, who had to approach Milius about being involved in War of the Worlds.

"But what would he do?" Rorion asked me.

"Any fucking thing he wants."

Never did I harbor any allusions that Milius was going to start keeping hours in my little office at the corner of El Prado and Sartori, nor did I think that he would go out on pitch meetings with me to potential investors and sponsors.

I knew that Milius was very successful in the film business and, from what I could tell, he was also fairly wealthy and incredibly busy. So the chance to make a little money off of War of the Worlds probably wouldn't be a motivating factor, and the prospect of devoting large chunks of his time to our fighting tournament would likely turn him off.

I told Rorion that what we needed from Milius was his support. You don't make a career in Hollywood like his without being incredibly smart and creative. I knew that he was bound to have a lot of ideas that we could to use. But even more importantly, just like in the movie business, having a big name attached to your project opens up a lot of doors that would otherwise stay closed. Make that locked and bolted shut.

Rorion agreed that he would set up a meeting for us at the Gracie Academy with Milius, but that I should do most of the talking. Before we met with him though, I felt that we needed something to show Milius, rather than just profit projections and marketing plans. Clearly, as someone who had made a career for himself in movies, Milius was a visual thinker.

I contacted Deb Stanley, a former co-worker of mine from the direct marketing business, about having her husband, Mike, do a sketch. He was an accomplished artist, and also a martial artist, who I knew would get what I was talking about.

I met with Mike and outlined the whole concept. I told him that War of the Worlds was going to be an epic event—one that would hopefully spawn a franchise. All of these different fighting styles from across the world coming together for a one night, single elimination tournament. We hadn't booked anything with Lulu yet for Brazil, and we were nowhere close to having a date set. But I wanted this to look like a real fight poster for a real event, so I told Mike to make it appear as though the tournament would take place in Rio de Janeiro on October 31 of the upcoming year, 1993. I really liked the theatricality of holding our event on Halloween night.

Mike and I also talked about my inspiration for War of the Worlds coming partially from Pankration of the Ancient Olympics. Was there a way that he could create this using a classic motif? Something that made fans think of the Time of Antiquity?

"So, if we had a kickboxer facing off against a grappler on a Greek pedestal–that might work, right?" Mike asked.

"Exactly."

Mike and I then riffed on what styles of fighting we could include on the poster. We needed 16, as that would be the number of fighters in the tournament. Between the two of us though, we could only come up with 15. I then figured that perhaps one of the styles could have two representatives.

Mike clearly understood my vision, and I put him straight to work. When Mike showed me his finished product, it was even better than I'd hoped. It did in fact seem like a real fight poster for a real event. Standing on what looked like the Parthenon in Greece, with mountains silhouetted in the background, were two fighters. They were face-to-face, drawn in all white. The fighter on the left was bare-chested, with a fist cocked, knee raised and poised to strike.

The fighter on the right was in a gi, and in the process of throwing a head kick, which his opponent was simultaneously attempting to block. The force of their battle was shaking loose the foundation of the fighting pedestal, as the rubble was flying into the air. Framed by two rising columns, in gold letters were the words, "War of the Worlds, World Hand-to-Hand Fighting Championship, Rio de Janeiro, Brazil, October 31, 1993."

At the bottom of the poster, written on the fighting pedestal were the 15 styles of fighting that Mike and I had come up with: "Boxing, Hapkido, Jiu-jitsu, Judo, Karate, Kempo, Kickboxing, Kung Fu, Pencak Silat, Sambo, Savate, Shoot fighting, Sumo, Tae Kwon Do and Thai Boxing." Below that was: "Presented by Mills/Niemeyer and W.O.W. Productions."

I'd told Mike that it couldn't hurt to give Lulu's company a free pop, since there was a chance that we would be working with them. In addition to the poster, I also had Mike do some sketches of crowns that we could award the winner. I figured that championship belts were for boxing and pro wrestling, and trophies were for karate tournaments. We were going to go big in every way—literally crown the king of the fighting world.

I was drawing from the Gracies, boxing, vale tudo and my own wild ideas.

But my biggest inspiration was Pankration. I had it in my head that I was going to be bringing back something from the classical world. I took Mike's finished work to Rorion, who loved it as much as I did.

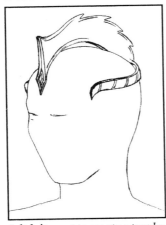

Photo courtesy of Art Davie archives/W.O.W. Promotions

These were going to be my only props in our pitch to Milius. I knew that I would also have my well-rehearsed explanation of what War of the Worlds was all about. And as my ace in the hole, I would have Rorion by my side.

On a Tuesday night just before Christmas, after Milius had finished his private lesson with Rorion, the three of us met in Rorion's office. I started by telling Milius that I had read in Eldridge Cleaver's 1967 book, *Soul on Ice*, that the real Mr. Universe was the world heavyweight boxing champion. We were going to create a title that would be bigger than that.

I didn't want to create a trophy or a belt as an award for the winner of our tournament. So I had Mike Stanley draft this sketch for a crown.

"I love it," Milius said immediately.

I then let Milius know that we weren't asking him for any money. What we wanted was his input, as much or as little as he would be willing to give us. Milius seemed open to the idea from the start, and I could tell that he loved the imagery of the classical world: mythological Greece, Pankration, the ancient Olympiad, all of it.

"What exactly do you need from me?" Milius asked.

I answered with a job title that I knew from my days in advertising, "To be the creative director."

Without hesitation, Milius told Rorion and me that he would be glad to lend his name to War of the Worlds, and that he wouldn't accept any money from us whatsoever. Milius didn't even blink. With most hotshot Hollywood players, it's going take a lot of tap dancing to get them to commit to anything. Meeting after meeting after meeting. And then there's the army of attorneys, agents, managers and assistants who have to get involved. But with Milius, one quick conversation at the Academy was all that it took. Towards the end of the meeting, Milius said, "This is the search for the real Superman." Clearly he got it, right then and there.

I could tell that Gracie Jiu-Jitsu was something extremely personal and meaningful to Milius, and that his respect for Rorion was the main reason why he said yes to us.

I wasn't sure if my impassioned pitch and Mike Stanley's fight poster and crown sketches had even mattered. But I really didn't care. I had gotten Rorion on board, and now Milius was in the fold. There was still the business plan to write, a tournament's worth of fighters to find, and $250,000 to procure. But one-step at time. And John Milius as creative director for War of the Worlds was, without question, a huge step.

On January 5, 1993, Milius sent a letter to Rorion at the Academy, in care of W.O.W. It didn't matter to me that it was only addressed to Rorion, and not to both of us.

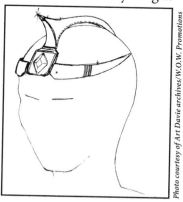

Photo courtesy of Art Davie archives/W.O.W. Promotions

This was the second crown design from Mike Stanley. Both were eventually featured in my 65-page business plan.

The contents, which was written on his A Team Productions letterhead with the word "Conan" on the top of the page, were confirmation of his commitment to us. Pure fucking gold. In it, Milius wrote:

"I appreciate your invitation to be involved in this project. I feel it connects the present to the past by recreating the classical Greek and Roman contest of Pankration. I believe that I can contribute to make this tournament a World Class Event. Therefore, I am eager to serve as the Creative Director."

We were on the road. Picking up speed and heading toward our prize.

I now felt like Carl Denham, the producer character in the classic 1933 film *King Kong*. I'm dripping with enthusiasm, and I sound a bit crazed. I'm telling people that War of the Worlds is going to be an overwhelming success—just like the giant ape that Denham discovered on Skull Island.

"We're millionaires, boys! Why, in a few months, his name will be up in lights on Broadway! Kong! The Eighth Wonder of the World!"

I just tried not to dwell on the end of the film, when King Kong falls to his death from the top of the Empire State Building.

CHAPTER 7

THE NEW YORK BANKEES

A HANDFUL OF PATIENCE IS WORTH MORE THAN A BUSHEL OF BRAINS.
— DUTCH PROVERB

BACK in 1982, when Pat Strong pitched Rorion on his World Freestyle Fighting Championship idea, he envisioned it as a one-off event that would be done for the home video market. The producer who tried to set up the rematch between Rorion and Benny "the Jet" was thinking about the same thing. And even Rorion, when I explained my plan to him—the one that finally got him to say yes and join me—initially thought that I was talking about creating a videotape. He was focused in this direction, based on all of the money that was pouring in from the Brajitsu, Inc., tapes.

But from the earliest stages of the work that I did for my World's Best Fighter proposal to Wisdom Imports, I saw this as a live television broadcast. There was definitely money to be made in home video sales, as I had clearly demonstrated to Rorion with the *Basics of Gracie Jiu-Jitsu* series, but it seemed like chump change in comparison to what could be reaped through TV. Perhaps you strike a deal with Blockbuster or Hollywood Video, but really, how many tapes are you going to sell?

Television on the other hand could generate sums into the multi-millions of dollars. You could get a rights deal from a network like

ESPN or HBO, where they pay you a fee to air your events. I knew there was no way to get the event on broadcast TV, but cable was a possibility. My main focus though was Pay-Per-View television, which if successful, would take us into the financial stratosphere. I needed to look no further than Don King and Bob Arum in boxing, and Vince McMahon, Jr. in pro wrestling, as shining examples.

To start pitching PPV and cable TV outlets, I needed to finish my executive summary and business plan. Now that Milius was on board, I had a name that I could include which would jump off of the page—one that would announce loud and clear that I wasn't some dipshit bringing them a karate tournament to be held in a shopping mall dojo.

I'd written plenty of business plans over the years for my various entrepreneurial ventures, and they usually took me anywhere from six to eight weeks to complete. You have to spell out, in painstaking detail, how you are going to actually make money with your crazy idea, and why someone should trust you with their hard earned cash. They go on and on and on.

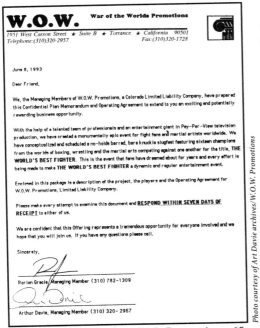

Photo courtesy of Art Davie archives/W.O.W. Promotions

This is the cover of W.O.W. Promotions 65-page business plan. Only 68 of these were ever distributed to investors.

But it took me just two weeks to crank out this 65-page business plan. I'd never been as fired up about anything in my life, as I was for War of the Worlds. The business plan was accompanied by a two-page executive summary, which would be used to gauge initial interest of the people that I was going to contact.

The first page read in full:

WAR OF THE WORLDS

The World Hand-to-Hand Combat Championship

The concept behind this event is quite simple:

*Millions are practicing various martial arts worldwide.

*Thousands are watching various martial arts worldwide.

*All the existing contests showcase only intramural competition. (i.e. taekwondo vs. taekwondo, karate vs. karate, etc.)

*Among fans and martial artists, there is one question that has always been asked: "Which art is the most effective?"

*Therefore, a competition that would draw boxers, wrestlers, kickboxers, as well as experts in karate, taekwondo, kung fu, judo, aikido, etc., and allow them to compete in an, open no-holds-barred event, would have very broad appeal. Such an event would create the world's hand-to-hand combat champion.

*Allowing the fighters to dress and compete according to their style would create tremendous fan enthusiasm. Because of its broad appeal to fight fans and martial artists, War of the Worlds is conceptualized as a theatrically staged world-class event. To this end, W.O.W. Promotions has recruited famed film director John Milius (Conan the Barbarian) to be the event's creative director.

At the top of the second page, I explained our format:

WOW is a single-elimination, challenge tournament with (16) entrants, drawn approximately from the following arts. They compete for $110,000 in prize money, and the title of the World's Hand-to-Hand Combat Champion.

I listed the styles of martial arts and combat sports that would be involved, listing the number of representatives from each:

Western Boxing, 1 representative

Kickboxing, 2 representatives

Wrestling (Greco-Roman or Freestyle), 1 representative

Okinawan/Japanese Karate (Shotokan, Goju, Kenpo), 2 representatives

Korean Karate (Taekwondo, Tang So Do, Hapkido), 2 representatives

Kung Fu, 2 representatives

Thai Boxing, 1 representative

French Savate, 1 representative

Jiu-jitsu, 1 representative

Aikido, 1 representative

Judo, 1 representative

Shoot boxing, 1 representative

As for this last entry on the page, shoot boxing, I had in mind the hybrid fighting that they were starting to do in Japan, which seemed to mix the worked aspects of modern pro wrestling, with the shoot aspects of the sport's long past.

I'd decided to up the total prize money to $110, 000, using a system based on:

$50,000 to the tournament winner

$22,000 to the tournament runner-up

$10,000 to the two losing semifinalists

$2,500 to the four losing quarterfinalists

$1,000 to the eight opening round losers

I set about cold calling everyone that I could think in TV and PPV who might have even the remotest interest in giving War of the Worlds a serious look: HBO, Showtime, ESPN, even Prime Ticket, a regional sports cable channel based in Los Angeles.

Especially intriguing to me were HBO and Showtime, because both cable networks operated their own in-house PPV outlet, which they used for huge boxing cards. HBO's was called TVKO; Showtime's was named SET, and both knew how to bring in truckloads of money.

The 1991 world title fight between Evander Holyfield and George Foreman had 1,450,000 PPV buys for TVKO, grossing a reported $55 million. I figured if War of the Worlds could do a tenth of that business, we'd all be in pretty good shape.

I settled on a two-pronged attack for television, primarily targeting PPV outlets, while also going after cable channels. The broadcast

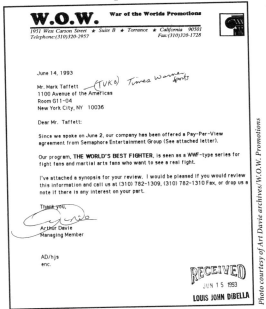

Here is the pitch letter to TVKO/HBO. Famed boxing TV pioneer Lou DiBella was forwarded this letter by Mark Taffett and he was the executive who turned me down.

networks ABC, CBS, NBC and the fledgling FOX seemed like a waste of my time. I just couldn't see Rickson choking some poor taekwondo guy unconscious, right after an all-new episode of *Murder, She Wrote*.

From my advertising career past, I was very comfortable with, and very capable of, getting decision makers on the phone. Cold calling without fear or hesitation was no problem for me. And so I went about it, going down my list. But my time in the ad business had also made me very aware that rejection is a big part of the game. Get used to it, because you're going to hear "no" a lot more than you hear "yes."

And the rejections came quickly from HBO and Showtime, which also meant TVKO and SET. The head of sports programming for HBO/TVKO, Lou DiBella, let me know that there was a memo floating around their offices in New York that said if a guy came to their door pitching anything that had to do with kickboxing or martial arts—slam the door in his face.

Jay Larkin, a senior VP and executive producer for boxing at Showtime/SET told me that he'd be more interested if I was pitching him a show on "*marital* arts" rather than martial arts.

Michael Aresco at ESPN and Terri Quinn at Prime Ticket, both asked me to send them my two-page executive summary, and said they'd be in touch. I understood that these could be polite blow-offs, but I mailed them the exec summary just the same. At least they hadn't said "no" right away like DiBella and Larkin.

As far as PPV, I'd only scratched the surface. It was no doubt a booming enterprise that expanded far beyond the boxing offered up on TVKO and SET. There was pro wrestling, music and comedy concerts, and lots of oddball events like Jimmy Connors vs. Martina Navratilova in a tennis exhibition from Caesar's Palace in Las Vegas, and a basketball one-on-one competition from Atlantic City featuring Dr. J and Kareem Abdul-Jabbar. None of these fell under the HBO or Showtime umbrella.

Back at the Torrance Public Library, I found, and then read over 200 articles on the PPV-TV industry—literally everything that they had. A name that kept popping up as an emerging force in the business was Semaphore Entertainment Group (SEG).

On April 14, 1993, exactly one year and one day after I signed my contract for the 22.5 percent commission on the *Basics of Gracie Jiu-Jitsu* tapes with Rorion, I called SEG in New York. Cold.

I asked the receptionist for Campbell McLaren, who I knew from my research, was SEG's Vice President of Original Programming—the guy who was tasked with finding new shows. I was put right through to Campbell, and after a brief introduction, I started in—laying it on thick.

Borrowing from Milius, I told him that what we were doing was, "The search for the real Superman." I didn't let Campbell catch his breath. Academy Award nominee John Milius was our creative director, my partner was Rorion Gracie of the Brazilian family who had created an unbeatable fighting style. And the guy who designed the UN Building, well, his relative, was our promoter, and we were going to do our first event in Rio—probably on Halloween night.

This would be the real deal, featuring 16 of the best martial artists and combat sports athletes from around the world. There would hardly be any rules. Fights to the finish, consequences be damned. This just wouldn't be sports, it would be spectacle. And best of all, this wasn't going to be a one-time thing. War of the Worlds was built to be a never-ending series of tournaments to discover the latest and the greatest king of combat.

That was my big finish, because my research had shown me that what SEG lacked was a franchise. Everything that they did was a one-shot: New Kids on the Block, Andrew Dice Clay, the Judds Farewell Concert. SEG had a few hits, and some big misses, but absolutely nothing that would keep the same customers coming back time and time again. I was a native New Yorker talking to a guy in New York, and I knew that I couldn't be humble.

"The train is leaving the station, Campbell. Either you'll be with me for the first event, or you'll be watching it at home on TV."

"So you're going to do this event, if we don't get involved?" asked Campbell.

"Absolutely. I've had discussions with HBO and Showtime, and ESPN is currently reviewing my proposal."

It got very quiet on the other end of the phone. Then Campbell asked if I could fax him my proposal for War of the Worlds. I told him I'd do it as soon as I hung up, and that I'd also overnight him both *Gracie Jiu-Jitsu in Action* tapes, so that he'd be able to see the type of fighting that I was talking about. At that moment, I knew that I had my PPV partner. All I had to do now was close the deal. Two weeks later, on

April 27, I received a fax from Campbell, in which he wrote:

"Dear Art: Thank you for all the information on War of the Worlds, the World Hand-to-Hand Combat Championship. I am definitely interested in pursuing this event as a Pay-Per-View television show. I think there is tremendous potential in the War of the Worlds and am anxious to begin working with you and Rorion. We should schedule a meeting in the next few weeks. I will call you soon to set up a convenient date."

Campbell arranged our meeting for the first week in May, at the SEG headquarters on 57th Street in Manhattan, and said that they would pay for my entire trip. I told Rorion about the meeting, but didn't even ask him if he wanted to go. He probably wouldn't have anyway—too busy, not interested, this wasn't his world; those sorts of things would have likely been his response. I knew that by and large at this point, he was happy to leave the driving to me. Rorion wished me good luck, and that was that.

On my flight out from Los Angeles, I started to wonder if War of the Worlds could really take off. Getting shown the door by HBO and Showtime was wholly expected, but it hadn't exactly boosted my confidence. I had a solid two-page executive summary, a killer 65-page business plan, an outstanding fight poster for an event that did not yet exist, Milius as our creative director and Rorion with the Gracie name and reputation. And now I had a meeting across the country with a legit PPV-TV outlet, serious enough to bring me out on their dime.

What I didn't have though was an actual set location and date for our first event, or the 16 fighters that we needed for the first tournament. I figured that Rickson was in for sure, but I'd never actually bothered to ask him, and I wasn't positive that Rorion had yet either. And there was the matter of the $250,000 that I'd always felt that we needed to raise, of which we had so far brought in nothing. But maybe SEG would chip in $250,000 or even more? I really didn't know what to expect.

A young, cute receptionist greeted me when I entered the SEG offices. Behind her were small cubicles with lots of intense folks hunched over computers. Campbell came out and greeted me warmly: he was not what I'd expected. An executive with a slightly bohemian edge to him, he was quick-witted, fast-talking and New York cool. He had on a tweed jacket with patches on the elbows and his hair was unfashionably long. Campbell was chubby and looked like he had been a hippy in his earlier days. He also looked like he had done his share of mind-altering drugs. I liked him immediately.

Campbell was my entry point, but I knew that he wasn't the final decision maker. That was SEG owner, president and CEO Bob Meyrowitz, who Campbell said I'd meet in a bit. First, he wanted to introduce me around the office. There was Michael Pillot, the in-house producer for SEG's broadcasts. Balding, and with a constant smile, Pillot looked a lot like the creative directors and art directors that I had worked with throughout much of my professional life in advertising.

Next up was Stephen Loeb, SEG's chief financial officer—the guy who made out the checks. Loeb struck me as the quintessential New Yorker, sarcastic and very funny. He looked like Central Casting had hired him to play the skinflint in charge of a big company's money.

On then to David Isaacs. Slim, of average height and clean-shaven, he struck me as quiet, self-assured, intellectual and very smart. It wasn't actually explained to me what Isaacs did at SEG. Apparently, he had both a law degree and a finance degree from Harvard, and he'd previously worked for Bertelsmann's Music Group in Europe—better known in the show business world as BMG. I knew from my research back at the Torrance Public Library that BMG was SEG's big financial backer. Something about the PPV concerts with the music superstars. And I knew that BMG was the largest privately held entertainment company on the planet, so perhaps Isaacs was their man at SEG. Neither Campbell nor Isaacs explained further, and I didn't ask.

Then there was Michael Abramson, a guy I knew immediately. Not literally, but I'd bought advertising time for clients from salesmen exactly like Abramson for years. Sales studs like him were the backbone of radio and TV stations across the country, selling commercial time, which allowed the creative types to be creative. Abramson's office was small and crammed. It looked impossibly disorganized, but not chaotic. He was a husky guy, with his jacket off and his tie loosened. A fast talker with plenty of New York smarts, who I liked right off the bat.

"There's more than 20 MSOs (multi-system operators), and more than a thousand cable systems in the U.S. and Canada. I close them on our shows. I'm on the phone following up on a kit, like this," Abramson said as he held up a package about one of SEG's upcoming PPV broadcasts.

It was Abramson's job to get the local cable providers from California to Maine to push SEG's product. I understood it completely. It also turned out that Abramson did more than PPV. Campbell escorted me around the corner, and there was a recording studio right there in SEG's offices. It turned out that they cut the syndicated radio program, *The King Biscuit Flower Hour*, there every week.

King Biscuit was a rock radio institution that began in 1973, and aired every Sunday night on more than 300 stations across the country. It featured concerts that were specially recorded for the show, with artists ranging from Eric Clapton to the Grateful Dead to U2.

Abramson's job on this program was to close radio stations in North America, and from what I could see, he was really good at it. He'd better be, because *King Biscuit* was the creation and baby of his boss, Bob Meyrowitz.

I was next introduced to Mary Corigliano, a marketing coordinator who seemed smart, and was very attractive. I could tell this well-dressed blonde, young woman was a big asset at SEG. Mary handled herself like she would eventually be running the whole show.

I'd done my homework on Meyrowitz, trying to get a handle on the guy, and more importantly his needs for SEG. A magazine article that I'd read explained that SEG was searching within the PPV television milieu for a franchise. Concerts, both music and comedy were, by definition, one-night stands. Almost nobody was going to pay to watch the same performer multiple times in a year. And the sporting events that they'd produced, such as the Martina Navratilova vs. Jimmy Connors tennis match in Las Vegas had failed to be SEG's ticket to the pot of gold at the end of the rainbow. Nothing on their roster was a series of ongoing events such as TVKO and SET had with their non-stop line up of boxing world title fights. SEG had thus far failed to find a franchise to call their own.

I could immediately tell from the vibe at SEG, that Meyrowitz was, without question, "the Man." The way that Campbell and all of the employees spoke of him, and genuflected when his name was mentioned, made it clear that Meyrowitz had a large and well-developed ego. Everyone there deferentially referred to him as "Meyro," as though it was a title more than a nickname. When I was ushered into Meyrowitz's office, after being made to wait a considerable amount of time, Campbell and I then waited some more for him to get off the phone.

Meyrowitz was impeccably dressed. His suit and tie looked like it cost more than most people pay for rent or a mortgage. His hair was dark, cut fashionably and his beard was well trimmed. He came across as a modern day business buccaneer. Finally, he was ready to greet me, and started right in. Meyrowitz began expounding on what SEG did, and I mainly listened. He had strong opinions about everything, and mentioned that he'd been nominated for a Cable ACE Award for a Bette Midler special that he'd executive produced. Then he told me that he understood War of the Worlds, since he'd boxed as kid.

"I know fighting. I don't know the martial arts, but I know fighting," he said. "There were people who thought that I could have been the first Jewish heavyweight champ if I'd stayed with boxing,"

I figured that he had forgotten about Max Baer, as well as reality, but I kept my mouth shut. He was big, well over six feet tall, with an imposing physical presence. But Meyrowitz certainly didn't strike me as the sort of guy who liked to mix it up in the ring or on the street. But what could I say? I just smiled and nodded.

Then we got into why I was there, and I could tell that his level of preparation on me was nowhere close to the prep that I had done on him. It struck me that this was Campbell's pet project, and that he was the one who brought me out to New York, not Meyrowitz. But Campbell just sat there in deference to his boss, hardly saying a word.

I started talking about Rorion and his family's history. Meyrowitz asked me about their style of fighting, and I used a phrase that Rorion was fond of, "With the Gracies, they need time to cook a guy." What this meant when Rorion said it—and what I was trying to convey to Meyrowitz and Campbell—was that their technique could be a slow-build. The takedowns and positions, the transitions and submissions often took time—it was not like a one-punch knockout in boxing.

This completely stopped the discussion cold. As soon as I said it, I realized that it was going to take thirty minutes of explanation on my part. Campbell—my advocate—looked at me like he didn't know what the hell I was talking about. And Meyrowitz wasn't about to be drawn into an esoteric discussion that only a martial artist or a serious fan would understand. I could see he wanted to keep his eyes focused on the big picture, which was how he could make money with War of the Worlds.

Sensing that I was losing Meyrowitz, I then mentioned that I was a fellow cigar aficionado, turned on to Cubans by Milius. They all smoked cigars in the office, and when I first arrived, Campbell had offered me a Punch Black Prince, which I happily accepted and lit up. Meyrowitz warmed to this part of our discussion. But as I sat in his office, our mutual love of cigars notwithstanding, I sensed he wasn't so sure that this venture was going to work. But I also felt that he just might be willing to take a flyer on Campbell's say-so.

Meyrowitz said that we should get our respective attorneys together to see how a deal could be structured. It hit me that I didn't know anything about how a deal was done in this industry, and that I'd never gotten around to putting an attorney on retainer. I hadn't even bothered to register W.O.W. Promotions as an LLC, or anything else for that matter. It existed only on paper, sharing an address with a martial arts school in Torrance, California.

I called Rorion at his office back at the Gracie Academy, and told him that SEG seemed preliminarily interested, and that they were preparing a deal. But let's not start popping the champagne corks yet. What that deal would propose and offer, I had no idea. All I did know for sure was that we had to get our shit together, and right away. After our meeting, Campbell and Isaacs took me out for a meal at McCormick & Schmick's at 52nd and 6th Ave., where I got a taste of the sort of life these show business types led. There was a huge platter of Dungeness crab, thick, rare T-bone steaks and icy Bombay Sapphire gin martinis. I had no doubt that these guys knew how to fly first class. With their connection to BMG, I started to think of SEG as the New York Bankees.

As soon as I got back to Los Angeles, I packed up my car, withdrew a few thousand dollars in cash from my personal account, grabbed my 9mm Glock 17, and hit the road for Denver. There was no way Rorion was going to make the trip, as he was wall-to-wall with the Gracie Academy, but he agreed that we'd split all of my costs.

I was headed there to first and foremost register W.O.W. Promotions as an LLC in the state, then locate a local attorney for us, and finally scout possible venues. Rio was feeling more and more to me like a really expensive and possibly disastrous idea.

W.O.W. Promotions, LLC, officially moved from a paper company to a real one on May 12, 1993. I hired Mark Field to be our attorney in Denver. He got us an accountant, J.A. Olsen & Associates, and I set up our company checking and savings accounts with First Bank at 17th and Broadway.

While there, I tracked down Karyn Turner, the kickboxing promoter with the Coors beer sponsorship, with whom I'd spoken three-and-a-half years earlier when I was trying to figure out my World's Best Fighter pitch to Wisdom Imports.

I asked Karyn about local fighters and possible venues. She told me that I should really look at McNichols Sports Arena, home of the Denver Nuggets. I still hadn't ruled out working with Lulu in Rio, but Colorado, with its legal tolerance for bare-knuckle fighting and now the home state of W.O.W. Promotions, LLC, was making more and more sense. Booking a venue would have to wait, as would setting a date for our inaugural event, but I did like the idea of playing a 17,000-seat NBA building.

Without question, there was a need for at least one hometown hero type in our tournament of 16 fighters, no matter where we held War of the Worlds. A local "champion" would help to not only sell tickets, but also energize the crowd. Karyn gave me a number of names, but at the top of her list was Pat Smith, a guy who was really making his mark on the Denver fight scene. Karyn said that he'd just won the Sabaki Challenge, which I knew was a huge bare-knuckle, full-contact karate tournament held annually in the city. He was also a pro boxer, and Karyn told me that he absolutely looked the part.

I went to watch Smith work out at Tiger Kim's Academy, and he instantly reminded me of the boxing knock-out artist Cleveland Williams, who fought Muhammad Ali for the world title in 1966. Smith was impressive: quick, athletic, and powerfully built at 6-foot-2 and about 220 lb. But he also struck me as a bit weird, kind of volatile, and paranoid. He told me about his win at the Sabaki Challenge, and that he'd been working with the noted boxing trainer Bobby Lewis, who had served as the U.S. Olympic coach in 1972.

Smith then said to me that he had a record of 250-0, which I found amusing, and wholly predictable. I'd heard talk around the Gracie Academy that Rickson was 400-0. What Smith didn't know was that after Karyn Turner recommended him, I quickly did a little research and discovered that he had at least two losses as a pro boxer. His personal record keeping didn't deter me though, as I hit it off pretty well with him, despite his edgy vibe.

As for his style, Smith said that he was a black belt in tae kwon do, and had also trained in robotae, which was taught to him as a kid by a school janitor. I'd never heard of robotae in my life, but like his 250-fight winning streak, it would do for now.

I told Smith that the winner's check would be for $50,000, and that was good enough for him. Just like that I'd successfully recruited my first fighter.

As soon as I drove back to Los Angeles from Denver, I hired Donald Delano Moss (a Loyola law school grad) in Burbank as our entertainment lawyer. Fields was our guy in Denver, but that was for W.O.W. Promotions, LLC things, like setting up our bank accounts and drawing up a fighter contract for Pat Smith. Business lawyer things. Moss was the guy who was going to have to go head-to-head on the forthcoming SEG contract, with their lead counsel, who just happened to be Meyrowitz's brother, David.

We got Moss just in time, as Campbell was right back on the phone requesting another meeting at SEG in New York, now with Rorion accompanying me. Meyrowitz wanted to meet my partner, and he wanted to talk about finalizing our deal for War of the Worlds. Campbell said that they'd pick up the tab again, and that we were all moving in the right direction.

At this point, I got the feeling that Campbell needed War of the Worlds more than War of the Worlds needed Campbell. While it didn't look promising, I hadn't yet heard back from ESPN and Prime Ticket which meant I might still have a shot with them. I'd come this far, picking up Rorion and Milius along the way. If it wasn't SEG, I'd find someone else. I wasn't sure who or when, but I did know that War of the Worlds would not live or die based on the whims of Campbell McLaren and Bob Meyrowitz.

I hadn't just done my homework on Meyrowitz; I'd done it on Campbell as well. He had a producer's mentality and seemed to have an understanding of what an audience would want. So, when I first ran my concept for War of the Worlds by him on the phone, he shot a lot of smart questions at me. I'd discovered in talking to him that in his search for new shit, he'd looked into midget pro wrestling, monster trucks, Mexican luche libre and other marginalia. Campbell's job as Vice President of Original Programming for SEG was based on his getting shows on the air, which would generate a lot of PPV buys, and thus a big profit for Meyrowitz.

The concerts they had been doing had huge talent fees, plus the legal costs for clearing the usage of the music. The top comedians didn't have the music clearance issue, but they still commanded big paychecks. Stars sold PPVs, but they also cost a hell of a lot of money. I suspected that SEG wasn't making a big profit on these. And anyway, you could only go to the well with New Kids on the Block so many times.

Campbell had graduated from Berkeley, did a stint at MIT, and had studied with Richard Leacock, the famed film documentarian. He had gone on to be a key player in the development of the Catch A Rising Star comedy nightclubs. This made sense, because from my first cold call, Campbell had struck me as a frustrated comedian. Whether or not he lacked the moxie to get up on stage, or decided early on that his future was in the business side of entertainment, I didn't know for sure. But, he was a funny, wisecracking guy and an out-of-the-box thinker.

At this point, W.O.W. Promotions hadn't really cost Rorion and me anything. We had my car trip to Denver, the fee of setting up the LLC, and the small amount that we'd paid to our lawyers Moss and Fields, and to the Denver accountants. But that was really it. I was still working out of the office down the hall from my apartment, and Rorion was still based at the Gracie Academy. He was there until 10 p.m. most nights, teaching classes and running the Academy business. Then he had his traveling Gracie Jiu-Jitsu seminars, and the cash that continued to roll in from the Brajitsu, Inc. videotapes.

Neither he nor I were collecting a salary from W.O.W. Promotions, which would have been ridiculous, since we would have been paying ourselves out of our own pockets. Absolutely no outside money had come in. My income came from the sales of the *Basics of Gracie Jiu-Jitsu* tape series, with my 22.5-percent commission deal with Rorion proving to be more lucrative than ever.

So while I wanted to do a deal with SEG, and get War of the Worlds launched, I wasn't about to roll over for them, and certainly not for Meyrowitz. But it was exciting to be going back to New York again.

When we reconvened in Meyrowitz's office, this time with Rorion in tow, it became instantly clear to me where this was headed—they were going to offer us a sweetheart deal, with them being the sweethearts. Of this I was certain. Meyrowitz came out of the music business, which is notorious for ripping off talent. And in this set up, Rorion and I were the talent. I wasn't about to start negotiating on our behalf, that's why I'd hired Moss. But I kept thinking that our lawyer back in sunny Burbank, California, was going to get eaten alive by Meyrowitz and his lawyer brother David, who impressed me right away as being very good at his profession.

Aside from talking in general terms about their offer, Meyrowitz kept telling Rorion that he knew fighting. He kept going on about this, almost obsessively.

"Now, I don't know anything about your jiu-jitsu or the martial arts, but I know fighting. When I was a kid, people thought that I'd become the first Jewish world heavyweight boxing champion."

At one point, Rorion shot me a look, and I thought that I was going to piss my pants.

We ended the meeting without agreeing to anything, other than that they'd be sending us a formal offer. As we parted, I realized that I could relate to Meyrowitz. In a weird way, I sort of liked him, although I certainly didn't trust him. We were both native New Yorkers—actually growing up fairly close to each other in Brooklyn.

But Meyrowitz couldn't relate to Rorion at all, and vice versa. It wasn't that they were from different countries; it was like they were from different planets. Rorion made it clear that he thought Meyrowitz was an egomaniacal idiot with all of his "I know fighting" talk. And I got the strong feeling that Meyrowitz viewed Rorion as nothing more than a dumb fighter. This wasn't true, of course. Rorion wasn't dumb by any measurement. He was actually very smart.

The David Meyrowitz drafted and Bob Meyrowitz issued SEG contract to "W.O.W. Productions" (we were of course W.O.W. Promotions, and I tried not to take offense) dated June 3, 1993, offered a five-year deal. Clearly, both Campbell and Meyrowitz shared my unwavering belief that War of the Worlds would be a continuing series of fighting tournaments—a franchise, rather than a one-night stand.

The contract stated that SEG would be "producing and acquiring all rights and title in and to a video production of a live martial arts competition tentatively entitled War of the Worlds: The World Hand-to-Hand Championship. This would take place, on or about October 30, 1993, in Denver, Colorado"

SEG never seemed to warm to my Rio de Janeiro idea, and at my two meetings in Meyrowitz's office, I never pushed the issue. The costs were going to be exponentially higher than doing a live PPV broadcast from the continental 48, and there were all of the hassles and headaches that Lulu told us that we'd face. So much for my dream of meeting an exotic, round-assed, Brazilian beauty.

I had enlightened Campbell and Meyrowitz on W.O.W. being registered as an LLC in Colorado, and on the state government's lack of oversight and regulation when it came to prize fighting. I'd also told them that if we did Colorado, the only city to consider was Denver, since any place else in the state would make our event feel small and minor league.

I had long felt that there was a nice symmetry to holding the first War of the Worlds on Halloween night. There was something of a freak-show element to what we were going to be doing, with fighters of all shapes and sizes doing battle. And I thought it would be a cool homage to the infamous radio adaptation of the H.G. Wells novel, in which a young Orson Wells scared the bejesus out of a gullible American public, by making them think that Martians had landed in New Jersey, and were taking over the world. *War of the Worlds* was the Mercury Theatre's 1938 Halloween episode.

But Campbell had explained to me that the big nights in the PPV-TV business were Fridays and Saturdays. Halloween 1993 was going to fall on a Sunday, so the tentative date was dropped back to the day before, October 30.

There were parts of their contract offer that I really liked. First and foremost was SEG's five-year option, which would escalate our guaranteed advance from $50,000 per event in 1993, to $150,000 per event by 1997. I was also pleased to see that they had written in an option to do two more events in 1993, three events in 1994, and then up to four events in 1995, 1996 and 1997.

But there were also some serious red flags. For starters, Section 2 of the contract stated that, "W.O.W. shall provide and pay for all production costs required by the live event and these live event costs shall in no event be the responsibility of SEG."

So in other words, we'd have to pay the fighters purse, arena rental, travel, hotel, meals, logistics and security—basically for everything apart from the PPV broadcast. From the beginning, I told Rorion that we'd need to raise $250,000 to get this thing off the ground. But now with SEG wanting in as our partner, I felt that they should absorb at least some of these costs. Namely the $110,000 total prize money that I'd proposed.

I also was troubled by Section 4: "SEG shall have the exclusive right to sell, distribute, perform, exploit, advertise and market the production throughout the world in any and all media whatsoever, in perpetuity, subject only to payment to W.O.W. of such royalties and other compensation as set for below."

Reading this, I suddenly wished that we had David Meyrowitz on our side, and SEG had Don Moss. And I realized that despite my long career in advertising, marketing and promotions, this stuff was over my head. And I was the guy who Rorion was counting on to get us a great deal.

He'd told me, "Whatever you decide, Arturo. You know how to negotiate. After all, look at the deal you squeezed out of me on the tapes."

The "royalties and other compensation set forth below" was our guarantee of $50,000 on the first event, and $50,000 if we did one or two more the rest of the year. Then the escalators went up to the $150,000 guarantee in year five of the deal in 1997. This I could understand.

What really concerned me though was Part B of Section 5, which said that we'd get $25,000 if "the production's initial Pay-Per-View broadcast attains a buy rate of at least 0.5 percent based on preliminary buy rate reports. And SEG would pay us $75,000 if "the production's initial Pay-Per-View broadcast attains a buy rate of at least 1.0 percent based on preliminary buy rate reports."

I didn't have any idea where the "preliminary buy rate reports" would come from. Would they be from an independent source or would they be from SEG's internal numbers? I didn't want Rorion and me to turn into those musicians who are in a never-ending financial and legal argument about how many records were actually sold.

But the kicker was how SEG was proposing to pay us in Section 6, Clause C of the contract which read in full: "50 percent of all revenues after SEG fully recoups all costs associated with the video production (including, but not limited to, all third party costs for production, marketing, advertising and talent) and receives a 12-percent return on investment."

So we'd get 50 percent of what, exactly? I had no doubt that this was where they would kill us with their accounting. I'd already sized up their CFO, Stephen Loeb. He was in that job for a reason.

I had long heard the legendary show biz story of how the actor James Garner sued Universal Studios over the hit television series that they owned, and he starred in, *The Rockford Files*. In 1983, three years after the show went off the air, Garner filed a lawsuit against Universal for $16.5 million, claiming fraud and deceit. Basically, that Universal had cooked the books in order to cheat Garner out of his back-end money. It took until 1987 for the suit to settle, which was for a sum that Garner was legally prohibited from revealing.

Our W.O.W. Promotions backend money was the 50 percent spelled out in Section 6, Clause C of SEG's contract offer, and I knew that if a star like James Garner could get royally fucked, what chance did Rorion and I have?

I decided that my play was to not sign the contract, and be amicable in not doing so. I'd keep this moving along with SEG—their proposed October 30 date was less than five months away—by continually telling Campbell and Meyrowitz that our attorney Don Moss was working through everything. They were acting like the contract was signed, sealed and delivered, and were already putting their plans in place for the live PPV broadcast of War of the Worlds.

At this point, I realized that it was time for W.O.W. Promotions to hire its first employee, and I knew who I wanted to get. If we were ever going to be a real company, it had to be more than just Rorion and me. We did have our creative director, but since he had agreed to lend us his name and support, we hadn't yet sat down with Milius to talk about War of the Worlds. And I always knew he would be just a consultant, at best.

So I approached Kathy Kidd, who'd pitched Rorion and me back in February, trying to sell us a booth at the United States Martial Arts Association trade show in Pasadena, which was scheduled to take place in a few weeks time. Kathy was very professional, polite, and I had already made note of the fact that she was also a very attractive blonde. The quintessential girl-next-door, with a voice that could melt butter.

Kathy told us that martial artists such as Jeff Speakman, Frank Dux and Frank Trejo would be in attendance, and that 60 booths had already been purchased by companies like Century Martial Arts, Otomix and Kwan. And they were going to be holding a preview screening of *Dragon: The Bruce Lee Story*, which wasn't scheduled to hit theaters until May.

Kathy thanked us for our time, and we told her that we'd think about it, and be in touch. But as much as I liked Kathy, I explained to Rorion that the booth price of $750 was just too much. We would be better served in spending that amount of money on a new direct mail campaign, rather than a trade show booth. The Brajitsu, Inc. tapes were flying out the door as it was, and while the event sounded fun, it would be tough to recoup our investment. We'd of course had great success at the Long Beach International Karate Championship the summer before, but the Brajitsu, Inc. mail order business had really grown since then. And a booth at Long Beach cost a lot less than what Kathy was asking for Pasadena.

Photo courtesy of Kathy Kidd

Rorion agreed, then said, "I saw the way she was looking at you. And the way you were looking at her. She's your type. I bet you two get together. What do you think?"

I ducked the question. When I called Kathy later that day to let her know that we decided to pass on a booth, she graciously invited me to the trade show as her guest.

This is Kathy Kidd, our first employee. Kathy had been a marketing/event promotion powerhouse when I persuaded her to join our merry band in the summer of 1993.

When I attended the following month, I discovered that Kathy was not only a salesperson, she was also the event coordinator. She told me that she worked as an independent marketing and promotions coordinator, and that the United States Martial Arts Association was just one of her clients. What impressed me most about Kathy was that she was working the event while suffering from the flu. I hung out there for half the day, and she never once complained or slowed down. Kathy just kept busting her ass, and with a constant and genuine smile.

What I saw in Pasadena was a confident woman, who was also an extremely hard worker with the talent for bringing together lots of different people on a project, and solving problems as they arose. This convinced me that I needed Kathy Kidd to work for W.O.W. Promotions. She understood sales, marketing, promotions, event coordination and travel. For our first employee, above all else, I needed a smart organizer who knew the martial arts world, and she had that covered.

Having not seen nor even spoken with Kathy since the Pasadena martial arts trade show three months earlier, I gave her a call. After very brief small talk, I asked her out to dinner, not making clear if this would be business or pleasure. I met Kathy at a great little Italian restaurant in Torrance, the Via Firenze, which had excellent pasta, veal and a sophisticated wine list. I discovered that Kathy was very knowledgeable about wines and let her order a bottle. As the evening wore on, I told her all about my dream for War of the Worlds, and how it was now about to become a reality. She sat there listening attentively, with real or pretend stars in her eyes. I was blown away by her enthusiasm and personality.

The electricity between us was palpable, but I tried to keep it all business. I had an agenda and that was to recruit her to the team. There was no one else I was considering for the job. When I walked Kathy out to her car after dinner, it felt like there was a mutual attraction—a vibe. But since it seemed like we would now be working together, I pushed the thought out of my mind.

There was no denying though that something was going on. I vowed to make sure that this wouldn't interfere with the project. Kathy, without saying it, seemed to agree, and took the role of event coordinator that I offered her, which was really the role of chief operations officer. It was arranged that I'd pay her out of my own pocket until we brought in some investment capital. And just like that, we were on our way.

I was now Kathy's boss, and there was an unbelievable amount of work ahead for both of us. It was early June, and SEG's proposed date of October 30, 1993 for the first War of the Worlds was just over four-and-a-half months away.

I knew that even if Don Moss was able to get us a much better deal than the one that SEG was proposing, we'd still need a lot of cash. Maybe, just maybe, Meyrowitz would agree to pay for some or the entire $110,000 fighter purse, but no way was he going to pay for the rest of our costs, including Kathy's salary.

I told Rorion that it was now time for us to make a presentation to potential investors, and that he should lean heavily on his students. They all worshipped Rorion and the Gracie Family, and they would make for a friendly room. I worked my Rolodex, inviting anyone and everyone that I could think of too.

We sent out the invites, made calls and the following week Rorion and I welcomed 68 potential investors to the backroom of the Gracie Academy for our big W.O.W. Promotions presentation. Rorion's wife Suzanne, and his office manager, Helen, greeted the attendees and got them signed in. They then gave everyone their own copy of the 65-page business plan that I had written. Even though we didn't have a signed contract, when I told Campbell about this planned meeting, he offered to fly out from New York and attend. I didn't think twice about taking him up on his offer. Campbell's presence would demonstrate that this wasn't just some pipe dream, it was real, and it was going to be broadcast live across the U.S. by Semaphore Entertainment Group on Pay-Per-View TV.

Rorion got up to speak. First he thanked everybody for coming, presented the basic idea of War of the Worlds, introduced Campbell (who very briefly explained SEG's role and their "$400,000 commitment" to the first event), Kathy, and then me. I talked for an hour, and pitched like I had never pitched before. I caught both Rorion and Campbell looking at me as if to say, "You're on fire!"

Our goal was to raise $250,000. Rorion and I had agreed that he would own 50 percent of W.O.W. Promotions, I would get 40 percent, and the remaining 10 percent would be divided up by our investors.

We decided that a full share would cost $12,500, and an investor could come in for any portion of that sum.

I wasn't thrilled about our ownership distribution, as the 45-45-10 split that I'd proposed to Rorion seemed fair to me. But he balked, and I just wasn't in the mood to fight with him. We were too close now, and I was ramping up for the battle with Meyrowitz that was sure to come.

Not everyone who showed up that June night was serious. There were a lot of tire-kickers and kibitzers. But by the end of the evening, 24 individuals and three couples—24 were Rorion's people (mostly Gracie students) and three were mine—pulled out their checkbooks. The smallest amount purchased was a 1/10 share for $1,250. We'd raised $112,500, under half of our target amount. But at least we had operating capital, and 30 new allies who had joined the cause.

With our fresh money and Kathy on board, I felt that it was finally time to get W.O.W. Promotions into a real office. There was no room for Kathy at my personal office down the hall from my apartment, and it made us look like a joke that the W.O.W. Promotions address was also the address of the Gracie Academy. It would have been an even bigger joke to host meetings there with our new investors, potential sponsors, and any of the SEG guys who might fly in to see us. I didn't like the prospects of us being taken seriously as businessmen, when people were rolling around on mats, sweating and grunting just a few feet away.

On Monday, July 5, I located a small space at 1616 Gramercy Ave. in Torrance. It was far from spectacular, but it was a lot more impressive than having our headquarters in an apartment building or a martial arts school. Our new office was only a few blocks from my home, and about 100 yards from the back entrance of the Gracie Academy. We were right next to an AFL-CIO union hall, By Brazil, a churrascheria (Brazilian barbecue) that the Gracie family loved, and Lucio's Mexican restaurant.

Lucio's was a down and dirty establishment with some of the namesake's hunting trophies on the wall. Lucio himself doubled as our landlord. With Kathy's help, the W.O.W. Promotions headquarters was stocked with a computer, printer, fax machine, three telephones and a few pieces of used furniture. There was a good-sized waiting area with space for a receptionist, and two offices. Kathy settled into the smaller office, and the bigger one became mine. I found a huge blue conference table at a second-hand furniture warehouse, which I felt could serve as the focal point of the office, as well as my desk when there were no conferences scheduled.

Rorion had no interest in claiming either office for himself. If he had, I would have stuck Kathy in the waiting area. No doubt she would have settled there with a smile on her face. But I knew that Rorion would never relocate from his own office at the Academy. Rorion may have been the majority owner of W.O.W. Promotions, but the Gracie family business remained his primary focus.

As hands off as Rorion was about almost all things concerning War of the Worlds, he was all over it when I asked him if he could recommend a good candidate to be my secretary. He immediately told me about Sherry Santos.

I'd seen Sherry many times around the Gracie Academy, and even though I didn't really know her, I had no problem in offering her the job based solely on Rorion's endorsement. She was the wife of Fabio Santos, a black belt from Brazil, who worked as an instructor at the academy. Fabio was a great guy, and very personable, but he looked like a movie villain due to a long knife scar that covered most of one side of his face. Sherry was tall, blonde, and freckled who came across as an earth mother type. And she was very sweet and polite, which I knew would go a long way with the people who I hoped would be coming in to meet with Kathy and me.

When I offered her the job, Sherry asked me if there was a dress code, since she was a "T-shirt and jeans kind of girl." She knew that Kathy always wore business clothes, and that I was a dress-up guy: pin-striped and solid suits in shades of gray and blue, wingtip shoes, rep and foulard ties, all of that. This was the uniform that I wore from my earliest days in advertising, and I'd never looked back. But I figured that it was a new era for me now, so I told her that I was cool with what she called her "laid back clothes." I told Sherry that I would, however, continue to wear my suits, if it was all the same to her.

Then Sherry asked me if she could bring her best friend to work with her every day—a big, shaggy golden retriever named Grizz. When

I said yes, Sherry's smile lit up the office. She was in, and W.O.W. Promotions had welcomed its second employee.

Rorion and I were excited to tell Milius about the money that we'd generated, our new office space, and our two W.O.W. Promotions employees. We knew that a proper sit down was needed with our creative director, as it was now the second week in July, and time was running short. Rorion saw him weekly for their private lessons at the Gracie Academy, but they never really discussed War of the Worlds. When I did see Milius on occasion at the Academy, it never felt right for me to bring up business to him. I knew that he was really Rorion's guy, and I didn't want to be a pain in his ass. Milius had allowed us to use his name, which had no doubt helped with both SEG and our new investors.

I asked Rorion to set up a meeting, and Milius invited us to his office at Sony Pictures Studios in Culver City. In addition to filling in Milius on SEG and our capital raise, we wanted to discuss the fighting area for the event with him. After all, as the director of *Conan the Barbarian*, Milius had Arnold Schwarzenegger doing battle in a pit—imagery that I absolutely loved. His time was always tight, so I knew that we had to get every idea that he had. Milius' office was located in the legendary Thalberg Building on the Sony lot, and I was struck by how small it was. But it looked like all of the producers and writers housed there had similar sized lairs.

Right away I spotted a stand-up humidor for his cigars. Milius was smoking, and so was Frank McRae (a Milius buddy who had played briefly for the Chicago Bears and had acted in the Milius directed film, *Red Dawn*) who was there in his office that afternoon. I accepted a Montecristo from Milius, who knew better than to offer one to his Gracie Jiu-Jitsu instructor. Just the thought of them made Rorion turn green. Every once in a while, as the meeting progressed, Milius would go to the door

ARTHUR DAVIE

1616 GRAMERCY AVENUE. TORRANCE. CALIFORNIA 90501
(310) 782-6373   FAX (310) 782-6374

Photo courtesy of Art Davie archives

W.O.W. Promotions business card. I was thrilled we were moving forward and no longer relying on my little office on Sartori Ave. or the Gracie Academy to present ourselves to the world.

and blow smoke down the hallway.

"I like to piss off the Disney pukes," he explained, which made me laugh.

Rorion had to keep getting up to go outside for a breath of fresh air.

Milius said that he liked the idea of a stadium styled pit, straight out of *Conan*. Then he talked about the idea of Roman or Greek classical columns to set the stage. He loved that look on our mock-up poster, the one that Mike Stanley had created, and thought it would work. Rorion and I both nodded. Any idea was a good idea at that point. The October 30 date was closing in fast, and we still had a lot to figure out.

Milius thought that perhaps the gladiatorial approach would be the ticket. He told us that we should have cheerleaders, but that we'd call them "vestal virgins." He also thought that we should get a mascot, something like the USC Trojan. As Milius was cranking in to high gear, the phone rang. Julie Ann, Milius' secretary, answered it, then came in and announced, "Moses is on the phone." Charlton Heston wanted to speak about some National Rifle Association business.

When Milius concluded his call with Heston, he started to talk to us about Helene "Leni" Riefenstahl, the German film director and photographer widely known for directing the 1935 Nazi Party propaganda film *Triumph of the Will* and *Olympia* (about the 1936 Olympics) which had often been cited as a major influence in modern sports cinematography. Milius mentioned that in *Triumph of the Will* they had secured 140 anti-aircraft lights for the rally in Nuremberg and aimed them at the night clouds to form a cathedral of light—the shining columns went all the way up to the heavens. Perhaps, he announced, we could do something like that. Milius was on a roll, throwing in white horses and a marching band for good measure.

"Art, this is going to create a new Excalibur. The ring you design is a version of Excalibur, where an unknown man puts his hand on that sword and pulls it free to achieve immortality. This is a mythic situation you're creating. You've got to think big! You're not putting on the tiddlywinks championship here. This is the World Hand-to-Hand Fighting Championship."

Milius then told us that Alexander the Great was a patron of the fighting arts, and that after a huge feast, the Pankration fighters would be brought out to entertain. And that Darius, the King of Persia, had a team of bodyguards called the Immortals, who were so invincible that when they went to the Olympic Games to compete in Pankration, they all returned with the laurels. This, Milius exclaimed was what War of the Worlds should be about.

Listening to Milius, I kept thinking back to my conversation earlier in the week with Michael Pillot, SEG's live broadcast producer. Pillot had methodically explained to me about camera placement, lighting and the positioning of the fighting area in relationship to the in-house crowd. Not once did he mention vestal virgins.

Milius was in free association mode now, spit balling ideas left and right, as well as talking about films past and present. When the conversation turned to why Frank McRae should have been cast as Lennie in the 1992 film remake of *Of Mice and Men* instead of John Malkovich, I thought that it might finally be time for us to go.

Rorion looked half-dead from all of the cigar smoke, and as much as he liked Milius, I could tell that he wasn't all that certain about his ideas. But there was something that I loved about that pit from *Conan the Barbarian*; I just wasn't sure how it would work. As much as I liked Milius before that meeting, I liked him even more after it. In the land of Hollywood cool, he was the coolest.

As the summer of 1993 progressed, I fell into a regular routine of working on the event, I'd speak to Campbell two to three times a week on the phone, take and make calls with various other SEG people, and see Rorion every Tuesday and Friday. Tuesdays were casual conversations, either proceeding or following my private lessons with Royler. Fridays were the day when Rorion would make the very short walk to W.O.W. Promotions from the Gracie Academy.

Once he arrived at my office, we would then go to By Brazil for a consistently amazing meal cooked by a woman who had known Hélio back in Brazil. I'd always have two agendas to discuss: our marketing and direct mail campaigns for the ever-growing series of Gracie Jiu-Jitsu instructional videotapes, and of far more importance to me, the current state of affairs on War of the Worlds.

We'd start out on track with the Brajitsu, Inc. videotape business, but once we got to War of the Worlds, Rorion just wasn't that interested in the nuts and bolts of the operation: the arena, the date, the 14 fighters that we still needed to recruit, the fighting area, the advertising, the marketing, the sponsorship sales that Kathy was working on, none of it. As for the still unsigned contract offer from SEG, Rorion was happy to let Don Moss and me get it all sorted. What he really wanted to talk about was Gracie Jiu-Jitsu and the Gracie Diet.

Rorion would recite his often told stories of how his father had fought pro wrestling legend Wladek Zbyszko to a draw in 1934; had challenged "The Brown Bomber," boxing's world heavyweight champion Joe Louis to a vale tudo match in 1947 to no avail; and in 1955, had gone three hours and 42 minutes in an epic contest against his former student Waldemar Santana. And Rorion would go on and on about how you should never combine starches, and how bananas mix well with all other sweet fruits, but not with acidic fruits.

I just couldn't get him to lock in and fully focus on War of the Worlds. Whether it was his constant 12-hour days at the Academy, Brajitsu, Inc., his ever expanding travelling seminar business, the responsibilities that came with being a husband, father, brother, and oldest son of Hélio; or some combination thereof, I didn't know. But what I did know was that Rorion just didn't seem to have the level of interest in War of the Worlds held by Kathy, Sherry and me.

At one of our weekly Friday lunches at By Brazil in late July, I broached one of my growing concerns about War of the Worlds with Rorion. I'd always envisioned the tournament as being comprised of 16 fighters. Single elimination with the opening round, quarterfinals, semi-finals, and final—15 fights total all in one night. The 16-fighter concept had been spelled out in both our two-page executive summary and 65-page business plan. But two factors began to make me think that an eight-man tournament was actually the way to go.

First, both Campbell and Pillot had drilled into my head that we had a two hour, 50 minute broadcast window. We absolutely couldn't go even one second over. Something about SEG having to buy additional satellite time, and the local cable systems cutting off the live PPV broadcast signal if we went beyond that allotted period of time. I just didn't see how we could get all of those fights to fit into a sub-three hour show.

Second, I'd long since settled on our total prize money for the 16 fighters at $110,000—with $50,000 to the winner. But if we dropped the size of the tournament field to eight fighters, then we could greatly reduce our fight purse. $50,000 to the tournament winner seemed like a sum that I couldn't move away from without hurting our credibility, but by eliminating the number of fighters, I'd be cutting down the number of fighters who would have to be paid. This was a real concern in light of our $112,500 capital raise, and with SEG not budging on our request to have them pay all or part of the prize money.

"We only have Rickson and Pat Smith so far," I said to Rorion. "I can find us 14 more fighters, but that's not my concern."

I was then ready to lay out my argument for reducing the tournament field from 16 fighters to eight, when Rorion cut me off.

"Rickson is not going to be fighting in War of the Worlds, Arturo. I've selected Royce to represent my family."

Rorion stated this so matter of factly, that at first I didn't fully comprehend what he was saying.

"What? Royce? But, Royce? Did Rickson get injured? Is he okay? Royce?"

I'd known that over the past few months, there was some kind of tension between Rorion and Rickson. I'd seen the family champion around the Gracie Academy a lot less than usual, but since we opened the W.O.W. Promotions headquarters on Gramercy Avenue, I was pretty much only there now for my weekly class with Royler. I had heard whispers that Rickson was starting to pilfer students from the academy, giving private instruction in his garage and keeping all of that money for himself. Rorion was paying all of the family salaries and bills out of the money that was being generated by the Gracie Academy and the Brajitsu, Inc. tapes, so this would have obviously been a real betrayal.

Rorion and I had become close, as business partners and as friends, but rarely would he discuss anything personal with me. I knew that there were always Gracie family dramas and traumas, which would develop and resolve in a constant cycle. But Rorion would never confide in me about the private life of the Gracies, and I never was interested in looking behind that curtain.

It just wasn't any of my business. But this tournament was my business—our business: Rorion, SEG, Milius, the 27 investors, and me. I pressed him on why Rickson would not be fighting in War of the Worlds. He was going to be our anchor fighter, our superstar, and I felt that I was owed an explanation.

Rorion and I had an unspoken agreement that he would select the Gracie representative for the tournament, but I just assumed that it would be Rickson. He was far and away the best athlete and fighter in the family, and he had legitimate vale tudo experience in Brazil, including those two wins over the mighty Rei Zulu.

Rorion said that he had indeed discovered that Rickson had been pirating students, and not turning in the money to the family pot. So he confronted Rickson, and was assured by his younger brother that it would not happen again. And then Rorion kept hearing that it was happening again. But the final straw between them was a massage that Rickson's wife, Kim, had gotten. As the oldest son, Rorion was tasked with pooling all of the Gracie money, paying the bills, and then doling out the wages. But the bills had to relate to the academy, and the family's key living expenses: insurance, rent, food and things like that—not personal extras.

Rickson tried to get Rorion to reimburse him for Kim's massage. Rorion refused because he felt this cost had nothing to do with the Gracie Academy or the family's real expenses. Rickson told Kim what Rorion had said. Kim told Rickson to stand up to his big brother. And well, now Royce was going to be fighting in War of the Worlds. I figured that there were probably other issues at play, but this was all that Rorion would reveal.

I guess I wasn't as shocked that Rickson was out, as much as I was that Royce was in. Since my earliest days at the Academy, I picked up on the sibling rivalry between Rorion and Rickson, and how there was this unspoken struggle to be Hélio's favorite, and the family's heir apparent. But in spite of all of this underlying tension, I always figured that Rorion would choose Rickson to represent Gracie Jiu-Jitsu in War of the Worlds. Never once did I think that Royce would have even been preliminarily considered.

From my experiences, I always thought that Royce was a sweet, simple soul. He was now 26, but had always seemed like a teenager to me, dating back to our first encounter. He never said much, and he seemed firmly under the guidance and control of Rorion—teaching classes all day long, and then cleaning up the Gracie Academy with a broom and mop. Royce lived in a tiny space over the garage at Rorion's house, with two piranhas that he kept in a hexagon-shaped fish tank as his roommates. Rorion once told me the story of taking Royce with him to an out-of-state seminar. When they returned, Royce discovered that only one roommate remained, as he'd forgotten to ask someone to feed his fish.

Royce didn't have a car or even a checking account. On Saturdays, after classes were done and Royce had completed his clean-up duties, he would shyly slip into Rorion's office at the Academy, and patiently wait for his weekly allowance. When I would be in there talking with Rorion, Royce would stand off to the side, not saying a word. Once Rorion had acknowledged his kid brother's presence, he would open the safe, pull out a few twenty-dollar bills, and hand them to Royce. With a smile on his face as bright as a lit-up Christmas tree, Royce would head over to the beach, where he would flirt with the girls, surf and have a bite to eat.

I got the impression that Royce worshipped Hélio as much as the other brothers did, and that he worshipped Rorion like none of the other brothers did.

Royce didn't seem as if he'd ever been in a street fight in his life. There was no question that he was a solid black belt, and as Ethan Milius would surely attest, an excellent instructor. And I had seen him easily choke out some karate and kung fu types at the academy in a number of Gracie Challenges. He was well built at 6-foot-1 and 175 lb., but he just never struck me as a real fighter, the way that Rickson, Relson, Royler and even Rorion did.

When I'd watched Royce roll on the mat with Rickson, it looked about as competitive as my training sessions with Royler. He just wasn't anywhere near Rickson's level, but in all fairness, I didn't know who was.

A lawyer friend of mine who trained in Gracie Jiu-Jitsu once said to me that Royce seemed like the perfect guy to babysit your kids. No way did I ever see him as a killer.

I really liked Royce—he was a sweet kid and always very friendly. But it seemed to me that he was about to be in way over his head. It wasn't my call though—it was Rorion's. For all of his, "whatever you decide Arturo," attitude on almost everything concerning War of the Worlds, this was his decision to make—well, with the input of Hélio, no doubt. But it certainly had nothing to do with me.

So if Rorion said it was going to be Royce, then it was going to be Royce. Case closed.

Once I gave it some thought though, I could see that with Rickson now out of the running, Rorion really had no option but to choose Royce. It was almost a decision by default. Rolker and Robin were persona non gratis—I didn't even know if they had ever been to the U.S., or how often Rorion spoke to them.

I had only met Relson a few times, and I really knew him more by reputation. The talk around the academy was that while Rickson was the best fighter in the Gracie family, Relson was the meanest. If the shit went down for real, on the street or in a bar, Relson would fuck you up. He apparently lived in Hawaii with a beautiful girlfriend, and only made it out to Southern California on occasion. One time Rorion had let it slip to me that Relson "likes to party," but never said more on the subject. For whatever reason, Relson may have been a wild card in Rorion's eyes who just couldn't be risked as the Gracie Jiu-Jitsu emissary to the world.

Through his role as my instructor, I'd really come to like and respect Royler. He had gotten me up to blue belt, which was no small feat, considering my lack of natural jiu-jitsu and grappling abilities. Despite all of his easy victories in the Gracie Challenge, the fact remained that Royler was 5-foot-8 and around 145 lb. The "invincibility" of Gracie Jiu-Jitsu aside, Rorion was smart and experienced enough to understand that if a much bigger and stronger opponent got on top of Royler—and if that opponent had even rudimentary grappling knowledge—things might not go well for his younger and smaller brother. He knew that I was talking about getting a wrestler and maybe a sumo wrestler into War of the Worlds.

As for himself, Rorion had never once floated the idea that he would be the family representative in the tournament. He was 42 years old, and while I knew that he could still whip some serious ass, he had really transitioned from a fighter into a businessman since his "toughest man in the United States" exploits had been reported by Pat Jordan in that 1989 *Playboy* article. Rorion often joked with me that he wanted to trade his Gracie Jiu-Jitsu black belt for an expensive silk tie like mine.

Beyond all of that, I felt that having an owner of W.O.W. Promotions actually fighting in War of the Worlds, would have made it look like a rigged event. I knew that it was going to look like a set-up as it was with one of his brothers in the tournament, but to have Rorion himself would have looked to the other fighters, and to the public, like we'd stacked the deck.

So of the seven Gracie brothers, that only left one real candidate: Royce. And once I got over my initial shock, I realized that I didn't care. As I'd felt from the beginning, it truly didn't matter to me who won War of the Worlds, because for me, this was never about promoting Gracie Jiu-Jitsu and the Gracie family name. My warm feelings for Rorion and the Gracie family aside, this was about creating a new franchise in the world of fighting. It wasn't meant to be an in-house sales campaign, like the ones that I'd been creating for the Brajitsu, Inc. tapes. No doubt Rorion's feelings on this were polar opposite from mine, but so what? This was not the Gracie Challenge, and I never wanted it to be.

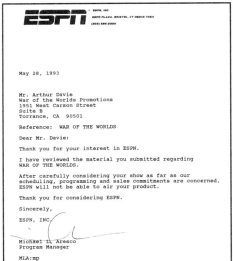

I finally got the word from ESPN that our fighting tournament was not ready for prime time.

From my experience as a student at the academy, I knew first-hand that Gracie Jiu-Jitsu was incredibly effective and dominant. But I also understood that no fighting style was unbeatable. The Grandmaster Hélio had himself been submitted in his competitive past, which only bolstered my belief that in a real fight, anything could happen. And that, at its core, was what I had always envisioned, initially for the World's Best Fighter, and now for War of the Worlds.

Meyrowitz and his lawyer brother David flew to Los Angeles to meet with Rorion, our attorney Don Moss, and me in the first week of August. We were closer to that "tentative" October 30 date, but no closer to a signed and executed contract between our two groups.

I knew that my Plan B television options were evaporating, as I had received a letter dated May 28, (just before SEG sent their contract offer) from Michael Aresco, program manager at ESPN, which stated "After carefully considering your show as far as our scheduling, programming and commitments are concerned, ESPN will not be able to air your product."

And on July 13, lowly Prime Ticket officially passed on War of the Worlds, as Program Coordinator Terri Quinn cheerfully concluded in the letter, "Please feel free to submit a proposal should you find that you have other product to offer in the future."

I, of course, wasn't about to let Meyrowitz, his brother David or Campbell know about these rejections, nor was I going to tell them that if things fell apart with SEG, I'd start my search anew for a broadcast partner. I wanted to do a deal with SEG, and get War of the Worlds launched sooner rather than later. But the deal was going to have to make sense for my side, and not just theirs.

The August meeting was at the W.O.W. Promotions office, and we all sat around my big blue desk/conference table. Meyrowitz, David, Moss and I negotiated and debated and threatened and discussed all day long. I sent out for deli sandwiches and we ate. We talked some more. Finally, we all shook hands, and agreed to keep moving forward with War of the Worlds, even though absolutely nothing was finalized.

At this point, I thought that October 30 was going to be a tough date to hit. But I was locked in to Denver, and felt that once we got into late November and then December, the strong likelihood of snow would wreak havoc on our

PRIME TICKET.

July 13, 1993

Arthur Davie
W.O.W. Promotions, Ltd.
1951 West Carson Street
Suite B
Torrance, CA 90501

Dear Arthur,

Thank you for submitting "War of the Worlds" for Prime Network's consideration. This is not something that Prime is interested in distributing on a national basis, therefore, we will not be able to provide clearance. However, I have enclosed a list of programming contacts at each of our regional networks should you decide to contact them individually.

We appreciate your interest in Prime Network. Please feel free to submit a proposal should you find that you have other product to offer in the future.

Sincerely,

Terri Quinn
Programming Coordinator

Enclosure: Programming contacts
VHS

Photo courtesy of Art Davie archives/W.O.W. Promotions

In early July 1993, even Prime Ticket kicked us to the curb. They wouldn't distribute our event on a national basis, but shunted us off to their regional affiliates.

travel and logistics. So I set my mind on early-to-mid-November. There was really only one place in Denver for me to consider, and that was the city's major indoor venue. Anything else would have been an image killer, and given the perception that we were a low-rent event.

Campbell told me that the first weekend in November was a no-go, as Saturday, Novenber 6 was the date set for the boxing heavyweight championship rematch between Riddick Bowe and Evander Holyfield in Las Vegas, to be broadcast live on TVKO Pay-Per-View. There was no way that we could launch War of the Worlds in the shadow of that massive fight, which would lock down all of the PPV buys.

From my cold call to the 17,000-seat McNichols Arena, I found out that the Denver Nuggets would be hosting the Golden State Warriors on Saturday, November 13, but the day before was available for booking. I negotiated the price down to $4,000, and our date for War of the Worlds moved from "tentative" to firm. Campbell told me that November 12, 1993 worked great for him. If only everything was this easy with SEG, my New York Bankees.

CHAPTER 8

SHARKS AND GOLDFISH

A FISHING ROD IS A STICK WITH A HOOK AT
ONE END AND A FOOL AT THE OTHER.
— SAMUEL JOHNSON

SO with an unsigned contract offer from SEG, two fighters, an arena deal and a date, I now put all of my energy into filling out the tournament bracket. Kathy was working dutifully on sponsorship sales, and said that she had a lead on Gold's Gym. Rorion was doing his thing at the Academy, and repeatedly told me that he was fine with whatever fighters and fighting styles I recruited. After all, who could beat Gracie Jiu-Jitsu, even with Royce as the representative?

I then approached Rorion to officially lock in my role as matchmaker.

"What does a matchmaker do?" he asked me.

"Sets the matches. I'll decide who fights who. Are you OK with that?"

"Do you think you can get all the fighters, Arturo?"

"I can get everyone we need. You've chosen Royce. I've already gotten Pat Smith, and I'll get the rest. Trust me."

"And you'll match them?"

"Absolutely. If we have you do it, we'll get a ton of shit. It'll look like your rigging things for Royce to win," I responded.

"Actually, I'm not worried about any of these guys. We have always taken them down and choked them out. No problem. I'm good with you doing the matchmaking."

I felt relieved that Rorion seemed to grasp the big picture. And I felt grateful, as even though I had plenty on my plate, this was a job I wanted.

I thought that Meyrowitz might have some ideas on who he'd like to see, but he exclaimed to me on the phone, "Jiu-jitsu, kung fu, taekwondo—it's all moo goo guy pan to me." And I was reluctant to bother Milius about his views on the matter. In truth, he was a pretty loyal Gracie man and wasn't really into the different martial arts. I knew Milius would just want me to get the biggest, baddest, and toughest guys I could find.

With my mind made up about a tournament consisting of eight fighters instead of 16 (a number that SEG fully endorsed), I set out to find the remaining six men needed to complete the bracket for War of the Worlds.

I used a shotgun approach in reaching out to the martial arts world—spraying pellets in all directions. By 9 a.m. every day, I was behind my big blue desk making calls, putting out feelers and sending letters and faxes, to fighters, managers, agents, promoters, martial arts schools and gyms. And I contacted 38 separate organizations and sanctioning bodies—ranging from the United States Tang Soo Do Association to the World SAMBO Committee to the International Pencak-Silat & Puklulan Federation. And I was back at the Torrance Public Library, scouring books, magazines, newspapers and even microfiche, for anything and everything that might prove useful.

If I was lucky enough to get someone on the phone, or in the extreme rarity, actually receive a returned call, it usually went downhill from there. Most listened very quietly, and then told me they would either get back to me (which I knew they wouldn't), or that this just wasn't something that they'd be interested in.

I heard, over and over again:

"Who are you?"

"Who do you represent?"

"What is it exactly that you want?"

"Why are you calling me?"

And on multiple occasions I was told something along the lines of, "You'll never get this off the ground. People have been talking about this for years. It never goes anywhere."

A huge positive was when the voice on the other end of the phone said, "Well, good luck" as opposed to the usual brusque hang-up without a goodbye.

What bothered me the most was when I would hear some version of, "This would be bad for martial arts." I heard that a lot.

I thought that perhaps I could spread the word by speaking to reporters from the top martial arts magazines. But none of them would bite. The closest that I came was a phone call with Jim Coleman, the executive editor of *Black Belt*. But Coleman seemed repulsed by War of the Worlds, as though I was going to be corrupting the nation's youth with my plan to stage "dirty fighting."

I got used to rejection. I was knocking on the doors of established martial arts organizations and dojos, and these guys were set in their ways. To them, I was a newcomer, an outsider. What did I know? But, I was too stupid and stubborn to take their rejection as final. I had a vision. All I had to do was recruit enough people to get this off the ground. If I could do that I knew everybody would see what this actually was, and we would be flying at that point. The problem was to make sure that I enlisted enough viable brave souls to join this ship of fools with me as the navigator.

Undeterred, I purchased a series of quarter page ads in the magazines *Black Belt*, *Inside Karate* and *Inside Kung Fu*, which heralded the $50,000 first prize, and dangled the chance to "Compete as one of the toughest punchers, kickers and grapplers in the world in this full-contact, no-holds-barred tournament" and, "Show yourself to the world." Some of the ads specified that a fee of $100 had to accompany the application. Rorion was always listed as the matchmaker, with the Gracie Academy phone and fax numbers included.

I did this figuring that Rorion's name had a hell of a lot more credibility than mine in the fight world, and even if the prospective fighter had never heard of Rorion or Gracie Jiu-Jitsu, at least his call would be answered at a martial arts school. When the messages and faxes came in to Rorion, he would then pass them on to me.

Aside from the Rorion as matchmaker sleight of hand in the ads, I also squeezed the truth in three other ways. I listed the date of the event as October 2, figuring that this would get fighters off their collective asses a lot faster than if they knew we weren't actually going to be fighting until November 12. I was running out of time, and I needed to fill six spots in the tournament bracket.

I also wrote in the ad that the fighters would compete in "A pit designed by famed film director John Milius." Anything to motivate the talent.

And I listed the name of our event as "World's Best Fighter." SEG was expressing to me the same concerns that I had long held about the name War of the Worlds—that it opened us up to a copyright infringement claim related to the H.G. Wells book, the 1953 Paramount film or both. Meyrowitz, Campbell and SEG's main sales guy Mike Abramson, all thought as well that War of the Worlds didn't sound like a fighting tournament. Their attitude, which made sense to me, was that a brand new event had to have an obvious name—one which would let people know immediately what they were going to see. World's Best Fighter met that criteria, but it didn't pop enough for them, or any of us really. It just sounded too bland.

Here is a 1993 advertisement I placed in various martial arts magazines soliciting fighters for our no-holds-barred event.

From studying Tex Rickard and Mike Jacobs, legendary boxing promoters from the first half of the 20th century, I knew that to create buzz and sell tickets, you needed a shark. This was an extremely talented fighter who you built up carefully by feeding goldfish, also known in the boxing parlance of the Rickard/Jacobs era as a "tomato soup can." Eventually, when your shark was ready, you matched him up against another shark—with one portrayed to the public and media as the hero, the other as the villain. These were the biggest fights of all. Look no further than the two heavyweight world title bouts between Jack Dempsey and Gene Tunney that took place in 1926 and 1927 as a classic example of this approach.

Even with my concerns, Royce was a shark, a baby shark perhaps, but a shark nonetheless. Pat Smith looked like a shark, but the more that I talked to him on the phone, the more he seemed to have the mental frailty of a goldfish. Smith could go either way.

The fake October 2 event date seemed to serve its purpose. To my great relief, the magazine ads proved to be a success, and the replies started trickling in. We even received more than a dozen $100 checks in the mail from hopeful fighters, including one from Trent Jenkins, a Sabaki Challenge veteran from Denver.

One of the first calls was from Kevin Rosier, who said that he had experience as a pro boxer, and was the three-time World Kickboxing Association (WKA) super heavyweight champion. He told me that he could knock out anyone in the world with his "big right hand," but that his fighting career had been derailed by dirty promoters.

I did some digging on Rosier, and on paper, he looked to be the real deal. His stat sheet said he was 6-foot-4, 245 lb., with a 79-inch reach, and his WKA championship claims checked out. And I really liked Rosier, who seemed sweet and endearingly dopey. His only ask before signing the contract was that he would be allowed to bring his wife out to Denver with him, which was no problem for me. I just wasn't sure, though, if Rosier really understood the no-holds-barred aspect of the tournament in which he was now set to fight. I marked him down as a goldfish, since he seemed to have no clue when it came to grappling.

Soon after Rosier, I got a call from Scott Bessac, who said that he fought out of a gym called the Lion's Den, which I'd never heard of, but I thought had a great name. The Gracies often called the rear-naked choke the mata leão, which is Portuguese for lion killer. This would be an easy fight to sell.

But after a 15-minute conversation, Bessac said to me, "Mr. Davie, honestly, I don't think I'm right for this event. The guy you want is the leader of the Lion's Den—my instructor, Ken Shamrock."

Bessac told me that Shamrock was a pro wrestler in Japan, who also did real fights, and was without a doubt, "the man." I got Shamrock's number from Bessac, and quickly started my research on the guy. I discovered that his real name was Ken Kilpatrick, and that he had been adopted by Bob Shamrock, who ran a group home for troubled boys.

After being a star high school football player in California, Shamrock became a pro wrestler—working small shows in the U.S. before moving on to Japan. He began to make a name for himself in that country's Fujiwara Gumi promotion, which was part of the strong-style pro wrestling movement. As I understood it from my research at the Torrance Public Library, strong style was a form of pro wrestling, that while still predetermining the winners and losers, employed a rough and realistic looking approach.

Occasionally, strong style would cross over into the realm of real fights, either by accident or design. In 1992, Shamrock had easily defeated Don Nakaya Nielsen in Japan, submitting the kickboxer in less than one minute with a key lock. By most accounts, this mixed match fight was completely real, a shoot.

Shamrock was definitely making a name for himself on the Japanese fight scene, and when I got him on the phone, I knew immediately that Bessac was right. He seemed to be "the man."

He told me that he had a fight coming up on September 21 in Urayasu, Japan against Masakatsu Funaki as part of the first event of Pancrase. I had already done my homework, and knew all about this start up, named in honor of ancient Pankration. From what I could tell, it looked to me like it was going to be the midpoint between strong-style pro wrestling and what we were going to do. As I understood it, Pancrase was going to have a number of fairly restrictive rules that I wouldn't have ever considered, such as making closed fist punches, kicks to the head of a standing opponent and knees and stomps to the head of a grounded opponent all illegal.

Also, a fighter would be able to escape a submission hold by grabbing the ring ropes up to a set amount of times. And I kept hearing that there were definitely going to be works in Pancrase, often when a fight was going to feature one of the big Japanese stars. I confronted Shamrock on all of this, and he told me that what he was doing in Japan was "mostly real." I then shot back that the World's Best Fighter/War of the Worlds—whatever we were going to call ourselves—was going to be "all real," and I asked him if he could handle it.

Photo courtesy of Art Davie archives/W.O.W. Promotions

Here's the War of the Worlds poster created by my friend, Mike Stanley. We were going for the classical look of Pankration with this sketch that I used to attract John Milius into joining us.

The World's Best Fighter—this was the first working title for what became the Ultimate Fighting Championship

5 January, 1993

WOW Productions
1951 W. Carson Street, Suite B
Torrance, CA 90501

Dear Rorion:

Congratulations on the development of your concept for the "War of the Worlds" Tournament to be staged in Rio de Janeiro, and tentatively scheduled for 30 October, 1993. I appreciate your invitation to be involved in the project. I feel it connects the present to the past by recreating the classical Greek and Roman contest of Pankration.

I believe that I can contribute to make this Tournament a World Class Event. Therefore, I am eager to serve as the Creative Director. I look forward to our next meeting to work out the details.

Sincerely,

John Milius

cc: Art Davie

A-TEAM PRODUCTIONS   3630 RIVERSIDE DR., BURBANK, CA 91505   (213) 843-6000, EXT. 3675

Here is the January 1993 letter from film legend John Milius agreeing to become our event's creative director.

April 27, 1993

Mr. Art Davie
War of the Worlds Promotion

VIA FAX: 310-782-1310

Dear Art:

Thank you for all the information on the War of the Worlds hand to hand combat championship.

I am definitely interested in pursuing this event as a Pay-Per-View television show

I think there is tremendous potential in the War of the Worlds and am anxious to begin working with you and Rorion.

We should schedule a meeting in the next few weeks. I will call you soon to set up a convenient date.

Sincerely,

Campbell McLaren
Vice President, Original Programming

Photo courtesy of Art Davie archives/W.O.W. Promotions

This is the letter from Semaphore Entertainment Group (SEG) that began the key relationship to launch the UFC. With SEG as our TV partner, our event would conquer PPV television.

Bob Meyrowitz, CEO of Semaphore Entertainment Group. "Meyro," as his troops called him, was an experienced TV producer as well as a syndicator of radio content. He proved to be a tough adversary for me throughout the first Ultimate Fighting Championship.

Photo courtesy of Art Davie archives

BE THERE TO SEE
THE ULTIMATE FIGHT!

JIU-JITSU vs. TAEKWONDO vs. KARATE vs. KICKBOXING vs. SUMO vs. SHOOTFIGHTING vs. SAVATE vs. BOXING ... Who will be the

ULTIMATE FIGHTER?

Never in the history of unarmed combat have all of the fighting styles come together in a ring designed for no escape.

Match by match, style vs. style, these 8 world champions will challenge each other until only the ULTIMATE FIGHTER is left standing. THERE ARE NO RULES!

Royce Gracie (Jiu-Jitsu) 5' 1", 180 lbs. Brazilian & World Light Heavyweight Champ	**Pat Smith (TaeKwondo/Robotae)** 6'2", 217 lbs. 1993 Sabaki Challenge Heavyweight Champ	**Art Jimmerson (Boxing)** 6'1", 196 lbs. IBF North American Cruiserweight Champion
Gerard Gordeau (Savate) 6' 5", 216 lbs. World Heavyweight Champion	**Zane Frazier (Kenpo)** 6' 6", 230 lbs. WKF Super Heavyweight Champ	**Ken Shamrock (Shootfighting)** 6' 0", 220 lbs. #1 Shootfighter in Japan
	Teila Tuli (Sumo) 6' 2", 410 lbs. 3 years Pro Sumo	**Kevin Rosier (Kickboxing)** 6'4", 265 lbs. WKA & ISKA Super Heavyweight Champ

LIVE ON PAY-PER-VIEW FROM
McNICHOLS SPORTS ARENA IN DENVER COLORADO
FRIDAY, NOVEMBER 12, 1993
Call your cable company to order and enjoy it at home!

W.O.W. PROMOTIONS

Fight Hotline:
(310) 782-6373

TICKET & ROOM PACKAGE

VIP

- Ringside $50 ticket
- Deluxe reserved room at Fight Headquarters Hotel (3 nights/4 days)
- Autograph / Photo session with fighters afternoon of fight
- Post fight cocktail party
- VIP tickets to Saturday night Black tie masked ball and supper! (mask included)

Total $359 one person / $499 two people

Deluxe

- Reserved $25 ticket
- Deluxe reserved room at Fight Headquarters Hotel
- (3 nights / 4 days)

Total $269 one person / $319 two people

AIRFARE

Special UFC Package rates · must be booked 7 to 14 days in advance for best prices.
For reservations or info call Elaine at Katella Travel and ask for the UFC Package.
Call (Outside California) 1-800-528-5858
(In California) 714-771-1270 Today!

For event tickets only call the box office (303) 640-7333 or TICKETMASTER (303) 757-6766

Photo courtesy of Art Davie archives/W.O.W. Promotions

Note the ticket/room packages and the pricing; it was designed to make it attractive to attend and we got a fair amount of Southern Californians to come. Where it says, "Special UFC packages" is the first time the UFC acronym was used instead of the Ultimate Fighting Championship.

Here I am standing in front of the W.O.W. office in Torrance. This little cubbyhole was the birthplace of the UFC. You can tell how proud I am on this July afternoon.

Photo courtesy of Art Davie archives

Photo courtesy of Art Davie archives

Rorion and I explaining the rules (or lack thereof) at the fighter's meeting on Thursday night. We have lost control of the meeting at that point and the room was bedlam.

Photo courtesy of Charlie Anzalone

This was taken at the UFC press conference on Thursday, November 11, 1993. From left to right, that's Campbell McLaren of SEG, NFL legend Jim Brown and shootfighter Ken Shamrock.

Here is Bill "Superfoot" Wallace addressing reporters at the UFC press conference on Thursday, November 11, 1993. To his left is Hall of Fame football legend Jim Brown and to his right is Rorion Gracie, my partner in W.O.W. Promotions.

From left to right, that's the Gracie family champion, Rickson Gracie, with the owner and CEO of Gold's Gyms worldwide, Pete Grymkowski and Rickson's wife, Kim. Taken right after the UFC press conference. Grymkowski was one of America's leading bodybuilders when I got out of the Marines in 1970 and was regularly featured in Iron Man *magazine. At 5-foot-10, he weighed about 230 lb. in contest condition.*

Photo courtesy of Charlie Anzalone

That's big Kevin Rosier on the left, commentator Bill "Superfoot" Wallace in the middle and Rosier's manager, Charlie Anzalone, on the right. Taken right after the press conference, Rosier was probably ready for lunch. Anzalone was from Buffalo, Rosier's hometown, and showed up to support his man. Charlie was somewhat of a legend as a disc jockey known in dance clubs from Buffalo to New York City as "Captain Disco."

Photo courtesy of Charlie Anzalone

Sumo wrestler Teila Tuli kneeling with his brother and his two cousins behind him. They were four big, strong Hawaiians who loved to party.

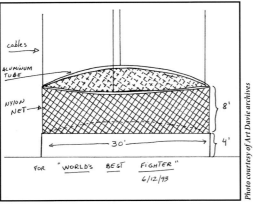

Photo courtesy of Art Davie archives

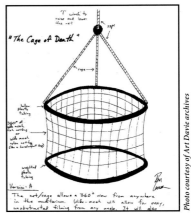

Photo courtesy of Art Davie archives

Here is a sketch I did in June 1993 of the cage/ring which was just at the beginning of its development. My artistic abilities leave much to be desired.

The Cage of Death. This sketch was supplied to Rorion and me by a student at the Gracie Academy. The concept was a bit too complicated to be workable, but it showed the level of interest that our event was having with everyone.

Photo courtesy of Art Davie archives

Here is the octagon-shaped cage being set up for the first time. The date is November 11, 1993 and the place is McNichols Sports Arena.

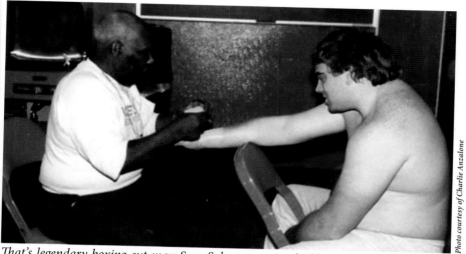

Photo courtesy of Charlie Anzalone

That's legendary boxing cut man Sam Solomon taping kickboxer Kevin Rosier's fists. It was a thrill for my brother Matthew and me to get to know Sam. We couldn't resist asking him which famous boxing matches were fixed, because he knew where all the skeletons were buried.

THE ULTIMATE FIGHTING CHAMPIONSHIP

Official Event Program Guide   Price $4.00

THE ULTIMATE FIGHTING CHAMPIONSHIP

HERE ARE NO RULES!

WOW PROMOTIONS

SEG

IFC

McNichols Sports Arena
Denver, Colorado
November 12, 1993

Photo courtesy of Art Davie archives/W.O.W. Promotions

Here is the front cover of the Official Event Program Guide sold at McNichols Sports Arena. Note the price of $4, which was a lot in 1993.

Age:	29
Height:	6'2"
Weight:	217 lbs.
Neck:	17 ½"
Chest (N):	43 ½"
Chest (E):	46"
Biceps:	14 ½"
Forearm:	14 ½"
Wrist:	7 ½"
Fist:	12"
Waist:	36"
Thigh:	26"
Calf:	16"
Ankle:	9 ½"
Reach:	75"

Pat Smith

PATRICK SMITH PICTOR AND FOOTAGE
COURTESY OF THE SABAKI CHALLENGE

PATRICK SMITH
Home: Denver, Colorado

WKC #7 Ranked Super Heavyweight Kickboxer
3rd Degree Black Belt Robotae
1st Degree Black Belt Tae Kwon Do
1993 Sabaki Challenge Heavyweight Champion
1993 Kyuk Too Ki Heavyweight Champion

Amateur Kickboxing Record:	250-0, 240 KO's
Professional Kickboxing Record:	15-0, 13 KO's
Professional Boxing Record:	1-2, 1 KO

Age:	29
Height:	6'0"
Weight:	215 lbs.
Neck:	17 ½"
Chest (N):	47 ½"
Chest (E):	50"
Biceps:	17 ¾"
Forearm:	13 ½"
Wrist:	7 ½"
Fist:	12"
Waist:	32 ¾"
Thigh:	25"
Calf:	16"
Ankle:	9"
Reach:	73"

Ken Shamrock

KEN WAYNE SHAMROCK
Home: Lockeford, California

Japan Pancrase Association #1 Submission Fighter (Shootfighting)
1986 Toughman Champion, Redding, California
1990 Toughman Champion, Stateville, North Carolina
1990 Toughman Champion, Hickory, North Carolina

Professional Shootfighting Record: 24-3-2

TALE OF

Age:	29
Height:	5'11"
Weight:	195 lbs.
Neck:	17"
Chest (N):	40"
Chest (E):	44"
Biceps:	14 ½"
Forearm:	12"
Wrist:	8"
Fist:	11 ½"
Waist:	34"
Thigh:	22"
Calf:	15"
Ankle:	9 ½"
Reach:	74"

Art Jimmerson

ARTHUR JIMMERSON
Home: St. Louis, Missouri
Nickname: "King Arthur"

IBF North American Cruiserweight Boxing Champion
WBC #10 Ranked Cruiserweight Boxer
1983 National Golden Gloves Boxing Champion (Middleweight)
3 time St. Louis Golden Gloves Boxing Champion (Middleweight)

Amateur Record:	125-14
Professional Record:	29-5 20 KO's

Age:	26
Height:	6'1"
Weight:	178 lbs.
Neck:	16 ½"
Chest (N):	37"
Chest (E):	39"
Biceps:	13"
Forearm:	11"
Wrist:	7 ¼"
Fist:	11 ½"
Waist:	32"
Thigh:	22"
Calf:	14 ¼"
Ankle:	9 ½"
Reach:	78"

Royce Gracie

ROYCE GRACIE
Home: Torrance, California and Rio de Janeiro, Brazil

Federação de Jiu-Jitsu do Rio de Janeiro World Light Heavyweight
Champion
4th Degree Black Belt Jiu-Jitsu

Amateur Record: 51-1

Age:	30
Height:	6'6"
Weight:	230 lbs.
Neck:	17 ½"
Chest (N):	46"
Chest (E):	47"
Biceps:	19"
Forearm:	12"
Wrist:	8 ½"
Fist:	12"
Waist:	32"
Thigh:	26"
Calf:	16"
Ankle:	12"
Reach:	75"

Zane Frazier

ZANE FRAZIER
Home: North Hollywood, California

WKF Super Heavyweight Kickboxing Champion
4th Degree Black Belt American Kenpo Karate
4 time International Karate Champion

Professional Record: 10-0, 9 KO's

Age:	31
Height:	6'4"
Weight:	265 lbs.
Neck:	21"
Chest (N):	52"
Chest (E):	54"
Biceps:	19"
Forearm:	15 ½"
Wrist:	8"
Fist:	13"
Waist:	40"
Thigh:	28"
Calf:	19"
Ankle:	11"
Reach:	81 ½"

Kevin Rosier

KEVIN ROSIER
Home: Buffalo, New York

ISKA North American Super Heavyweight Kickboxing Champion
3 time WKA World Super Heavyweight Kickboxing Champion
1990 World Karate Association World Super Heavyweight Champion
1989 All Japan World Karate Champion
1987 United States Kung-Fu Karate National
    No-Rules Tournament Champion

Professional Record: 66-8, 66 KO's

THE TAPE

Age:	35
Height:	6'5 ½"
Weight:	216 lbs.
Neck:	17 ½"
Chest (N):	42"
Chest (E):	45"
Biceps:	15 ½"
Forearm:	13 ½"
Wrist:	7 ¾"
Fist:	12"
Waist:	34"
Thigh:	24"
Calf:	16"
Ankle:	10"
Reach:	78"

Gerard Gordeau

GERARD GORDEAU
Home: Amsterdam, Netherlands

1992 World Champion Boxe Français Savate
1989-1991 European Champion Boxe Français Savate
1978-1985 Dutch Champion Karate

Professional Record: 27-4

Age:	24
Height:	6'2"
Weight:	410 lbs.
Neck:	22 ¾"
Chest (N):	59"
Chest (E):	65"
Biceps:	23 ½"
Forearm:	16"
Wrist:	10"
Fist:	13 ¾"
Waist:	59"
Thigh:	32"
Calf:	22 ½"
Ankle:	12 ½"
Reach:	76"

Teila Tuli

TEILA TULI
Home: Honolulu, Hawaii
Nickname: "Mr. T"

Sumo Wrestler - 2 ½ years Japanese Professional Sumo
Association Makushita Class

5 years amateur Sumo

This was a copy of a full-page ad I ran in martial arts magazines urging fans to watch our tournament. There were no photos to be had of mixed match fighting, but my partner Rorion Gracie owned a photo of two Brazilian vale tudo fighters and we used that as the central image for this ad and the UFC fight poster.

Photo courtesy of Susumu Nagao

Here is the 425-lb. sumo wrestler, Teila Tuli with the referee Joao Alberto Barreto in the very first bout in UFC history on Friday, November 12, 1993.

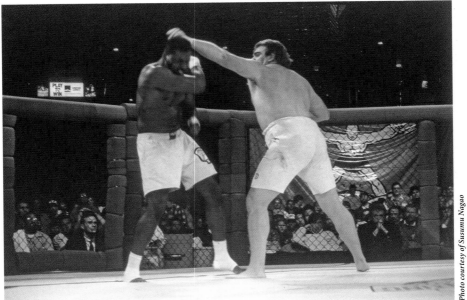

Photo courtesy of Susumu Nagao

Kickboxer Kevin Rosier and kickboxer Zane Frazier exchange punches in the second bout in UFC history.

Photo courtesy of Susumu Nagao

Rosier stomps Frazier's head twice to win the bloody bout. You can see the white towel that had been tossed into the cage to indicate that Frazier was done. It was a brutal punch-up that excited the live crowd, but was really more an artless Pier 6 brawl than a contest of two great martial artists.

Photo courtesy of Susumu Nagao

Jiu-Jitsu black belt Royce Gracie squares off against professional boxer, Art "King" Jimmerson in the third bout in UFC history. Jimmerson decided, at the last minute and unknown to me, to only wear one glove. It didn't help him as Royce closed the distance and took him to the ground where Jimmerson was soon helpless. A big disappointment for me. I had hoped for a true battle royal between these two very different stylists.

Photo courtesy of Susumu Nagao

Muscular Ken Shamrock, the shootfighter, grapples muscular kickboxer, Pat Smith on the mat. Smith's lack of grappling skills quickly caught up with him and he got caught in a heel hook in one minute and 49 seconds.

Photo courtesy of Susumu Nagao

Here is Royce Gracie at the moment of ultimate victory. Note the big check for $50,000 with my signature at the bottom. From left to right: me, Relson Gracie, Royce, his girlfriend Marianne and eldest brother, Rorion.

Royce Gracie, the light-heavyweight jiu-jitsu master, reigned supreme at the inaugural Ultimate Fighting Championship. Here he is with the gold medal that I had designed. A true champion.

Photo courtesy of Art Davie archives

Shamrock responded exactly how I was hoping, that he would absolutely be able to handle it, would win the $50,000 first prize, and would show the world what he could really do with his grappling and submissions.

How could I resist? He was built like a Greek God, at 6 feet, 215 lb., with a 47-inch chest, huge biceps, bulging muscles everywhere and with a model handsome face. He called himself a "shoot fighter" and he had that top-of-the-marquee name, Ken Wayne Shamrock. Not only was he a shark, he was a shark who might just be able to swallow Royce whole.

I knew that I needed at least one European stand-up fighter, to help give us some instant legitimacy and credibility. Unlike their U.S. kickboxing counterparts, who primarily focused their kicks above the waist, the top European guys employed the Asian style of attacking the entire body, with ferocious kicks to their opponent's legs as a hallmark. I discovered that the Western epicenter of this fighting style was the Netherlands, and that there were two gyms in Amsterdam that had pioneered Muay Thai boxing in Europe—Thom Harinck's Chakuriki Gym and Jan Plas' Mejiro Gym. They threw knees, elbows, fists and feet, just like they did in Bangkok. It was pretty brutal stuff.

No inquiries were coming in from Amsterdam or anywhere in Europe, so I started making overseas calls. The star of the Plas gym was Ernesto Hoost, and I went after him hard from my big blue desk in Torrance. But Hoost wasn't available, having already booked a fight in Japan doing kickboxing. To his credit, he was going to honor that commitment.

As an alternative, Plas offered me up a legitimate tough guy named Gerard Gordeau. In addition to being a bad ass in Muay Thai, Gordeau was also a world champion in Savate. He had the combat sports pedigree, having fought across Europe and in Japan. And the guy was built to knock people out at 6-foot-5 and 215 lb. with a lean, long, sinewy physique. Plas asked me if I minded that Gordeau's second career was working as a leg breaker for the brothel and porn show owners in Amsterdam. Minded? I told him that was a huge bonus. Just like that, I figured I had another shark.

One of the first fighters that I reached out to was Benny "the Jet" Urquidez, thinking that he'd love the chance to settle the score in his long-standing feud with Rorion, this time by potentially getting a shot at his foe's kid brother, Royce. I called "Blinky" Rodriguez, Benny "the

Jet's" brother-in-law, and asked him to see if he was interested. "Blinky" got back to me, and told me that Benny "the Jet" said, "I'm a professional fighter, and these guys are all amateurs. The Gracies are not in my class. I've already proven myself."

I thought that Dennis Alexio would be a perfect fit. He was arguably one of the greatest kickboxers in the U.S., a serious martial artist, and an actor who had starred opposite Jean-Claude Van Damme in the 1989 film *Kickboxer*. When I got him on the phone in Hawaii, Alexio was quick and to the point, then hung up without saying goodbye. He shot me down immediately.

So did Bart Vale, a Japanese pro wrestling contemporary of Ken Shamrock's in Fujiwara Gumi. Hailing from Miami, Vale was an impressive 6-foot-3, 250 lb., a black belt in Kenpo, and had fought in RINGS, a Japanese promotion that struck me as being a lot like Pancrase—maybe the fights were real, maybe not. But Vale told me "no" as well, just like Alexio, without a real explanation.

Then there was Peter Aerts, a tall, young Dutchman who was the World Muay Thai Association Heavyweight Champion, and fought out of Thom Harinck's Chakuriki Gym, the rival gym of Jan Plas where Gordeau trained. I thought it would be perfect to have two devastating strikers go kick for kick and elbow for elbow in one of our fights. But Aerts passed as well. As successful as he was, we probably couldn't have afforded him anyway. I realized more than ever that my job was to get the best of the best, provided they didn't live in the financial stratosphere.

I always made it a point to keep Rorion updated at our weekly Friday meetings on what fighters I had signed or was pursuing. His attitude was always the same: "Whatever you think Arturo."

Always, except when I mentioned the name Emin Boztepe. I first became aware of Boztepe a couple of years earlier, when Rorion had off-handedly told me about his encounter with the Turkish-born, California-based martial artist.

Boztepe had apparently been running his mouth about his unbeatable martial arts style, and the 300 street fights that he had won. Somehow Rorion heard about this, and offered to fight him in a full-on, and thus far mythical, Gracie Challenge—my $100,000 against your $100,000, winner take all.

According to Rorion, Boztepe declined, wound up getting an attorney involved, and threatened to sue for defamation of character or some such thing. So when I mentioned the idea of trying to recruit Boztepe for our tournament, Rorion laughed and reminded me of their nearly litigious past. I figured the guy wasn't worth the trouble, and I was getting my fill of lawyers with David Meyrowitz, so I decided to drop my Boztepe idea right then and there.

Rorion did mention though, to my great surprise, that he had a lead on a fighter who I should check out. He'd been turned on to him through his working friendship with Frank Trejo, with whom Rorion had conducted joint grappling/striking seminars. Trejo taught the striking, and for good reason. He had a record of 21-1 as a pro kickboxer, and a martial arts background in both Shotokan and American Kenpo. Trejo thought that his guy, Zane Frazier, was just what we were looking for. The undefeated Superheavyweight Champion of the World Kickboxing Federation, Frazier looked like someone who could have a career as an action movie star, at 6-foot-6, 235 lb., with 19-inch biceps.

Best of all, Trejo said that he had witnessed Frazier beat the shit out of Frank Dux (of *Bloodsport* infamy) earlier that year at The Second Annual Draka Martial Arts Trade Show held at the Century City Plaza Hotel in Los Angeles. Apparently Dux came at Frazier, who responded by delivering several unanswered punches to the "undefeated Kumite champion," and then throwing him over a table.

When Rorion told me about Frazier, I suddenly realized that I had actually met him in March, when I was Kathy Kidd's guest at the United States Martial Arts Association trade show in Pasadena. Frazier had come up to me and gushed that he was the guy who had beaten up Frank Dux. I liked Frazier and decided, based on Trejo's recommendation, to give him the "green light" right then and there.

I could tell straight away that he was very smart. But Frazier seemed too smart for his own good, asking me all sorts of questions about the other fighters who I was signing, the rules, the mile-high altitude in Denver, the equipment that they would be allowed to wear, and on and on. The guy was spooking himself before the fight. And the more he talked, the more I thought that he was moving from shark to goldfish.

At this point, I had six of the eight fighters I needed: Smith, Royce, Rosier, Shamrock, Gordeau and Frazier.

One afternoon, I got a call from a woman with a foreign accent.

"Master Ishii wants to meet with you and Master Gracie."

I knew instantly that Master Ishii was Kazuyoshi Ishii of K-1, which was the fighting promotion that he launched in Tokyo back in March. Ishii was a Kyokushin black belt turned highly successful businessman, who had billed his new promotion as something of a kickboxing, Muay Thai, and full-contact karate hybrid. I didn't see them as our competition, as K-1 was strictly about striking—no grappling or ground fighting was allowed. But I also knew that they had already recruited some amazing stand-up fighters from Asia and Europe, many of whom I thought would be ideal for our tournament.

His assistant set an appointment for breakfast at the Beverly Wilshire Hotel. There were rumors of Ishii's "influential connections" in Japan, and I had no idea why he wanted to meet with us. But the invite was irresistible. Rorion and I strode into the hotel lobby, where another assistant immediately came over, and escorted us to Master Ishii's table. In Japan his disciples all called him "Kancho," and I made sure to refer to him that way. He smiled at the courtesy. We talked about the martial arts in Japan and America, and Ishii soon inquired about our upcoming event. Clearly, the word had gotten out in Japan. As Ishii spoke, I got the feeling that he looked upon us as little brothers, since, in his mind, Japan was the true home of martial arts. He was quick to point out that he believed stand-up fighting was far better entertainment that what we were planning.

"I do not do what you do. We do not have grappling in K-1. Striking only. Much better," Ishii said in his halting English.

But despite Ishii's claims of superiority, Rorion and I understood that with our forthcoming no-holds-barred, all styles welcome fighting tournament, we had scooped Master Ishii and the Japanese.

"This is just like when your dad stole jiu-jitsu from them." I whispered to Rorion, while elbowing him in the ribs.

"My dad didn't steal it. He improved it," Rorion whispered back, then smiled.

We bid farewell to Master Ishii after a big shot breakfast of bacon and eggs at the most expensive hotel in LA, and got back to work.

Later that night, I thought about what Rorion had said, how his dad had improved jiu-jitsu. This was what we were now attempting to do: improve what was already out there in the martial arts and combat sports worlds. We had literally gone back to fighting's past in an attempt to bring something fresh to the modern world, right here in the U.S. I understood that the Japanese would be worried by our plans. And I also understood that numerous people in our country were worried as well. My wide array of phone calls in the search for fighters had shown me the opposition and ill will that was out there, and coming our way.

It really seemed to me that the martial arts community in America was a backwater. As a nation, we had come late to the party that had started centuries earlier. Instead of tradition, we had been reared on things like the *Karate Kid* and *Kung Fu* with David Carradine. The general public was clueless. And martial artists in the U.S. believed the shit they'd read in magazines like *Black Belt*. Fantasy stuff peddled by charlatans and hustlers. It was a culture of martial arts strip mall gurus who were happy to babysit middle class kids after school, all the while selling the aura of invincibility. On this, Rorion and I were absolutely united. He wanted to expose the flaws in the striking arts, and I wanted to expose the con men. To me, this would be a viable sub-text of our event.

We would not only crown the new king of fighting, we would also reveal the flakes and bullshit artists of the martial arts world.

A sport that I'd long been intrigued by was the Indonesian martial art penjak silat, which to me, looked legit. When I asked Rorion if he had heard of this fighting style, he laughed, and accused me of making it up. Kathy had heard of it though, and told me that through her previous work on the martial arts trade show circuit, she had met Alberto Cerro Leon, a Spaniard who claimed to be the first non-Indonesian penjak silat world champion. Kathy still had his contact information, and I asked her to arrange a meeting. Alberto and his beautiful manager, Eleni, came to the W.O.W. office, and seemed like a pair of European movie stars. If Antonio Banderas and Mike Tyson had their DNA combined, the result would have looked a lot like Alberto.

I made my pitch, emphasizing the $50,000 first prize. But Alberto seemed extremely cautious, and said that he wanted to see how the first event turned out before committing.

"Come on Alberto. This is the opportunity of a lifetime. Show the world that you are the real master of the universe."

But he wasn't having any of it.

"Perhaps next time my friend," were his parting words.

I still needed two more, and I was determined that one of those final places would go to a pro boxer. There was a bit of a historical precedent in my thinking, as Hélio had issued a public challenge to World Heavyweight Boxing Champion Joe Louis in 1947. Rorion had recounted that story to me more than once during our Friday meetings at the By Brazil restaurant. Even though the idea was quickly dismissed by the Louis camp, it presented a fascinating image in my mind. And fastforwarding five decades, it posed the same question with different participants: Could Royce slip the punches of a powerful and accurate heavyweight, in order to get inside for the takedown?

The dream was Mike Tyson, but "Iron" Mike was serving time in an Indiana penitentiary on a rape conviction. Even if he had been a free man, there was no way that we could have afforded Tyson. Our first place prize money was of course $50,000, and Tyson had reportedly earned $22 million for his 91-second destruction of Michael Spinks in 1988.

I would've loved to have had other top heavyweights such as Evander Holyfield, Riddick Bowe, George Foreman or Lennox Lewis, but because of the money issue, I never pursued them. Even if I could have scrounged up a $100,000 appearance fee—which would have been all of the money in the world to guys like Pat Smith and Kevin Rosier—that sum would have been equivalent to spare change in the couch cushions for those A-list boxers.

But I pressed on, looking down the boxing food chain, as I hustled and made more calls. It quickly became clear to me that boxing people thought martial artists were a joke. Compared to boxers, no martial artist or kickboxer had ever made the kind of money earned by a superstar like Tyson, Muhammad Ali and Sugar Ray Leonard. And to them (and so many others as well), money was the measure of an athlete.

Also, the boxing crowd seemed to feel that their fighters actually took a punch as opposed to the "touch & giggle" scoring systems used in numerous martial arts. In their world, if a guy couldn't make it as a boxer, then he became a kickboxer. More than one boxing guy laughed me off the phone about the punching power of "black belts." A trainer at Kronk Gym in Detroit said that I was "chasing rainbows" in trying to find a real boxer to get into the ring with martial artists.

Another boxing trainer told me, "No rated heavyweight is going to waste his time on that shit."

I heard pretty much the same speech when I called Joe Frazier's Gym on North Broad Street in Philadelphia. But I was able to make two good contacts there, cut men Leon Tabbs and Sam Solomon (who had been in Sonny Liston's corner in Miami Beach when he lost to Cassius Clay née Muhammad Ali in 1964). I kept their names handy, feeling that they'd be perfect to work our event.

To me, getting a ranked heavyweight boxer would really excite the fans. And, it would answer the eternal question that helped get me started on this quest: who would win between a boxer and a grappler? I wanted to see how Royce would do against a guy who landed left hooks and right crosses for a living, even though I didn't say this to Rorion.

I simply had to have a boxer.

Thinking that SEG might provide the cash I needed, I turned to Meyrowitz.

"Would you guys be willing to pay an appearance fee for a boxer?"

"If you can get someone with name value for little or no money," was his blunt response.

I looked into Randall "Tex" Cobb, the one who had run roughshod on the set of the Milius produced *Uncommon Valor* until he ran into Reb Brown. He felt to me like an inspired choice.

The guy had been both a professional kickboxer and boxer, best known for his horribly lopsided 15-round, unanimous decision loss to Larry Holmes for the world heavyweight title in 1982. Afterwards, a disgusted Howard Cosell had said that he would never work as a commentator on boxing again. "Tex" then quipped to the press, "If it gets him to stop broadcasting NFL games, I'll go play football for a week, too." In addition to *Uncommon Valor*, "Tex" had acted in a number of other films including *Raising Arizona* and *Fletch Lives*, and was a larger than life character.

Mark Gastineau was another possibility. He had racked up 107-and-a-half sacks and five Pro Bowl selections in a 10-year career as a defensive end for the New York Jets. After the NFL, Gastineau extended his fame in 1991 by becoming a pro boxer, and then dating Brigitte Nielsen (ex-wife of Sylvester Stallone and an actress in *Rocky IV*). He had big hair, and an even bigger ego. Gastineau was the quintessential love-to-hate big-mouth athlete.

And then there was Mitch "Blood" Green, best known for his second fight against Mike Tyson, which took place outside a 24-hour clothing store in Harlem. Their first fight had occurred in 1986—in a boxing ring—with the pre-world champion Tyson defeating Green in a 10-round, unanimous decision. Two years later, Green got his rematch, which resulted in him receiving a closed left eye, and a cut that required five stitches. For his part, Tyson suffered a ripped shirt and a fractured right hand from blasting Green in the face. Green filed a $25 million lawsuit against Tyson, and became an instant media darling, as he recounted the street fight, and his hatred of "Iron" Mike. A New York jury eventually awarded Green $45,000, which was $15,000 more than what he'd earned in his first fight against Tyson.

Before I could get too deep into negotiations, Meyrowitz shot them all down, feeling that "Tex", Gastineau, and Green would want fat guarantees. He reiterated to me that he would consider paying for a boxer, but it had to be a boxer with legitimate credentials in the sport. And one who was willing to fight for peanuts.

Through my numerous calls to the boxing world, I was eventually given the name of Earnest Hart, Jr. as a person who I should contact.

Hart held black belts in a number of martial arts, including Kenpo and taekwondo. And he was a legendary welterweight kickboxer who won his first PKA title at age 21, and was once tabbed as one of the "Top Ten Kickboxers of All Time" by *Inside Karate* magazine. Hart was fast talking, funny, and he knew boxers, managers and attorneys associated with the sport in his hometown St. Louis.

Hart put me in touch with representatives for James "Bonecrusher" Smith and Leon Spinks, and I went to work. Both Spinks and "Bonecrusher" had been recognized boxing world heavyweight champions, but were now on the downside of their respective careers. Spinks won a gold medal at the 1976 Summer Olympics, and two years later stunned the world by defeating Muhammad Ali in a 15 round split decision to take the WBA and WBC titles. He lost the rematch to Ali the following year, and then proceeded to win just three of his next six fights. It was all downhill from there.

"Bonecrusher" had scored a first round knockout victory against Tim Witherspoon in 1986, which gave him the WBA title. Seven months later "Bonecrusher" was defeated by Mike Tyson, which started him on a four-fight winless streak. He would never be in the world title picture again.

I went back to Meyrowitz and asked him how much he would be willing to pay for one of these former title holders. Even long-faded champions like Spinks and "Bonecrusher" wouldn't come cheap. Meyrowitz liked the idea, and told me $5,000 as an amount that could work for him. But the $100,000 asking price of both Spinks and "Bonecrusher" didn't meet this financial criterion, so I kept looking.

I circled back to Earnest Hart who put me in touch with St. Louis-based attorney Phil Adams, who handled a number of boxers, the most prominent of whom was Art "King Arthur" Jimmerson. His nickname made me smile, and think of Milius with his Excalibur talk. I smiled even more when I started researching Jimmerson's boxing career. At 5-foot-11 and 195 lb., Jimmerson kind of looked like a heavyweight, if you squinted. The guy was good; he'd won the National Golden Gloves middleweight title in 1983, but had the misfortune of ending up as a cruiserweight, the boxing weight class that runs from 176 to 200 pounds.

Cruiserweights are forever stuck in a boxing financial dead zone, as they're seen as not as fast and exciting as the smaller guys and not as powerful and awesome as the heavyweights. So you could have a great career in this weight class, and still not reap the rewards of fame and fortune. And this was Jimmerson in a nutshell. His record was 29-5, he was on a 15-fight winning streak, a legit top-10 cruiserweight and in

This is Earnest Hart, Jr. from St. Louis, Missouri, a championship kickboxer and pioneer mixed martial artist, who was instrumental in connecting me with various heavyweight boxers.

Photo courtesy of Earnest Hart, Jr.

talks to fight the great Tommy "Hitman" Hearns. But he still needed money, and unlike his top-10 heavyweight counterparts, a grand prize of $50,000 was, for him, a lot of money.

We started talking, and true to his sport, Jimmerson wanted an appearance fee. He asked for $30,000, I countered with $10,000, and went around and around until we finally arrived at $17,000. Meyrowitz gave his approval and his cash reluctantly, and then there were seven. To Meyrowitz and the boxing fans like him, this was the Great White Shark of the tournament. But my experience at the Gracie Academy told me that one-dimensional "King Arthur" was likely going to be just another goldfish.

I had often wondered how a world-class wrestler would fare on the ground with one of the Gracies. What they lacked in submissions, they would no doubt make up for with takedowns and positional control. My Mike Tyson in this sport was Alexander Karelin, who the previous summer in Barcelona had won his second consecutive Olympic gold medal in the Greco Roman wrestling superheavyweight division. Between his Olympic triumphs, Karelin had captured three straight world championships. But penetrating the bureaucracy of Russia to bring their sports hero to Denver seemed about as likely as getting Tyson an early release from prison just so he could fight for us.

So instead, I set my sights on the greatest wrestler in the history of the U.S., Dan Gable. After going 181-1 with two NCAA championships, Gable captured gold in freestyle wrestling at the 1972 Summer Olympics without dropping a point. But I wasn't looking for the 44-year-old coach of the famed University of Iowa's wrestling program to fight for me, I was looking for Gable to tell me who should. If anyone could get me a world-class wrestler, it was Gable. After numerous, unreturned phone calls, I started leaving messages for his assistant, Tom Brands. But he never called me back, either.

I figured fuck it; I have Shamrock, and while he's not a straight wrestler, the guy knows how to grapple. So, I moved on.

As for trying to sign a big name from American pro wrestling, the thought entered my mind, and then exited just as quickly. For starters, someone like Hulk Hogan or Ric Flair would have sought big money. Likely not as big as the dollar amount that the top heavyweight boxers would have looked for, but still well out of our budget range. And who knew if any of these guys could actually fight? Unlike Shamrock and even Bart Vale with their strong-style Puroresu matches in Japan, the era of shooters in Western pro wrestling seemed to have died out with old-timers like Lou Thesz and Ed "Strangler" Lewis. Plus, having a star from the WWF or WCW would have announced "work" to the fight public. I didn't need the aggravation, and I certainly couldn't pay for it anyway.

Having struck out with Olympic wrestling, I turned my attention to the Olympic sport of taekwondo. The king of that mountain in this country was Herb Perez, who had won the U.S.'s only gold medal in the sport at the 1992 Summer Games. I reached out to Perez and offered him $10,000. I figured that I had to come with something, and that Meyrowitz would never turn down writing a check to an American Olympic hero. But Perez wasn't interested, and didn't even counteroffer. I had the feeling that the honchos in Olympic taekwondo were down on his participation in our rough-and-tumble event.

For quite some time, I had been harboring the idea of getting a sumo wrestler. On the mock-up poster that Mike Stanley did for me, sumo was listed as one of the 15 fighting disciplines. I'd seen sumo and found the athletes astonishing, weird and compelling. And they were certainly strong and enormous. Plus, the sport had the air of the exotic about it. I could envision a 400-pound sumo wrestler chasing after Art Jimmerson or lying on top of Royce. That would be a spectacle.

If we really were going to have a wide open tournament featuring all the fighting arts, well then, we'd have to showcase the minor ones too. And sumo, as far as North Americans were concerned, was about as minor as it gets. Apart from the scene in *You Only Live Twice* where Sean Connery, as James Bond, has a knock-down, drag-out fight in a high-tech office with a sumo wrestler, I knew that most Americans had virtually no exposure to the sport.

I wasn't sure how a sumo wrestler would do in a real fight, but the sheer audacity of putting one in the tournament got to me. When I ran the idea by Rorion, he didn't know what to make of it, but said, "Hey, the old man grappled to a draw with Wladek Zbyszko (the famous Polish strongman and wrestler). He weighed 280 lb. So, why not?"

But everyone who I asked told me to forget it: sumo is a very closed subculture, and there is no chance that they'll let you in. Undeterred, I started calling Japan, and with my Brooklyn accent, it went nowhere fast. I felt like I was talking to owls, "Who, who, who?"

I did get someone on the phone at a Tokyo newspaper who spoke passable English. But the journalist told me that I was wasting my time.

"You no have luck getting sumo. Sumo is for Japan. Very proud. Understand?"

I remembered reading back at the Torrance Public Library that the sumo leagues in Japan were now recruiting Hawaiians to the sport, and so I decided to change course. I tracked down John Jacques, the honcho of the American Amateur Sumo Association. Jacques was based in California and had substantial credibility in the sport. He was a recruiter for the big sumo organizations in Japan, sending them massive men from the Hawaiian Islands. When I called Jacques and explained to him what I was looking for, he told me to look no further.

"I've got a guy, Teila Tuli, who got into the Makushita 2 class. And that's up there a bit. He's the real deal, but he ran into a few problems in Japan, and is now back living in Hawaii."

Jacques told me that he would call Tuli on my behalf, and gauge his interest. At 6-foot-2 and 420 lb., the man known as Takamishu in sumo, and also as Taylor Wily in Hawaii, was a perfect representative of sumo for our tournament, as far as I was concerned.

Tuli had been unbeaten in his first 14 official sumo bouts, winning two consecutive yūshō (tournament championships). While he'd never reached the upper echelon of the sport, Tuli had achieved some semblance of success in Japan, and his credentials were more than solid.

Jacques told me that Tuli wanted $10,000, plus airfare from Honolulu to Denver for his brother and two cousins as well. I countered with $6,000 plus the travel, and we had a deal. As physically imposing as Tuli was, I questioned if he had either the overall fighting skill or conditioning to do anything other than look scary. Was he nothing more than an enormous goldfish? I amazed myself that I was first able to convince Campbell on this idea, and then get Meyrowitz to shell out $6,000 for an unknown quantity like Tuli.

Locking in our eight tournament fighters gave me an incredible sense of both satisfaction and relief, but then I realized that I still had more work to do. There was a serious likelihood that a fighter could win his bout, but then be too injured, too exhausted, or both, to continue on in the tournament. I had to get an alternate, who would be on stand-by, and ready to jump in at a moment's notice.

Jim Mullen was a 23-year-old taekwondo black belt who had contacted me after seeing our ad. He had a solid kickboxing pedigree, but at just over 200 lb., lacked the size of my other two American representatives of that sport, Rosier and Frazier. He seemed like a nice kid though, and I offered him a spot as my alternate, which he quickly accepted. Hedging my bets, I then decided that I really needed two alternates, just in case everything went wrong.

Rorion asked me one Friday what I thought about Jason DeLucia. "The kung fu guy. Nice kid," I said.

DeLucia was a stylist in Five Animals Kung Fu and had studied aikido. He first came to the west coast trying to get Steven Seagal to fight him, after the action film star had made some bold claims in a martial arts magazine. He was of course never able to get anywhere close to Seagal, so DeLucia then went to the Gracies in search of a fight. He was given Royce as an opponent, and summarily defeated, but not without showing a great deal of heart. The fight was included as part of the second *Gracie Jiu-Jitsu in Action* tape, as a showcase for Royce. But watching it, I couldn't help but admire how doggedly determined DeLucia had been, despite getting pummeled.

After this loss, DeLucia became absolutely obsessed with Gracie Jiu-Jitsu. I got to know him a little bit at the Academy, and I always liked how he carried himself.

DeLucia had been lobbying both Rorion and me for a place in the tournament. So when Rorion mentioned him as a possible alternate, I thought he was a worthwhile choice. DeLucia was so determined and tenacious, I figured he would walk to Denver, just for the opportunity to be on stand-by.

With that I now had my 10 fighters, eight for the tournament and two alternates. But what I still didn't have was a signed contract with SEG. In the business world of sharks and goldfish, I couldn't help but wonder how Bob Meyrowitz viewed me.

CHAPTER 9
IS THIS LEGAL?

THE GODS ARE ON THE SIDE OF THE STRONGER.
— TACITUS, Histories, Bk IV, 17

THE third week in August 1993, Campbell flew out to LA to meet with me. He said that was the reason, but I suspected he actually had other business, and was squeezing me in. I was happy to see him nonetheless, as we had very quickly developed a friendly working relationship through our regular phone calls. Campbell was due to stay at the Chateau Marmont, but ended up at the Mondrian. Both of these were fancy "show business" hotels that producers and stars frequented. When I hooked up with him at the Mondrian close to dinnertime, he told me that he wasn't here to talk about the contract. That was for Meyrowitz and his brother David. Rather, he had pressing issues of his own, namely what were we going to call this thing, and what were we going to use as the fighting area.

I was resigned to the fact that, legally, War of the Worlds just wasn't going to fly. And then there was the issue raised by Campbell and everyone at SEG that War of the Worlds just didn't sound specifically like a fighting competition. As much as I liked the name, it was really always a working title. At times, I found myself using World's Best Fighter again, almost subconsciously hedging my bets. But Campbell didn't like that name either—too generic. And Meyrowitz, the SEG broadcast producer Michael Pillot, and the SEG sales guy Mike Abramson, all felt the same.

Just before Campbell flew out from New York, Abramson came up with the name Ultimate Fighting Championship. It was his brainstorm and his alone, and it just felt too long, too convoluted to me.

Over the phone, Abramson had tried to be persuasive.

"Ultimate. There is nothing beyond ultimate. Think about that, Art. Nothing above and beyond ultimate."

I actually loved the words ultimate, fighting and championship, just not in that three-word sequence. But I couldn't think of a better alternative. Campbell said that he was on board with this name, and Meyrowitz thought it worked as well. I told Campbell that I'd talk to Rorion about it, who I knew would probably have no strong opinion one way or the other.

As for our fighting area, Rorion did have strong opinions. Repeatedly he had told me that he didn't care what we used, as long as it wasn't a boxing ring. Rorion had fought in them personally, and had seen them used in vale tudo fights in Brazil, including with his dad and his brother Rickson. In Rorion's opinion, they just didn't work when grappling was involved. And it was without question that grappling would be involved as far as Royce was concerned. Rorion felt that a boxing ring allowed a grounded fighter to slide under the ring ropes for a quick exit, or tie himself up in the ropes to avoid being taken down.

Photo courtesy of Art Davie Archives

I didn't really care how this would affect Royce, but I did care about the flow of the fights. Rorion made a lot of sense. We needed brutal action, not stalling and escapes. Campbell bought into this logic when I relayed Rorion's sentiments.

"But what would we use then, wrestling mats?" he asked me. Campbell's

Here I am with Campbell McLaren while we were both still sober. We loved Cuban cigars and single malt scotch in those days—although he was a Cohiba fan and I favored the Montecristo #2.

brother-in-law had apparently been a wrestler, and he'd gone to him for some ideas.

Inspired by Milius and all of his talk of spectacle and grandiosity, I'd been thinking about this quite a bit. Rorion and I had already spread word around the Gracie Academy that any ideas were welcome—no matter how unrealistic or outrageous.

One of Rorion's students proposed something he called "the Cage of Death." It featured a mesh enclosure suspended from the ceiling, which would be dramatically lowered from the rafters to surround the fighting mat, and then locked into place. I thought this was pretty cool, and incredibly theatrical. The guy gave me his notes and a sketch. Seeing it on paper, I liked the Cage of Death even more. But it would require a lot of precise coordination and solid engineering that I wasn't sure we could accomplish.

On my own, I came up with three ideas. The first was a circular grappling mat, which would be bordered on the outside by electrified copper flooring panels. My thought was that a fighter would be discouraged from fleeing or even backpedaling, as he would know that a small jolt of electricity was waiting for him. The shock would be nothing major; just a little tingle similar to what happens when a person touches an electrified fence. I floated this idea by Rorion, and he in turn mentioned it to one of his students who was a doctor.

"Are you guys trying to kill someone?" was the M.D.'s terse reply.

The doctor explained that if a sweaty fighter landed stomach first on the electrified panels, he could possibly suffer ventricular fibrillation—a rapid contraction of the heart—which could cause a heart attack or even sudden death. So I moved on.

My second idea felt truly revolutionary to me, and I was curious to see if I'd found the answer. We'd build a huge Plexiglas box, open only on top and with a door created on one side. The fighters would have no way to escape the battle, and the view of the in-house and PPV television audiences would never be obstructed. With a look of disbelief, Rorion asked me about the flooring, and I told him that it would probably be Plexiglas as well.

"And you think this would be a good idea for fighting on the ground, Arturo?"

He, of course, had a valid point. It would be very uncomfortable, especially for Royce, who was just as offensive and effective fighting off of his back as he was on top of his opponent. Holding closed guard with a 220-pound man on top of you while lying on hard Plexiglas, was not a pleasant proposition. And how about my enormous sumo wrestler Teila Tuli potentially slamming someone down onto the floor? Plus, I started thinking back to my conversations with Pillot about the numerous bright lights required for the broadcast. Clear, shiny Plexiglas was going to look like the surface of the sun on TV, although I did love the thought of putting a camera below the fighters, and shooting upwards for a really unique view.

My third idea also involved a grappling mat, but this time it would be surrounded by a moat, filled with water, and sharks or piranhas. Again, an incentive for both fighters to keep moving forward. It would be a gimmick, as we'd use sand sharks or lemon sharks, neither of which are particularly threatening when it comes to humans; or piranhas that would be well fed, thus making them about as dangerous to the submerged fighters as catfish. But what a gimmick it would be.

My enthusiasm, though, quickly gave way to the cold, hard and un-sexy world of logistics. We would have to transport all of those fish from who knows where to the venue. And we'd have to fill up the moat with water, adding a lot of time to the set up. How practical would this be, event after event? I didn't even mention my sharks and piranhas concept to Rorion.

At that point, I had nothing concrete for Campbell when we met at the Mondrian, other than a lot of Milius-inspired "think big" ideas. Since I felt we were inventing this thing as we went along, it seemed appropriate to offer up anything and everything that came to mind, no matter how out-of-the-box. Campbell and I smoked cigars and sipped single malt as we riffed on what the fighting area could be. It was a laugh-filled night, and I felt a definite "show business" vibe hanging out with my hippy-dippy pal from back east.

"Why didn't you wind up staying at the Chateau Marmont?" I asked him at one point.

"Too many echoes from my misspent youth," Campbell said with a wink and a grin.

"Drugs?"

"Well, you know you can still get a contact high from staying there. That's where John Belushi bought it," Campbell darkly joked, about the famed comic actor who had died from a drug overdose at that hotel in 1982.

The next night, Rorion and I took Campbell to meet Milius for dinner at Schatzi in Santa Monica, which was owned by Arnold Schwarzenegger. Once a month, Cigar Night was held at Schatzi, and a who's who of Hollywood would turn out to eat and smoke and smoke some more. We had chosen Schatzi for just this reason, as all of us were cigar aficionados, apart from Rorion of course.

Milius was in outstanding form, telling one showbiz story after another. Campbell was entranced and entertained. Rorion meanwhile looked as though he was about to pass out, as he was the only one of the 90-plus diners who did not have a cigar in hand. He continually excused himself to get fresh air outside.

Schwarzenegger worked the room, shaking hands, and carrying a big prop cigar. He was amazing, like a politician running for office.

At one point in the evening, Schwarzenegger and Sven Ole Thorsen came to our table. Thorsen was one of Schwarzenegger's closest pals and a co-founder of Cigar Night at the restaurant. As well as being an actor, Thorsen was a bodybuilder and power lifter, and had won the title of Denmark's Strongest Man in 1982. He'd had roles in a number of films that starred his Austrian buddy, including *Conan the Barbarian*, *The Running Man* and *Total Recall*.

Schwarzenegger greeted his Conan director by throwing up his arms theatrically and exclaiming, "Ah, the Milius!"

Milius introduced us, and when Thorsen asked Rorion, who he knew from the movie business, what we were all working on together, he mumbled, "We're... uh... doing something with fighting."

I had never seen Rorion this subdued—ever. I didn't know if it was the evening's star power or cigar smoke, but he barely said a word. Milius said plenty, but very little had anything to do with the issues still undecided for our fighting tournament. Our creative director was an outstanding dinner companion, but we, as a group, didn't move the needle very far forward.

It had been an enjoyable evening, but it just wasn't much of a working session.

Campbell and I agreed that he'd take my half-formed theories on the fighting area to Pillot when he returned to the SEG offices. As the TV producer, Pillot would have to take into consideration our input plus whatever parameters and issues would be involved with the live PPV broadcast.

When Campbell was back at his office in New York, he called and asked me again what I thought about the name proposed by Abramson. I still wasn't crazy about "the Ultimate Fighting Championship," but the posters, press kits and marketing materials all needed to get made, and they were on hold until we got this issue settled. So I gave Campbell my consent, but told him that it just wasn't catchy enough. I felt that the name needed to be shortened, but I was bereft of ideas. So the Ultimate Fighting Championship it was. I knew that I should have been more pro-active, given my ad agency experience. I had sold and created product names for a number of client companies. But when the chips were on the line with what to call my pet project, I came up short.

On this call, Campbell also told me he had talked to Pillot about all of my ideas, concepts and theories regarding our fighting area. To make sure we were heard, I then drafted a fax with a list of bullet points for a designer to use in its creation. It was based on Rorion's anti-boxing ring position, plus considerations from me about the canvas and the padding underneath. I also suggested in this fax that the fighting area should be at least 30 feet in diameter—six feet bigger than a standard world championship boxing ring.

Pillot then gave my list, along with his TV production requirements, to two set designers in California he had worked with in the past: Greg Harrison and Jason Cusson. Pillot told them that we wanted it to look almost primitive, incorporating the feeling of ancient Pankration and the Roman Coliseum.

Soon after, I was shown four preliminary design sketches that Harrison and Cusson had created. The first looked like a standard boxing ring, but instead of ropes, a wall of thick fencing surrounded the perimeter. The fence, which started on the floor, and extended a few feet above the canvas, was topped with barbed wire. In the four corners of the ring were lit torches for obvious dramatic effect.

The second sketch also featured what seemed like a boxing ring, but this one had an inner fighting area that was enclosed by a thick rope netting, similar to what would hang behind home plate at a baseball stadium. The netting was held in place by support poles anchored just outside the four corners of the ring.

The third depicted the fighting area with an elevated circular mat. In essence, a raised platform. The mat sloped down to be surrounded by an inside circular walkway, with a circular chain link fence around the perimeter.

The fourth and final sketch that I saw employed an octagon shape, enclosed by a chain link fence, and surrounded by an outer catwalk. It was elevated, just like a boxing ring, and had two entry gates placed on opposite sides, which could be locked shut. I immediately felt that this was our winner, as did Harrison, Cusson, and everyone at SEG.

As we hit September and two months out from our November 12 premiere date, things were rolling. Moss was making real headway with Meyrowitz and his brother David in the negotiations. Just after Campbell departed from LA, Moss had successfully been able to negotiate that SEG, and not W.O.W. Promotions, would pay the full bill for the design and construction of the fighting area. It was a small victory in the larger war that was still raging over the unsigned contract between our two sides.

Kathy Kidd was even better than I had expected, and she had assembled a support staff that came to include her gal pals, Sally Starr and Terry Parr. Collectively, their names sounded to me like the roster of some Ivy League sorority. Kathy also hired Elaine McCarthy as our travel coordinator. Elaine owned Katella Travel with her mom, and was the wife of John McCarthy, the LAPD cop I knew from the Gracie Academy.

Jeff Black, the VP of music at SEG, gave me the number of Barry Fey, a guy who he said could really help us with local ticket sales.

Fey was a living legend in the concert business, and the fact that he was based in Denver, made him an ideal choice. He was known as the "Rockfather," and had first established himself by bringing big name English music acts to the U.S., including The Rolling Stones, Led Zeppelin and The Who. Three times Fay had been voted Promoter of the Year by *Billboard* magazine, and one of his crowning achievements was U2's show at Colorado's Red Rocks Amphitheatre, which was the basis of the 1984 concert film *Under a Blood Red Sky*.

I had, of course, never promoted a fight or a music concert, so I was all for the idea. Plus, with everything going on, I was in no position to start hawking tickets in Denver.

Meyrowitz then followed up Black's call, and said that I should personally reach out to Fey, and sell him on our event.

When I got Fey on the phone, I told him all about the Ultimate Fighting Championship, as well as the uniqueness of our fighters and the fights themselves.

"Think of this like one of your big rock concerts. Lots of theatrics and fireworks to get the crowd going."

I then went on to tell Fey that while I knew that "the real money" was in the PPV broadcast, the in-house show was still very important to me.

With that, Fey suddenly got very quiet, and soon after ended the call.

Thirty minutes later, my phone rang, and Meyrowitz was on the line.

"What do you mean by fucking up a deal with Barry Fey? Do you know how fucking hard it is to bring a Barry Fey to the table? What the fuck is with you?"

I had never heard Meyrowitz lose his cool like this before, even in our contract negotiating sessions.

"I'm spending a lot of fucking money to make this work. I don't need you running around like a bull in a China shop with Barry Fey!"

Apparently, I had insulted Fey by denigrating the live event and its revenue potential. I immediately called him back, said that I was sorry if I had offended him in any way, and told him that I felt fortunate he wanted to be involved in our event. To his credit, Fey accepted my apology, and we quickly moved on. I had no doubt that Fey knew that the "real money" was indeed in the PPV broadcast, and not his in-arena ticket sales. But this was a guy who had made his living, and his reputation, by staging amazing live shows. And he wasn't about to let some fast-talking fight promoter from Torrance, California demean his bread and butter.

With the Fey crisis averted, Campbell called me and said that I should also contact Zane Bresloff, who was the World Wrestling

Federation's promoter in the Rocky Mountain states. Fey and Bresloff knew each other, and had both done business with Meyrowitz.

Bresloff and I hit it off immediately, and on our second phone call, he impressed me with his insight.

"Art, I looked over the list of the fighter bios that you sent me, and either your jiu-jitsu guy or this Shamrock character will win the whole thing."

"How do you figure that?" I asked.

"Easy. None of these other palookas know anything about grappling. The best grappler always wins."

Even though Bresloff had come to me from the world of pro wrestling works, he seemed to possess a fundamental understanding of fighting that was lost on Meyrowitz.

Fey, Bresloff and I quickly formed an alliance, in which W.O.W. Promotions would get a $25,000 guarantee, and then our two sides would split everything 50-50 that came in from ticket sales above that sum.

Despite the PPV broadcast being my absolute priority, I didn't want us playing to rows upon rows of empty seats at the massive McNichols Arena. I knew that would be an instant mood killer, and immediately register as a huge red flag for our live TV audience. I was happy with the deal, as I had two guys who knew how to sell tickets, and were financially incentivized to bust their ass. Plus, they were both there in Denver, and were paying us a sizeable guaranteed advance regardless of what happened.

In our contract with Fey and Bresloff, I was able to negotiate a clause that let W.O.W. Promotions control some of the best seats in the house, as well as sell travel packages to the Ultimate Fighting Championship, which would be coordinated through Elaine McCarthy. My idea was to target our investors, students at the Gracie Academy, and the database of names that we'd assembled through the Gracie videotape sales.

For the local Denver market, Fey and Bresloff set their ticket prices at $10, $15, $20, and $25. We offered our market two travel packages, the "Deluxe" which cost $269 for one person and $319 for two; and the "VIP" which went for $359 for a single, and $499 for a double. The VIP Package included a seat (or two) in one of the first two rows (listed at $50 per ticket), three nights at our headquarters hotel, an autograph and photo session with the fighters, a post-fight cocktail party and a masked ball and supper the night after the fights.

In writing up this one-sheet brochure, I wanted it to be as concise as possible. I'd already used the word "ultimate" twice in the copy, and I didn't want to be redundant. I was also running out of room at the bottom of the page. So I shortened the Ultimate Fighting Championship to "UFC." I hadn't used this three letter abbreviation previously, nor had I heard anyone else refer to our event by this shortened name. To me, UFC had a nice concise quality to it, like NFL or NBA. I just wasn't sure if it would take hold, as no one really knew what those letters meant out of context.

Right after I got a handle on the tickets, we landed our first sponsor, and it was a good one. Through Kathy's original contact, I'd been able to meet with Pete and Paul Grymkowski, the brothers who owned Gold's Gym Enterprises, Inc., based in Southern California. As part of the deal, our fight poster would be hung in Gold's Gym locations across the U.S., we would get Gold's Gym merchandise for our use in marketing, and the Grymkowski Brothers would attend our first event in Denver along with a number of their senior executives. They also put out the word in their company's monthly magazine which featured a photo of Pete, Rorion, Derek Barton (their marketing VP) and me.

Pete had been a well-known bodybuilding champion on the North American scene, who quickly became a darling of *Iron Man* magazine. In 1979, along with two partners, Pete purchased Gold's Gym. The following year, he brought in his brother Paul to help run the business, and soon after they launched a national and international licensing and franchise program. Within a few years, there were Gold's Gyms all over the world, and the Grymkowski brothers were multi-millionaires.

This deal further motivated me to get SEG the necessary materials to create our poster for the Ultimate Fighting Championship, the design and cost of which had been negotiated as their responsibility. What they needed from me were any relevant photographs and brief fighter bio information, such as records and titles.

For their part, SEG put an artist to work on creating the logo for the Ultimate Fighting Championship. It was contractually their responsibility to both design and pay for it, although I was able to offer my input. I asked Rorion his thoughts on the matter, and just as I expected, he told me that he would be good with whatever I liked.

In attempting to create the quintessential iconic image of the tournament, SEG came back to me with a bald fighter, in red trunks and a gold belt, with both fists extended. The fighter was straddling a globe, which had a yellow banner in front, on which was written in bold all capital red letters "Ultimate Fighting Championship." In the lower right hand corner, also written in red caps, was a phrase I had given SEG, "There Are No Rules" which was followed by an exclamation point, for obvious emphasis.

My tagline aside, I didn't love the logo that SEG created, but I didn't hate it either. I thought it was decent, and I was expecting a lot more from them than decent. But I felt that I had much bigger concerns, namely the matter of the still unsigned contract. The logo I dubbed "Mr. Clean," in reference to the famous cleaning products' illustrated pitch man, would have to do.

As the staff at SEG got busy putting together the promo kit that would be sent to cable systems across the country, it came to me for approval. With my background in advertising, I felt that I could properly evaluate what they were doing. Ad slicks and posters were marketing tools I had a great deal of experience with. There was a lot of discussion over what photos to use on the official fight poster, with numerous opinions offered. Since there was obviously no existing footage of our event, I knew that we had to improvise.

SEG asked me for pictures of all eight tournament fighters, but I told them that no one knew who any of these guys were, so we should just go with one really cool photograh that screamed "fighting." Rorion suggested that we use a photo he owned of a vale tudo fight in Brazil between Fabio Gurgel and Denilson Maia.

I didn't think that it was perfect, but SEG said that it was good enough for them to use as the poster's centerpiece image.

Collecting the fighter bios was a hilarious experience for me. Pat Smith had already told me about his record of 250-0. Kevin Rosier said that he had 66 wins, all by knockout. When I was recruiting fighters, it quickly became apparent that everyone was a world champion or a 10th degree black belt or on a 100-fight winning streak. Usually the fighters claimed that it was all of the above.

Outside of professional boxing, there just wasn't much in the way of official and standardized record keeping in combat sports and martial arts. And there was an alphabet soup of organizations, federations and sanctioning bodies, all with their own recognized titleholders. Rather than become the Hall of Records, I figured that I'd let the fighters claim whatever they wanted. They could prove it in our tournament.

I was sensitive to what we could say about Royce, other than he was a Gracie Jiu-Jitsu black belt. Rorion provided me with info from an organization in Brazil that claimed Royce was their world light-heavyweight champion, had a record of 132-1 as an amateur, and 13-0 as a professional. I wanted to say, "What the fuck is this? When was Royce a pro? How and where did he become their champion?"

But I remembered my newfound philosophy, and kept my mouth shut, while doing my best to suppress a laugh. I especially liked that Rorion included one defeat on his brother's record. This made me think of the dictators who announce to the world media that they have won re-election with 99 percent of the vote, fearing that if they claimed to have received 100 percent of the vote, nobody would take them seriously.

As I was so focused on my deals with Fey/Bresloff and Gold's Gym, travel packages, the fight poster, and fighter records, it didn't hit me right away that my contact with Campbell and everyone at SEG was starting to taper off. But then I realized that our regular phone calls were happening with less and less frequency since Campbell and I had met at the Mondrian. And when we did talk, more often than not, it was me dialing him in New York and not the other way around.

I confronted Campbell, and he told me, "Art, you always see conspiracies on our part when you don't get your way."

This didn't reassure me, and instead made

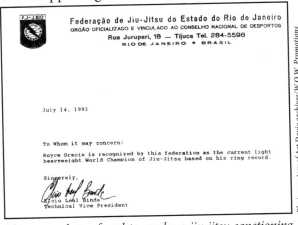

FJ-J.RIO

Federação de Jiu-Jitsu do Estado do Rio de Janeiro
ORGÃO OFICIALIZADO E VINCULADO AO CONSELHO NACIONAL DE DESPORTOS
Rua Jurupari, 18 — Tijuca Tel. 284-5598
RIO DE JANEIRO • BRASIL

July 14, 1993

To Whom it may concern:

Royce Gracie is recognized by this federation as the current light heavyweight World Champion of Jiu-Jitsu based on his ring record.

Sincerely,

Lício Leal Binda
Technical Vice President

Photo courtesy of Art Davie archives/W.O.W. Promotions

This was a letter faxed to me by a jiu-jitsu sanctioning body in Brazil testifying that Royce Gracie was their light-heavyweight champion. I wasn't positive that this wasn't just a gift from a Gracie family pal in their hometown.

me think of something that I'd once heard: "It's not paranoia if they're really out to get you."

For all of the progress that we'd made with SEG since our meetings at their offices in May, and our meeting at the W.O.W. office during the summer, we still didn't have a deal. In theory, they could pull out at any time, and there wasn't a thing that Rorion and I could do about it. I didn't really think this was a possibility, as Meyrowitz, Campbell, Pillot, Abramson and everyone at SEG had put in a lot of money, time and work on the Ultimate Fighting Championship. But still.

So, on September 15 I faxed a two-page letter to Meyrowitz outlining my complaints. I broke them down into six areas, which I underlined for emphasis—"lack of regular professional communication," "sloppy execution," "you're not giving the project 100 percent," "you're not treating us like a partner," "we are concerned about your staffing adequacy," and "strained relationships."

I then gave a summary of gripes under each of these six headings, such as the write-up of the Ultimate Fighting Championship that SEG sent out to cable systems across the country had "18 typo and factual errors, including the misspelling of Rorion's name!" and "no one in your organization seems to be in charge of the UFC when Campbell is preoccupied with overseas trips and jury duty. Jury duty?!"

In conclusion, I wrote:

We're not threating to pull out of either the November 12 show or the five-year commitment. But as I have told Campbell, we are unhappy with aspects of your performance composed to the picture which was painted for us and to which we responded by agreeing to your 6/3/93 offer. And we're not pleased when it comes to how we're being treated. Knowing what we do today, we are very concerned that this long-term commitment will be mutually beneficial given the current circumstances and climate. We think it has to improve or it jeopardizes the project's success. We need to talk and we suggest that you tell us when. We feel strongly that our attorney be present for this conference call.

I made the document from both Rorion and me, and I had him sign it just above my signature. Rorion wasn't overly concerned, as he felt that this was just posturing on my behalf to get us a better deal. And I was posturing to a certain extent, including when I put in this letter that we had agreed, in principle, to their original contract offer of June 3. But I didn't feel that SEG was giving us their best effort, at least not anymore, and combined with their decreased frequency in communication and the never-ending contract negotiations, this had me genuinely concerned.

Rather than answer me personally, Meyrowitz had Campbell respond to my letter. He told me not to worry, that SEG was fully behind the Ultimate Fighting Championship, and that the lawyers Moss and David would get everything sorted. There was still a huge elephant in the room—the lack of an actual agreement between W.O.W. and SEG—but it seemed that the elephant had at least moved a few inches.

I felt a lot better after getting my frustrations out via fax, and Moss told me we were getting closer. SEG was slowly making concessions, and as tough as Meyrowitz and David had been, it was clear to Moss that they were determined to do this deal.

By the end of September, SEG was more engaged, and they sent me a copy of our official Ultimate Fighting Championship poster. The Gurgel/Maia photo was front and center, surrounded by a black border with red stars and the names of the eight tournament fighters in reversed type. Down the left side—top to bottom—were the names of Royce, Smith, Tuli and Frazier. Listed down the right side of the poster—top to bottom—were Gordeau, Jimmerson, Rosier and Shamrock.

Below each fighter's name, a few lines of bio information were listed, mixing fact and fiction. For Shamrock, it read: "220 lb. 6-foot-0, Lockeford, CA, #1 ranked shootfighter in the world, Japanese Pancrase Association." I let Royce have his 13-0 record, but I couldn't go with 250-0 for Smith. It was just too ridiculous, even for a fight poster built on over-the-top hype. So I had sent SEG his combined documented pro boxing and pro kickboxing records, which worked out to 17-2, and that's what was listed.

Written in thick reversed type over the Gurgel/Maia picture was, "The Ultimate! Sumo vs. Kickboxing vs. Karate vs. Jiu-Jitsu vs. Tae Kwon Do vs. Boxing vs. Savate vs. Shootfighting. Who will be the Ultimate Fighter?" In the bottom right corner was the four-word tagline, inspired by my days in the ad business, that I had suggested to SEG: "There Are No Rules!"

It was a take-no-prisoners positioning statement, but there were, of course, going to be some rules. We weren't going to let a fighter get repeatedly kicked in the balls or have his ear bitten off on live TV. But if young guys thought those brutalities were a possibility, then they just might be inspired to buy a ticket or call their local cable company and place an order.

As we hit October, there were still jobs on the Ultimate Fighting Championship that needed to be filled—the referee and the television commentators.

The ref would be our call, and the commentators would be a joint decision between W.O.W. and SEG, which really boiled down to Campbell and me. For some time I'd been thinking about "Judo" Gene LeBell to be our referee. It would be an homage to the brief and scattered past of 20th century mixed match fighting, as LeBell had of course choked out the boxer Milo Savage in 1963 and 13 years later refereed the Muhammad Ali vs. Antonio Inoki debacle in Japan. LeBell was a no-bullshit, old-school tough guy who wouldn't be intimidated by any of the fighters. But Rorion shot his name down as quickly as I brought it up.

In 1983, Rorion had a bit acting role and some stunt work on an episode of the Robert Wagner TV series *Hart to Hart*, on which LeBell was also working. As Rorion told it, the two hit it off, and he was invited by LeBell to come to his school and roll with some of the better students. Apparently, Rorion choked them all out, one after the other. LeBell got more and more pissed off, and started dismissing Rorion's obviously impressive grappling and submission skills. So Rorion challenged LeBell to have a go with him on the mat, but his host declined. Words were exchanged, and that was the end of their very brief friendship.

No way now after all those years was Rorion going to do anything for LeBell. I didn't argue, as Rorion so rarely raised his objections to any of my ideas. But I didn't know who else to get. There were big name boxing refs like Mills Lane and Richard Steele, but I didn't think that I could interest them, and even if I could, I figured they'd likely know nothing about ground fighting and submissions.

Rorion told me not to worry, as he had two old friends back in Brazil who would be perfect. Hélio Vigio and Joao Alberto Barreto were both Gracie Jiu-Jitsu black belts who he said would understand the intricacies of the fights we were going to stage. Neither spoke English, but Rorion assured me that it wouldn't matter, as the two men would have a commanding presence that would produce immediate respect from the fighters.

I agreed, but then went about doing some research. The fact that they'd be giving instructions in Portuguese was a bit troubling, and so to was the cost of their flights from Brazil to Denver and back. I had to be certain that these guys could do the job.

From what I could find, Barreto was a big footnote in the annals of vale tudo. Sometime around 1960, Barreto was fighting in a match on the Brazilian television program *Heróis do Ringue* (Heroes of the Ring). Barreto apparently caught his opponent in an arm bar, and when his opponent refused to submit, Barreto broke his arm. This led to a big public outcry in Brazil, and the show was soon off the air.

What I read about Vigio was a bit more troubling. The term *Esquadrão da Morte* (death squad) kept coming up, but I could never tell if this was fact or opinion, and these stories were in Portuguese, a language in which I was far from fluent. I did, however, find a solid bit of reporting in English from an extremely credible source. An Associated Press story, dated July 24, 1987, detailed a Rio de Janeiro police team rescuing a woman and her daughter from gunmen, "led by Brazil's best-known man-hunter, Police Chief Hélio Vigio."

Maybe there was another guy in Brazil named Hélio Vigio. Maybe this was the right Hélio Vigio and he was a brave protector of the public from the criminal element. Or maybe it was something far different. I had no way of knowing and I certainly wasn't going to press Rorion. Vigio and Barreto were his friends, and Rorion said that his father was in favor of them as well. That was good enough for me and I stopped digging.

I knew that finding our television commentators was going to be a far more involved process. Rorion suggested we use Rod Machado, a student at the Gracie Academy who'd been a host of the straight-to-video series *ABC Wide World of Flying*. I didn't think Machado had the star power that we needed to be one of our main broadcasters, but I figured we could bring him in on Royce's fights to discuss the intricacies of Gracie Jiu-Jitsu. He was good-looking, well-spoken and in possession of a head of hair usually found on local TV news anchors.

The guy who I thought would be perfect was Chuck Norris. He was a martial arts legend in the U.S., arguably second only to Bruce Lee; an action movie star in films such *Way of the Dragon, Lone Wolf McQuaid*, and *The Delta Force*; and had a new television series on CBS, *Walker, Texas Ranger*. As far as I was concerned, Chuck could be our play-by-play commentator, color analyst, back stage interviewer, anything he wanted. I'd pay him just to show up in Denver, sign autographs and wave at the camera.

Rorion had gotten to know Chuck fairly well from the seminar circuit, but seemed lukewarm on my idea of bringing him in for the broadcast. I kept persisting, and finally Rorion admitted to me that they'd had a slight falling out over money a few years back. Something about Rorion being hired by Chuck to do a seminar for his students, Rorion bringing along a couple of his brothers, and Chuck thinking he had contracted to pay only Rorion, not an entire troop of Gracies.

It didn't seem like a big deal to me, so I kept pressing Rorion until he relented. It was finally arranged that we'd drive over to Chuck's house in Tarzana, and give him our big pitch, with both Rorion and me armed with index cards that contained the key points of the Ultimate Fighting Championship. But when we pulled up to the huge Norris family compound, Rorion turned to me and said, "Let me go in there by myself. I need to talk to him first. Patch it up with him. I think it's best if I do this by myself. When I need you, I'll come out and get you. OK?"

I reluctantly agreed to wait in the car, and sat there idly playing with my index card for 30 minutes until a dejected looking Rorion returned.

"How did it go?" I asked.

"Not good, Arturo."

"Oh. What happened?"

"Well I told him all about the event, and the fighters, and the Pay-Per-View, but he just kept shaking his head

Legendary martial artist and film star Chuck Norris and kickboxing champ Earnest Hart, Jr. Rorion Gracie and I went to Chuck's house in 1993 to ask him to be a commentator. He declined saying, "Is this legal?" Given our untested idea and his considerable status, I was not surprised or upset.

and asking me, 'Is this legal?' He kept asking me that over and over again, 'Is this legal?' He just couldn't get past that, so we finally shook hands and I left."

"Wait a minute, Rorion. He kept asking you if it was legal? How many times did Norris ask you this?"

"Can you believe it? I think he said it at least six times. Every time I made a point that was on the card, he said the same thing," Rorion replied with a shake of his head and a bemused laugh.

Apparently, Chuck just couldn't believe that we would be allowed legally to do what Rorion was telling him that we were going to do. Bare-knuckle, no-holds-barred, virtually-everything-goes fighting. And no way was a superstar like Chuck Norris going to be involved with something that the local police chief, Governor or National Guard probably would rush in to shut down at any minute. This entire illicit affair just wasn't for him. I understood. If I was in Chuck's position, I probably would have said the same thing.

I decided not to mention any of this to Campbell. But I knew that he wanted a "classic All-American tough guy" in the mode of Chuck Norris, to work on the commentary team. Campbell had been going on and on about getting this type, as he felt it would add the right tone to our broadcast. We started going back and forth, offering up names like the actors Charles Bronson and Steven Seagal, retired NFL linebacker greats Sam Huff and Ray Nitschke, even former boxing heavyweight world champion Ingemar Johansson, who was actually Swedish, not American.

None of those guys—especially Johansson—seemed like the right fit. Then on a call, Campbell told me that he'd had a revelation, "What if we get Jim Brown?" If there was ever a "classic All-American tough guy," it was Jim Brown. An NFL Hall of Fame running back who left football at age 29 for a full-time film career, Brown was always his own man. He did what he wanted, and said what he felt, consequences be damned. I loved Brown as a player, and I thought he was a solid actor, especially in films like *The Dirty Dozen* and *Ice Station Zebra*.

Campbell was agreeable with our choice of Rod Machado, and I certainly wasn't going to veto the great Jim Brown. He said to leave things to him, and a few days later, Campbell told me he'd signed Brown for $10,000 to be our play-by-play commentator.

Brown was going to be the main guy, and Machado was going to have a small role. We still needed one or two color analysts, and this is where I had my own revelation. Bill "Superfoot" Wallace had been on a rant about how kickboxing should only be for men. He'd said this in a number of interviews, and even written a couple of articles in martial arts magazines expressing this view. Wallace had made his name as a top kickboxer and competitor in full-contact karate. He was *Black Belt* magazine's Man of the Year in 1978, and had claimed John Belushi as one of his students.

Firing back publicly at Wallace on behalf of female fighters was Kathy Long, a champion kickboxer, who was *Black Belt's* 1991 Woman of the Year. She was very pretty, known by the nickname "The Queen of Mean" and seemed comfortable speaking her mind—at least as far as Bill Wallace was concerned. I thought that they'd create a really entertaining point/counterpoint dynamic on the broadcast, and Campbell agreed.

After locking in both Wallace and Kathy, Campbell asked me what I thought about using Brian Kilmeade as our reporter on the broadcast. He was a young guy who worked with Jim Brown on his radio show in Southern California, and Campbell felt that the kid had solid potential. That was fine with me, especially since SEG was paying for our stable of commentators, which now numbered five.

We still needed a ring announcer, though, and I had just the man for Campbell. Back in May when I'd driven out to Denver to set up W.O.W. Promotions as an LLC, I heard a familiar name on the radio. It was Rich "The G Man" Goins, and it was making me crazy trying to figure out how I knew it. Then I recalled that I'd learned about Goins from a promotional stunt he did in 1990 for his radio station KRFX, Denver's 103.5 FM "The Fox," which garnered national attention. For 33 days across November and December of that year, Goins camped out atop a billboard, refusing to come down until the Denver Broncos broke their losing streak.

I knew that having a local radio personality as our ring announcer would be great for ticket sales, as he'd no doubt give us loads of free publicity by continually talking about his upcoming gig in the Ultimate Fighting Championship. Campbell loved the idea, even more so that "The G Man" wouldn't require a flight or hotel room as part of his deal.

To me, this was going to be as much a rock concert as it was a sporting event, so I didn't want the usual suspects on the microphone. This certainly wasn't boxing or pro wrestling, and I felt that we absolutely couldn't have anybody from those worlds. And I really believed that a top boxing guy like Jim Lampley would feel compelled to demean our fights and fighters at every turn, with constant reminders that this wasn't the sweet science. We never could have afforded him anyway, nor someone at his level such as Bob Costas, Pat Summerall or Al Michaels. Even if we could have paid them enough money, and convinced them to do the show, (both scenarios I knew were highly unlikely) none of them would have known the first thing about what they were looking at, apart from the punches being thrown.

Campbell pointed out to me continually that we needed people who actually knew martial arts, even if they didn't really know broadcasting. With Wallace and Kathy Long, that is exactly what we now had. I could only hope that Brown, with his movie and radio talk show experience, could be the glue to hold the broadcast together.

I'd been procrastinating on putting together the rules and regulations, but as we hit mid-October, I knew that it had to be done. Rorion wasn't going to do it, and no one at SEG would have even known where to start. To quote the great pro wrestler and pro wrestling commentator Gorilla Monsoon, Meyrowitz, Campbell and company, "Didn't know a wrist lock from a wrist watch."

Earlier in the summer I had mentioned to Rorion that we needed to create a sanctioning body to govern our fights, not just for the first event, but for all of the events moving forward. Pro boxing had the WBC, WBA and IBF; international wrestling had FILA; and every combat sport and martial art on the planet had a litany of regulatory agencies almost always abbreviated down to three or four letters.

Because we would face no governmental oversight whatsoever in Colorado, Rorion and I were really in the position of being both judge and jury. This was our event. We owned it, promoted it, and hired the fighters. So we needed to set the rules and regulations, but in an official looking capacity.

I proposed to Rorion that we create the International Fight Council (IFC), for which he would be Commissioner. It would be a paper company—but it would create an air of authenticity to the fighters as well as to the general public. We talked about eventually getting attorneys, doctors and famous martial artists on board to one day make it a real sanctioning body. For now though, it would just be the two of us.

I figured that having Rorion listed as the Commissioner would give us the same cache as when I'd listed him as matchmaker in the martial arts magazine ads I had created to find fighters. And just like in that search, I knew that the responsibility of the IFC would actually fall to me, because Rorion just wasn't interested in such minutiae.

He'd let his voice be heard on having Royce represent Gracie Jiu-Jitsu in the Ultimate Fighting Championship, not using a boxing ring for our fighting area, and employing his family friends Vigio and Barreto as our refs. But otherwise, his attitude had pretty much been, "Whatever you think is best, Arturo."

So in my untitled role with the non-existent IFC, I set about drafting the rules and regulations for the Ultimate Fighting Championship on my dark blue IBM Selectric II typewriter.

They read:

A. *Five rounds, five minutes each, two minutes rest between rounds*

B. *Fight to be held in a 30-foot octagon*

C. *Fighters wear clothing according to their style, as long as it complies with IFC rules. Rorion Gracie, IFC Commissioner and the referees to inspect each fighter prior to event.*

D. *Fight can be stopped as follows:*

1. *Knockout (standard 10 count)*

2. *Submission*

3. *Tapping out with the foot or hand on the mat at least three times*

4. *Corner man throwing in a towel*

5. *Choke-out*

6. *Doctor's intervention*

7. *Disqualification*

8. *At referee's discretion (eye gouge, groin shot, biting)*

E. *All punches, kicks, knee and elbow strikes, joint locks and/or chokes are permitted.*

F. *Target areas for all strikes include head and body with the exception of the eyes and groin.*

G. *6- or 8-ounce boxing gloves or Kempo gloves are optional if a fighter's art employs closed fist strikes to the face and head, otherwise bare knuckles are permitted.*
1. *Taping of wrist must end one inch away from the knuckle. Tape should be placed on top of any wraps.*
2. *Shoes–boxing or wrestling shoes allowed if the fighter does not use any kicking.*
3. *Types of supports that are permitted (show examples).*
4. *No shin guards or arm pads.*
H. *Fight shall not be interrupted in the event of a clinch or fall to the mat. Referee will determine when to break if the fight is stalled. If both fighters intentionally stall, they will both be disqualified without pay.*
I. *No point system is in effect; fight shall continue into overtime rounds until one fighter is declared the winner.*
1. *Overtime–unlimited number of five-minute rounds until winner is declared. Two-minute intermissions.*
J. *This is a single-elimination tournament; there are no weight classes.*

In writing the rules, there were three things that I felt were of huge importance. First, the referee could not stop the fight, except in the event of disqualification. I'd seen far too many boxing matches end in controversy because the actions of the ref overshadowed the actions of the fighters. No way did I want an early stoppage or a bad judgment call to start derailing our fights, especially when we'd be using two guys from Brazil who I'd never met, and who didn't speak English.

Second, was how our fights could actually end, which I gave serious consideration. I knew from training in Gracie Jiu-Jitsu that the tap out and verbal submission were always great options. And from my lifelong love of boxing, I thought the 10-count for a fallen fighter would work great to determine knockouts. And it was only fair and safe that the fighter's corner, or in worst-case situations our doctors, could stop the fight—just not the referee. I also knew that we had to have rounds with time limits.

I couldn't afford a Hélio Gracie vs. Waldemar Santana-like three-hour, 42-minute grapple fest to ruin the night, with two grounded fighters patiently and non-violently waiting for the smallest of openings to the delight of absolutely no one. By having five-minute rounds, I figured this would give a fighter stuck on the bottom a chance to start again on his feet when the new round began. But technically, these would be fights to the finish, as the number of rounds were uncapped. SEG had given us a hard two hours and 50 minutes for the live PPV broadcast which we absolutely could not exceed. But I figured that none of the fights would go longer than three or four rounds. Or so I hoped, as otherwise, we'd all be fucked.

And third, I wanted every fighter to be able to use the uniform and equipment of the sport that they were representing. Jimmerson could wear his boxing gloves, Shamrock his wrestling trunks, Royce his gi. This would starkly illustrate the different backgrounds and styles of the fighters, and the uniqueness of our mixed match event. I figured that it would be really unfair for a fighter to be able to kick with shoes, especially to the head, so I wrote that they could be worn so long as kicks weren't thrown.

I wasn't sure about shin guards or elbow pads, as these would be protective devices. If we allowed them, then someone would eventually want to wear amateur boxing headgear. Same thing with taping the knuckles. A boxing glove was sort of neutral, but a properly taped hand would allow a fighter to unload devastating blows with limited damage to his fists. The only thing allowed to be worn for protection would be the cup.

Originally, I liked the idea of a standardized dress code, which I envisioned as a type of fighting G-string; sort of like the mawashi that is worn in sumo. I wanted to pay homage to ancient Pankration and their nude fighters. When I mentioned this to Rorion, he looked at me in disbelief and said, "My brother won't be wearing that." He then laughed and joked about Royce having a "thong" up the crack of his ass. End of discussion, as I knew he was right.

Despite the tag line that I'd written for our event, I always knew that we had to have rules. I just didn't want too many. Basic human decency really—no eye gouges, groin strikes or biting. Everything else was fair game. I ran my rules and regulations by Rorion, and he gave them his quick blessing, with no questions asked.

In late October, Campbell and I had a conversation about some cool giveaways that we could use for our sponsors and selected VIPs. It was decided that W.O.W. would create this merchandise, which we would sell at McNichols Arena. I hired the brother of a Gracie student who lived in Denver, and owned a silk screen business, to create our official Ultimate Fighting Championship apparel. He was into martial arts, and seemed really excited for the opportunity to be involved.

We went over my order of a couple thousand T-shirts and sweats in different colors and sizes. The guy then told me that for $750, he would also deliver two big, vinyl Ultimate Fighting Championship banners, which could be hung at McNichols Arena.

I settled on a 30- by 30-foot banner, which I figured we could put up outside the venue, and a 20- by 20-foot one that could be placed above our fighting area, in full view of the television cameras.

A few days later, Campbell and I came up with the idea to create event jackets, which we conceived of as being solid black in color, with our "Mr. Clean" Ultimate Fighting Championship logo prominently featured on the front. Campbell found a guy in New York who could fill this order, and got one made for himself, Meyrowitz, a few of the top executives at SEG, Rorion, Kathy, Jim Brown and me. Campbell added to the list a couple of extra jackets, and I claimed one for the son of our biggest investor.

The kid was a student at the Gracie Academy, and we gave it to him as a Bar Mitzvah present, which I knew would impress all of his friends.

Just as I felt that everything was finally coming together, our first alternate Jim Mullen called to inform me that he was injured, and thus was going to have to pull out. Mullen was very apologetic, and I believed his story—he didn't strike me as the type of guy who would be overcome by a bad case of nerves. I contemplated rolling the dice and just going with DeLucia as the only stand-by. But I quickly realized that I couldn't afford to risk our entire tournament process by not having two injury replacements lined up. It would be Murphy's Law, and it would no doubt come back to bite me in the ass.

I phoned Karyn Turner in Denver and told her of my predicament, which had to be resolved immediately. At this point I didn't need her to find me another Pat Smith, just a warm body, preferably one who was local and thus wouldn't require a flight and hotel room. The name she came back with was Trent Jenkins. He'd fought in the Sabaki Challenge, just like Smith. But unlike him, he'd never won it. And, unlike Smith, Karyn told me that Jenkins wasn't an emotional wreck.

"Look," she said, "He's not a great fighter. He's a journeyman, really. But Trent is right here in Denver, and he's reliable. Whenever I have a fighter fall out, Trent is a guy I can call on to do the job on short notice. He's solid that way."

I then remembered I had actually spoken to Jenkins back in the summer, after he had sent in his fighter application and $100 check, as requested by one of our magazine ads. He had struck me then as a very bright and articulate guy, but one who lacked the fighting pedigree that I was looking for. But as we now approached zero hour, I was more than happy to give Jenkins this opportunity, and he was more than happy to accept.

All that was left for me to do now was sign the deal with SEG.

At this point, their original contract offer of four pages from June 3 had ballooned to 26 pages. I still felt that Moss was wearing gloves in his negotiations with Meyrowitz's brother, David, who seemed to be contesting with bare knuckles. But Moss had gotten concessions on a number of points, some big, but most small. SEG was paying for the fighting area, and the guarantees of $17,000 to Jimmerson and $6,000 to Tuli. They had taken on the design and costs of the fight poster and logo, and had allowed W.O.W. to create our own merchandise and souvenir event program to be sold on fight night at McNichols Arena, for which we could keep the potential profits.

And SEG had upped their guarantee for future events, and lowered the period of exclusivity should we part ways. What they wouldn't budge on though was Section 6, Clause C from their original contract offer: "50 percent of all revenues after SEG fully recoups all costs associated with the video production... and receives a 12-percent return on investment."

This was where I knew that we could, and most likely would, get fucked by the internal SEG accounting, which would determine the 12 percent, and thus our 50 percent. But Meyrowitz and David just wouldn't give an inch. I figured that they had to pay BMG for their use of advanced funds, and that plus a profit for SEG constituted the 12 percent. No matter what we proposed, their side rejected. This was a template they had long been using with their shows and events, and they were loath to abandon it.

With Moss and I finally coming to the realization that this was a dead-end street, I decided on a different approach. My new proposal was that after the first Ultimate Fighting Championship, SEG would pay the entire fight purse for every event moving forward. Not just the guarantees, but the tournament prize money as well. With a field of eight tournament fighters, and two alternates, I had structured the payouts so that the winner would receive $50,000 (as I had always envisioned), the runner-up would get $15,000, the two losing semifinalists would earn $4,000 a piece, and the four opening-round fight losers would each take home $1,000. That totaled $77,000, which I knew all too well was a crushing expense for us. And while I hadn't guaranteed DeLucia and Jenkins anything to be on stand-by, I figured that if they were called upon, I'd have to pay at least a $1,000 to one or both of them.

I knew that both the prize money and the guarantees would need to keep rising, event after event, if we were going to keep attracting quality fighters. Whoever won on November 12 would probably want more money, or at least the potential to win more money, upon their return. And the opportunity for more cash just might mean we could get someone like Bart Vale, Peter Aerts or Herb Perez to consider our offer.

The response from SEG was, "No fucking way." The fight purse was our expense, and we were to be thankful that they'd forked over the appearance money for Jimmerson and Tuli.

On the first day of November, I met with Kathy to double check that we had everything in place. My event coordinator turned unofficial W.O.W. Promotions chief operations officer and her team had done a masterful job of locking down all the facets of travel and logistics. The dozens of flights were booked, as were the three shuttle vans, and the scores of rooms at the Executive Tower Inn and Suites, which was just two miles from McNichols Arena. We needed a hotel for the week of the event which was centrally located in Denver, and the right price. But most important, the hotel had to be cool with the fact that we were bringing fighters to town who were not particularly house broken.

On Sunday, November 7, Rorion and I boarded a plane at LAX to fly to Denver, despite the ambiguity of the contract situation. My partner didn't seem concerned at all. He had unwavering faith (or perhaps he was just disconnected) that Moss and I would get everything worked out. Rorion's sole concern was making sure that his kid brother would be properly prepared physically and mentally to win the tournament and showcase the indomitability of Gracie Jiu-Jitsu to the world.

When Rorion and I arrived at the Executive Tower Inn for check-in, I was struck by how small the hotel lobby was. This made me worry that a log jam of tense fighters and their respective camps would pile up there. We didn't have the budget for a five-star hotel, and even if we did, I didn't think that a high-dollar place would want to play host to our motley crew. So this would have to do.

I'd already let Kathy know that she was to schedule twice daily meetings, 7:30 a.m. and 11:30 p.m., which would begin the next day. After seeing the tiny lobby, I knew that I had to tell her to stay vigilant, and be ready to diffuse volatile situations at all times. I was given the master suite with an attached conference room, which I planned on making our base of operations for the week.

Now that I was in Denver, I called my T-shirt guy. He was still working on printing our shirts and the sweats. I pleaded, "Please don't hang me out to dry on this." He kept reassuring me that while he was a "little behind" he would deliver. I got off the call muttering to myself that he wasn't a "little behind," he was a "little asshole."

On Monday, the fighters began arriving in Denver from all corners of the map. Elaine McCarthy was in charge of the travel arrangements, and had been told by Kathy to book the fighers on alternating floors, to avoid potential confrontations.

Early in the day I was notified by hotel security that there was a near scuffle in the lobby, but they didn't know the names of the participants. They just knew that it was "those fight people."

Among our W.O.W. Promotions event staff in Denver were two guys who I had hired specifically for the week, both of whom I knew from the Academy: Milius' son Ethan and Clay McBride.

Rorion and I had offered Milius $10,000 as a thank you for his inspirational work as our creative director. It was actually a thank you for letting us use his name, which had helped open a lot of doors, none bigger than SEG's. But just like he had told us back in December when he signed on, Milius would not accept any money from us. We also offered to pay all of his expenses to join us in Denver for fight week, but he politely declined, saying he was too busy. So I arranged to have a gift-wrapped box of Montecristo #2 Cuban cigars sent to his office.

Hiring his son, Ethan, as my assistant in Denver for the week was not a thank you to Milius, but rather a reflection of how much I thought of the kid. He was a dedicated student at the Gracie Academy, and had also started working there in an entry-level capacity. I knew that Ethan was someone who I could trust to get things done for me, even menial things, and with a smile on his face.

Clay McBride had been lobbying me for quite some time about having a role at the Ultimate Fighting Championship. He was a bright guy, a martial arts encyclopedia, and a good writer. I was continually impressed that despite having polio as a child, Clay never had a woe-is-me attitude. What cinched it for Clay was when he gave Rorion and me a two-page summary he had written as to why we should give the tournament winner a medal rather than a crown.

"Crowns are for beauty pageants," Clay had stated, and I knew immediately that he was right.

I loved the Olympic imagery of awarding a medal. It was unique and at the same time familiar.

Rorion had a student who worked as a jeweler, and we hired him for the job. I poured over books at the Torrance Public Library on military medals, looking at the British Victoria Cross, the United States Navy Cross and the German Cross—all of which were based on the cross pattée, which has arms narrow at the center and broader at the perimeter. The form appears very early in medieval art. Using this as the basis, I sketched out a rough design, adding the inscription, "Per Aspera Ad Astra" (Through Adversity to the Stars).

Our jeweler did an outstanding job, making it from pure 24-carat gold, with the care of a highly skilled craftsman. He only charged us for the raw materials.

Without a real role for Clay, but incredibly impressed with his medal idea, I offered him the chance to be our in-house photographer and writer for the event. I told Clay that he would be tasked with helping Pillot and the commentators with their research and background notes on the fighters. He'd also serve as our archivist, who would document everything along the way through his photos and words.

Clay immediately accepted, but then told me that he had to get something off of his chest.

"Well, Art. Now don't take this as criticism, but I don't see any stars from the real martial arts in this tournament. There's nobody from Asia. No kung fu expert from China or a judo champion from Japan. That sort of thing."

I took a deep breath and explained to Clay how far and wide I had searched to find the right balance of fighters, emphasizing the numerous difficulties and rejections that I'd faced along the way.

Clay listened patiently, and then said, "It's just that, well, it seems you have a fixation on big guys."

"Come again?"

"Could it be that since you're a smaller guy that you're subconsciously selecting guys like your kickboxer Rosier, and that sumo wrestler? Maybe this a Napoleonic Complex type of thing with you."

I smiled at this point, as I had no intention of playing Freudian games with Clay. I respected him in a lot of ways, but I could see from this conversation that above all else, he was always going to be a martial arts "purist." Part of why I liked Clay so much was he always held to his ideals, and he wasn't afraid to let his strong opinions be heard, even when they were far from tactful.

Trying to surround myself with as many allies as possible, I also flew in my kid brother Matthew, as well as my close friends Jon and Adrianne Pannell, and Les and Prentice Smith. Prentice of course was the one who had given me the

Photo courtesy of Art Davie Archives/W.O.W. Promotions

The UFC medal awarded to the first Ultimate Fighter. I created the design and wrote the inscription. A talented jeweler, a Gracie Jiu-Jitsu student, crafted the medal in 24-carat gold. The idea for a medal, rather than a crown, was Clay McBride's.

War of the Worlds idea the year before, which now seemed like a very, very long time ago. And Jon and Adrianne were investors in W.O.W. It seemed only right that they were all there with me in Denver.

Rorion and I saw Elaine McCarthy's husband John in the hotel lobby on Monday, and Rorion offered him a job. I'd never really gotten to know McCarthy all that well at the academy, but he had always struck me as a quality guy.

"Would you mind guarding the championship medal for the week?" Rorion asked.

McCarthy accepted, and since he was a highly respected LAPD officer, I had no doubt that our medal would be safe.

When I told Kathy about this later that day, she laughed, and said that McCarthy was going to have his hands full. I asked why, and Kathy told me that in addition to McCarthy serving as a training partner for Royce in Denver, she'd heard rumors that Rorion had enlisted McCarthy as his private security guard. Apparently, Rorion's cousin Reylson Gracie (the son of Carlos) had been making some threats. And from the gossip that Kathy had heard from her staff, Rorion was concerned that Reylson was going to show up in Denver looking for the type of fight that didn't involve jiu-jitsu, but perhaps bullets. I stopped Kathy, and said to her that I didn't even want to know if any of this was true. There was already far too much for me to worry about, without getting involved with yet another Gracie Family melodrama.

Just prior to arriving in Denver, I secured two gyms for our fighters to use for fight week: Jones' Tai-Kung Fu-Karate on Sheridan Boulevard, and Tiger Kim's gym on Steele Street (the place where I'd first watched Pat Smith train six months earlier). Both gyms had boxing rings, heavy bags, speed bags and mats. My cousin, Nancy and her husband Sean Mahany, who were both bodybuilders, owned and operated the Powerhouse Gym on East Alameda. They graciously agreed to give our fighters and their camps access to the barbells, dumbbells and Nautilus equipment, all free of charge. Between these three facilities, I felt confident that we had everyone's training needs covered.

Pat Smith and Trent Jenkins, of course, lived in Denver, which in theory meant that I didn't have to worry about them as much as the eight fighters flying into the city. I took Karyn at her word on Jenkins, and never gave the guy a second thought. Smith, though, was a different story. I'd tried to stay in regular contract with him since he signed his contract back in May, but he was a hard man to keep tabs on.

Every time I called, his number had changed or was disconnected, or I was told by a female voice that he'd moved. And when we would finally speak, he always seemed paranoid and prone to misunderstandings. It became clear that Smith didn't completely trust me, which made me lose some trust in him. I made sure he was given a room at the Executive Tower Inn, and I told Kathy and her crew to keep close tabs on his whereabouts. I felt that if anyone was going to flake out, and not show up on Friday night, it was going to be Smith.

"Why do I gotta be at the hotel?" he whined to me.

"Because I've got confidence you're going to rock the house Friday night and I want you close by," I lied to him.

Royce, by contrast, was someone who I didn't have to worry about at all. He had Rorion for that, as well as four of his other brothers with him in Denver. Rickson was there as Royce's main trainer and chief second, despite all of the past issues with Rorion. I found it so odd that it could have been or perhaps should have been Rickson representing Gracie Jiu-Jitsu in the Ultimate Fighting Championship. Yet, because of the family tensions, he was bypassed by Rorion for Royce. And yet Rickson was there as Royce's mentor, and acting as though he and Rorion were completely cool with each other. I decided then and there that I would never be able to figure out the family dynamics of the Gracies from top to bottom.

Joining the family reunion in Denver were Royler and Relson who had flown in from Hawaii, and Rolker who had arrived from Brazil. And of course Hélio was there, hovering over his sons like Zeus on Mt. Olympus.

I had no doubt that Hélio was going to be in Denver to see Royce attempt to defend the Gracie Family honor, but now he also had an official role. Back in August, I told Rorion that we'd need to fill time between the semi-finals and the tournament final. The fighters were no doubt going to require at least a few minutes to rest and recover, and we had to show something to both the in-house crowd and the

PPV audience. My idea was to honor Bruce Lee as a pioneering martial artist, and invite his widow, Linda, to accept an award or plaque on his behalf, and perhaps say a few words.

Rorion, though, suggested that we do this for his father. I thought about it, and decided that this had both pluses and minuses. Hélio was, like Bruce Lee, a pioneering martial artist. But unlike Lee, he didn't have much name recognition to the general American public, or even to the martial arts community. There was no doubt in my mind that Hélio was a legend deserving of the honor, it's just that he was a virtually unknown legend outside of the tiny world of Gracie Jiu-Jitsu. I also thought that giving him an award would create the impression that the Ultimate Fighting Championship was nothing more than a Gracie event bought and paid for.

But this was extremely important to Rorion, and I felt I understood why.

Months earlier I had actually met Reylson Gracie, son of Carlos, nephew of Hélio, maker of alleged threats to Rorion. We hooked up in LA, started talking, hit it off, and then decided to continue our conversation over coffee. Reylson said that he wanted me to better understand my business partner and friend. "I will tell you Arturo what you don't know about Rorion," he announced with a conspiratorial wink.

"One day, Rorion went to his father and asked him, 'Why am I dark and you and my mother are so white?' Well, the truth was that Margarida, Hélio's first wife was not Rorion's birth mother. Nor Relson or Rickson's. His real mother, the one whose egg was fertilized by Hélio and who carried him in her womb, was Isabel Soares, who was also called Belinha. She was the maid and she was dark."

"Holy shit. Really? Is this true? What happened then?" I asked.

"Rorion went ballistic. He was furious at his father. Pissed that this had been kept from him all those years. This is why he came to America. He was fleeing. He was angry with his father."

I was never able to verify Reylson's story, and I certainly wasn't going to ask Rorion about it. Rarely had Rorion spoken to me about his personal life, although he had told me that when he arrived in the U.S., he possessed nothing but the clothes on his back. After hearing

Reylson's version of events, I thought that maybe Rorion was only able to forgive his father after he had accomplished enough on his own to gain a sense of personal vindication. And then once he forgave Hélio, perhaps Rorion was determined to prove to his father that he was better than the old man's other six sons—first and foremost Rickson. Who knows? But Reylson's story at least gave me another perspective in regards to Rorion's unrelenting drive to please his father.

So I let my friend and partner have his way with Hélio and the award. Although it would be the father receiving the honor, I knew that this moment was actually going to be a lot more important to the son.

CHAPTER 10
THERE ARE NO RULES

NECESSITY HAS NO LAW.
— WILLIAM LANGLAND

AS the fighters began arriving in Denver, I decided it was best that I personally pick up Tuli, his brother and two cousins at the airport. Tuli and I had never met, nor even talked on the phone, as all of my dealings to sign him had been with John Jacques. From what Jacques had told me, this was going to be Tuli's first trip to the mainland U.S., and he was very distrustful of people he didn't know.

As I waited for Tuli and his entourage to arrive, I laughed to myself about what he could have said in anticipation of our meet-up. "I'll be the 400-lb. Hawaiian guy with three other enormous Hawaiian guys. And what do you look like?"

I knew he would be impossible to miss, and not long after arriving at the airport, I spotted Tuli with his menacing scowl.

"Teila, I'm Art Davie," I said as I extended my right hand. In my left hand was an envelope containing 60 crisp $100 bills. Jacques had told me that Tuli didn't like checks, so I came prepared.

Without saying a world, Tuli took the envelope from me, opened it, and then stared at the cash. With that, a huge smile spread across his broad face, which caused his brother and two cousins to begin smiling too. The ice had cracked, and just like that Tuli shook my hand, as though I was his best friend in the world. As the five of us piled into the van I was driving, as part of our rented three van fleet, I felt very thankful that I hadn't tried to squeeze this crew and their luggage into an economy car.

I drove back out to the airport to get Kevin Rosier, for the sole reason of seeing for myself if the reports that I'd been receiving about him being out of shape were indeed true. When I spotted him standing by baggage claim, I thought for a moment that Teila Tuli had an identical twin. Dating back to our very first conversation, Rosier had always insisted that he was "about 265."

When I saw Rosier at the Denver Airport, I immediately said to him, "Kevin, I'm Art Davie. What the fuck happened to 265 pounds?"

He sheepishly replied, "Well, I guess I'm up to around 285 now."

"Bullshit, your left leg weighs 285."

I knew that I was getting a behemoth in Tuli, but that wasn't the deal with Rosier. He was supposed to be an in-shape, mean heavyweight kickboxer. Instead he looked like Poppin' Fresh the Pillsbury Doughboy.

Rosier wasn't with his wife, and I asked him where she was, since her attendance in Denver was part of his contract. He told me that he changed her to a later flight, and that instead of going to the hotel with me, he was headed out to Loveland, Colorado in a rental car to see his ex-wife. I shook my head thinking that in addition to being out of shape, Rosier had a soap opera going on.

Gordeau and Shamrock both arrived from outside of the country, in-shape and all business. Flying in from Amsterdam and accompanied by his trainer, Gordeau carried only a small duffel bag and a lot of cigarettes. Upon meeting him at the airport, he struck me as relaxed and cool as any human could possibly be—like he had come to Colorado for a week of sight-seeing.

I asked Gordeau if he needed anything from my staff or me, and he responded, "No problem, Art Davie."

Shamrock had flown straight to Denver from Japan, where on Monday he had submitted Takaku Fuke in just 44 seconds at Pancrase's third event. He was with his adoptive dad, Bob, who immediately stood out to me as a first-class guy. Seeing Shamrock in person, with his athletic grappler's physique, I felt, more than ever, that this was the fighter who might just beat Royce at his own game. He was now 3-0 in Pancrase, and regardless of what those fights were or weren't, Shamrock was absolutely oozing with confidence and muscular swagger.

On the other end of the spectrum were Jimmerson and Frazier. From the moment that he arrived with his wife, Jimmerson seemed off to me. When I first saw him at the hotel, I couldn't tell if he was wildly overconfident, as in "I'm going to knock all these motherfuckers out," or scared shitless.

SEG had already paid him his $17,000 guarantee, and I could only hope that he was still going to be a hungry and motivated fighter.

Upon seeing Frazier in the hotel lobby, I commented to Rorion that "he seemed more nervous than a virgin on her wedding night." All Frazier wanted to talk about with me was the mile-high altitude in Denver, the cold weather, his breathing issues and his runny nose. I felt like he was subconsciously building excuses for why he was going to lose, all the while desperately trying to convince himself that he was going to destroy everyone in his path. He also kept complaining to me about Rorion's involvement with the Ultimate Fighting Championship, and how he was angling to make sure that Royce won. I tried to reassure him that I absolutely didn't care who won, and I promised him that all of the fighters were going to be treated fairly and honestly. But Frazier persisted and said, "Rorion's trying to make us all look bad on national TV."

Although I didn't say it to Frazier, I understood how he and all of the fighters could feel that the deck was being stacked for a Royce victory. His big brother was an owner of W.O.W. Promotions, and listed as both "Matchmaker" of the Ultimate Fighting Championship and "Commissioner" of the IFC. I was struck by the irony of how I originally felt I needed Rorion as my partner to give me credibility in order to stage a mixed match fighting event, and now his presence was potentially undermining my credibility and the credibility of the event itself.

Outside of my assurance, what reason would Frazier and the other fighters have to believe that I wasn't in on a pro-Gracie conspiracy? Without question, I knew that for Rorion, the Ultimate Fighting Championship was primarily a vehicle to showcase the superiority of Gracie Jiu-Jitsu to the outside world. But all I wanted was to get our deal with SEG signed, and then score big with ticket sales and PPV buys. It truly made absolutely no difference to me if Royce won the tournament, or got knocked out in ten seconds. The event was the thing that I knew would last. Fighters come and go.

It was clear that DeLucia was thrilled to be part of the tournament, even as an alternate. So once I found out that he had checked in to the hotel, I left it at that. If anyone would keep their head down and mouth shut, it would be DeLucia.

When Campbell arrived in Denver from New York, I was surprised to see that he wasn't with Meyrowitz.

"Where's Bob?" I asked.

"Oh, he decided not to come."

"Why not? What's the deal?"

"Actually Art, I think... uh... he was afraid that someone might actually get killed Friday night, and he didn't want to be there if it happened."

I did, however, feel that I had Campbell's full support, despite all of our ups and downs over the past seven months. I'd grown to really like him, and I felt that he liked me. At times his level of involvement surpassed Rorion's. But then he would disappear, leaving me with the impression that the Ultimate Fighting Championship was, for him, a bit of an afterthought. Campbell wasn't a principal like Meyrowitz, Rorion, and me and he had a lot of irons in the TV fire. I knew that our project was just one of many for him.

But to his credit, Campbell had kept moving everything forward from my original cold call and cold fax to him on April 14, 1993. Now we were both in Denver, about to see this to fruition, or so I hoped. There was still the matter of that unsigned contract though.

Before I dealt with my seemingly never-ending SEG issues, I had to settle things with Fey and Bresloff, my local promoters in Denver. Wednesday was the day that I was due to pick up the $25,000 advance guarantee from Barry Fey at his office in Englewood, just south of the city. No matter how many tickets were sold, they had to deliver this payment to us. It was in the contract.

Fey and Bresloff had swamped the city with flyers and posters advertising "DEATH", "MUTILATION" and "THE END OF CIVILIZATION AS WE KNOW IT," in hopes of whipping up interest. I knew that SEG's advertising approach was aggressive, but this was clearly on an entirely different level. Fey had told me earlier that he liked that our fighter contracts I had drafted listed "death" as one way that a bout could end. So he took that idea, and built their local ticket sales campaign around it, but apparently to little effect.

I knew though that I was dealing with a guy from the rock concert business and a guy from the pro wrestling business, two industries not known for their unwavering honesty. I also knew that Fey and Bresloff were used to playing hardball, and intimidating their various business associates. They owed me $25,000 for the guarantee that we'd agreed to, and it was now time to collect, regardless of what they claimed.

I wasn't in the mood to play, so I asked Rorion to send me a Brazilian to act as my "aide." Rorion enlisted Rickson to go with me to Fey's office, and he seemed happy to oblige. As I was ready to head out, I ran into Campbell, and we started talking about Fey and Bresloff. At one point during the conversation, my Glock 17, which I had shoved into my waistband, "printed"—it became visible. Campbell immediately went silent, and his face turned pale white. He was a New Yorker, and the super restrictive gun laws there meant to him that only criminals and cops had guns.

After a long pause, he asked nervously, "Why are you armed?"

"No big deal. I just like to have my little friend along when I carry cash."

So, with my Glock, my chutzpah, and Rickson, I set out to get what we were owed.

As soon as Rickson and I arrived, Fey started right in about all of the money they were going to lose, and how he wanted to renegotiate our deal.

"$15,000 is fair," Fey said. "That's what I think I want to pay. This event isn't selling so good."

This newspaper clipping shows the ad that the local promoters we hired—Barry Fey and Zane Bresloff—employed to sell tickets to the live event. Note the mention of "7 Bone Crushing Bouts."

"That's not our problem. That's your problem," I responded, as Rickson sat silently, and kept his killer eyes on Fey.

"Art, you're acting like a little gangster, bringing your goon with you to shake us down."

I understood where he was coming from. In Fey's world, this was how the game was played. He didn't get to be the top concert/event promoter in the Rocky Mountain states by being a push-over. Neither Fey nor Bresloff, who remained pretty quiet during our meeting, had any idea who Rickson was, but they could tell that he was not a person to be fucked with. We went back and forth, and I finally agreed to take a $23,000 cashier's check, which they issued on the spot. As Rickson and I drove straight to the bank, we shared a laugh about him being my mob enforcer. With Rickson by my side, I could have left my Glock in the hotel safe.

When we arrived back at the Executive Tower Inn, Kathy told me that things were reaching a boiling point, and that she and her staff were doing their best to keep everyone separated in the undersized lobby. Apparently, in the latest of numerous incidents, Tuli's two cousins were ready to throw down with a couple of the Gracies, and Pat Smith kept walking around glowering and trash talking—generally trying to intimidate everyone.

Then there were complaints from both Zane Frazier and Pat Smith that Carlos Valente, one of Rickson's black belts, had been videotaping their workouts and sparring sessions at Tiger Kim's and Jones' Tai-Kung Fu-Karate.

A few minutes later, I ran into Frazier, who was coming back from a run.

He immediately starting griping about the weather, and the altitude, and his breathing problems.

This made me think of a conversation that I had earlier with our broadcast producer Pillot about the fighter entrances, which would involve them walking through smoke.

I had asked him if this could potentially be a problem for anyone, and he had told me not to worry.

But now speaking with Frazier, I began to worry. He once again struck me as a man who was looking for an excuse as to why he'd lost—before the fights even began. I certainly didn't want to hear after the event that Frazier was blaming defeat on our smoke machine, or anything other than his own performance.

I genuinely liked Frazier, and I knew that he was a smart cookie. But he seemed increasingly nervous, and skeptical about everything that we were doing.

Part of my overall job description for W.O.W. Promotions included the roles of booker and matchmaker, and in this regard, I had to keep all of the fighters focused and on track. I wasn't anyone's manager, so I didn't care who won and lost. My loyalty was to the Ultimate Fighting Championship itself, which meant that I had to work towards delivering great fights. So I had to create a level of trust and confidence with all 10 fighters, and put them in a position to give their absolute best effort. But I fully understood that I was walking a fine line, because if favoritism was to become involved, then I was suddenly a manager.

With a guy like Frazier, I felt that I had to support him, but only to a certain point. I knew that it would be a calamity if any of the fighters grew jealous of perceived special treatment, or far worse, believed that I had a rooting interest in their opponents. This approach was, of course, not available to Rorion, since as the big brother to Royce, he undeniably had a horse in this race.

I did my best to remain a booker/matchmaker, and not become a manager, when Tuli told me that he forgot to bring a pair of both fighting and workout shorts to Denver. I asked Kathy to take him, his brother and cousins on an excursion in one of our vans, so that they could find something in a size 60. Kathy then drove all over the city, while Tuli's brother and cousins pounded down beer after beer in the van.

After becoming thoroughly lost in the eastern Denver suburbs, Kathy and her Hawaiian companions finally made it back to the hotel. As soon as she arrived at the Executive Tower Inn, Kathy told me that there was some sort of issue regarding Rosier that I needed to address with his manager, Charlie Anzalone. Known as "Captain Disco" during his days as a nightclub DJ in Buffalo, New York, Anzalone was a fast-talking guy with a nervous twitch in his face. He struck me as a crazy party-animal type, and I immediately liked him.

I figured that Anzalone wanted to talk to me about Rosier's eating habits. I had already been advised by Kathy about the ever increasing room service bill that Rosier was racking up for pizzas and muffins, and I really wasn't too concerned. Rosier was horribly out of shape, and there was no way that he was going to be fit and trim come Friday night. So it really didn't matter to me now what he ate. I became pretty much resigned to Rosier being a blimp when he informed me on Monday that, "my best diet for a fight is brown rice with hot sauce, and Snickers bars washed down with a Dr. Pepper."

But Anzalone told me that the issue at hand involved Rosier's other big appetite. Apparently, access to both his current and ex-wife during the week wasn't enough for him, as Anzalone had walked in on Rosier and some barely legal girl in bed together naked.

"Don't worry Charlie, I'll keep a close eye on Kevin, and you do the same. He's a problem child."

I didn't feel that there was anything else that I could say or do.

Later that Wednesday afternoon, I gave an interview to a reporter from KUSA Channel 9, the NBC affiliate in Denver. I told him that facing their fears and stepping up to the challenge marked our athletes as special.

"Isn't this brutal?" the reporter then asked me.

"Men have been competing in hand-to-hand fighting contests since 648 B.C., and most societies found such contests a safety valve."

I didn't think he was convinced. Our advertising that blared around town, courtesy of Fey and Bresloff, proclaimed that the Ultimate Fighting Championship would be the most brutal show since the Christians went winless against the lions.

After the TV interview, I met in my conference room with Rorion, Jim Brown and Bill Wallace. It started as a casual opportunity for everyone to get better acquainted, but the energy level in the room quickly escalated.

Wallace suddenly stood up and demonstrated what he would do if he was competing in the tournament, instead of commentating. He was used to commanding the floor from his seminars, and he quickly hit full speed. I made eye contact with Rorion, and I could tell that he thought Wallace was a full-of-shit idiot.

I then turned towards Brown and saw that the look on his face was priceless. In addition to being arguably the best and the toughest running back in the history of the NFL, Brown conducted numerous leadership workshops with Crips and Bloods gang members. A glimmer of a smile appeared, and Brown slightly pursed his lips. Even though I hardly knew him, it was clear to me that he felt about Wallace just as Rorion and I did. For his part, Wallace carried on, completely oblivious to his less-than-impressed audience.

After Wallace finally left, I asked Brown who was the toughest man he had ever met in show business.

After some additional prodding, Brown finally responded, "Charles Bronson. I don't know if he could fight. I never saw him throw down, but he gave off a heavy vibe that he could."

I smiled, remembering that Campbell and I had very briefly contemplated approaching that hard-as-nails film star about a job as one of our commentators.

It was important to me that I routinely stopped by the fighters' hotel rooms unannounced at night, just to see how they were doing, ask if they needed anything, and to get a handle on their mental state. As I made my rounds on Wednesday night, my knock on Tuli's door was answered by his brother, who invited me in. Sitting on a stool completely naked in the darkened room was Tuli, who was being rubbed down by his two cousins with a concoction that smelled like cat piss. I recognized it as dit da jow, an analgesic liniment favored by martial artists—a mixture of aromatic herbs like myrrh and ginseng, used to stimulate circulation and reduce pain and swelling.

"Hello, Mr. Davie."

"Hey Teila. I'll come back later. You're busy. Take it easy," I said as I beat a quick retreat.

My brief visits to Jimmerson's room had already shown me that this knockout artist had turned into a nervous kitten here in Denver. Word had gotten back to me that John McCarthy had taken Jimmerson to a workout area, and it had gone horribly wrong for the boxer.

Apparently Jimmerson said, "What are you going to do when I'm shooting a jab at you like this?"

As Jimmerson then fired off his lighting quick jab, McCarthy stepped back, just out of range, and quickly shot in for a double leg takedown. After hitting the mat, McCarthy moved effortlessly to the mount position, raised his fist above the flattened Jimmerson, and said, "Now what are you going to do?"

I didn't bother to check up on Royce, as Rorion and Rickson had him sequestered away. They didn't want anyone outside of their tight inner circle, including me, to enter the hotel suite in which they had laid down mats brought in from the Gracie Academy. Through W.O.W. Promotions, we'd booked and paid for a suite, and I was really concerned that the other fighters would find out about this, only adding to their case of Gracie favoritism. I knew that it was an unfair advantage, and now I kicked myself for having agreed to this when Rorion suggested that we cover the costs.

Just before our 11:30 p.m. staff meeting that night, Campbell pulled me aside to let me know that Jim Brown didn't feel that he could handle the play-by-play duties. He wanted to shift over to be one of the color commentators, which came with far fewer on-air responsibilities.

"Why don't we just move Bill Wallace to play-by-play," I suggested to Campbell. "The guy loves the sound of his own voice, so it's probably a better fit anyway."

Campbell had already come to that conclusion, and when we called Wallace in his hotel room, he didn't hesitate in accepting the larger role.

Late that night, I sat down alone to make out the tournament bracket. Rorion told me that whatever I decided was good with him, as did Campbell. For Rorion, this was because he truly believed that Gracie Jiu-Jitsu was unbeatable, so it didn't matter who Royce fought and when. For Campbell, it was because the fights and the fighters had always been my domain, and he wasn't going to start interfering now.

Of the eight tournament fighters, I felt that only Royce, Shamrock and Gordeau had a realistic chance of claiming the $50,000 first prize. I didn't want grappler versus grappler in the Final, as this could be a boring grind-fest that would end the night on a bad note. So I knew that I had to put Royce and Shamrock in the same half of the draw.

I had long ago made up my mind to pit Royce against Jimmerson in the opening round. Rorion had really intrigued me with his oft-told story of Hélio's challenge to Joe Louis back in 1947, and I wanted to see how Gracie Jiu-Jitsu would fair against someone who really knew how to punch. What if Jimmerson blasted Royce with an uppercut or big hook when Royce invariably closed the distance? Could Royce get past Jimmerson's thudding jab as McCarthy had in sparring? If Royce took Jimmerson down, I knew it would be a quick sprint to the finish line, but the possibility of Royce getting hit by a pro boxer was pretty intriguing. Even though it was clear to me that Jimmerson was an emotional mess, he did possess legitimate knock out power in both hands.

Seeing how Smith had behaved at the hotel all week in Denver helped me decide to match him against Shamrock in the opening round. While Smith was loud-mouthed and cocky, Shamrock was quiet confidence and cool. I liked Smith, and after all, he was the very first fighter that I had signed. But he was also a bit of a bully, and I couldn't help but think that it would be interesting to see him humbled by Shamrock.

I then thought Gordeau versus Frazier and Tuli versus Rosier for the two remaining first round bouts. Gordeau against Frazier would be a contrast of North American and European kickboxing styles, and Tuli facing Rosier would produce a freak show between the two behemoths.

But in the thin mile-high air of Denver, it seemed very likely that both of my super heavyweights would be exhausted in a matter of moments if there wasn't a quick victory for one of them. Inevitably, the pair would just move around in slow motion after that.

Also, I remembered hearing Gordeau say to a radio reporter that morning that he was always being compared to a bullfighter, using agility and skill to defeat larger opponents throughout his career. This made a real impression on me. Who was more of a bull than the giant Hawaiian? So I decided that it would be Gordeau vs. Tuli and Frazier vs. Rosier.

Those two fights would open the night, as I figured that they'd likely be the most violent, and we needed to grab both the in-arena and PPV television audiences right off the bat.

Royce against Jimmerson would be third, and then Shamrock vs. Smith would conclude the opening round. I didn't want Royce going last, as it might give off the impression that he was the "main event" fighter—leading to more grumbles of Gracie favoritism.

Gordeau would be in the top half of the draw, likely meeting either Royce or Shamrock in the Final. Of course anything could happen—in fighting everyone always has a puncher's chance—but I had to project the course of the night as best as I could, based on everything that I knew about the physical, mental and emotional states of my eight fighters.

On Thursday—the eve of the event—I began the day by getting the fighters' stats to the broadcast production team. Despite there being no weight classes, and no weight limits, we needed the information for the show, plus Clay McBride wanted it for our archive. I'd previously had the eight tournament guys fill out a "Tale of the Tape" form, which we included in our official program to be sold at McNichols Arena. My mailed questionnaire was inspired by my love of boxing, and the personal stats that were always given for the sport's world title fights. I had our fighters list everything from age and height, to the size of their wrists and forearms. This was on the honor system, thus Rosier's self-reported weight of 265 lb.

That afternoon, we held a press conference in the hotel's main ballroom. I had offered my services, but Campbell thought it best that SEG's main sales guy, Mike Abramson, serve as the host. Abramson had apparently been adamant with Campbell that he would be the most qualified to convey what the Ultimate Fighting Championship was about to the assembled media. Campbell had seen me pitch to a room full of investors, and he knew I could move an audience. But it was clear to me that SEG wanted control.

Rorion didn't care, and I had bigger fish to fry, so we let Abramson take the reins. There was a great turn out by the local media, with TV stations KUSA and KMGH (the ABC affiliate), and radio stations by KS-104, (where we had been running ads) KAZY, KRFX and KBPI, all in attendance. The "national" media was represented by a few martial arts magazines, and no one else. Abramson talked all about the brutality that was certain to occur the following night, and used the line that he took from Fey/Bresloff about the Christians and the lions.

After Abramson gave his spiel, he introduced Rorion, Campbell, and me. Campbell got up and discussed the media and the marketing plans surrounding the Ultimate Fighting Championship. It became painfully clear that the local reporters didn't have a clue as to what we were actually doing. Virtually everything that they knew about the Ultimate Fighting Championship came from our local "fight-to-the-death" ad campaign, courtesy of Fey and Bresloff. What the Denver TV and radio newshounds seemed to be interested in was the blood and gore aspect of our forthcoming event. The martial arts magazine writers acted as though we were bringing shame on the world of fighting, by abandoning honor, traditions, customs and civility.

We even had a couple of Japanese journalists on hand, and they seemed upset that we were trying to bring the martial arts together in one mixed event.

When Campbell finished, it was my turn to speak, and I brought up the connection to Pankration and the Olympic ideals of the Greeks. The media members were not impresssed.

I then unveiled a device that measured the "power-of-the-punch." An inventor and self-promoter type from Alaska had called me the previous month, and told me he had designed and built a device that measured the power of a fighter's punches, kicks, knees and elbows. I was intrigued, but not enough to spend any money. After a few minutes of negotiations over the phone, the guy agreed to fly to Denver at his own expense, and in return, I would feature his gizmo at the event. I figured that the perfect place for such a stunt would be at the press conference.

The media types perked up when I introduced the Alaskan, and he mounted his contraption on a pillar. Bill Wallace, immediately rose from his seat, and announced that he was going to demonstrate the force of his legendary kicks. Jason DeLucia got up next, and out-scored Wallace by a sizeable margin. Shamrock then took a turn, and threw a huge elbow, which registered just below DeLucia's kick. I asked Gordeau if he wanted to have a go, but the Dutchman passed, telling me that he was going to save his strength for when it mattered. It was an amusing side show, and a clip actually aired on the local news.

After the press conference ended, I made the short drive to McNichols Arena. Pillot was there, setting things up for the PPV broadcast, which was now just under 30 hours away. I was thrilled to see that the two huge vinyl banners which featured our logo were in place. It had been money well spent. The smaller banner was displayed inside the Arena so that it would be clearly visible every time our PPV broadcast director Mark Lucas went to what he called his "number one camera."

The fighting area itself, designed by Greg Harrison and Jason Cusson, had been unpacked, and then assembled on the arena floor earlier in the day. The grips were still making adjustments, and when I saw it for the first time, I was actually speechless. As good as Harrison's sketch was, I felt that the amazing combination of artistry and engineering was even more impressive, more breathtaking in person. The 30-foot octagon shape encased by gray padding, the black plastic-covered chain link fence, the clean white canvas with 2-inch thick padding and our logo prominently featured in the center—all combined to strike the right balance between primitive and futuristic.

After quickly huddling with Campbell, Pillot, Abramson, and Lucas for a broadcast production meeting, I hurried back to the hotel. In my suite, using the IBM Selectric II that I'd lugged out to Denver from my W.O.W. office, I typed up the agenda for that evening's fighters meeting. This one-page document included the rules and regulations that I had written a couple of weeks earlier, and was required to be signed by all ten of our fighters. By giving their acknowledgment and consent, there would be no doubt as to what they were going to be getting themselves into the following night.

At 7 p.m., we gathered everybody in one of the hotel conference rooms for the fighters meeting. The room was set up classroom style with a head table at the front for Rorion and me. It was shoulder-to-shoulder and ass-to-ass with the fighters, their respective camps, staff from W.O.W. Promotions and SEG, our commentators, event personnel, VIP guests and assorted hangers-on. Absent was anyone from the City of Denver and the State of Colorado. I never expected representatives from those governments to come, but now left to our own devices, I was really struck by just how much we were flying under the radar.

I had sold our insurance broker Gagliardi Insurance Services in San Jose, California on the idea that we were doing a "full-contact" tournament. They were old hands at working with boxing promoters and didn't ask many questions. I also felt that the management personnel at McNichols Arena were equally clueless, as though we were going to be doing some kind of karate event, like the Sabaki Challenge. All of the fighters and their entourages seemed a bit on edge as they came into the room and found seats. Everyone knew that at the end of the meeting, I would be announcing the opening round match-ups and the bout order. There was a lot of posturing going on, and also a lot of eye contact avoidance. It was a mix of fear, nerves and pure testosterone.

I handed out a copy of the agenda, made a few opening remarks, and then introduced Rorion, who gave a very brief welcome. I stood back up and acknowledged our two Brazilian referees, Dr. Alan Brakup (a Gracie Jiu-Jitsu student), and the two outstanding boxing cut men I'd flown in from Philadelphia, Leon Tabbs and Sam Solomon.

I then turned things over to Campbell, who proclaimed, "There will be a million eyeballs on this show. Give it everything you've got."

After Campbell, it was Pillot's turn, and I made it clear that he deserved everyone's full attention.

"Tomorrow night, this man, our broadcast producer Michael Pillot, is the boss. It's his job to get this all done in two hours and fifty minutes."

Pillot went over the dress rehearsal, which was scheduled for the following afternoon, and then gave the basic rundown of the actual event from a TV timing perspective.

I could tell that we were starting to lose the group's attention and interest by the time I introduced Derek Barton, who was head of marketing for Gold's Gym, our lead sponsor. After Barton said a few words, I then cued Rorion to go over the rules and regulations, and told our audience that aside from his role with W.O.W. Promotions, he was also the "Commissioner of the IFC."

Rorion stood up, nervously cleared his throat and started in. In a low monotone, he announced that there were three basic rules: no eye gouging, no biting and no groin strikes,

Immediately, Zane Frazier shouted, "Why not? I can throw groin strikes in Kenpo."

"Give me a break," Rorion retorted. "This is going to be on TV. No groin strikes, Zane."

"Well what about a cup? Can we all wear a cup?" Frazier asked.

"Yes," Rorion replied sharply.

Frazier shot back, "Well what about hand wraps? It says right here on the sheet that the tape has to be one inch below the knuckles. I want to tape my knuckles."

And just like that, it was on.

From his front row seat, Frazier began acting like the jail house lawyer of the group.

I was fascinated to see where everyone had plopped themselves. Gerard Gordeau was predictably in the last row. He looked incredibly disinterested, and stayed quiet. Teila Tuli, his huge brother, and cousins were in the back as well, against the far wall. Royce was in the middle, surrounded by his father and brothers, eyes locked on Rorion.

Jimmerson was seated close to the door, and yelled out, "Man, I'm a boxer. I have to have my hands wrapped. This is bullshit."

Shamrock, who had hardly said a word to Rorion or me all week, suddenly spoke up, and said that he wanted to wear the boots that were part of his Pancrase gear.

"If you kick, no shoes. Otherwise, it's OK!" Rorion said, his voice rising.

"Well, what about shin guards?" asked Shamrock, as he wore those in Pancrase as well.

"No shin guards, no elbow pads!" I could tell that Rorion's temperature was rising.

"Can we wear knee wraps?" was Shamrock's next question.

"Yes, knee wraps are allowed, as long as they're not padded."

Campbell gave me a look to indicate that this was going awry.

Pat Smith then piped up, "Can we wear a mouthpiece? It's not in the rules."

"You can wear a mouthpiece if you want," Rorion responded.

"Even though it's not listed on the sheet?" asked Frazier. "Well, how about boxing gloves?"

"Yes on mouthpieces, and yes on boxing gloves if they're 6- or 8-ounce gloves. It's written right there on the sheet."

Rorion really seemed to be losing his composure now. He didn't have the patience for this type of thing.

Taylor Wiley

AGENDA FOR FIGHTERS' MEETING
11/11/93

I. Welcome to the Ultimate Fighting Championship

II. Introductions
 A. Referees
  1. Helio Vigio
  2. Joao Alberto Barreto
 B. M.D. - Alan Brakup, M.D.
 C. Cutmen
  1. Leon Tapps
  2. Sam Solomon
 D. Semaphore
  1. Campbell McLaren, General Manager
  2. Michael Pillot, Producer
 E. Gold's Gym Corporate
  1. Derek Barton

III. Rules & Regulations
 A. 5 rounds, five minutes each, 2 minute rest between rounds
 B. Fight to be held in a 30' octagon
 C. Fighters wear clothing according to their style, as long as it complies with IFC rules. Rorion Gracie, IFC Commissioner, and the referees to inspect each fighter prior to event.
 D. Fight can be stopped as follows:
  1. Knockout (standard 10 count)
  2. Submission
   a. Tapping out with the foot or hand on the mat at least 3 times
  3. Corner man throw in a towel
  4. Choke-out
  5. Doctor's intervention
  6. Disqualification
   a. At referee's disgression (eye gouge, groin shot, biting)
 E. All punches, kicks, knee and elbow strikes, joint locks and/or chokes are permitted.
 F. Target areas for all strikes include head and body withe the exception of the eyes and groin.
 G. 6 or 8-ounce boxing gloves or Kempo gloves are optional if a fighter's art employs closed fist strikes to the face and head, otherwise bare knuckles are permitted.
  1. Taping of wrist must end 1 inch away from the knuckle. Tape should be placed on top of any wraps.
  2. Shoes - boxing or wrestling shoes allowed if the fighter does not use any kicking.
  3. Types of supports that are permitted (show examples)
  4. No shin guards or arm pads
 H. Fight shall not be interrupted in the event of a clinch and/or fall to the mat. Referee will determine when to break if the fight is stalled. If both fighters intentionally stall, they will both be disqualified without pay.
 I. No point system is in effect; fight shall continue into overtime rounds until one fighter is declared the winner.
  1. Overtime - Unlimited number of 5-minute rounds until winner is declared. 2-minute intermissions.
 J. This is a single elimination tournament; there are no weight classes.

IV. Bout order and match-ups

ACCEPTED: Taylor Wiley AKA Teila Tuli

This is sumo wrestler Teila Tuli's copy of the Fighters' Meeting Rules. Note his signature on the bottom.

"So we can wear boxing gloves, but can't tape our hands," Frazier shot back. "That doesn't make any sense."

"If you're in a street fight, are you going to wrap your hands?" was Rorion's reply.

I thought to myself, if you were in a street fight, you probably weren't going to be wearing boxing gloves or a gi, but I kept that thought to myself.

"How about if we tape half an inch below the knuckles?" Frazier countered.

"No! It's already been decided. Look at your sheet. One inch below the knuckles."

Frazier then yelled, "This whole thing is rigged for your brother to win."

Now all hell broke loose.

Rorion tried to restore order by yelling, "You can wrap your hand one inch below the knuckle!"

There were calls for allowing a half-inch below the knuckles, then a quarter-inch, then across the knuckles. Frazier led the charge, and shouted that he was being held back by a jiu-jitsu guy who didn't know how to punch.

At this point, Rorion and I had completely lost control of the meeting. The fighters and their camps were all loudly arguing, and I could see that this whole event was coming apart before it had even started.

Everyone, with the lone exception of Gordeau, was going crazy, and Rorion was completely swallowed by the moment.

It then hit me like a full on punch to the face that I'd made a terrible miscalculation. From the fighters' perspective it was bad enough that Rorion was one of the people in charge of the Ultimate Fighting Championship, but now he was also the rules director of an obviously made-up sanctioning body. The fighters couldn't help but ask how Rorion could possibly be impartial when his brother was in the tournament, representing the style of fighting created by his father and uncle? I was the one who personally wrote the rules—not Rorion—but he was the one standing in the front of the room, listing and defending them.

Of course Rorion wanted Royce to win. Of course he wanted to showcase Gracie Jiu-Jitsu. Of course he wanted to honor his father's legacy. I knew all of this without a doubt. But Rorion never interfered with me when it came to the integrity of the event: the rules, the equipment, the match-ups, the fighters that we signed. But God almighty, did this look bad.

I tried to restore order, but I couldn't be heard over the wall of chaos. I looked over at Michael Pillot and his face said, 'You better put a cork in this. Now!'

Rickson started saying something, and then quickly jumped to his feet. When I saw this, I realized that the next thing that happened was likely going to be disastrous.

Then Teila Tuli, in the most dramatic and theatrical of gestures, stood up and announced, "I just signed my paper. I don't know about you guys, but I came here to party. If anyone else came here to party, I'll see you tomorrow night at the arena." He then slammed his signed paper down on the table. The sound reverberated throughout the room.

With that, it became eerily quiet. And then the Gracie brothers started applauding. Then Trent Jenkins started applauding. And within seconds, everyone, apart from Frazier, was applauding.

The tension was completely sucked out of the room, and that was the end of the arguing and debating. I quickly announced the match-ups and bout order, reminded the fighters to sign the paper in front of them, just as Tuli had already done, and thanked everyone for attending. Meeting adjourned.

As he was exiting the now emptying conference room, Gordeau said to me, "I sign the paper and now I go. Everyone wants to debate what is allowed and what is not allowed. Americans, they talk a lot. But if you have no rules, you are finished explaining in two seconds."

Rosier then came up to me.

"That was hilarious. All the guys going over the hand tape and everything else. I was just hanging back. I had a root canal today, so I'm on medication."

Afterwards, Kathy, Elaine, Clay and I went for a drink at the Brown House, a famous Denver watering hole and hotel. When we sat down, we noticed that Democratic pollster and commentator, James Carville and his wife, Republican strategist, Mary Matalin were seated nearby. It was that kind of joint. I definitely needed to blow off some steam, as

I felt we all did. I started teasing Kathy that since she was doing such a bang up job, I was going to give her a raise.

With that, Clay started pestering me.

"Well, what kind of an offer are you going to make to Kathy? Come on Art. How much?"

I announced that I was going to give Kathy a title, instead of a raise, and she and I kept joking back and forth.

Clay began looking more and more irritated, and said, "Why don't you two get a room and settle it."

"You up for that Kathy?" I asked laughing a bit.

"We don't have time, boss. There's a staff meeting still on the agenda tonight. How else can I get a promotion if I start missing staff meetings?" she fired back.

It became clear to me that Clay seemed to be attracted to Kathy, just as I was. I could sense that Elaine had picked up on this as well. I finally paid the bill, and we headed back to the hotel for our final meeting of the day, with Clay barely saying a word.

That night as I struggled to get to sleep, I kept thinking about the debacle of our fighters meeting, and how it had completely gone off the tracks.

I'd written the rules and regulations for the Ultimate Fighting Championship with the sole purpose of creating the best and fairest fights possible. I wanted everyone to have an equal chance at victory (and feel they were being treated fairly) whether they came from Gracie Jiu-Jitsu, kung fu, boxing, sumo or whatever. That was the only way that this thing was going to work.

Mixed match fighting had failed to break through to the mainstream because everything always got negotiated to death. I needed to look no further than Antonio Inoki on the mat for 15 rounds against Muhammad Ali in 1976, throwing kicks while on his ass, because the rules made it virtually impossible for him to stand and fight his fight.

My mindset was that a fighter should be able to wear whatever they wanted, as long as it didn't create a weapon or protection, and do whatever they wanted, as long as it didn't cross the line of humanity. I was determined that the Ultimate Fighting Championship was going to be a place where absolutely anyone could come in and do their thing, and then see if it really and truly worked.

And then it hit me that this core philosophy of mine was the major reason why so many gyms, managers, organizations, sanctioning bodies and fighters themselves had not hesitated in given me a blunt, "No!" when I approached them. Martial arts and combat sports were pretty much based on your style being dominant, and every other style being worthless—a sham. So many of the guys who I reached out to were the kings of their own little fiefdoms—heroes in their own tiny realms. No one challenged their dominance; to their followers, they were the unbeatable masters.

There was a lot more risk than reward for these guys to be given the chance to show the world that what they did really worked. A loss meant that maybe they weren't all that they'd claimed. An ass kicking meant that they were pretty much full of shit, and so too was their fighting style. It wasn't just a matter of pride and reputation, it was a matter of money. Teaching and training your fighting style was ultimately business—and absolutely no one wanted their business labeled as a fraud. I had real admiration for my eight tournament fighters and two alternates. They all had the balls to step up, and despite all of the bitching and debating, were now ready to put themselves on display to the world—consequences be damned.

I concluded that I had almost blown all of this by going along with Rorion being in charge. My own fault. If it wasn't for Teila Tuli, I felt that the Ultimate Fighting Championship might have been derailed on the eve of the event.

Friday, the day of the fights, arrived early. I set my alarm for 6:30 a.m. to be ready for our early morning staff meeting, but I was awake by 5 a.m. Even before the Ultimate Fighting Championship was set to go live on PPV at 7 p.m. local time in Denver, we had to do the walk through dress rehearsal with all of the fighters that afternoon, supervised by Pillot.

And there was, of course, that matter of our unsigned contract, which I'd been trying not to think about all week. Moss had been battling over the phone daily with Meyrowitz and David, and he didn't think that there was anything more that we could get. They'd made their concessions big and small, and Moss told me that he felt that it was now time for me to sign. As I saw it, my alternatives were to hold the Ultimate Fighting Championship without SEG broadcasting it that night, postpone it, or cancel it all together. I'd come too far to cancel, and a postponement would only prolong my misery with SEG. After such a move, I doubted that Meyrowitz would welcome me back to the negotiating table anyway.

Legally, I could still hold the event—untelevised—but I knew that it would be a financial disaster to do so. Gone would be our SEG guarantee, and our sponsorship money from Gold's Gym, as well as our smaller advertiser, Otomix martial arts gear. The fighters had all signed their contracts with the understanding that the event would be aired live across the U.S. on PPV-TV. This would be a serious breach on our part. And I didn't like my chances of getting us another broadcast partner once word got out that we'd abandoned SEG at the altar on wedding day. With a vengeful Meyrowitz leading the charge, there was no question that word would indeed get out. I knew for sure that we'd be industry poison.

But the leverage that I had was that SEG could not legally broadcast the Ultimate Fighting Championship without a signed contract. Campbell had let that slip. They would have wasted hundreds of hours, and tens of thousands of dollars in getting to this point, with nothing to show for it. And they would badly tarnish if not ruin their reputation with the myriad of cable systems across the country that aired SEG events. I knew that as a content provider in the PPV-TV world, they had to deliver as advertised, or there would be serious hell to pay.

Now in the final stage of this prolonged game of chicken, I was prepared to swerve at the very last second, but my instincts told me that Meyrowitz would veer out of the way first.

Before the start of the day's 7:30 a.m. meeting, I looked at our fight program which we'd be selling at McNichols Arena for $4 that night. I felt bad for Jenkins, who as my second alternate I figured most likely wouldn't get to fight in front of his hometown crowd, and also didn't even make it into the program. By the time he replaced the injured Jim Mullen, we'd already shipped our finished pages to the printer. All we could do was type "WITHDREW!" diagonally in all capital letters across Mullen's picture and profile.

On page one was a letter of welcome and introduction that I addressed to our McNichols Arena crowd, which stated:

Hundreds of fighters from Asia, the Americas and Europe were reviewed to select the eight brave and skilled men who battle tonight. Many were called, but few were chosen.

I concluded:

See which style is the best on this night and who is the man worthy of the title–THE ULTIMATE FIGHTER!

At the early morning meeting, Campbell let me know that we absolutely had to get the contract signed. He told me that we'd all be fucked if I refused, and that this wasn't just about me. There were a lot of people who were now involved in this, himself included, and Campbell said that I needed to think about that. I told him that we'd get everyone on the phone later in the day and get everything finalized, but first we needed to get through Pillot's walk through with the fighters. The contract would work itself out.

Before heading to McNichols Arena for the dress rehearsal, I checked in on Rorion, who along with his dad and brothers, was holding a Gracie Jiu-Jitsu seminar at the hotel. It was open to the public, and when I arrived, I asked Rorion if he was worried about giving away the family secrets so close to fight time.

"No, Arturo," he told me. "We have to get the whole world on board."

Our commentators Jim Brown, Bill Wallace and Kathy Long were there to observe Gracie Jiu-Jitsu up close and in person at the seminar. To her credit, Kathy Long was willing to humble herself, and got on the mat—which was clearly not her fighting domain. She wanted to expand her knowledge as a martial artist, and also get an understanding of what Royce would be trying to utilize that night come fight time.

Rather than join in, Wallace leaned back against a folding table and kept making comments to no one in particular about how he'd successfully counter every move from Gracie Jiu-Jitsu.

"I could show you how to reverse that."

"That would never work in a real fight against me."

"Let's see how they'd deal with one of my kicks."

At one point, I caught Jim Brown staring at Wallace with a look that mixed amusement with disgust.

That afternoon at McNichols Arena, the fighters and their respective camps began to arrive, as Kathy Kidd worked diligently to keep everyone separated, out of fear that the bouts would start early. We had told them the day before that they would need to bring what they would be wearing that night. The plan was for Kathy to show them their dressing rooms, and then let the fighters go inside the octagonal fighting area, which they would all be seeing for the first time. After that, Pillot would have them rehearse their entrance walk, which he needed for timing purposes for the PPV broadcast. I now just hoped that everyone would follow this plan, and make my life easy for a change.

I had originally wanted Tuli to wear his traditional sumo outfit—the mawashi—in the Ultimate Fighting Championship. But Tuli declined, as he was afraid that it would be ripped off, and give the world the sight that I'd seen earlier in his hotel room. Instead, he wanted to wear boxing trunks, but after Kathy's fruitless search, he settled on some awful Polynesian skirt thing.

Rosier showed me what he was going to wear, and I thought it was a joke. They looked like the bottom half of a pair of white long underwear that had been shrunk in the wash. Jimmerson's boxing trunks looked great, solid black with his last name across the front waistband in white letters.

I continued checking out the remaining fighters doing their walkthroughs, with Royce going last. When I headed to the van for a ride back to the hotel, Todd Hester came running up to me. Todd was a cool guy who I would often see around the Southern California martial arts scene, and had gotten to know fairly well. He'd flown out to Denver at his own expense, and Rorion had given him an all-access pass.

"Art, you're not going to believe what I just saw," he said. "Royce absolutely lost it after rehearsal."

Todd went on to tell me that after everyone had cleared out, he watched Royce and Rickson walk back into our fighting area. They knelt on the mat facing each other, and Royce just started crying inconsolably. Rickson then tightly embraced his brother, the way a father holds his sobbing child who has just awoken from a terrible nightmare.

What Todd had to say actually didn't surprise me at all. The crushing pressure of the moment was squarely on the shoulders of Royce, and I seriously doubted that he'd asked for any of this. Without question, this wasn't about him, it was about his dad, his brothers, his uncle— the entire Gracie family and legacy. At that point, I truly believed that Rorion should have made amends with Rickson, because this was going to be far too much for poor, sweet Royce to bare.

I took the short two-mile ride from McNichols Arena back to the Executive Tower Inn, so that I could change into my tuxedo, and then have the big conference call that I understood was going to decide the fate of our SEG deal, and the night, one way or the other. I was trying to keep my composure, as I knew that this was the decisive battle.

As I now waited in my suite for the phone to ring, I turned to Ethan and said, "We're doing fine on time. Just get my monkey suit all set to go."

I then asked him to put the studs in my tuxedo shirt, and pin on the dress service medals I'd been awarded as a Marine in Vietnam.

"What's with the medals, Art? That's going to look cheesy."

"Ethan. Damn it. Just do it!" I was surprised by the sharpness in my voice, and I immediately apologized.

Soon, the phone rang, and I was joined on the line by Moss, who was in his Burbank law office; Meyrowitz and his brother David, who were in New York; and Campbell who was in his room, one floor below me. I lit a Montecristo #2, poured myself a shot of single malt scotch and settled in.

Immediately, I could tell that Meyrowitz was wired, but was trying his hardest to remain calm. Meyrowitz clearly didn't want to piss me off, but acting like this was against his nature, and I thought it must be killing him.

I wasted no time in laying it all out for Meyrowitz.

"I'm good with everything else Bob, but SEG is going to have to pay all fighter purses after tonight. That's prize money and guarantees. It's just part of talent costs. And fighters are the talent for this show."

The call dragged on and on, extending past the hour mark. We kept going over this issue, with SEG offering to pay varying percentages of the fight purse, none totaling the 100 percent that I demanded. Either Meyrowitz was going to blink first, or I was. This was about the future of the Ultimate Fighting Championship, but without tonight, there would be nothing.

Finally, Meyrowitz let out a huge exhale, and then agreed to pay the full cost of all fighter purses for every Ultimate Fighting Championship after this first event.

"OK, Art. You win. Are you happy? I hope you're fucking happy!"

The contract was faxed to my hotel room, and I signed it at 5:47 p.m.—seventy-three minutes before our on-air time.

I was right on the verge of caving in, but Meyrowitz lost his nerve and caved first. There was no time to celebrate though, as I had to get my ass back to McNichols Arena, and watch my dream now finally become a reality. But then I decided that there was time for one more glass of scotch.

All the work of the last year; all of our grief and struggles were finally coming to this moment. Kathy had set up a car for Rorion and me, and Ethan joined us. I was bubbling over inside with excitement and nerves. I could tell from Ethan's reactions that he knew Rorion and I were tight. Rorion wasn't saying much, but the muscles in his jaw kept working. I was manic. What if it all came apart in the last minute? I had the feeling that anything was possible. We were on new ground here. I tried to look cool; I had to. But I felt the tingle that comes from not knowing what's going to happen next. It was the most exciting feeling in the world. I had a checklist with me, and I knew, that with plenty to do, I'd be busy.

When Ethan and I arrived, I could see that a decent crowd had formed outside the entrance gates and ticket windows. We'd given out almost 1,000 comps, distributing them to our friends, family, acquaintances, and business associates, as well as radio stations, gyms, and martial arts schools around Denver. But there actually seemed to be paying customers there as well.

Once inside, I gave Ethan my briefcase, which I told him was my "baby" for the night. It contained my Glock 17, the fighter contracts, our W.O.W. Promotions checkbook and $3,000 in cash.

"Whatever you do, don't let my baby out of your sight. Handcuff it to your fucking wrist if you have to."

"Don't worry, Art. You always worry, just like my dad."

My first order of business was to check in at the television production truck, which served as the command center of our live PPV broadcast. Seeing the constellation of monitors and control panels, as well as Pillot ruling the deck like an admiral, made me fill with adrenaline. I looked over at Mark Lucas, our director, and he said to me "break a leg." I figured that I had finally made it in show business and smiled at him. Pillot and Lucas were live TV veterans, with hours and hours of big shows under their belts, but I could still sense their excitement. Just like all of us, they were about to step into the great unknown.

I then headed back inside McNichols Arena to see if William "Buzz" Reifman (who was a nurse) and Dr. Joel Cooperman, our emergency medical team, had arrived. I had mandated that all of our fighters were tested for AIDS. The pair were regulars at working boxing events in Denver, and when I found them by the fighting area, I handed the negative test results to Dr. Cooperman.

From there, I went to visit all of the fighters in their dressing rooms.

Frazier looked terrified, and seemed really agitated. I felt like he was already thinking about all of the reasons why he was going to lose, and why it would be our fault.

"How are you doing, Zane?"

"Man, I just hope my breathing problems don't start up."

Rosier was joking around, and had a big smile on his face. He was wearing his fighting long underwear, which he had pulled about a foot above his waist, like a 90-year-old man. Somehow they were both baggy and way too tight.

"Are you really going to wear that Kevin? Is there nothing I can do to change your mind?" I asked.

I couldn't help but like Rosier and his goofy enthusiasm.

Throughout our early conversations, and even when he arrived in Denver, I wasn't sure that Shamrock realized that the Ultimate Fighting Championship was going to be a full-on shoot. But seeing the intensity on his face told me that he now knew exactly what he was getting into, and that he was ready to roll. In his bright red Pancrase/Puroresu trunks, Shamrock looked like a bodybuilding champion. And I thought he looked like he might be our tournament champion as well.

Gordeau was smoking, and had the demeanor of a man waiting for a city bus to take him on his mundane daily commute.

"Is everything good, Gerard?"

"No problem, Art Davie."

Royce was with his dad and brothers in the marquee dressing room, which had been given to him by Rorion. It was far and away the biggest, and it was the only one that had a television monitor, on which Royce could watch the live PPV feed. I could only hope that Frazier didn't see where Royce was housed. Whatever Rickson had said and done during his apparent breakdown earlier in the day seemed to have worked, because Royce looked focused. I couldn't get very close to him though, as he had a phalanx of Brazilians guarding him like he was the Pope.

Tuli was with his brother and two cousins and seemed nervous.

"Are you ready to party?" I asked him, thinking he would appreciate the reference to his comment at the fighters meeting of the night before. He could only offer up a weak smile in reply.

Pat Smith was bouncing off the walls, repeatedly shouting to himself that he was going to "fuck motherfuckers up tonight." I thought that if we were giving out a self-doubt award, he would have finished second, just behind Frazier.

I then stopped by Jimmerson's dressing room and asked him to show me his gloves, as they couldn't be bigger than eight ounces.

"I didn't bring no gloves. I need a pair. And I need some shoes too."

It took me a moment to comprehend what I was hearing. Jimmerson was a top 10 cruiserweight in the world, and the guy we had paid a $17,000 appearance fee. He was here to represent boxing, and he hadn't bothered to bring his gloves, or even his shoes. And he was just now telling me about this? What the fuck?

I wanted to curse him out, but I caught myself, realizing that it was pointless. He wasn't offering an explanation for his lack of proper packing, and even if he had, it wouldn't have mattered at this point.

I immediately got Kathy on her walkie-talkie and told her about our latest emergency.

"Kathy, huge crisis. You've got to get on the phone now and find me a pair of regulation boxing gloves for Jimmerson. And shoes. Get the Yellow Pages out and start calling sporting goods stores. If you can't find boxing shoes, get Jimmerson some good running shoes. The asshole didn't bring anything!"

Kathy quickly located a sporting goods store in the nearby suburb of Arvada, but everybody on her staff was totally committed to dealing with other pressing issues. Undaunted, I called my kid brother, Matthew, who was still getting dressed at the hotel. He was looking forward to an enjoyable evening of kicking back and watching the fights.

I yelled at him to grab a cab and get down to the arena as fast as humanly possible. When he arrived 20 minutes later, I opened my wallet and took out three one hundred dollar bills.

"Here's the address. It's a sporting goods store. They're open and waiting. Take this cash, grab a cab outside the arena and get over there. All you got to do is pay the man and then get back here yesterday."

As I now waited for Matthew to return, I went to check on my two alternates, but could only find DeLucia. He seemed fairly relaxed, and thanked me again for the opportunity. I had sympathy for him, being stuck in such a weird limbo state. Jenkins had not arrived yet, and that had me worried. Karyn Turner said he was dependable—which was supposed to be Jenkins' best attribute as a fighter. No one had any idea where he was, and I asked Kathy to find out what the hell was going on.

Soon, Matthew returned with 10-ounce boxing gloves and a pair of black Nike high tops, fresh off of the shelf. In his rush to get to the sporting goods store, Matthew had forgotten to take his credential with him. When he returned to McNichols Arena, the security guards wouldn't let him in. They thought that he was some nut who showed up at the fights with boxing gloves and shoes, as though he was looking to join the fray.

Kathy had to be called on her walkie-talkie to restore order.

I went back to Jimmerson's dressing room, and I again resisted the temptation to ask him what he was thinking by not bringing his gear with him to Denver. The boxing gloves that Matthew had bought for him were bigger than what I'd stipulated could be worn in the rules. But at this point, I didn't care.

I doubted that Royce, Rickson, Rorion, Hélio or any of the Gracies would complain, as they all viewed Jimmerson as a clueless idiot.

As he had all week in Denver, Jimmerson looked completely befuddled. I actually almost felt bad for him, as he seemed so utterly lost. When I gave him the gloves and shoes he looked at me quizzically and said, "Running shoes?"

"Yeah, beggars can't be choosers," I mumbled to myself as I headed for the door.

I then ran into Kathy, who told me that our official T-shirts and sweats still hadn't arrived. I was assured that everything would be there on fight day—that the entire order would be personally delivered to McNichols Arena by 3 p.m.

At this point all I could do was laugh, and say to Kathy, "This never fucking ends."

From there, I headed down to the service entrance to double check on the gear, and finding no vendor unloading my official merchandise, I headed back towards the arena floor. In the subterranean bowels of McNichols, I then ran into Sam Solomon, our elderly cut man from Philadelphia. Sam was apparently lost, and seemed a bit disoriented in his unsuccessful search for the dressing rooms. I thanked him again for being with us, gave him a hug, and then steered him in the right direction. It was an honor to have him working our fights, but I couldn't help but notice that Sam was obviously at the end of a long and distinguished career.

Making my way up the inner stairs, I bumped into Rorion. I hadn't spent much time with him all week, as he had been consumed with getting Royce ready. Rorion was wearing his tuxedo, with a white silk scarf draped around his shoulders. Tall and lean at 6-foot-2 and 165 lb., he looked like a million dollars. I now told him that the deal with SEG was finally signed. I had been so preoccupied with my own thoughts on the ride over from the hotel that I hadn't brought it up. Rorion didn't seem overly elated, and said he always knew that I'd get it all worked out. We then looked at each other in our tuxedos, which we'd bought together at the Del Amo Fashion Center in Torrance, and were silent for a long moment.

Then Rorion spoke.

"Arturo, we did it. Can you believe it?"

"We did make it, Rorion. It's been a bumpy ride, but we're here. And we're going to have a great show tonight."

With that, we hugged and then slapped each other on the shoulders. I knew that we were never more like brothers than we were on that staircase deep inside McNichols Arena, just a few minutes before the start of the Ultimate Fighting Championship. Walking in step with my friend and partner, we headed for our front row seats as the fights were about to begin.

CHAPTER 11
THE FIRST UFC

VICTORY BELONGS TO THE MOST PERSEVERING.
— NAPOLEON BONAPARTE

Quarterfinal #1—Gerard Gordeau vs. Teila Tuli

EXACTLY four years to the month when I first started working on my pitch to Wisdom Imports for the World's Best Fighter, the Ultimate Fighting Championship took flight with the twenty-six second destruction of an enormously fat Hawaiian by an icy cold Dutchman.

It was quick, brutal, a freak show, and undeniably real. I thought to myself that anyone who believed that this was going to be just another WWF-type pro wrestling rip-off, or some Japanese strong-style work, was given a harsh dose of reality. Any and all doubt evaporated into the Denver night when Gordeau's full force leg kick landed flush into Tuli's face, made all the worse because Tuli chose not to wear a mouthpiece.

When Joao Alberto Barreto stopped the fight, even though the rules clearly stipulated that the referee could not stop any fight except for a disqualification, it looked sloppy as hell, but it was also painfully real. In the midst of this chaos, I thought that you couldn't fake this level of disorganization and dissent if you'd wanted to, and you certainly couldn't fake those two crushing strikes to the face.

Once Gordeau was officially declared the winner and everything had settled down, I was overcome with a sense of embarrassment that I had actually thought that he'd given a Nazi salute prior to the fight. I now realized that he had acknowledged the four corners of McNichols Arena in a classic martial arts gesture. Gordeau was through to the semifinals, and just like that, we were on our way.

Quarterfinal #2—Zane Frazier vs. Kevin Rosier

As Rosier made his entrance walk towards the arena floor, he became blinded by the lights and smoke that Pillot had arranged, and hit his head on the lighting grid. The impact of the blow almost knocked Rosier out. But undeterred, he kept right on walking.

At the opening Bell, Rosier came out charging, and forced Frazier, who was almost 100 lb. lighter, to immediately start backpedaling. These two kickboxing "world champions" then started throwing down like we were holding this fight in the McNichols Arena parking lot.

Rosier quickly landed a huge, sloppy, and entirely effective overhand right, which put Frazier in real trouble. More right hands and a knee followed, and Frazier dropped to the mat. I thought that had Rosier known even the first thing about submissions, he would have taken Frazier's back, and looked to sink in a choke. But all that Rosier really knew was brawling, and he followed Frazier to the ground with a barrage of punches.

Frazier surprisingly countered by exploding back to his feet, with Rosier right back up with him.

From there, both fighters started punching and kneeing each other with reckless abandon and little technique. Frazier then turned things in his favor by landing a crushing knee into Rosier's cup. Every man at McNichols Arena—first and foremost Rosier himself—let out a loud groan in reaction to this illegal shot, which Hélio Vigio allowed.

Suddenly, Frazier was looking really good, as he landed powerful knees to the head and body, while also throwing some pretty effective punches.

But seemingly without warning, his gas tank hit empty. Rosier then appeared as though he knew that his moment was at hand.

Just seconds before, Frazier had been dancing and moving, but now he was standing almost dead-still, hands at his waist, mouth wide open, and chest visibly heaving.

Frazier began a slow retreat, as Rosier came forward, closed the distance, and started landing jack-hammer right hands. As his opponent fell into the fetal position, Rosier continued to land crushing punches to the top, side, and back of Frazier's head.

Two absolutely brutal foot stomps followed, the first of which actually bounced Frazier's head off of the canvas, and the towel was thrown in.

I laughed to myself that fat ass Kevin Rosier won this fight largely through superior cardio. As he'd guaranteed, his huge right hand was a factor as well.

The day before the fight, Rosier told me, "I'm like Rocky Marciano. I can take a huge punch and keep on coming. So think of me as Rocky Marciano."

I had said to him in response, "You're so big, I think of you as two Rocky Marcianos."

But true to his word, Rosier took a huge punch, as well as a pretty vicious nut-shot, and kept on coming. After four minutes, twenty seconds of utter fucking brutality, Kevin Rosier had advanced in the tournament. The crowd was losing their mind with bloodlust.

Quarterfinal #3—Royce Gracie vs. Art Jimmerson

Just prior to the third fight of the night, I moved from my front row seat to the TV production truck, to get a sense of the live PPV broadcast. As I was watching the fighter entrances on the wall of monitors, I saw that Jimmerson was only wearing one glove.

I turned to Pillot, and started saying, "Oh shit, oh shit, oh shit!" without realizing that those words were coming out of my mouth. What I never wanted was for any of our fights to look like a joke. And Jimmerson attempting to fight a Gracie Jiu-Jitsu black belt—or anyone for that matter—with just one boxing glove looked like a huge fucking joke.

Our director Lucas turned to me, and asked what this was all about.

All that I could think of was that Jimmerson had worked out that from his orthodox boxing stance, he would be able to grab Royce's gi with his ungloved right hand, and then repeatedly hit Royce with his gloved lead left hand, while Royce stood perfect still. I had no idea what was in Jimmerson's head.

This one-glove decision was absolute clown stuff, but there was nothing that I could do. Even if I had been in my front row seat, I would have been helpless to act. All that I could do now was watch unfold what I knew would be a train wreck, as I also tried hard not to think about Jimmerson's $17,000 guarantee.

Royce came out with a front kick to Jimmerson's lead left leg. In the countless hours that I'd spent at the Gracie Academy, I don't think that I'd ever seen Royce throw more than ten kicks total. I figured that this must have been something that Rickson had thought of in his role as Royce's chief strategist and trainer: establish the low kick almost as a jab, to back off the boxer. It worked beautifully. After a series of kicks, Royce shot a quick double leg takedown, dropped Jimmerson, and gracefully moved into side control at the completion of the takedown.

From there, he quickly stepped over into full mount, and I figured that it was time to start the countdown clock to Royce's victory.

Jimmerson literally had no idea what to do once he was put on his back by Royce, and both fighters knew this immediately.

All that Jimmerson could think of was to body lock Royce from the bottom position—a move greatly inhibited by his one boxing glove. Jimmerson then desperately tried to scoot backwards with the full weight of his opponent on top of him.

Out of what I could only assume was frustration, mixed with genuine fear, Jimmerson then tapped out. And then he kept tapping out again and again, as Barreto was completely oblivious to the surrender.

Royce finally had to tell Barreto that Jimmerson had conceded, and that the fight was now over.

The time was two minutes, eighteen seconds. Royce had won by submission without actually applying a submission hold. Jimmerson did not land a single punch, neither with his gloved nor ungloved fist.

The Denver crowd could not make sense of what had just happened, and responded to the finish with a chorus of boos. Only Jimmerson seemed more confused.

Royce didn't care about the crowd reaction, and neither did Rorion, Rickson and the rest of the family. This was Gracie Jiu-Jitsu at its most basic and effective, and it had worked flawlessly, sending Royce on to the semifinals.

Quarterfinal #4—Ken Shamrock vs. Pat Smith

Even though I had balked at using Smith's "250-0" record on our fight poster, I told Rich Goins to announce it during the fighter introductions. I knew that it would play really well here in Smith's hometown, and the live TV audience would certainly take note.

The stare down was intense, and the first really good one that had occurred all night.

Smith looked ready to unload his taekwondo/robotae on the man he dubbed "some goofy wrestler from Japan," who he was certain would crumble in short order.

With his hands held high, Shamrock moved forward and immediately shot inside. A quick body lock led to a wrestling lateral drop, and Smith was on his ass in about 10 seconds flat. To my surprise, Smith knew how to close guard, a basic position of Gracie Jiu-Jitsu. This, however, looked to be the only thing that Smith knew about ground fighting.

Slowly and methodically from Smith's guard, Shamrock postured up, threw a few strikes and then sat back for a heel hook.

Lacking submission defense of any kind, Smith countered by grabbing Shamrock's toes, and elbowing Shamrock's shin and calf. Completely undeterred, Shamrock fully locked on the heel hook, forcing Smith to tap out at the one-minute, 49-second mark.

Smith then stayed on the canvas for a long time, partly due to the pain of experiencing what was no doubt his first ever leg lock, and partly from the humiliation of failing so spectacularly in front of his Denver fans.

Unsure as to what had just happened to their guy, the crowd responded with a hearty round of boos. They had come to see Pat Smith kick people in the head, not have some guy in red Speedos pull on his ankle.

In response, Smith challenged Shamrock to keep fighting, as though this was a best two out of three falls pro wrestling match from the 1950s. I understood that in reality, Smith was just trying to save face. He knew that he'd lost, and he knew that he'd submitted to the excruciating painful heel hook.

There was nothing to argue, but Smith argued anyway.

Shamrock was the clear winner, and he was the final semi-finalist. The chant of "bull-shit, bull-shit" didn't seem to bother Shamrock in the least, as he headed back to his dressing room.

Semifinal #1—Gerard Gordeau vs. Kevin Rosier

As I watched him await the fighter introductions, I noticed that Rosier had a huge glob of Vaseline over his badly swollen right eye. In defeating Frazier, he had taken a great deal of punishment. For his part, Gerard Gordeau came into this semifinal with both his right hand and right foot wrapped in medical tape. I asked Dr. Cooperman about this, and he told me that Gordeau had fractured his hand from punching Tuli in the eye, and had fragments of Tuli's tooth embedded in his foot from that horrific kick to the mouth.

Looking at Rosier, I got the impression that beating Frazier was enough for him, and now he just wanted to go sit in the crowd, and drink beers the rest of the night.

But here he was, honoring his commitment, instead of dropping out.

This fight was going to be a stylistic match-up of American kickboxer vs. European kickboxer, and I didn't think that Rosier had a chance.

The contrast of styles as well as experience was immediately evident, as Gordeau's first combination of the fight was a left hand-right low kick. Rosier tried to answer with an attempted low kick of his own: toes down, and aimed at Gordeau's ankle, which brought the word feeble to my mind.

Gordeau circled out, reset, and then stepped in to deliver a full force kick to Rosier's left thigh.

Despite being a kickboxing "World Champion," Rosier had the look of a man who had never been kicked in the quadriceps before, at least not with that type of power and technique.

Gordeau then loaded up another kick, and as Rosier made an attempt to check it, Gordeau went under the raised left leg, and crushed Rosier's back right plant leg without mercy.

The Dutchman then went in for the kill, and landed a huge right hand that dropped Rosier against the base of the fence. Gordeau then proceeded to pummel Rosier, who kept trying to get up, only to be literally beaten back down by his opponent.

Rosier had fought his way back against Frazier, but this was clearly not Zane Frazier, and I knew that there would be no late rally.

Sensing the end of the fight, Gordeau delivered a vicious elbow to the head, and then a stomp to Rosier's ample gut. Rosier rose up and tapped the mat in submission, which the ref Vigio missed completely. Gordeau did see the tap, and mercifully walked away from his annihilated opponent. The towel was thrown in a few seconds later, which was spotted by the referee.

Gordeau had followed his twenty-six second squash of Teila Tuli with a 59-second demolition of Rosier, which earned him a place in the final.

I felt certain that Gordeau had engaged in tougher battles on the streets of Amsterdam against unruly brothel and hash bar owners who were late on their debt payments. In two fights, he had thrashed a pair of men who weighed in at a combined 740 plus pounds, and he hadn't even been hit.

I said out loud, to no one in particular, "Fuck, who's going to beat this guy?"

Semifinal #2—Royce Gracie vs. Ken Shamrock

While both Shamrock and Royce possessed a grappler's base and mentality, it was clear from what they wore that they came from two very different styles.

The visual contrast was amazing: lanky Royce in his spotless white gi, muscular Shamrock in his flashy red trunks.

As dismissive as the Gracies were of all other fighting styles, I knew that Rorion took Shamrock very seriously, and felt that he could be his brother's toughest opponent. He didn't tell me much about Royce's week of training in their Executive Tower Inn hotel suite, but Rorion did say that Rickson had special drills that he was putting Royce through, so as to be ready for Shamrock in case they fought.

By contrast, I got the feeling that Shamrock thought that Royce was a skinny karate guy with a worthless black belt, and that he clearly hadn't done his homework on Gracie Jiu-Jitsu. Shamrock had been grappling with monsters in Japan, and whether those fights were shoots, works, or somewhere in between, he knew how to move very large bodies around on the mat. Royce was giving away almost 40 pounds in weight.

Just like he had done against Jimmerson, Royce opened with a quick low kick. But rather than play around, he immediately followed the kick with an attempted double leg takedown. Shamrock effectively sprawled, and after a quick scramble, the two fighters were back on their feet.

Immediately Royce went for a second takedown, this time by clinching Shamrock, and pulling him into his guard. Right there, I saw a clear illustration of the confidence that comes from Gracie Jiu-Jitsu. Royce actually wanted to be on the ground, with Shamrock on top of him, feeling that he could now really go to work. From his open and active guard, Royce started landing rapid fire heel kicks to Shamrock's body.

The over-confidence of Shamrock was then evident, as from the top position, he dropped back for a heel hook, just as he had done against Pat Smith. But rather than lie there and elbow the shin, Royce followed Shamrock over, and immediately gained top position. This was as simple and reflexive as blinking for Royce, as it would have been for any Gracie Jiu-Jitsu black belt.

Shamrock then had open guard, but could do nothing with it. Royce landed two palm strikes to the side of Shamrock's head, and put heavy pressure on his grounded opponent's chest with his top game.

Seeming to having no interest in fighting from the bottom, Shamrock turned on his left hip and tried to hook Royce's right ankle, exposing his neck in the process. Like he'd probably done 10,000 times before at the Gracie Academy, Royce locked on a rear-naked choke, then positioned his opponent on all fours, and got him to submit.

Once again, our Brazilian referees fucked up the ending of a fight. Shamrock clearly tapped, not once, but five times on the mat, yet Vigio failed to see any of this.

As with Barreto at the end of the Jimmerson bout, Royce had to tell Vigio that his opponent had submitted. I could see that Shamrock was thinking about acting as though he hadn't tapped, but Royce was having none of it, as he gave both the ref and his opponent an ear full. Either through a sense of sportsmanship, or perhaps more likely because Royce was still on his back, Shamrock admitted defeat, and the fight was over in fifty seven seconds.

With that, Royce was through to the Final. Rorion's baby brother was one big step closer to showing the world that Gracie Jiu-Jitsu reigned supreme, but the fearsome Gerard Gordeau was standing in the way.

Alternate Bout—Jason DeLucia vs. Trent Jenkins

I hadn't given a guarantee to my two alternates that they would get the chance to fight, nor had I given them a guarantee of money. Basically, they got a free ticket to hang out and hope that one of the eight fighters got hurt badly enough so that they couldn't continue. Or perhaps after seeing Gordeau kick Tuli in the face, hope to hell that they weren't needed.

Right after our opening bout, once order had been restored and Gordeau was officially declared the winner, I'd hurriedly run backstage to see if Jenkins had finally arrived, and make certain that DeLucia was still eager for his potential chance in the spotlight. The sheer savagery of that fight made me think more than ever, that we just might need one or both of our stand-by fighters after all.

I was relived to find Jenkins in his dressing room, and I asked him where he'd been.

"I'm really sorry about that. I was going to take the bus here, but it was running late, so my friend gave me a ride."

Any anger that I had built up towards Jenkins for his tardiness immediately went away. Karyn Turner had been right all along. The guy was so dependable and low-maintenance that he was willing to take a fucking city bus to the Ultimate Fighting Championship.

I genuinely felt that both DeLucia and Jenkins wanted their chance to shine, and I wanted to give it to them one way or another.

But through the six fights leading up to the Final, nobody had dropped out. I didn't need one injury alternate, let alone two.

What I did need now, however, was a time filler.

None of us, Rorion and myself included, really had any idea how long these fights would go.

Gracie Jiu-Jitsu was all about being patient—taking the time to "cook" your opponent, as Rorion had always said. Maybe they needed two minutes, maybe like a young Hélio on occasion back in Brazil, they needed two or three hours. As a boxing fan, I was schooled on 15-round fights. That's 45 minutes in the ring, plus 14 minutes for the between round breaks. Pro wrestling shoots from the early 20th century would routinely last an hour. My concern going in to our broadcast was fitting in the seven fights without going over our allotted PPV time of two hours, 50 minutes, that had been drilled into my head by everyone at SEG.

As it turned out, Gordeau took a grand total of eighty-five seconds to blow through Tuli and Rosier, in advancing to the Final. Royce needed exactly three minutes, 15 seconds to dispatch Jimmerson and Shamrock, and join Gordeau in the last bout of the night.

The longest fight thus far was the Rosier vs. Frazier slugfest, and that ran four minutes, twenty seconds. Our first six bouts hadn't even produced eleven minutes of fighting. We'd yet to see Round 2.

Making my frequent runs back to the TV production truck, I knew that the commentators were clearly struggling, and would no doubt have real difficulty in killing time on-air during an extended intermission.

From my front row seat, I saw that the McNichols Arena crowd—already confused and agitated by a lot of what they saw and largely failed to understand—was getting really restless. And they were getting drunker by the minute.

Gordeau had taken a lot of damage in pummeling Tuli and Rosier, getting a fractured right hand and a right foot full of jagged tooth shards. He needed a rest period, even if only for a few minutes. I got together with Pillot and he was in complete agreement about having DeLucia and Jenkins fight

I then reached Kathy on my walkie-talkie, and told her to get our alternates ready.

"Tell them that they'll both get $1,000, with an extra $500 to the winner. And I'll seriously consider putting both of them in the next tournament."

Unless the upcoming Shamrock versus Royce bout went really long, or the victor got injured, my plan was for DeLucia and Jenkins to fight each other as soon as the second Semifinal ended.

I then alerted Campbell to my decision, which he fully endorsed

After Royce defeated Shamrock in under a minute, the green light was given. I was happy to provide both alternates the chance to show what they could do, and even happier that we had a legitimate time filler before the final.

Jenkins was in front of his hometown fans in Denver, and even those who had no idea who he was, seemed eager to support one of Colorado's own.

For DeLucia, this fight was about proving something to himself, to me, and most of all to the Gracies. He felt he was no longer just a kid from kung fu who had been easily submitted by Royce in the backroom of the Academy, but was now a man who'd used their teachings to become a complete fighter.

Both Jenkins and DeLucia came out in full karate stances, and unloaded action film-style kicks, in that they looked great, but were largely ineffective. One of Jenkins' flashy head kicks missed the mark, but grazed the bridge of DeLucia's nose, opening a small cut. At that point, DeLucia seemed to say, "Fuck this karate bullshit," and drove in for a takedown, which morphed into an outside trip, and then into a full tackle of his opponent.

Jenkins fell on his ass, squirmed to his hip, and quickly shot back to his feet. But staying tight, DeLucia followed his opponent up, locked on a waist cinch, and pulled Jenkins on top of him, as both fell to the mat. In full control, and now in single-minded pursuit of a Gracie Jiu-Jitsu finish, DeLucia sunk in a very deep rear naked choke, positioned well below Jenkins' chin. With the panicked look on his face of someone who knew that he was caught, Jenkins quickly tapped out.

DeLucia claimed victory in 52 seconds, and no doubt hoped that the Gracie Family took note. But I knew that they were focused on just one thing—getting Royce ready for the biggest moment of his life.

Final—Royce Gracie vs. Gerard Gordeau

After the alternates fight, I went backstage to see Gordeau in his locker room. His right hand was grotesquely swollen, and he was limping pretty badly on his right foot.

"You can do this right, you can fight?" I asked him, as it occurred to me I probably should have had this conversation before sending Jenkins and DeLucia out to fight each other.

But it would have spoiled the night to have an untested and previously unseen alternate suddenly appear in the Final. We had to have Gordeau.

"You're good to go, right Gerard?"

"No problem, Art Davie."

I knew that Gordeau wasn't a ground fighter, and even if he did know something about grappling and submissions, it would have been a drop in the ocean compared with Royce's knowledge and experience.

Gordeau's way to beat Royce was to establish his devastating strikes, and keep the fight standing. But I could see clearly that he had a fucked up hand, and an even more fucked up foot. I thought this guy hasn't been touched in two fights, and his body is falling apart.

In effectively using his Gracie Jiu-Jitsu to reach the Final, Royce was fresh and ready, at least physically. I kept thinking back to what Todd Hester had told me earlier in the day about Royce's breakdown in front of Rickson, and I wondered if he could continue to hold it all together. This wasn't really about winning the tournament and the $50,000 that came with it—this was about defending the Gracie Family name.

Before the Final, the entire Gracie clan, Royce included, moved to the fighting area for Hélio's award ceremony. Rorion acted as master of ceremonies, and as soon as he started talking, a number of idiots in the Denver crowd started booing and jeering. I figured that they wanted to see more fighting, and not hear a speech.

But the grumbles quickly subsided, as Hélio stood there in his dark suit, looking incredibly dignified. His sons Rickson, Relson, Rolker, Royler and Royce lined up side by side.

Rorion proclaimed, "The fighting world respectfully addresses him as the Grandmaster Hélio Gracie. But my brothers and I are proud to call him father." This heartfelt statement was greeted by cheers and applause from the audience, who I doubted had any idea who Hélio was, but seemed to appreciate the ceremony. The old man's dignity was a factor too. He radiated quiet magnetism. Hélio then accepted a kiss on the cheek from Rorion, and then the plaque, which described him as the "first ultimate fighter."

It was a really powerful moment, and I knew how much it meant to Hélio, and the entire family—but no one more so than Rorion. It hit me that by agreeing to be honored in public by his oldest son, Hélio was officially passing the torch to Rorion. Hélio had always felt that it was he, above his other brothers, even Carlos, who had worked the hardest to popularize Gracie Jiu-Jitsu in Brazil. And now he was letting it be known that he felt that Rorion, above his six other sons, was the one most responsible for carrying his legacy of Gracie Jiu-Jitsu to the U.S., and now finally, to the world.

All that was left now for Rorion on this night, was to see Royce win the Final.

At the opening bell, Gordeau started slowly and methodically moving straight ahead, as he tried to cut the angles, and trap Royce against the fence. Royce backpedaled with his hands held high, and then exploded forward at Gordeau with a low kick into an attempted double leg takedown. Gordeau sprawled, causing Royce to adjust, stand straight up into a clinch, and go for an outside trip.

Gordeau defended that as well, and with Royce in tight, moved backwards, finally grasping his fingers in the chain links of the fence to keep himself upright. Royce then grabbed a body lock and positioned himself chest-to-chest with his opponent. Gordeau now had no room to throw his strikes, and was forced to think defense, rather than offense, as he desperately worked to keep standing. Not giving an inch of space as they battled against the fence, Royce went for another outside trip, and this time hit it. He then landed on top of Gordeau in full mount.

Flat on his back, Gordeau raised his head up, and bit Royce's right ear. This illegal action was predictably missed by Vigio. Royce responded with two quick head butts, and then thrust his forearm into Gordeau's jaw. Gordeau attempted to counter by applying a side headlock, as he moved to his right hip. Royce easily escaped the headlock, and then rolled Gordeau onto his stomach. He then slid his left hand under Gordeau's neck, but couldn't quite find the rear-naked choke. Royce released, gave Gordeau another quick head butt, and then went for a second attempt at a rear-naked choke, this time leading with his right hand. With his left hand, Royce then reached across the back of Gordeau's head, and grabbed his own gi at the right shoulder. Simultaneously, he pressed his head into Gordeau's, to fully lock on the submission hold.

With his right hand, Gordeau tapped the canvas, then tapped Royce's right shoulder, then tapped the canvas again. Royce refused to break the hold. Then Gordeau tapped the canvas with his left hand, and still nothing. I could tell that Vigio actually saw the submission, as he now moved in to pull Royce off of his beaten opponent. In full-blown panic, Gordeau slapped the canvas with both hands. Royce finally let go when the referee grabbed him, and then shouted at Gordeau for having bitten his ear. It was officially ruled over at the one-minute, 44-second mark.

Royce looked furious rather than elated. But Rorion was elated, as was Hélio, Rickson, and the rest of the family. The Gracie clan mobbed Royce, and they all celebrated triumphantly. They hoisted Royce on their shoulders and paraded him across the mat. When he passed by me, our eyes met, and I impulsively took his hand and kissed it. I then laughed at my out-of-character gesture, which had come from me being so thoroughly caught up in the moment.

Next, I looked for Ethan, who had been in his front-row seat next to mine the entire night, holding and guarding my briefcase. But now he was on his feet, having jumped up to join in the victory party. Without question, Ethan was thrilled that his role model and instructor had triumphed.

"Ethan!" I screamed. "Where's my baby?"

I could tell that what I was saying didn't register with him. Then a look of abject horror overtook Ethan's face, and he covered his mouth with his hand.

"My baby, Ethan. My briefcase. I told you not to let it out of your sight. Where the fuck is it?"

"Oh shit. Don't worry, Art, I know where it is. I gave it to Royce's cousin. I'll get it. I'll get it. I'll get it."

He then turned and started running at full speed.

We'd had an oversized prop check in the amount of $50,000 created

Photo courtesy of Ethan Milius

for the championship ceremony, which I was now supposed to present to Royce. But I couldn't find that either.

I spotted Kathy, and yelled at her, "Where's the fucking giant check?"

Calm and organized as always, she told me that it was backstage, and being brought out as we spoke.

Brian Kilmeade conducted the post-fight interview with Royce, who said, "I'm just Royce, I'm always going to be. There's no change in me, money or no money. I'm not here for the money, I'm here for the honor of the family."

Here is young Ethan Milius, John Milius' son. The night of the event he was by my side right up until the end.

There was no doubt in my mind that he had indeed honored his family.

I handed Royce the huge check, and Rorion put the tournament winner medal around Royce's neck. Surrounded by his dad and brothers, Royce finally allowed himself to smile—the first time that I had seen him do so all week.

Immediately afterwards, I walked back to the TV production truck to congratulate Pillot, Campbell and Lucas. They seemed pretty happy, especially that we'd gone off the air in just under 1 hour, 55 minutes. Campbell said that this would make selling the rebroadcasts a lot easier for them. Pillot wanted to tear down our beautifully constructed fighting area, and throw it away. He told me it was like a concert set, and that you always build a new one for the next show.

"Are you crazy?" I asked him. "Leave it to me, I already rented a storage place. We're not throwing it away."

I loved the job that Harrison and Cusson had done in creating it. It was perfect, and I thought it would be insane to go through the ordeal and the expense of building a new one.

Pillot, Lucas and Campbell all agreed that the commentators had a pretty rough night, especially our play-by-play man Bill Wallace. I knew that there were some awkward moments and gaffes from my constant trips back to the production truck, but I had no idea as to what extent, until they played back some clips for me.

Wallace opened the PPV broadcast in a very matter-of-fact tone with the words "Hello ladies and gentleman. You are about to see something that you have never seen before—The Ultimate Fighting *Challenge*. Hello, I'm Bill Wallace and welcome to McNichols Arena."

At this point he belched into the microphone, which made "McNichols Arena" sound like "Mcniquoolz Oreeda."

Wallace then continued with, "excuse me, McNichols Arena in fabulous Denver, Colorado. Along with me is Jim Brown, and I'd like to introduce you to what is called the Ultimate Fighting *Challenge*."

In his opening lines, Wallace had said the name of our event wrong—twice—and sounded like he almost threw up in his mouth, live on air.

And that set the precedent for Wallace's night.

He gave a wide array of pronunciations—all wrong—for Teila Tuli and Gerard Gordeau. He consistently mispronounced Jimmerson as "Jimm-AH-son", and Rosier (correctly Roe-zher) as "Roe-ZEER." Ignoring the Portuguese pronunciation of Royce, in which the R is said like the English H, as in "Hoyce," he called him Royce with a hard R—like Rolls Royce. He also referred to as him "Roy."

Wallace didn't fare much better with the names of his on-air colleagues, calling Rod Machado "Machacho," Brian Kilmeade "Kilmore," and Rich Goins "Ron" and "Rod." Not once in the entire broadcast did he correctly refer to him as Rich.

Our tournament bracket was "the chart," the instant replay was "the rematch," our fighting area was "the octagonal octagon," and our location in Denver was mentioned numerous times as being "a mile high up in the air," as though we were floating around in that cloud city from *The Empire Strikes Back*.

And over the course of the broadcast, Wallace had these gems as well:

"Sumo is very formal, because it's a very national sport of Japan."

"You have a Kenpo stylist against basically a kickboxer that uses the boxing techniques along with the kicking techniques of taekwondo of kicking."

"Pain hurts."

"It kind of *discomboberates* you."

"We're having boxing who is basically at a disposition."

"I'm an old person, if you want to wrestle we can wrestle."

"Most fights do (end up on the ground) because you're in a bar room and that bar's kind of slippery with all that, with all that beer on the ground, and all that glass down there and everything."

"The mouth is the dirtiest part of the human body. You wouldn't think so but it is."

"Now you're going to think how maybe those kicking techniques can set up some grappling techniques, or maybe create the opening that you need for the, what you might call the *kaboomer*."

"Most boxers when they enter the ring, they're nice and wet already."

And, "It's kind of ironic that Royce Gracie's going to wear his judo top."

Of course it was not a "judo top" and there was nothing ironic about Royce wearing it.

I knew that we had thrown Wallace in the deep end of the pool by asking him to switch with Jim Brown, and move from color analyst to play-by-play. But he had been so incredibly arrogant from the moment he arrived in Denver: dismissing Gracie Jiu-Jitsu at their seminar, not doing his broadcast prep work, acting like a know-it-all, and generally taking a condescending attitude with everyone in sight. It was hard for me to have any sympathy.

I'd hoped that Kathy Long would give it back to Wallace all night on air, as an adversary or contrarian, but she was just kind of bland.

Kilmeade was absolutely clueless in his fighter interviews, asking questions that would have seemed inane coming from an 8-year-old.

Machado and Goins were decent, but both seemed nervous, and a bit overmatched.

For his part, our superstar Jim Brown had very little to say, especially anything of real substance.

But towards the very end of the show, Brown did utter something extremely profound, "What we've learned tonight is that fighting is not what we thought it was."

CHAPTER 12
MONSTERS BALL

AN HONOR IS NOT DIMINISHED BY BEING SHARED.
— LOIS McMASTER BUJOLD

AFTER departing the TV production truck, I headed to the dressing rooms, where everything was still pretty chaotic. Absolutely everyone was exhausted at this point, myself included. After the first two bouts, with four fighters injured and only two ambulances, Kathy had ordered up a third ambulance. Later, she was so convinced that every fighter was going to need an ambulance, she called 911 to beg for additional medical help. Kathy actually had to send one of the fighters to the hospital in a taxi, as things began to spin out of control.

As I wandered around in the backstage area, I ran into Kathy, who had a drink in her hand.

"What are you doing? It's still showtime! Why are you drinking?"

But then I stared at her face, and I immediately shut up. Kathy looked like she had been in a war zone. We all did.

The next evening was our Grand Masked Ball and Supper, with all of the fighters, their camps, friends and family invited, as well as the staffs of W.O.W. Promotions and SEG and our VIP guests—basically everyone who had been involved in the Ultimate Fighting Championship who was with us in Denver.

Kathy had long since suggested the masked ball theme, as she wanted the party to feel like something truly special and elegant for all in attendance. She booked the main ballroom at the Executive Tower Inn, and distributed masks to everyone at the door. In an odd moment of serendipity, Sally Star had discovered that there was a hair dressers' convention taking place at the hotel, and they had a huge carnival mask as their central display. Sally asked if we could have it for our masked ball, and the hair dresser conventioneers were happy to oblige.

The party began at 8 p.m., and was listed on the invitations as "black tie." I didn't expect everyone to wear tuxedos and ball gowns—but I hoped that our guests would be encouraged to dress up, at least a little bit, to give the evening a touch of class.

W.O.W.
PROMOTIONS

V.I.P.
Invitation

Rorion Gracie
&
Arthur Davie
The promoters of

THE ULTIMATE
FIGHTING
CHAMPIONSHIP

Invite you to attend a

Grand Masked Ball
and Supper

Executive Tower Inn
8:00pm, Saturday
November 13th, 1993

Black Tie
Masks will be provided at the door

Photo courtesy of Art Davie archives/W.O.W. Promotions

This is the ticket to the Masked Ball & Dinner on Saturday, November 13, 1993. This was an opportunity for the fighters to relax and party. For the staff of W.O.W. Promotions and Semaphore Entertainment Group, who were almost as exhausted as the fighters, it was just as welcome.

Campbell walked in and looked completely wiped out, as well as fairly drunk.

"After a show, it's like I've given birth," he told me. "I need a day or two to come down. I'm OK but I've got to process this thing."

I looked at him and felt a tremendous kinship. He had become my friend and confidant throughout this entire process, despite all of our disagreements, and all of my frustrations.

"I can't believe you carry a gun. You're a fucking crazy cowboy, aren't you?" he said to me slurring his words.

Campbell then looked around the room, and in a very loud whisper said, "Art, there's a lot of people I don't know wearing masks here. This is like a fucking Fellini movie!"

I laughed, and then asked him, "So, are we a hit Campbell?"

"I think so, but we'll all know when the numbers come in on Monday. All we can do now is wait."

Back in late August when Campbell told me that SEG would price the PPV broadcast at $14.95, he also mentioned that the target was 50,000 buys.

"But I'll be pretty happy with 25,000, and so will Bob," he had said at the time.

I had no idea how many people had actually ordered the Ultimate Fighting Championship, and 24 hours after the fights, I still didn't have a sense of how we'd done. The live audience at McNichols Arena was decent with 3,013 tickets sold, and including the comps, 3,997 total people in attendance. But if we hadn't shrunk the seating area with piping and drapes, it would have looked empty on TV.

All I could do now was be optimistic. It was better than the alternative.

Rosier was the first fighter to arrive at the party, and he was wearing a circa 1975-looking tux, complete with a huge flower cummerbund. He looked as joyous as if he'd won the tournament, and greeted me with a huge hug. He then proclaimed that he was my long-lost son, and that he was now going to call me "Dad." Rosier then excused himself, and said that he wanted to go look for John McCarthy, so that he could challenge him to a pizza-eating contest.

Gordeau soon followed, and seemed as cool and expressionless as he had throughout the week. He thanked me for the opportunity, and seemed to feel really good about his performance as the runner-up, and the $15,000 check that came with it. Gordeau wore a T-shirt and tuxedo tie, as well as thick tape on his horribly swollen right hand. He was limping noticeably, and I was certain that his right foot was bandaged as well.

"Are you sure that you're okay, Gerard?" I asked him.

"No problem, Art Davie."

The Gracies then came into the ballroom, with Rorion leading the way. We both were wearing our tuxedos from the night before, and we laughed at the sight, as we gave each other a warm embrace.

Hélio looked happier than I had ever seen him, and Royce seemed incredibly relieved.

Shamrock wasn't far behind, arriving with his adoptive dad, Bob, and his wife, Tina. He appeared emotionally devastated, and really embarrassed. He told me that he was going to devote himself to getting a rematch with Royce, and then making sure that things went his way the second time around.

Frasier then appeared, and started in at me about the thin Denver air, and his breathing problems, and not being able to tape his knuckles, and the event being rigged for Royce to win. I was in no mood for a debate, so I thanked him for his involvement, and told Frazier that like the other nine fighters, he should be incredibly proud to have been a part of this.

"Benny Urquidez and Dennis Alexio could have been here. But they turned me down, and so did a lot of other guys. You had the balls to step up and take part in this Zane. That's a really big deal."

When Jimmerson showed up, he approached me, and began alternating between saying that he had done his best, and that he should have done things differently. I could tell that he was pretty humiliated. We both knew that he didn't earn that $17,000. The guy was a top ten cruiserweight in the world, and he never even landed a punch. I still couldn't figure him out. After almost an entire week together, Jimmerson remained a complete mystery to me.

Pat Smith looked angry and utterly distraught when he walked into the party. If anyone seemed relieved at the opportunity to hide their face behind a mask, it was him. Smith really believed that he was going to knock out everyone on his way to an easy $50,000. During the week at the hotel, he'd told me that he was "impervious to pain." This apparently excluded the wrenching pain from a well-applied heel hook, but I didn't bring that up. As flaky and volatile as Smith was, I couldn't help but like him. He told me that whenever I was ready for our second event, he would be back, and he'd win it. "I just have to work on this jiu-jitsu thing," he said.

I spotted Jason DeLucia and thanked him for being so flexible all week, and for stepping in to fight at the last second. DeLucia asked me if I would find a place for him in our next tournament, and I told him that I'd give it strong consideration.

The party was now rolling, with dinner, lots of drinks, a DJ and dancing. But I realized that we were missing Trent Jenkins and Teila Tuli.

Since Jenkins was a Denver local, I figured he had decided not to come back down to the hotel. This disappointed me, as I wanted to thank him for living up to his billing as a really reliable person. As was the case with his opponent DeLucia, Jenkins was in an awkward position as an alternate, not knowing if and when he'd fight. And just like DeLucia, when I needed him, he was ready—without complaint.

I asked Rorion if he knew where Tuli was, and he said that he'd find out.

Rorion quickly dispatched one of his brothers to Tuli's room. Apparently, Tuli was really embarrassed—embarrassed that he had been defeated, embarrassed that he was missing a tooth, and embarrassed that he didn't have any formal clothes to wear to the masked ball. After some prodding, Tuli finally put on a T-shirt and another Polynesian skirt thing and headed down. When he arrived with his brother and two cousins, Tuli asked me if he was welcome at the party.

"Of course you're welcome, Teila. This party is for you guys—the fighters."

"I'm really sorry about last night, Mr. Davie."

"Teila, you have nothing to apologize about. I'm so happy that you fought for us, and I know you did your best."

Just as had occurred at the Denver Airport at the beginning of the week when I gave him his $6,000 in cash, Tuli lit up with a huge smile.

The mood in the ballroom was celebratory, as all of the tension and anxiety that had built up throughout the week now disappeared. As I made the rounds with a single-malt scotch and a Cuban cigar, I noticed that there was no macho posturing

Photo courtesy of Art Jimmerson's personal collection

Rorion and I are addressing the crowd right before dinner. Masks were handed out at the door and almost everyone came in fancy dress or evening clothes.

going on, no tough guy antics of any sort. Instead, there was a sense of camaraderie, brotherhood even.

When everyone had arrived and the festivities were in full swing, I asked the DJ to kill the music, so that Rorion and I could say a few words.

Just as he had always been after a back-room Gracie Challenge at the academy, Rorion was extremely gracious to the defeated fighters. There was no gloating on his part, no "I told you so" type comments of any kind. His attitude of respect was shared by Hélio, Royce and all of the family members in attendance.

After Rorion thanked everyone, I then took my turn to address the ballroom.

"You fighters are like the X-15 test pilots of the 1960s, going into the stratosphere where no one has gone before."

I'm not sure that everyone got my analogy, but I thought it was fitting. We'd all just been a part of something that was pioneering, revolutionary even, and these were the men who put their bodies and reputations on the line, without fear or hesitation.

Royce Gracie and his beautiful girlfriend, Marianne. Both are wearing masks but Royce emerged almost without a scratch from the previous night's battles and doesn't need to cover up. That couldn't be said for many of the other fighters.

By 11 p.m., the liquor was flowing freely, and Tuli had become the life of the party, leading the way on the dance floor.

I was fascinated by the conversations that were going on: Royce and Gordeau, Jim Brown and Hélio, Tuli and Rosier.

From what I could see, everyone now looked to be having a great time, apart from Smith and Shamrock.

Smith seemingly couldn't take it anymore, and found me on his way to the exit.

"You'd better bring me back for the next one," he told me before pointing to Shamrock and saying "I'm gonna get that fucker," as his parting words.

Shamrock appeared as though he was trying to enjoy himself, but just couldn't. He still didn't seem to be able to process how that skinny kid in a gi had beaten him in less than one minute. Shamrock didn't look pissed off to me, as much as he looked disgusted.

Behind Rorion and the rest of the Gracies, I noticed Rickson seated at a back table. He was with his wife Kim, and looked even angrier than Smith and more miserable than Shamrock. I wasn't sure if I should visit. Rickson's son Rockson, also dressed in a tuxedo, was there at the table, as was Frederico Lapenda. A guest of Rickson's at the event, Lapenda was a suave looking Brazilian, who had flown in from LA to support his countrymen. I finally decided to stop by the table and introduce myself to Lapenda. I quietly asked him how Rickson was doing. Lapenda smiled, and let me know with a clear gesture that the Gracie family pot was about to boil over. I understood immediately.

I had already surmised from the looks, the hand-waving, and the raised voices that Kim was probably badgering her husband. It seemed to me that it was most likely about how Rickson should have been the Gracie in the Ultimate Fighting Championship, how that $50,000 should have been theirs, and how his big brother Rorion had fucked him out of his rightful place. I glanced over at Rickson, who seemed to be growing visibly more upset by the minute. He kept alternating between glowering at Rorion who was one table away, and trying to ignore his wife.

Once again, I realized that I would never completely understand the Gracie family dynamic. I thought that the Rorion-Rickson relationship was strained, until I saw them together all week in Denver, where everything seemed to be fine. Rickson was Royce's main trainer and chief second at the Ultimate Fighting Championship, and worked his ass off so that Royce would be properly prepared to win the tournament.

Photo courtesy of Art Jimmerson's personal collection

The legendary Rickson Gracie and boxer Art Jimmerson. Rickson, the family champion, didn't get to fight in the UFC, but coached/trained his younger brother Royce to the win. Jimmerson lost to Royce in the first round by submission.

But once Royce won, Kim was apparently furious that Rorion had chosen Royce over her husband. The spotlight was now on Royce as the family champion, and not on Rickson, where she felt it rightfully belonged. All I knew was that if things really got heated between the brothers, it was best that we all leave quickly and quietly. I shook hands with Lapenda and told him, "I look forward to meeting you again. Call me when you get back to LA." Then I excused myself and moved on.

The DJ cranked the music, the bartenders kept everybody's glass full, and Montecristo #2 cigars were smoked heartily by a number of us.

Just after 3 a.m., I led a conga line on the dance floor, which included Tuli, Rosier and Kathy. Trying so hard to play gracious host, I realized that I had pretty much ignored my Girl Friday all night. I asked her to sit down with me, and I then got us both fresh drinks.

Kathy told me that after the fights had finished, she threw up in the bathroom from all of the stress. This shocked me, as I thought that Kathy was actually immune to stress—as she always seemed so calm and in control.

"You know, you're a pretty tough guy to work for."

"I couldn't have pulled this off without you," I replied.

We stayed talking until 4 a.m., when I noticed that the party was in its final stages. Rorion and Campbell had long since said their goodbyes, and only a hearty few remained. Kathy and I were laughing and drinking, and she said, "You know you really should go out with me. You know, like on a date. Don't you like me? I think you do."

"Would you like to continue this conversation in my room, Kathy?" I replied.

"I would, Art. Very much."

As we headed to the elevator hand in hand, I paused for a moment, but then kept walking, as I knew that I'd left my mask behind.

That's me leading a conga line at 3 a.m. as the festivities at the Masked Ball wound down. Some of the Gracie youngsters got in on the fun, too.

Photo courtesy of Art Jimmerson's personal collection

AFTERWORD
BY SEAN WHEELOCK

I first saw the poster for the Ultimate Fighting Championship at my gym—a Gold's Gym in Kansas City, where I was no doubt the scrawniest, youngest and least likely member. It immediately drew me in with its lineup of style vs. style match-ups, listing sports that I had heard of (boxing, karate, sumo, kickboxing) and those that I hadn't, which sounded incredibly exotic and mysterious (jiu-jitsu, Savate, shoot fighting, taekwondo). As a life-long fan of boxing, pro wrestling, action movies and fistfights in general, how could I resist the tantalizing question that was asked on that poster: "Who Will Be The Ultimate Fighter?"

My mom didn't even hesitate when I asked her if she'd spend the $14.95 for the Pay-Per-View broadcast. She was my regular benefactor for all things Evander Holyfield and WrestleMania, which cost far more than this out-of-nowhere oddity. Well, not quite out of nowhere. I had read a few articles in fight magazines about these new kinds of bouts that were happening in Japan, which one writer had described as "real pro wrestling." The names Bart Vale, Volk Han, and Akira Maeda were mentioned, and I was thoroughly mesmerized. But I was also old enough to be skeptical. Real pro wrestling? Seriously?

It hadn't been that long before that I'd fully bought into the world of kayfabe—the illusion that pro wrestling was indeed real. Every match, every feud, every angle. I was a total mark as a kid, regularly attending

Thursday night Central States cards at Memorial Hall in downtown Kansas City, Kansas, and devotedly watching the weekly Georgia Championship Wrestling on WTBS and the monthly WWF shows on USA Network. I believed every second.

Now older and a bit wiser, when I heard about these fights in Japan, and then saw this poster for the Ultimate Fighting Championship, I wasn't quite convinced. Sure, convinced enough to ask my mom to pony up for an added charge on our Tele-Cable bill, but not fully in.

But still, I had to see for myself. There was literally no way that I was going to miss the chance to watch real fights on live TV. Genuine no-holds-barred throw downs.

On the big night of November 12, 1993—a Friday that I remember clearly—I popped a blank VHS tape into my Sony VCR, hit the record button, and settled in. Unlike all of the boxing and WWF Pay-Per-Views that my mom bought for me, I didn't invite anybody over for this one. Looking back, I think that I was kind of embarrassed—not that I loved fighting, all of my friends did—but that I may have been suckered in by a full-on work. It was one thing to buy a pro wrestling show, as we all now knew the score on those. But on this, I just wasn't sure.

My worst fears seemed to be realized as soon as the live Pay-Per-View began, with the incredibly cheesy production values, and the unintentionally hilarious commentary. I was a long way from being a professional broadcaster then, but I already knew that opening a show as the lead announcer did by calling the event the wrong name, and then belching into the microphone, was not a mark of quality.

It got worse when I saw the fighters for the opening bout: an enormously fat Hawaiian guy and a tall, skinny, balding guy. These two looked just like the prelim jobbers of my childhood, who I had seen toil in the Central States circuit. Fuck, I knew it. This was just another pro wrestling show. A complete rip off.

But then something absolutely incredible happened. The enormously fat Hawaiian guy charged at the tall, skinny, balding guy, got clipped by a clean upper cut, and dropped on his ass. In an instant, the tall, skinny, balding guy unloaded a full-on kick to the enormously fat Hawaiian guy's face. Even in those low-def TV days, I could see a tooth go flying into the crowd on impact. It got even better as the tall, skinny, balding guy re-set, and then threw a hard, clean, bare-fisted punch directly into his now helpless opponent's eye, which was immediately bloodied.

I had never seen anything like this in my life. No one had, not on live TV anyway. Even Mike Tyson at his baddest-man-on-the-planet-best could not come even remotely close to delivering the level of shock and violence contained in that brutal head kick delivered by the man who I came to know as Gerard Gordeau.

There was no doubt now—this was all real, and in that instant, I was fully hooked. Chaos followed, which made it even better, and even more real, as a scripted show would never have appeared so disorganized and out of control. People poured into the cage, the referee seemed clueless, everyone was arguing, and the enormously fat Hawaiian guy, who I quickly learned was named Teila Tuli, was actually hurt. Really hurt. So hurt in fact that the fight was over, just like that.

In less than 30 seconds, the world had been introduced to the sport that would come to be known as mixed martial arts, but didn't even have a name on that autumn night. If Art Davie had asked his friend, Academy Award nominated screenwriter John Milius, to script the opening of the first Ultimate Fighting Championship, it couldn't have gone any better. Cringe-inducing violence, followed by utter pandemonium.

Oh yeah, this was real, this was my new favorite sport, and this was going to alter the direction of my life moving forward. I know three other people who watched this broadcast live on Pay-Per-View as I did, and I don't think that it's a coincidence that all of us have gone on to careers in the MMA industry (one of those three is the outstanding fighter and UFC veteran Ben Saunders). There was something so raw, so mesmerizing, and so real about the first Ultimate Fighting Championship that you were either going to be repulsed or captivated. I was, of course, captivated, and I have been ever since.

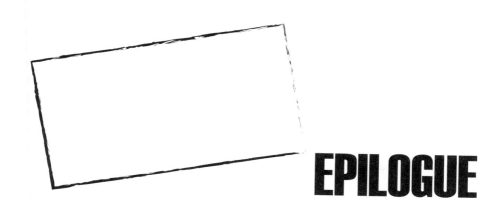

EPILOGUE

ZEUS DOES NOT BRING ALL MEN'S PLANS TO FULFILLMENT.
— HOMER, XIX, 328

WE did 86,592 Pay-Per-View buys on the first Ultimate Fighting Championship and 286,256 buys at UFC 5. The first UFC was a big hit and the franchise just kept growing. How do you explain the success of the UFC? In succeeding years, the event spawned a new sport (MMA) and an entire industry. Students, teachers, lifestyle clothing companies, gyms, seminars, promotions, amateur and professional fighters are all now part of the scene spawned years ago by the success of the first UFC. It's amazing. Years later, I discovered a book that does a good job of explaining the phenomenon of the UFC and mixed martial arts, *The Black Swan*. It describes historical events that come as a surprise, have a major impact and are often rationalized after the fact with the benefit of hindsight.

The writer, Nassim Nicholas Taleb, who is an economist and philosopher, employs the metaphor of the black swan. For a long time people only thought swans were white. Black ones were extremely rare. Taleb explains the role of high profile, hard-to-predict, rare events— beyond the realm of normal expectations in the fields of science, literature, film, technology and politics. He also illuminates the bias that makes people blind to the massive role of the rare event in history. For me, that really describes the UFC and the advent of MMA. Very few believed it was possible and only now, years later, are people trying to understand and explain what happened.

But, after the first UFC, a firestorm erupted. The politicians and newshounds smelled blood and began dogging the event. The political opposition soon found a champion in Arizona Senator John McCain. He became the head cheerleader for the "stop-the-carnage-before-Western-Civilization-comes-to-an-end" movement. McCain called the UFC "human cock fighting" and was soon joined by such media powerhouses as the *New York Times*. McCain wrote a letter to all fifty U.S. governors asking them to ban the UFC. Mayors in cities, including Denver, where we had staged events, soon found the UFC "objectionable" on moral grounds.

I just buried myself in my work as the event's promoter, booker and matchmaker.

But the need to hire both civil and criminal attorneys to keep the UFC going as the political and media pressure grew convinced me that we would eventually be squeezed to death. So, after UFC 5 I gave it a lot of thought and made a decision to sell the event to our Pay-Per-View partner, Semaphore Entertainment Group (SEG). I had to convince Rorion that it was the right decision.

To Rorion, the UFC was a means to an end. He saw it was a way to gain attention for Gracie Jiu-Jitsu and the event had truly supercharged his business. He didn't want to sell. To me the UFC was an end in itself—a franchise—but I was hearing the wolves howling for our scalps and the monster we had created. I also knew that Rorion was going to pull Royce out of the event because time limits and judges, which I was considering, were poison for the Gracie style. Rorion and I were heading towards a showdown.

The climax came on a sunny afternoon in April 1995. I asked Rorion to come over to the new W.O.W. office. After a few pleasantries, I got down to business. I asked him about Royce and the next UFC. Rorion was non-committal about Royce, but I could tell he was thinking about a hiatus for his kid brother.

And then, I talked about the rule changes I was considering: The referee would be given the authority to restart the fight. If two fighters were entangled in a position on the ground and the action had stagnated, the referee could stop the fight and restart the competitors on their feet. And I was considering gloves, which would allow strikers to hit harder. Rorion knew this spelled the end of the Gracies in the UFC.

As we argued, both of us understood that a line was drawn in the sand. I told Rorion that the political pressure was becoming worse and I did not see it getting any better. And the spectacle we had founded was going to morph into a sport. It was inevitable in my opinion.

Another reason I wanted to sell was that I wasn't sure that SEG wasn't screwing us. After five events, I was convinced that Bob Meyrowitz, an experienced concert promoter who knew the ins and outs of live event promotion better than I ever could, was padding expenses. I did not have a lot of proof because SEG always had a good explanation handy and any discrepancies I caught were corrected. But I still had a feeling Meyrowitz just considered Rorion and me talent and not real partners.

We rowed back and forth, and at one point, Rorion had tears in his eyes. I think he felt betrayed by me. But I prevailed and a deal was struck with Meyrowitz. He had always wanted to buy Rorion out. Earlier, he had asked me if that was possible and I said, "No, you can buy W.O.W., but not our individual shares."

When we distributed the proceeds, Rorion wanted to give our 27 investors, most of whom were his students, more than the 10 percent originally allocated to them. Unhappy with the original split with Rorion, I insisted that any bonus for the investors had to come from him. In the end, I got 40 percent, Rorion received 35 percent and our investors got 25 percent. I felt it was fair to everyone and that I had earned the lion's share.

Two weeks after the sale of W.O.W.'s assets to SEG was concluded, Meyrowitz called and asked me to come on board as booker and matchmaker. I took over as Commissioner of a new sanctioning body, The Ultimate Fighting Alliance, and began to install the rules necessary to morph the UFC from a spectacle into an actual sport. Meyrowitz and I had not talked about him hiring me at all during the sale, but I knew he would have to hire me. I had created the event.

Meyrowitz was convinced that he and SEG could weather the political storm and was thrilled to be able to buy W.O.W.'s stake. I was glad to sell. I stayed on board as a contract employee—doing the booking/matchmaking and acting as UFA Commissioner for a total of 18 UFC events until January 1998.

When asked later by Tad Friend, a writer doing a story about the UFC for *New York Magazine* in 1996 why I decided to sell to SEG, I coyly said, "I had a million reasons."

The curtain call came at a surprise dinner Kathy Kidd had organized for Royce at his favorite restaurant in Redondo Beach in April 1995. I convinced Rorion that we should buy a real samurai sword from Japan, emblazon it with the event logos memorializing Royce's victories in the UFC and present it to him.

The dinner was bittersweet. I remember Clay McBride, our scribe and investor, was at the bar with his wife. I joined them for a drink. But it was clear that I had become the enemy by forcing the sale to SEG and some hard words were exchanged. A little later, Royce was duly surprised by the party, as he thought he was just joining some friends for dinner. He got misty when we presented him with the sword. It was a sweet moment. But that dinner marked the end of my relationship with Rorion and the Gracies. Nevertheless, the tall, magnetic Brazilian and I have remained on friendly terms over the years, I'm glad to say.

One good thing that came out of the UFC for me was Kathy Kidd. After we sold our share of the UFC to SEG, I began to date her exclusively. She and I were married on New Year's Eve, 1995. John and Elaine McCarthy were in attendance, but no one else from the UFC came.

Kathy and I stayed together for several years. She had become my closest friend and we still worked best when we were tackling a business project. One of the ventures we attempted together was a Las Vegas stage production bringing Bruce Lee to life as a hologram. Another project

Kathy Kidd and I were married on New Year's Eve 1995. This photo was taken at a restaurant in May 1996 in Henderson, Nevada.

Photo courtesy of Art Davie's personal collection

was a proposal to the city fathers to stage a monster laser show and light up the Vegas Strip on New Year's Eve in 1999. We parted as a married couple in 2002 but have remained close ever since. I still consider her one of my best friends.

In 2001, Lorenzo and Frank Fertitta along with Dana White formed a company (Zuffa LLC) and bought the UFC from Bob Meyrowitz. Over the next few years they did a great job moving it into the mainstream. For the 20th anniversary show in November 2013, they invited Meyrowitz, Rorion, Campbell, David Isaacs and me to be their guests. Everyone but Meyrowitz came, and it was grand to be there beside the Octagon once again with Rorion. In the years following my exit from the UFC, I never attended another UFC show or produced another MMA event.

I crossed Chuck Norris' path again in 2004 when I pitched him a TV pilot called *Spear*, about a rodeo rider turned bounty hunter. There were a lot of us in his living room that day and during a break, someone mentioned the UFC. Chuck turned to me and, in front of everybody, announced, "I was wrong about that." It was a generous gesture. For me, besides being a star, Norris turned out to be a gentleman with a lot of class.

For the 20th anniversary, magazine and TV media from three continents approached me to talk about the old days. Interviewers asked me if I ever had any reservations or regrets about selling. *Sports Illustrated* asked me how I felt about being out of the picture. I told them that I was driving down Sunset Boulevard in LA a few years ago and spied a billboard advertising the UFC. I said, "It's like being a divorced father and watching someone else raise your kid," and then I added, "The light changed and I moved on."

Sean Wheelock, the play-by-play commentator for the UFC's main competitor, Bellator, approached me about a book that would tell the story of the first UFC. Sean kept insisting that if I hadn't started that quest, MMA would never have happened. Several others had approached me over the years about doing a book, but for some reason nothing came of it. The book you are reading now would not have happened if not for this persistent, talented sports commentator and super MMA fan. Sean persevered, much as I had 20 years earlier.

One last thought: I always knew that other than soccer, martial arts are the one truly global sport. Almost every country has some form of it. And everybody on the planet loves a good fight. It's in our DNA. MMA was destined to become huge.

That about sums it up for me. I'm grateful for what life has delivered. Most people don't get that much. When I was interviewed by FOX TV in the U.S. for a 20-year retrospective on the UFC, I said, "It was a great ride and a great experience; and I'm sorry I didn't take the full ride. But down deep, I know that long after I'm gone, MMA will still be around. Few men can say that much of what they do in life will survive them. This will survive me."

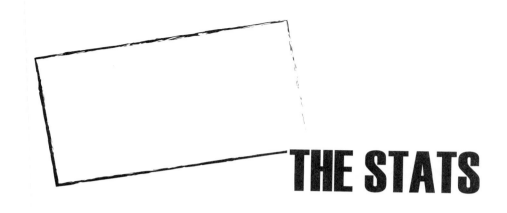

THE STATS

THE ULTIMATE FIGHTING CHAMPIONSHIP
November 12, 1993
McNichols Sports Arena
Denver, Colorado

Quarterfinals:

Gerard Gordeau def. Teila Tuli, TKO (head kick and punch), 0:26 Round 1 (Referee: Joao Alberto Barreto)

Kevin Rosier def. Zane Frazier, TKO (punches and stomps), 4:20 Round 1 (Referee: Hélio Vigio)

Royce Gracie def. Art Jimmerson, Submission (full mount), 2:18 Round 1 (Referee: Joao Alberto Barreto)

Ken Shamrock def. Pat Smith, Submission (heel hook), 1:49 Round 1 (Referee: Hélio Vigio)

Semifinals:

Gerard Gordeau def. Kevin Rosier, TKO (elbows and stomp), 0:59 Round 1 (Referee: Joao Alberto Barreto)

**Rosier submitted via tap out due to strikes. Referee Barreto failed to recognize submission, thus the fight was recorded as a TKO.

Royce Gracie def. Ken Shamrock, Submission (rear-naked choke), 0:57 Round 1 (Referee: Hélio Vigio)

Alternate Bout:
> Jason DeLucia def. Trent Jenkins, Submission (rear-naked choke), 0:52 Round 1 (Referee: Joao Alberto Barreto)

Final:
> Royce Gracie def. Gerard Gordeau, Submission (rear-naked choke), 1:44 Round 1 (Referee: Hélio Vigio)

Total Fight Purse:
> $102,500
> Royce Gracie: $50,000 (as tournament winner)
> Art Jimmerson: $18,000 ($17,000 guaranteed; $1,000 as losing quarterfinalist)
> Gerard Gordeau: $15,000 (as tournament runner-up)
> Teila Tuli: $7,000 ($6,000 guaranteed; $1,000 as losing quarterfinalist)
> Kevin Rosier: $4,000 (as losing semifinalist)
> Ken Shamrock: $4,000 (as losing semifinalist)
> Jason DeLucia: $1,500 (as winning alternate)
> Zane Frazier: $1,000 (as losing quarterfinalist)
> Pat Smith: $1,000 (as losing quarterfinalist)
> Trent Jenkins: $1,000 (as losing alternate)

Attendance:
> 3,997 (3,013 paid; 984 complimentary)

Pay-Per-View Buys:
> 86,592

W.O.W. PROMOTIONS INVESTORS
> Michael Dash, Zane Rothschild, Mark Fiocco, Edward Bowman, Stephen & Deborah Maxwell, Clay McBride, Samuel Rand, Dr. Jeffrey Hudson, Gary Fiocco, Dr. Edward Gewiss, Mr. & Mrs. Bresler, Richard Bresler, Stanley Kuliga, Marvin Silver, Brion Pollock, Jonathan & Adrianne Pannell, Maria V. Fulay, Brent Fichter, Clayton T. Kirio, Virgil Thomas, Charles E. Espania, Jr., Christopher R. Laird, Ronald Kosakowski, Mark T. Lieberman, Randolph R. Krager, Vance Inouye and Mei-Fing Chiu.

INDEX

ACKNOWLEDGEMENTS

THERE are many people to acknowledge and thank for their help and participation with this book. So, if I left anyone out, please accept my sincerest apology. But, as near as my aging memory permits, here is a list of the people who helped with or inspired this book:

Campbell McLaren, Rorion Gracie, Kathy Kidd, Les & Prentice Smith, Bill Stinde, John McCarthy, Gerard Gordeau, Teila Tuli, Jason DeLucia, Trent Jenkins, Charlie Anzalone, Mark Fiocco, Richard Bresler, Frederico Lapenda, Earnest Hart, Jr., Reylson Gracie, Todd Hester, Jake Rossen, Ethan Milius, Dave Mandel, Russell Naftal, and Brett Kawzynski. I'm also in debt to Bob Snodgrass, my publisher who believed in this book from the beginning, Jim Bradford, my editor and most of all to Sean Wheelock, whose help and support made this book possible.

AUTHOR BIOS

ART DAVIE comes from the advertising agency world. He was an account executive and copywriter in West Coast advertising agencies in the USA for many years.

But that was before he had an epiphany in 1993 and created The Ultimate Fighting Championship (UFC) that pitted boxers, wrestlers and martial artists against each other to discover the king of combat sports. The UFC franchise, which exploded on Pay-Per-View TV, and is still going strong decades later, spawned the worldwide sports phenomenon known as mixed martial arts (MMA). In addition to being the UFC's creator, Davie was the co-producer, booker, and matchmaker, and he served as the Commissioner of Ultimate Fighting.

Davie attended New York Military Academy, St. John's University and Pace College in New York. After military service in the Marines in Vietnam, Davie worked with youth gangs in New York City. He owned a

car dealership and an advertising agency in San Diego. He currently makes his home in Pahrump, Nevada and serves as an example of rugged entrepreneurism

For more documents, photos and info on the first UFC and to contact Art Davie, go to www.isthislegalthebook.com

Photo courtesy of Russell Naftal

SEAN WHEELOCK holds the distinction of being the only person to serve as a play-by-play commentator on the FIFA World Cup, the Super Bowl, U.S. Open tennis and world championship fights in mixed martial arts.

Wheelock is the play-by-play commentator for Bellator MMA, which airs nationally across the United States and Canada on Spike TV. Prior to joining Bellator in 2010, Wheelock worked as the commentator for Pride FC, Affliction and the M-1 Challenge.

One of the best known American voices in both MMA and soccer, Wheelock's broadcasting work has taken him to over 25 countries, including Germany, for the 2006 FIFA World Cup.

Wheelock has served as the British Broadcasting Corporation's North American sports correspondent since 1996, and has called three Super Bowls for the BBC.

A lifelong Kansan, Wheelock lives in the Kansas City suburb of Shawnee, Kansas with his wife Kelly, originally of England, and daughters Ellee and Hadlee.

This is his second book.

Photo courtesy of Eric Coleman

BABY
S.T.E.P.S.
to better
Sleep#

How to gently coach your child to peaceful naps and rested nights

BABY S.T.E.P.S. to better sleep#

- One-size-fits-all doesn't work - Find your sleep solution today!
- Including a 30% off coupon for Baby Sleep Site membership

Nicole Johnson
Lead Baby Sleep Consultant

The
BABY SLEEP SITE®
Helping you and your child sleep

Baby S.T.E.P.S. to Better Sleep

Copyright © 2016 Kiddy World Publishing
Written by: Nicole Johnson
Cover and internal design by: Andrei Andras
ISBN 978-15-40587-95-4
NUR 853

Pick Nick's Brain LLC
7385 North State Route 3
Suite #127
Westerville, OH 43082
United States

CONTENTS

FOREWORD

It's no accident that the first word of this book's title is "baby". That perfectly captures what's so unique about this particular book, and what's so unique about Nicole Johnson herself. Nicole's approach to sleep coaching is so unique and so effective simply because she puts your baby first. Your child's unique temperament, personality, and sleep challenges are at the forefront when you use Nicole's sleep coaching approach.

I should know; I've experienced it firsthand! My oldest daughter did not sleep well. At a year of age, she still required attention many times during the night. I remember crying in the bookstore as I read sleep books that didn't really address my individual needs. The books all implied there was only one right way and that I was failing if I didn't do it that way. Someone finally referred me to Nicole's website. The first thing I read was how children's and parent's temperaments need to be considered when developing a sleep plan. That was such a relief to me, and with that consolation, I was able to follow through with a plan that made sense for my family.

During my 10 years of experience as a pediatrician, I have seen first-hand the toll that chronic sleep deprivation takes on families. One of the most common concerns parents have is about their children's sleep. Parents are often fighting with each other and feel they aren't able to parent as well during the day because of sleep deprivation. Children are also not always able to function during the day when they are tired. When families are struggling with school or behavior issues, the first thing I ask them about is sleep.

Baby S.T.E.P.S. to Better Sleep is an excellent resource for exhausted parents of sleepless babies and toddlers. It gives parents all the tools they need to create a custom approach to sleep coaching; in fact, there's an entire chapter that offers step-by-step instructions on how to create your own sleep coaching plan. The book also includes a number of helpful reference charts, including bedtimes and nap times, overall sleep needs by age, and sample daily sleep and feeding schedules. Best of all, however, is Nicole's incredibly personal and down-to-earth tone. Throughout the book, Nicole weaves in stories from real parents just like you who have struggled with frustrating sleep issues - and she shares her own story of striving to help her firstborn son sleep, too.

I regularly recommend The Baby Sleep Site to parents. Parents tell me that the resources and plans helped them understand and improve both the child's and parents' sleep. I can't thank Nicole enough for creating such a warm and thorough resource while encouraging parents to meet their goals without sacrificing what's important to them.

Carolyn Nichols, MD, FAAP

CHAPTER 1:

INTRODUCTION

While we hope most babies will "sleep like a baby," unfortunately, many do not sleep soundly all night long and take lengthy, luxurious naps every day. If someone would have told me my baby's sleep schedule was going to be complicated, I would not have believed them. What could be complicated about a baby's sleep schedule? As it turns out, a lot! Some babies wake up many times a night, take short naps, seem to fight sleep, and in the process, exhaust their parents. While most parents are concerned with their baby's well-being, it's also very difficult to be the best parent you envisioned you'd be when you're running on fumes. After all, how imaginative, patient, or happy can you be when you haven't slept more than a few hours at a time for months on end?

The problem of sleep deprivation is widespread and debilitating. In fact, when I surveyed over 250 moms on the subject, they were eager to share their experiences! Here are the top five responses I received when I asked how sleep deprivation affects their daily lives:

- Sleep deprivation affects how they interact with their older children. Many parents reported being more irritable and impatient with their toddlers or preschoolers after several nights of interrupted sleep.

- Sleep deprivation affects their relationships with their spouse/partner. An overwhelming number of parents reported that they were short and irritable with their partner as well after prolonged nights of interrupted sleep.

- ⊘ For parents who work outside the home, sleep deprivation can take a serious toll on work performance. Many parents we polled reported poor work performance due to drowsiness and an inability to focus while on the job.

- ⊘ A number of parents reported that sleep deprivation tends to make their existing mental and physical health problems worse. For example, parents who struggle with depression reported that their depression is worse when they're sleep deprived. Additionally, parents reported that health issues, like heart disease and diabetes, were worsened as a result of chronic sleep deprivation.

- ⊘ Many parents reported heightened anxiety even when anxiety had never been an issue before. The anxiety tends to center around the start of a sleep time, such as before naps and at bedtime.

This book will help you tackle the most common sleep problems babies and children have in the first few years of life. Your baby will grow and change tremendously, and that rapid change requires constant adjustment on your part, including adjustments in how you handle daytime and nighttime sleep. The act of being proactive with your baby's sleep habits is called sleep coaching. Just as we coach our children to have manners at the table or successful study habits in school, we can also coach our babies to help build healthy sleep habits, There are many ways to coach a baby to sleep better. Sometimes, there is only one method that works for a particular baby, while some babies will make positive changes regardless of which strategy you use.

How do I know so much about sleep coaching? It's simple: I was once a sleep-deprived parent, and I had to sleep coach my own children! My eldest son in particular was not a "natural" when it came to sleeping and needed a ton of help to learn healthy sleep habits. Through my sleep coaching experience, I became passionate about helping other exhausted parents. After a lot of encouragement from friends and message board visitors who had sleeping babies with my help, I opened The Baby Sleep Site®, an online resource that enjoys millions of visitors from around the world and offers personalized sleep coaching help. Now, my team and I have personally helped tens of thousands of families, and countless more have seen success with our online materials. Over the years, we've developed a unique approach to sleep coaching called the S.T.E.P.S. method:

Sleep
Training through
Education and
Planning in
Steps

The S.T.E.P.S. method is a holistic approach that first considers a baby's or toddler's routine, schedule, nutrition and environment; educates caregivers on the most important sleep concepts and tools; customizes a sleep coaching/training approach based on the child's temperament and parent's philosophy; and finally, tackles challenges in an exclusive step-by-step method for maximum results. We typically break sleep coaching into a day-by-day plan that is unique for different situations, depending on the goals, specific sleep problems, and the baby. You may start with one particular method and then "graduate" as you go through this journey. Don't get "stuck" thinking once you start one method, it will always be the right one at any particular phase. Your baby is ever changing. In this book, we will help you create your own personal sleep coaching plan.

Can you learn much of what is in this book for free by searching online and reading other books? Yes, you can learn some of the facts, but let me save you some time. There is a lot of "noise" out there and a lot of conflicting advice. Many other sources will tell you to do it their way or suffer the consequences. Other sources will scare you into thinking you shouldn't work on sleep at all, and still others will leave you more confused than when you started. Not only that, but sometimes it's not the knowledge that's stopping you from making improvements. Putting everything together is the real challenge. Putting everything together in a holistic way is not always easy. This book is about helping you find the right journey for you and your family, filtering out the noise, and saving you time.

Simply put, my team and I have worked to create the most practical and useful book on the market about a baby's sleep habits, and this is that book! This book is different from others because our goal is not to teach you about the history of sleep or the difference between REM and nonREM sleep or to quote sleep studies. We are not here to tell you the "magic pill" you can take or the magic formula to solve all of your sleep problems. We are not going to tell you to do it our way or pay the consequences. We are going to give you the information you need to make your own informed choice for you and your family. In fact, you may read this book for baby #2 and get something completely different out of it than you did for baby #1. Quite simply, our babies are not robots and will need a unique solution to their sleep problems. If you're ready to learn more about your baby, let's get started!

CHAPTER 2:

GETTING REAL – HOW YOUR CHILD SLEEPS AND WHY YOUR CHILD WAKES

It may seem a little counterintuitive, but the first step in helping your child sleep well isn't to dig right in and try to fix everything at once. No, the first step is to learn how your child sleeps (because your child's sleep schedule is quite different from yours) as well as why it is your child wakes at night and in the middle of naps. After all, you can't fix what you don't know, so let's first take a look at your child's sleep patterns and get a better understanding of why interrupted sleep happens in the first place.

SLEEP PATTERNS

If there's one thing I've learned in my years spent working with families, it's that new parents are generally pretty stunned at just how quickly their babies change in that first year. Most babies triple their birth weight in that first year and grow about half an inch per month on average. And that's not all; in that first year, your baby's cognitive and emotional development is exploding.

Here's something that's important to keep in mind: sleep patterns also change quite a bit in that first year. However, in my experience, most parents aren't as knowledgeable about these changing sleep patterns as they are about their babies' physical and developmental milestones. So, without further ado, let's take a look at how your baby's sleep patterns will change in that first year of life!

Average Sleep Patterns by Age – Breastfeeding (or Babies Who Need Smaller Feedings such as Those with Reflux)

Age	Average Total Sleep Hours Per Day	Average Total Night-time Sleep Hours	Average Total Daytime Sleep Hours	Average # of Naps	Average # of Night Feedings	Average Longest Daytime Wake-fulness	Average Longest Night-time Stretch Hours
Newborn	15-18	Varies	Varies	Varies	Every 3 hours	30-45 minutes	3
4-6 Weeks	14-16	10	4-6	Varies	Every 3 hours	45-60 minutes	3
7-15 Weeks	14-16	10	4-6	4-5	2-3	45-120 minutes	5
4-5 Months	14-15	11-12	3-4	3-4	2	60-120 minutes	5
5-7 Months	14-15	11-12	2-3	3	1-2	2-3 hours	5-8
8-9 Months	13-15	11-12	2-3	2	0-1	3 hours	5-8
10-12 Months	12-14	10-12	2-3	2	0-1	3-4 hours	8-10
13-15 Months	12-14	10-12	2-3	1-2	0	3-5 hours	11-12
16-23 Months	12-14	11-12	2-3	1	0	5 hours	11-12
24-36 Months	11-12	10-12	0-2	0-1	0	6-12 hours	10-12
3-5 Years	10.75-11.25	9.75-11.25	0-1	0-1	0	6-12 hours	10-11

Please note that these are just general guidelines. All babies are different, so you should discuss this with your healthcare provider.

Average Sleep Patterns by Age – Formula/Milk Feedings

Age	Average Total Sleep Hours Per Day	Average Total Night-time Sleep Hours	Average Total Daytime Sleep Hours	Average # of Naps	Average # of Night Feedings	Average Longest Daytime Wakefulness	Average Longest Night-time Stretch Hours
Newborn	15-18	Varies	Varies	Varies	Every 3 hours	30-45 minutes	3
4-6 Weeks	14-16	10	4-6	Varies	Every 3 hours	45-60 minutes	3
7-15 Weeks	14-16	10	4-6	4-5	2-3	45-120 minutes	5-8
4-5 Months	14-15	11-12	3-4	3-4	1-2	60-120 minutes	5-8
5-7 Months	14-15	11-12	2-3	3	0-1	2-3 hours	8-10
8-9 Months	13-15	11-12	2-3	2	0	3 hours	11-12
10-12 Months	12-14	10-12	2-3	2	0	3-4 hours	11-12
13-15 Months	12-14	10-12	2-3	1-2	0	3-5 hours	11-12
16-23 Months	12-14	11-12	2-3	1	0	5 hours	11-12
24-36 Months	11-12	10-12	0-2	0-1	0	6-12 hours	10-12
3-5 Years	10.75-11.25	9.75-11.25	0-1	0-1	-	6-12 hours	10-11

Please note that these are just general guidelines. All babies are different, so you should discuss this with your healthcare provider.

Why Adequate Sleep Matters

As I've touched on already, babies and young children need a lot of sleep. Many people are surprised by how much sleep their children need. Many parents are under the impression that children sleep like adults do; that explains why many new parents assume that letting a three-month-old baby nap frequently during the day will cause the baby to sleep poorly at night. But because baby sleep is so different than adult sleep, the opposite is actually true. Keeping your baby up will lead him or her to be overtired, and when we are overtired, our bodies release hormones to fight fatigue (commonly known as "second wind"). Ideally, if you avoid letting your baby get overtired, he or she will tend to sleep more restfully and longer with less night waking.

Many people think that if you keep your child up until 9:00 p.m. or later, they will sleep later in the morning, and then, they are frustrated when this doesn't happen. Or say that the child does sleep until 7:00 a.m. but has only gotten 10 hours of sleep when he or she really needs 12 and is missing out on two full hours of sleep every night. The table above has shown you how much sleep your child will need until the age of 5. Now, let's see why it's important.

Adequate sleep helps your baby in many ways, and inadequate sleep has been shown to lead to a multitude of problems. Here are just a few reasons why your child needs adequate sleep:

- ⊘ Learning and Memory – Children who get enough sleep seem to learn more rapidly than those who are tired. Have you ever tried to learn something new when you're tired? It's hard! Babies and toddlers learn a vast amount of information in a short amount of time.

- Safety – Similar to how it is dangerous for you to drive in a severe sleep-deprived state, it can be more problematic for your baby to go up and down stairs, ride a tricycle, etc. when he or she has not slept enough. I always notice my boys are clumsier when they are tired.

- Mood – This is a big one for a lot of people. While some children won't get too cranky, some get downright monstrous. Behavior problems have been linked to sleep deprivation.

- Illness – Your body's immune system has more trouble fighting off illnesses when it hasn't gotten enough rest.

- Obesity – A Harvard study concluded that sleep deprivation in babies and toddlers might be linked to obesity. Our bodies release hormones leptin and ghrelin to signal to our body when we are full and hungry, respectively. When we don't sleep enough, leptin levels go down, and when you get a spike of ghrelin, you will get hungry and most likely eat when you should be sleeping. In 2012, the number of obese six- to 11-year-old children rose to 18% and the number of obese 12- to 19-year-old adolescents rose to 21%.

- Depression – It was once thought that sleep problems were a symptom of depression, but now studies are showing that sleep problems may precede depression. In other words, if you begin to have substantial sleep problems, The American Academy of Sleep Medicine (AASM) strongly recommends that you urgently go see a sleep specialist. Depression is the most common form of mental health problems, and it now considered as common in children as it is in adults. Each year, 17 million people suffer from depression and as many as 1 in 33 children may have depression.

What Is Sleep Coaching?

Try as we might, we, tired parents, simply cannot make our children sleep. You may have heard the saying, "You can lead a horse to water, but you can't make him drink." Well, we can lead our children to their crib or bed, but we cannot make them sleep! We can only provide the opportunity for sleep and help them learn the skills we all need to sleep well. The rest will be up to them. Sometimes, all we need to do as parents is get out of their way, and the rest will come. However, other times, we perpetuate the very habits we want to break. While some babies only need slight encouragement in order to learn healthy sleep habits, others will need more encouragement and lots of consistency, and of course, there are many children in between.

Once your baby is 12 weeks old and is no longer a newborn, you may begin to see that your baby develops specific preferences, and with those, he or she develops habits. You will want to establish healthy sleep habits similar to how you will eventually want to develop proper hygiene, manners, and study habits. As with anything, habits sometimes take minutes to learn and days or months to perfect. During this process, some parents find they need to coach their baby towards good habits, similar to telling your child to say "please" before you will give him or her the toy he or she wants (which you may need to remind him or her to do thousands of times). In regards to sleep, we call this "sleep coaching."

Sleep coaching has also been called "sleep training," but that term has a common mischaracterization that it will always mean letting your baby cry to sleep. It is just not true or that simple. Yes, some babies get frustrated or upset when you change a habit. The way they communicate is fussing or crying, but sleep coaching is so much more than simply letting your baby cry to sleep. Sleep coaching starts with respecting your child's need for sleep and doing your part to ensure your child gets the sleep he or she needs. Babies, toddlers, and young children need a LOT of sleep because it's important for their growth and development! When my eldest son was a baby, several people told me to keep him up during the day so that he will sleep more at night. Crashing due to exhaustion is not a healthy sleep habit, and it often backfires. Teaching healthy sleep habits is done with love, follow-through, consistency, and persistence. It is putting your child's need for sleep at a higher priority than other things you might have or want to do. Babies basically just eat, sleep, and poop in those early months. You wouldn't deprive them of food or a clean diaper, so I challenge you not to deprive them of their sleep, either. Whether you co-sleep with them, allow them to learn to sleep alone or anything in between, the main goal is for them to get the sleep they need. There is not one right or wrong way to help you sleep, but this book will help you find YOUR way.

I can't end this section without emphasizing what sleep coaching isn't. Sleep coaching is NOT laying your baby down in the crib, closing the door, and then letting your baby cry him or herself purple for the next eight hours! While a small minority of people may choose to "sleep coach" that way, by no means is that how sleep coaching will look for all families. The vast majority of families I work with want far gentler methods that minimize crying as much as possible, and I'm happy to report that virtually all of these families find success! While sleep coaching will likely involve a small amount of fussing (simply because your baby is protesting to the changes in his or her routine), by no means does sleep coaching have to involve endless wailing and tears.

I hope this helps relieve any fears you may have about sleep coaching. I know many parents are hesitant to begin sleep coaching at first for the simple reason that they're afraid any crying or fussing may be harmful to their babies. However, by utilizing more gentle methods, you can minimize fussing, which in turn can help you feel good about sleep coaching. Additionally, I like to remind parents often that sleep coaching that is done well is not harmful to their babies, nor is it harmful to your relationship with your child. So many parents harbor these fears, but provided you remain responsive to your baby during the process, sleep coaching will not have a harmful impact on your child or on your parent-child bond. In fact, if you sleep coach successfully, the high-quality sleep your child gets as a result will be hugely beneficial to your child AND to you (as it will allow you to get the sleep you need). When you are rested, you are more likely to be a better parent and are able to foster an even stronger bond with your baby.

Now that we know how much sleep your child needs and just a few reasons as to why it's important, and what sleep coaching means, let's review the most common and uncommon reasons for waking.

COMMON (AND NOT-SO-COMMON) REASONS FOR WAKING

Before we get into why your baby or toddler wakes at night, I want to reiterate that night waking is normal. In the early months of your baby's life, it's downright necessary for survival. But regardless of our age, even when we're past the need to eat during the night to survive and thrive, all of us wake occasionally at night. We need to be able to wake at night in some instances. For example, we'd all be in big trouble if we weren't able to wake out of a deep sleep at the sound of a fire alarm going off!

But what about the night waking that doesn't really seem to have a cause? What about those times when you wake up briefly to roll over and adjust your pillow and are awake for just a few minutes? Interestingly, this is something that humans of ALL ages experience, and there's a very simple explanation for it: it's waking between sleep cycles.

I won't get into a lengthy, technical explanation of the science behind sleep here, but here's the short version: our brain "sleeps" in cycles. We cycle in and out of light and deep (REM and non-REM sleep) several times throughout the night. As we are transitioning out of one sleep cycle and into the next, sleep is very light, and that's when we are most prone to wake briefly for no apparent reason at all. This is true for you, and it's true for your child, too. In my experience working with families, this is generally the least-known and least-understood cause of nighttime waking. It's also at the root of what we work on with sleep coaching, but there's more on that in the subsequent chapters of this book.

Setting aside sleep cycles for a moment, there are, of course, a number of other reasons why your child wakes at night. Some are very common while others are less so. Let's take a look at each...

More Obvious Reasons for Night Waking

- ⊘ Hunger - This tends to be the #1 reason why parents assume their babies are waking at night, and it's not without cause. Newborns need to eat around the clock, but even older babies need one (or possibly two) feedings at night.

- ⊘ Physical Discomfort - This one tends to be fairly obvious, too. Check for easy-to-spot sources of discomfort such as...
  - » Itchy garment tags
  - » Room temperature that is too hot/too cold (aim for 68-70 degrees Fahrenheit)
  - » Hair or string twisted around baby's finger or toe

- ⊘ Illness - Despite your best preventative measures, your baby or toddler will sometimes get sick. During an illness, be prepared for your baby or toddler to wake often, and provide all the comfort you can.

- ⊘ Teething - Growing a mouthful of teeth is hard (and sometimes painful) work for a baby. It can be difficult to spot early signs of teething, but watch for red, swollen gums as well as small, hard bumps on the gums.

- ⊘ Diaper Issues - There's really no way to prevent wet or dirty diapers from waking your baby, unfortunately. The best thing you can do is change diapers promptly and quickly. Keep in mind that if you are using disposable diapers, most babies make it through the night without a diaper change by 6 months of age or so unless they have a bowel movement or unless your baby is extra sensitive.

⊘ Digestive Problems - Gas and reflux can be very painful for a baby and will obviously disrupt sleep. Food allergies may be to blame; if that's the case, try a change in diet. For more help with digestive problems, see your baby's healthcare provider.

⊘ Nightmares/Night Terrors - This won't apply to younger babies, but if your little one is 12 months or older, nightmares (or night terrors) may begin to disrupt nighttime sleep.

⊘ Bedroom Is Too Noisy or Bright - Our brains associate light with being awake; that's why it can be a good idea to let your newborn nap in a bright room to sort out day/night confusion. Once your newborn has days and nights sorted out, it's best to keep your baby's room dark during sleep. As for noise, you can't teach a baby to sleep through noise despite conventional wisdom. Some babies and toddlers are just light sleepers, and every little sound wakes them up! For babies who are light sleepers, a white noise machine (or a white noise app) that masks external sounds can be crucial to a good night of sleep.

Less Obvious Reasons for Night Waking

⊘ Sleep Regressions - Simply put, a sleep regression is a phase in which your child who has otherwise been sleeping reasonably well suddenly starts waking often at night and waking early from naps or skipping them altogether. There are three in the first year of life (one at four months, one at around eight or nine months, and a brief one around 11 or 12 months) and two in the second year of life (one at 18 months and then another at the two-year mark). I'll explain more about sleep regression in the next section.

⊘ Parent-Dependent Sleep Associations - Many babies and toddlers rely on their parents to help them fall asleep at bedtime and/or at the start of each nap. Rocking, holding, and feeding to sleep are all examples of common parent-dependent sleep associations. We'll take a closer look at these kinds of sleep associations and how they interfere with sleep in the next section.

⊘ Napping Too Much - This one is really tough to spot, but it happens more often than you might think. Long daytime naps are a good thing until they interfere with night sleep. That's when you know your baby is napping too much. Remember, your baby's or toddler's overall daily sleep amounts tend to stay the same, but your little one will shift sleep from nighttime to daytime. So naps that are consistently too long will mean less sleep at night. That said, this is NOT a reason to keep your baby up for long stretches during the day; doing that will cause your baby to be overtired, which will actually make it tougher for your baby to sleep well at night.

⊘ Overtiredness at Bedtime - This goes hand-in-hand with the last point. While it may seem sensible to keep your baby up for hours during the day or to push bedtime later in the evening in the hopes that doing so will make your baby "extra tired" so that he or she will sleep through the night, this simply does not work. The reverse is actually true. Babies who go to bed late (or who have missed nap sleep during the day) tend to be overtired at bedtime and sleep worse than babies who go to bed early and who get the recommended amount of nap sleep during the day.

⊘ Food Allergies and Sensitivities - Food allergies and sensitivities cause a whole host of problems for your baby or toddler, including sleep issues. Food allergies and intolerances can cause a kind of "brain fog" that results in daytime drowsiness. The symptoms that food issues cause, such as gas and stomach cramps, can cause problems falling asleep at bedtime and staying asleep throughout the night.

⊘ Fear - This applies more to toddlers than it does to babies. Simply put, as a toddler's imagination grows, so does the propensity for imagined nighttime fears (think monsters under the bed). Bedtime fears can make the bedtime routine difficult and can produce a lot of bedtime stalling as well as night waking. It's best not to assume fear (or plant ideas) unless your toddler is specific about it.

⊘ Bedtime Is Too Early – This isn't generally a problem for most babies, but it can be for older toddlers. If your older toddler is still taking a long afternoon nap, for example, you may actually need a later bedtime. Plan for five to six hours of wake time between the end of your toddler's nap and the start of bedtime. If bedtime is any earlier than that, your toddler most likely won't be tired enough to sleep.

⊘ Unstable Morning Wake-Up Time – Allowing your toddler to get up too early can lead to habitual night waking in the early morning hours. Make sure you keep your toddler in bed until it's "time" to get up. For most toddlers, that is no earlier than 6:00 a.m. If he or she wakes any earlier, treat it just like it was 2:00 a.m. You would not start the day at 2:00 a.m., so don't start it at 5:00 a.m. either.

Sleep Associations – Is it harmful to rock your baby?

We can't really talk about reasons for waking without mentioning sleep associations. Sleep associations are pretty tricky, and they don't really fit neatly into our "more common" and "less common" lists. Here's why: the majority of babies and toddlers who struggle with sleep, in my experience, have one or more sleep associations that are at least contributing to (if not outright causing) their sleep challenges. So, in that sense, sleep associations are a very, very common reason for waking. However, talk to the average parent, and they have no idea what the phrase 'sleep associations' means; therefore, they wouldn't identify it as a reason for their child's sleep problems at all. So, in that sense, sleep associations are less common since they're rarely identified by parents as the reason for waking.

Like I said, tricky!

For our purposes, we'll consider sleep associations one of the most common reasons for waking, but to really see why, we have to first identify what sleep associations are as well as explain why they're so disruptive to sleep.

To start, let me ask you a few questions: Is it a bad idea to rock your baby? Can it be harmful to your baby? It depends. It is never a bad idea to cuddle your baby and give him or her lots of love and affection! It's only a problem when rocking your baby becomes a task that's difficult to sustain. It becomes harmful to the baby if you need to continually rock him or her all night long (i.e. every one to two hours), robbing her of adequate sleep.

How do you fall asleep?

What kind of routine do you do before you go to sleep each night? Do you watch TV? Do you talk to your partner? Do you read a book? Do you sleep on a pillow? These are the types of things you associate with going to sleep each night. What would happen if your power was out, and you couldn't watch the news or read your book? Would you have trouble falling asleep? Maybe. Maybe not. Would you have trouble going to sleep without your pillow? That might be more likely to give you trouble. Some sleep associations are stronger than others. What if you went to sleep with your pillow and covers and two hours later woke up and they were gone? Would you be able to go back to sleep without your pillow? Now, let's look at how this concept might affect your baby.

How does your child fall asleep?

Let's look at how many babies fall asleep. They might fall asleep while their mother or father is rocking them in a rocking chair as they're bundled up and very cozy in their parent's arms. They may fall asleep feeding, or maybe they doze off with the simple use of a pacifier. There isn't a problem with any of these methods of falling asleep until it is a problem for you.

From the time my son was an itty bitty baby, he loved to be walked, rocked, and nursed to sleep. He also loved napping in the moving swing. At first, this was not a problem. He would fall asleep quickly, and we'd put him down. However, several weeks later, I found myself rocking him for two to three hours each night to put him to bed. He'd fall asleep easily, but when I put him down, he'd wake up! Then, I'd need to repeat it every one to two hours when he woke up. It was exhausting! I didn't understand why until later on when I learned about sleep associations.

The problem with sleep associations lies in the fact that your baby needs YOU to recreate the environment in which they fell asleep. YOU become their "pillow," and when they wake up through sleep transitions (that we ALL have) and their "pillow" is gone, they don't know how to go back to sleep.

So, the key is to allow them to go to sleep the same way they will wake up periodically throughout the night when they wake between sleep cycles. If they wake up briefly and find you are gone, the movement has stopped (as with my son) or their pacifier is gone, they will wake up more and have to call out to you, so you can "help" them once again. This is like your child saying "Find my 'pillow' for me!!"

Rocking your baby, using a pacifier, nursing or drinking a bottle before bed are not bad things to do. If you don't mind rocking your baby for 10 minutes and he or she falls and stays asleep after you transfer him or her to bed, there is no problem. It's only when you can't keep up with the parent-dependent sleep association that it becomes a problem.

Keep in mind that your sleep fragmentation that makes you exhausted is no better for your baby than it is for you. If you are cranky, don't you think that, over time, he or she may be cranky, too? I would have LOVED to rock my son to sleep every night, and boy did I try over and over (unintentionally -- just in my nature). We slipped back into bad habits more times than I want to count, but it just became a hitch for him EVERY time. In the end,

I was able to continue to nurse him to sleep once he learned the necessary skills to go BACK to sleep throughout the rest of the night, but he did have to learn those first. With opportunity and practice, we can all learn a new way to sleep even without a pillow!

Some nursing mothers start to believe they should wean because the baby is becoming dependent on nursing to go to sleep. Please do not wean for this reason alone. Babies can form a sleep association with nursing, but they can also form one just as easily with a bottle, too. Either way, the key here is that a baby learns to fall asleep on his or her own regardless of the food source. I successfully nursed my eldest son for 12 months and also helped him learn how to fall asleep without it.

> My daughter learned to fall asleep only while nursing. At first, it was okay. She was getting me up two times a night. But then it was three, then four, and then five. That's when I knew something had to change. I had heard of sleep training but couldn't handle the agony of letting her cry. Fortunately, I did some reading on sleep associations and was able to use a gentle sleep coaching approach that I felt comfortable with. Within 3 nights, she was sleeping through the night, a full 12-hour stretch! I thought I'd died and gone to heaven. I was so happy at being able to sleep again!   **-Jamie**

COMMON SLEEP REGRESSIONS

We included sleep regressions in our list of less common reasons for night waking, and as we take a look at each of these common regressions, you'll see why. The thing to remember with sleep regressions is that they are firmly rooted in your child's growth and development. With sleep regressions, we see a child who may have been sleeping well enough suddenly start waking more frequently at night and/or taking shorter naps (or even skipping naps altogether). Note that these are different than growth spurts. Growth spurts tend to last just a few days and are tied to your baby's physical growth whereas sleep regressions can last for up to four to six weeks and are connected to the physical, mental, and even emotional development of your child.

Keep in mind that every child goes through these regressions in one way or another, but the effects will vary from child to child. While some children will experience major sleep disruptions at each of these periods, other children will seem to sail through them with relative ease. Still, others will have tough sleep challenges with one or two of these sleep regressions but not with others. Of course, HOW exactly sleep is disrupted at each of these regression phases varies greatly from one child to the next. So, the bottom line is this: how each of these regressions impacts your child's sleep is totally dependent on unique factors like your child's temperament, your parenting style, your living situation, etc. I will provide you with an overview of each regression phase, and then, you can apply this information as needed in a way that matches your child's unique needs.

The Four-Month Sleep Regression

This regression is one of the most notable sleep regressions. Why? Because this is also when your baby will start sleeping more like an adult, going through sleep cycles and cycling between light and deep sleep instead of staying in a deep sleep most of the time. We get tens of thousands of visitors at The Baby Sleep Site® who visit us when their babies are around this age. However, this regression can start as early as three months or as late as five months.

Only some babies will struggle to sleep through this regression. This is the time when sleep associations begin to become a "problem." When you used to put your baby to sleep, he or she would stay in deep sleep for most of the night; now, your baby must go through sleep cycles and often needs you to recreate sleep associations to stay asleep. For instance, your four-month-old may wake briefly an hour or two after going to bed (because he or she is cycling out of one sleep cycle and into the next), but when your baby wakes, he or she realizes that you aren't there feeding, rocking, or holding him or her the way you were at bedtime. This is a problem since you may always put him or her to sleep. Naturally, your baby cries for you; he or she wants to go back to sleep but needs your help. As his or her sleep patterns become more mature, he or she will have to cycle in and out of sleep multiple times per night, and if he or she relies on you for help falling asleep, this can mean that you'll be waking up multiple times at night.

The key thing to understand about this regression is that things will never go back to how they once were. This is a permanent change to how your baby sleeps, and thus, we need to help your baby learn how to sleep with his or her new brain development and learn the way he or she sleeps.

The 8- (or 9- or 10-) Month Sleep Regression

This sleep regression is, by far, one of the most frustrating for most parents because just when you think your baby is getting easier, this regression seems to hit, and it can be very disruptive. We see it start anywhere from seven months (which is a bit early) to 10 months old and lasts three to six weeks on average. During this stage of life, your baby will go through a fussy period and will become very mobile, which will likely include, among other things, pulling up to standing, crawling, walking with support, and/or cruising. With all of this new physical movement, it can be very difficult to sleep well. Babies often seem to "practice" their new skills in their sleep and sometimes do so without intending to, which makes them extra frustrated and fussy. As with four-month-old babies, many eight- to 10-month-olds who haven't yet learned to fall asleep independently will wake between sleep cycles and need help getting back to sleep.

Another contributing factor to this regression is something called separation anxiety. Many babies this age have developed a strong sense of object permanence. That is, they understand that when people or toys disappear from their line of sight, those people or toys aren't actually gone forever; they're just gone for a little while. This is a necessary mental leap for your baby to make; however, it can produce separation anxiety. You may find that your eight-, nine-, or 10-month-old is exceptionally clingy and cries every time you leave the room at nap time or bedtime.

Of course, your baby can be developing "quietly" in his or her mind, and you may not see physical signs of this regression right away. Either way, your baby is going through a lot of changes mentally, physically, and emotionally.

The 11-Month Sleep Regression

The 11-month regression is a bit of a hidden regression in that it's typically less disruptive than the first two and that it affects only naps, not nighttime sleep. However, it can definitely throw parents off! Our clients have often reported feeling frustrated because their baby is suddenly taking two short naps or skipping the afternoon nap. The most common response to this leap is to transition from two naps to one. However, both personal and professional experience has shown me this is usually a temporary blip. This sleep regression often, but not always, occurs around the time a baby learns to walk. Although it's tempting to transition to one nap, I typically advise to try keeping two naps for three weeks or so because many babies will go back to taking two solid naps until 15 to 18 months on average.

The 18-Month Sleep Regression

The 18-month regression is one of the most frustrating sleep regressions. Why? Because you thought you were going to have a smooth sleep schedule now that your baby is a toddler. Who knew you might feel like you have a newborn again once your baby starts waking up a lot at night and sometimes staying awake for hours? Also, in my experience, a growth spurt or increased activity can also often lead to renewed nighttime hunger.

Perhaps the biggest factor in this regression, however, is your toddler's growing sense of independence. As your toddler matures, he or she is realizing that he or she has opinions, too, and that newfound sense of self-will can lead to major limit testing and tantrum throwing around this time! And yes, that limit testing will definitely extend to sleep. You may find that your toddler begins resisting nap time and bedtime very strongly simply because he or she doesn't want to stop playing and go to sleep.

All of this can lead to a very frustrating four- to six-week period when you question whether you ever knew what you were doing as a parent, especially since toddlers have at least twice the stamina and stubbornness of a baby.

The 2-Year Sleep Regression

Around the two–year mark is often another change in sleep, and I can almost set a clock by it. Not all toddlers will experience it, but if yours does, it will most surely occur right around 22 to 24 months. Your now walking, talking toddler may start climbing out of the crib or require your presence while he or she falls asleep even if he or she has been a perfect sleeper up until now. In addition, the amount of time your toddler can now stay awake may increase to up to six hours, which can mean long, drawn-out bedtime routines. In reality, your toddler is trying to communicate to you that he or she truly can stay awake a bit longer, and no, he or she is not making it up. In addition, we often find that some two-year-olds start skipping naps, especially if a sibling is born. But, have no fear, your toddler will likely go back to napping until the age of three to four on average. Generally, though, he or she won't reduce his or her new ability to stay awake for longer periods.

Additionally, many toddlers go through big changes during the second year of life, including potty training, transitioning to a "big kid" bed, welcoming a new sibling, etc. Big changes like these can wreak havoc on your two-year-old's sleep schedule. Add to this the fact that nighttime fears, nightmares, and night terrors are starting to be an issue around this time, and it's easy to see why sleep is disrupted at the two-year mark.

MANAGING SLEEP REGRESSIONS

All of this information is helpful because, if for no other reason, you'll know what to expect, sleep-wise, as your child grows from a newborn to a toddler. However, what exactly are you supposed to DO about these sleep regressions? Yes, sleep tends to fall apart, but how is a parent supposed to respond to these sudden sleep disruptions?

Well, in general, here's what I tell my clients: if your child was sleeping well before the sleep regression and was able to self soothe and fall asleep independently at the start of a nap and at bedtime, then, likely, it's best to stick to what you normally do. In other words, don't abruptly change all your sleep routines and patterns in order to accommodate the sleep regression; if you do, your child will likely end up creating new sleep habits that you'll have to undo later. You may need to make a few changes here and there to accommodate the regression, but stick to your normal routine as best as you can.

However, if your child has never really slept well, it's generally a good idea to wait a few weeks for the regression to pass to work on sleep coaching if you are planning to start addressing sleep challenges.

> *When my son's sleep fell apart at four months, I honestly had no idea what was happening. I thought it was just a quick phase that would pass, but after about a month, I realized that this wasn't going away and that things weren't just going to get better on their own. I got to the point where I was so sleep deprived that I started Googling everything I could about four-month-old sleep, and*

that's when I learned about the four-month sleep regression! I'm so glad I learned about this regression; it helped me understand why my son's sleep turned upside down and also helped me understand what the changes to his sleep patterns meant.

-Jen

HOW TO FIX UNNECESSARY WAKING

We've covered a lot of the "whys" behind why your baby wakes at night or wakes too early from (or skips) a nap. The first step in solving a problem is to understand the root cause behind the problem itself. Now that you know the "why" behind the waking, we can talk about the solution.

First off, know that if your child's night waking is age appropriate and is happening due to hunger, there is no "fix." Additionally, if your child is waking because he or she is teething, is sick, or is going through a sleep regression, there is no "fix" for that, either. Rather, you'll want to do the best you can to comfort and soothe your child without creating any new sleep habits that you'll have to undo later. For instance, it's probably best not to co-sleep every night for two weeks when your child has the flu unless you want to make co-sleeping a permanent sleeping arrangement. Camp out in your child's room instead.

If your child is waking due to discomfort of some kind, that's easy to fix. Swap out scratchy jammies for softer ones, or change the temperature of the nursery slightly. Try overnight diapers if nighttime leaks are problem. Eliminate trigger foods if your child is struggling with food sensitivities etc.

This brings me to the most frustrating, troubling reason for interrupted waking, the one that's most difficult to overcome: sleep associations. The fact is that even after you've dealt with any kind of discomfort and set the stage for sleep perfectly, many of you will still have night waking issues to deal with because your child has one or more sleep associations. This is where sleep coaching comes in. When you sleep coach, you are helping your baby learn new expectations and habits as far as how to fall asleep, so he or she can learn to go BACK to sleep without your help. The first step is almost always to put your baby down while he or she is semi-awake (some will say "drowsy, but awake"), so he or she will learn what to do on his or her own. This is, unfortunately, harder than it sounds! That's, no doubt, one reason why there are many books and online resources dedicated to helping parents sleep coach.

SUMMARY

- ⊘ Your child's sleep patterns and needs change tremendously in the first three to four years of life. That's why it's key to understand how and when your child begins consolidating naps and feedings as well as when common nap transitions occur.

- ⊘ Adequate sleep isn't a "bonus" - it's a necessity! A child who's well rested is a child who is primed to grow and develop in a healthy way. By helping your child build healthy sleep habits early in life, you are laying a foundation for an overall healthier lifestyle as your baby grows.

⊘ Some causes of your child's nighttime waking are obvious (like hunger, a dirty/wet diaper, or a nursery that's too bright or too warm). But other causes are less obvious, including:

» Sleep regressions

» Too much nap sleep

» Overtiredness at bedtime

» Food allergies and sensitivities

» Too early of a bedtime (for toddlers)

» Too early of a morning wake time (for toddlers)

⊘ Parent-dependent sleep associations are usually the cause of frequent nighttime waking, but they aren't obvious to most parents. A parent-dependent sleep association is anything that your child relies on you to do in order to fall asleep (think rocking, feeding, or holding your child until he or she falls asleep). The problem lies in the fact that your child must have this association in order to fall asleep, so when your baby wakes between sleep cycles at night, he or she needs your help to fall back to sleep.

⊘ Sleep regressions are a normal part of healthy child development, but they can wreak havoc on sleep. Expect to see the following regressions:

» 4-month sleep regression - this is where your child's sleep habits change permanently and become more like an adult's; your child will start to have distinct sleep cycles.

» 8-10-month sleep regression - this one is tied directly to all the physical development your child is experiencing; expect both naps and night sleep to suffer.

» 11-month sleep regression - this one is, perhaps, the smallest of the regressions; your child will show signs of wanting to drop the second nap, but resist the urge to do so as most children aren't ready to drop to just one nap until between 15-18 months.

» 18-month sleep regression - this one is connected to your toddler's growing sense of independence as well as his or her newfound desire to test boundaries; expect both naps and night sleep to suffer.

» 2-year sleep regression - this one is linked to both your toddler's new sense of self as well as common 2-year-old transitions (like potty training, the birth of a sibling, etc.) and newfound bedtime fears.

⊘ While many causes of nighttime waking are fairly easy to resolve, parent-dependent sleep associations can be incredibly tough to break. The process of teaching your child to fall asleep independently without help or intervention from you is called sleep coaching, and it is a key step for many families who are working towards helping their children learn to sleep through the night and take more regular naps. Sleep coaching does not mean allowing your child to cry it out for hours on end; rather, there are a variety of ways to teach your child healthy sleep habits that are very gentle and that minimize fussing.

CHAPTER 3:

WHAT TO DO BEFORE YOU START "FIXING" SLEEP

Believe it or not, it's generally not a good idea to dive straight into sleep coaching. Why? Because there's a lot of groundwork that has to be laid before you start the actual process of working on sleep through sleep coaching. Parents who do this groundwork and lay a strong foundation for sleep coaching tend to see better sleep coaching success, and sleep coaching tends to go more quickly (often with less upset parents and babies). What's more, when you lay a proper sleep coaching foundation, you identify and address obstacles that can get in the way of sleep coaching (like schedule problems, health issues, etc.). Finally (and perhaps most importantly for exhausted parents), when you put in the work to lay a good foundation for sleep coaching, you may actually resolve some (or most or perhaps even all) of your child's sleep challenges! It's true; I've worked with families over the years who, by simply strengthening their sleep routines, making schedule changes, and tweaking feeding times and amounts, are actually able to resolve the sleep issues that plagued their families.

Pretty great, right? With some basic groundwork, you set yourself and your child up for sleep coaching success, and you may actually solve sleep challenges entirely. Now, let's take a look at exactly what this groundwork looks like and what you should focus on before you start sleep coaching.

GET TO KNOW YOUR BABY

This might seem like an odd way to start sleep coaching, but let me tell you, it is critical to understand your child's personality and temperament before you attempt sleep coaching. Temperament directly impacts sleep coaching; it'll direct what kind of sleep coaching method you use, how long the process will take, what kind of setbacks and challenges you can expect, and more.

First, though, let's take a look at what "temperament" means exactly. Simply put, temperament is how your child naturally reacts to situations and stimuli, as well as the child's mood, his or her ability to calm down, and your child's usual level of activity. It is widely believed that temperament is biological, meaning your child comes out of the womb this way. This means that from day one, the way YOUR baby reacts to being wet, hungry, or tired may not be like your friend's baby. Yours might be low-key and not get very upset, or your baby may scream loudly. You are not making it up that your baby might not be "laid back." Every baby is different, and your baby may simply be on the more intense end of the spectrum! You might wonder what you did or didn't do to cause this. I remember one parent telling me that her husband thought her post-partum depression after the birth of their son caused their baby to not sleep well. What a burden to bear! Let me assure you, you have no control over your baby's temperament. You can only "blame" your genetics.

One thing that is important for you to know, though, is that while you can't change your child's temperament, you can get to know it, which will allow you to generally predict how he or she will react to certain things. This will help you set your child up for success with many things in life, including sleep. If you know

your child has trouble with transitions, for example, yc
able to help him or her navigate those with minimal fu:
pact on your daily schedule. The best part of this is that you ᴄᴀɴ
reduce some of the stress once you KNOW your child's temperament because you won't constantly be trying to figure out why he
or she is reacting a certain way.

Finally, you should know that just because your child's temperament traits are inborn does NOT mean that what you do does
not matter. You will be able to emphasize your child's strengths,
help your child understand his or her own temperament, and
help your child learn how to handle his or her own reactions as
he or she grows up. By making changes to your parenting style,
depending on your baby's age and temperament and personality,
you will teach him or her the skills he or she needs and help him
or her be happy and comfortable in his or her own skin. Attempting to make your child ignore his or her temperament traits is
not only very difficult, but it teaches your child to not be him or
herself.

Temperament Traits

So how can you determine your child's temperament traits? And,
equally important, how will your child's unique blend of temperament traits impact your sleep coaching efforts and your child's
overall sleep? Let's take a look! But keep in mind your child can
fall anywhere along the spectrum for each of these traits.

Intensity

Your child's 'intensity' is simply how strongly he or she emotionally reacts. This includes both positive and negative reactions; you

can find intense babies squealing loudly with joy over the sound that a rattle makes and wailing loudly because the diaper is a little wet. Conversely, less intense babies tend to have a smaller emotional spectrum. We often use phrases like "laid back" and "easy going" to describe less intense children.

Now, how does intensity affect your baby's sleep and your sleep coaching efforts? If your child is a low-intensity baby, this means that it may really be much easier for you to put baby down awake from the very beginning and help him or her learn to fall asleep on his or her own from day one. Your baby may fuss a little or not at all before drifting off into dreamland. When your baby is no longer a newborn and decides to protest things he or she doesn't like, his or her protests will likely be fairly low-key. Regardless of which sleep coaching method you use, you can expect limited fussing, and that fussing will likely be pretty mild, making it easier for you to manage.

On the other hand, if your baby is a high-intensity baby, you can bet that it will be hard to leave him or her upset for anything longer than a couple of minutes when he or she is young. You may not need to turn on your monitor at night to hear your child down the hall when he or she wakes up for a midnight feeding! Your high-intensity baby might get more upset or angry when he or she wakes up between sleep cycles and can't go back to sleep. You may also need to take your time during your bedtime routine to help soothe your child before sleep. Sleep coaching may feel tough with a high-intensity baby as even a few moments of frustration on your child's part may lead to bouts of loud screaming. For this reason, it can take longer to fully sleep coach a very intense baby.

Persistence

Your child's persistence refers to his or her perseverance to get what's on his or her mind. For instance, how does your child respond when you ask to him or her to stop doing something that he or she is enjoying doing? When you take away the car keys, how long does he or she notice and protest? When your child has his or her mind set on something, how easy is it to get him or her to change his or her mind? Persistence might reveal itself when you take your eight-month-old's toy away to start a new game or when you try to get your two-year-old out of the bath when he or she isn't ready. A very persistent baby or toddler doesn't take "no" for an answer very easily.

How might your child's persistence affect his or her sleep? If your child is a less persistent baby, it will not likely be that difficult for him or her to get better sleep. Typically, less persistent babies and toddlers accept "no" for an answer and do not stay upset very long when you make changes. You may simply just need to commit to making changes. As you might expect, less persistent babies tend to respond pretty well to sleep coaching as they don't really mind changes to the sleep schedule and to their usual routines.

On the other hand, if your baby is a very persistent baby, you can bet that it will be harder to get more cooperation out of your child when he or she has his or her mind set on something. This means that sleep coaching tends to take longer and that any bouts of crying tend to be longer. How persistence works with intensity makes a difference, too; if your baby is low intensity and fusses for an hour, that might be "easier" for you to handle than if he or she is screaming at the top of his or her lungs for an hour (which is what a high-intensity, very persistent baby might do). Regardless of the method, your key to success will be to be more persistent than your child is. You might also notice that you need to keep setting firm limits during bedtime routines as he or she gets older and wants "one more book," "one more drink," or "one more" anything.

Sensitivity

Your baby's sensitivity level reflects how noise, temperature, taste, texture, other people's emotions, etc. impact your child. Your child's sensitivity (or lack thereof) can come out in a variety of places. For example, a very sensitive child might melt down if his or her sock is a little crooked. Another child might complain about loud noises or a light being too bright. If your child is sensitive, he or she might also pick up quickly on your stress or emotions. You might notice that your child starts acting "off" if you are under an undue amount of stress.

How might your baby's sensitivity affect your child's sleep? If your child is sensitive, he or she will most likely not be the baby or toddler that falls asleep in a room full of people or with a lot of noise. Some families need to remove night lights because the sensitive child may see the light and decide to play in the middle of the night. You may have to put away the dogs so that they don't bark during naps, and you may need to keep the noise level down in general. Contrary to what some believe, some babies do not simply "get used to it." Conversely, a less sensitive baby may have no problem napping in a noisy, brightly lit area. Additionally, sleep coaching your sensitive child might be more difficult. You might question whether your child is comfortable, what's wrong, and why no two days are the same. He or she might become overstimulated more easily and need to nap more often, but, your sensitive child's sleep is even more important. Sensitive children "take in" a lot around them, and that can be exhausting! However, it's also difficult for your child to settle down for the night, and therefore, your child's bedtime routine might need to be longer than normal.

Perceptiveness

Your baby's perceptiveness is how much your child notices things like people, colors, and noises. A perceptive child may forget directions or instructions you have given him or her because something else has caught his or her attention. In addition, your child might notice many things that other people don't, such as a rock in the grass that other kids would walk past. This is different than sensitivity; a sensitive child is impacted and affected by things like noise while a perceptive child may simply notice and be distracted by the noise (but not necessarily be upset or excited by it).

How might your baby's perceptiveness affect his or her sleep? Your child's perceptiveness will most affect sleep when it comes to naps, routines, and whether you use a nightlight in the bedroom. When you are doing your bedtime routine, your toddler may not be able to follow multi-step instructions, so you may need to break the routines into smaller steps. In other words, instead of asking your toddler to go get a diaper, get his or her pajamas, and come over to sit down, you might need to ask your toddler to get the diaper first and then get the pajamas. You also might need to take more time for the routine. Some toddlers might take longer to get through books because they will notice a lot of different things on each page of a book even if you've read the book 10 times before. This inquisitiveness should be encouraged but kept in mind to plan for how long it takes to get through the routine and set the start time accordingly.

When it comes to napping, your baby or toddler might look at the light dance on the ceiling from the sunlight shining through the window rather than go to sleep. It is likely your child might take longer to fall asleep than a child who is not as perceptive simply because he or she notices more in the room, especially when there is something new. It is because of this that you will want to put your child down for bed at least 10 to 15 minutes before you want him or her to be asleep.

You may or may not want to use a nightlight in your baby's room until he or she is old enough to care. Remember, your child was in the dark in your womb for a long time, and until he or she goes through certain developmental milestones, your child is too young to be scared of the dark.

Finally, as with your sensitive child, a perceptive child will likely take in a lot more around him or her and can get overstimulated and overtired, so keep that in mind when establishing the sleep schedule.

Adaptability

Your baby's adaptability refers to how quickly he or she adapts to changes in schedules and routine. Slow-to-adapt children often cry or fuss when one activity has to end and another one must begin. They can also get upset with changes in routine. Slow-to-adapt children may also not react favorably to surprises.

How might your baby's adaptability affect sleep? Your child's adaptability will most affect sleep when it comes to routines, naps, and nights. Many parents like to follow routines even when their baby is a newborn. For slow-to-adapt children, this can be your saving grace. Slow-to-adapt children crave routine and need to know what to expect next.

As you can probably guess, consistency is the most important aspect when it comes to your slow-to-adapt child. As easy and tempting as it feels to read just one book when you usually read three or to attempt to brush teeth before you put on jammies, it might just erupt into a meltdown or rough night for all. A bedtime routine and sleep schedules are a must, and regardless of what kind of sleep coaching methods you use, your success will be highly dependent on your ability to stay consistent.

If your child is slow-to-adapt *and* persistent, it will be challenging to set limits, but limits will be instrumental in tackling sleep problems as well as raising a happy and healthy child in the years to come.

Regularity

Your baby's regularity refers to how predictable his or her schedule is from day to day. There are some babies by whom you can practically set the clock - that's how consistent and regular their daily schedules are! They wake up at the same time every day and eat at the same times every day. They take naps at the same time every day, and yes, some even poop at the same time every single day. (Not surprisingly, these kids tend to be easier to potty train!)

By contrast, inconsistent children are very irregular. They wake up at different times every day. They get hungry at different times and nap at different times for different lengths every day. This can cause parents to rack their brains to figure out what they did wrong today or right yesterday, but the truth of the matter is that this is just temperament. As you can imagine, getting these children on a schedule can be very frustrating. While you can influence their schedule, they may never let you make it truly predictable.

How might your baby's regularity (or lack thereof) affect his or her sleep? If you have an inconsistent baby, toddler, or preschooler, it doesn't mean you shouldn't try to have a routine and a schedule. You might need to be a little more flexible, but even irregular children still thrive on routines and knowing what to expect next. You will want to come up with routines that are flexible for your child's temperament, but also don't push the entire schedule too off track. Moving your irregular child to a schedule will likely take longer given that his or her natural tendency is not to adhere to a predictable schedule.

If your child is slow-to-adapt and inconsistent, you may need to have a routine "shell." This means you have the same basic structure from one day to the next, but within that shell, there is lots of room for flexibility. With an irregular baby who may or may not be tired at "bedtime," you may need to be a little flexible with the bedtime routine. Of course, toddlers often try a lot of things to stall bedtime, so it is tricky to know the difference between stalling and inconsistency. Be flexible within 15(ish) minutes (more like five to 10 minutes for younger babies); just be sure you're not being so flexible that bedtime is happening way too late.

Sleep coaching inconsistent babies can be tough. After all, you can't really rely on patterns of behavior to tell you whether or not that cry is due to hunger or if it's just a regular, run-of-the-mill "please help me fall asleep" cry. This is why I generally recommend that parents track their children's sleep for a couple of weeks before starting to fix sleep problems or their schedule.

I speak with a lot of parents who are frustrated by their children's inconsistency, and I get that. It can be very frustrating indeed! But keep in mind that we, adults, might not do the same things every day at the same time either, so it isn't fair to expect robot-like consistency from our children. While inconsistency might be frustrating now, keep in mind that we need these irregular children. They're the ones who work the night shifts, the doctors who work 36 hours straight, and the pilots who fly the red eye. Our society needs all types of people, and that's why it's really a good thing we have all these different temperaments!

Energy

Your child's energy level refers to how much he or she sits quietly versus runs or moves around. Some children are always on the move, and the parents we work with often know this from a very young age. These are the children who almost always run and never walk. Many spirited children have high amounts of energy. These are the children who might roll over early, fall out of their chairs at the dinner table because they're so fidgety, and have trouble with long car rides without the ability to get out and run around.

How might your baby's or toddler's energy affect his or her sleep? If your child has a lot of energy, you will likely notice that he or she moves around a LOT during sleep. If you have a video monitor, you might think your child is awake with all the activity in there! Energetic children also tend to need longer bedtime routines as well as more time to settle down before a nap. When my son was a preschooler, I found that he really needed a one-hour bedtime routine. I tried repeatedly to make it shorter (because an hour is a long time to be helping a child wind down before bed), but I failed every time. The more I tried to rush through it, the more he pushed back and didn't cooperate. I found that, no matter what, he seemed to fall asleep no less than one hour after we started the routine. This means that it was up to me that we started on time if I wanted him to go to bed on time. I also had to have the lights out and have him "settled" 15 minutes before I wanted him to be asleep. He needed this unwind time no matter what. Long bedtime routines are a must with high-energy children with slow-to-adapt natures as you can't go through transitions too quickly. Many of our clients report their high-energy children never seem to stop moving until they are already asleep. However, if given enough time, your child will slow down, stop moving and fall asleep even if you don't think it will ever happen. The e-mails we receive reporting success when they thought it wasn't possible never get old.

First Reaction

When someone is presented with a new food, idea, social situation, person to meet, or place to visit, some people will jump right in and embrace the newness; others, however, are hesitant. Your child's first reaction is how he or she responds to one of these new concepts. An easy-going child will just jump in. This is not always a good thing, of course; they may be "jumping in" to mischief or into a potentially dangerous situation. Other children, by contrast, will likely initially say "no" to something new or be hesitant about the new idea, food, or person. The hesitant child might learn better by watching rather than doing or will simply hang back and watch for awhile before jumping in.

You will likely see this temperament trait very early on in your child's life. It's usually apparent in your baby's first reaction to a bath, a new food, a new highchair, the first day at a new daycare or school, or the first day of summer when he or she has to change from wearing pants to shorts. As I remind my clients, it is important to know this is your baby's or toddler's first reaction to something new; it's not the same as a final decision. Your child may warm up to the birthday party that he or she initially threw a tantrum about attending or the new food that he or she initially rejected. Sometimes, you just have to keep trying.

How might your baby's or toddler's first reaction affect his or her sleep? If your child is prone to react negatively to new things, you likely want to take changes slower. Allow your baby or toddler to warm up to an idea before you "throw" him or her into it. For example, if you're transitioning your baby to sleeping independently in his or her own bedroom, you probably want to spend time in your child's new room and crib before you expect him or her to sleep there. You might want to put your baby in the crib while you put away laundry or just to play for five to 10 minutes. While you don't want your child to necessarily associate the crib with a playground, having time to gradually adjust will help him or her start to feel comfortable in the new space.

If your child's first reaction is usually negative, keep in mind that, regardless of what kind of sleep coaching method you use, he or she probably isn't going to like it at first, no matter what you do. How you choose to handle this will likely be dependent on your parenting philosophy; some parents are more "rip the bandage off all at once" types and prefer to just jump into sleep coaching without much prior warning while others want to go more gradually and give their children tons of time to adjust. However you choose to approach it, the key will be to stick with it and commit to the method you choose 100% for at least one to two weeks before you give up on it. Consistency is key!

Mood

This isn't the most technical definition, but it works: your child's mood is generally how happy or smiley he or she is versus how serious or intense and cranky he or she is. You can think about this as your child's disposition. Is your child usually pretty happy and positive? Or is your child generally more intense and cranky? No child is entirely one or the other, of course, but many children tend to slant more in one direction than the other. A specific pattern of brain activity is responsible for your child's disposition.

How might your baby's or toddler's mood affect his or her sleep? Primarily, the number one important thing to keep in mind is that even if you have the happiest baby all the time, it doesn't indicate that he or she doesn't need more sleep. While many sleepy children get cranky, some do not, which can make it difficult to assess whether or not it's nap time. For these children, it is best to experiment with an age-appropriate schedule (see the sample schedules in the appendix) and find the right schedule for your child even when he or she is happy.

One Last Note About Temperament

It is important to note that every temperament trait described on the previous pages is necessary and has its place. While it can be easy for us to look at some of these temperament traits as positive and others as negative (and, in truth, some of these temperament traits produce behavior that is tough to deal with), it's key to remember that what may seem like "negative" temperament traits in your child can turn out to be real assets as your child grows. For example, the persistent toddler can drive his or her parents crazy, but the persistent adult is one who achieves his or her goals and works hard. The sensitive baby may be tough to pacify and keep happy, but the sensitive adult is one who is full of empathy.

In short, your child is 100% unique, and while some of his or her temperament traits may produce difficult and frustrating behaviors at various times, none of those temperament traits are mistakes. What's more, none of them can (or should) be changed; rather, it's your goal as a parent to work with your child's temperament, to help your child come to understand his or her strengths and weaknesses, and to embrace who your child is.

GET TO KNOW YOURSELF

Your child's temperament impacts sleep coaching greatly and yours does, too. Specifically, I've found that parenting style and philosophy have a big impact on sleep coaching. So, what kind of philosophy of parenting do you have? How will that philosophy impact sleep coaching? While reading this section, look within and do a self-assessment, asking yourself questions such as how much crying you may be able to tolerate, how patient you can be to see results, and whether you want to continue bed sharing. Knowing these things will help you shape the sleep plan you will craft later in this book. The following are the three common parenting philosophies I see most and how they relate to sleep coaching.

Attachment Parenting

Many people credit Dr. William Sears with defining the attachment parenting philosophy. Attachment parents are focused on sustaining and nurturing the deep bond between parent and child. There is a strong emphasis on respecting the child and adhering to "baby-led" practices. Many attachment parents practice bed sharing, prioritize breastfeeding, and are proponents of baby wearing. Although some attachment parents are reluctant to "work on sleep," you can align your philosophies with sleep coaching. For example, I work with some families who focus on gently and gradually resolving sleep associations while still sharing a bed with their child (partially or full time). They may help their baby learn to fall asleep without being held upright and learn to sleep next to them or help them learn not to expect feedings throughout the night but continue to bed share.

Other attachment families I work with are ready to transition the baby away from the family bed and into a separate sleeping space but want to do it gently and gradually. Rebecca was one such parent:

> *I can honestly say that 'meeting' Nicole and getting her help was the answer I'd been looking for. Nicole had given me a multi-step approach to getting my son to disassociate the breast with falling asleep at nap time and from there another step-by-step approach to get him disassociating the breast with falling asleep at night and then to get him into his crib completely away from my bed. From there, we were going to work on getting him into his own room and getting him to allow being put to bed by other people (his own father included).*
>
> *I am grateful to report that within three to four weeks, my son was taking two one-and-a-half- to two- hour naps in his own crib (with all four sides up) and being put down with NO breastfeeding at all and completely awake/sitting up. NO TEARS. Not only that, but the bedtime issues were resolved almost on their own just utilizing some of the same*

methods we'd come up with to fix the napping issues. Something I expected to take months took mere weeks, days even.

My son is now, and has been for quite some time, sleeping 12 hours a night and two one-and-a-half- to two-hour naps a day. No more night waking or nursing to sleep. All 98% tear free. Any change as major as the one my son experienced is most likely going to cause some degree of sadness and invoke tears, depending on the sensitivity of the child. For the changes and benefits I see now in my son's sleeping habits, the 10 minutes he cried for a couple of days is so worth it, and I was completely against ANY amount of crying around 'sleep training.' With Nicole's help and understanding, I was able to truly coach my son in the most gentle and personalized manner I could ever find.

—Rebecca

Authoritarian Parenting

Authoritarian parenting tends to be considered an "old school" style of parenting. Simply put, authoritarian parents value immediate and unconditional obedience to authority and believe that the key to raising happy, productive children is to break their strong will and to immediately punish disobedience. In my experience, the struggle for authoritarian parents who sleep coach tends to be that they jump straight to cry-it-out methods too early and that they generally try to force a rigid schedule too early. This particular parenting philosophy emphasizes that the child is expected to adapt to the family's needs and to the parent's guidance, so authoritarian parents may jump too quickly to extreme methods and harsh schedules that may work for the parents but are not age appropriate for the child. Depending on the child, this may or may not be conducive to good sleep for everyone. Adaptable children may do very well, but persistent, slow-to-adapt children may struggle a lot.

Authoritative Parenting

While they sound similar, authoritative parenting is quite different from authoritarian parenting. Authoritative parenting, like authoritarian parenting, puts parents firmly in the "driver's seat," so to speak, but the similarities end there. Authoritative parents focus on setting limits on behavior rather than on requiring children to conform to a specific set of rigid rules. Authoritative parents tend to be pragmatic about their limit setting and also work on reasoning with their children and explaining the rationale behind the limits and expectations. Authoritative parents are just as likely to explain and reason with a child as they are to punish with consequences. Authoritative parenting focuses on reminding the child of his or her responsibility to abide by the limits while at the same time respecting the child's own rights and emotional needs.

Authoritative parents are generally pretty well prepared for sleep coaching. They recognize the double truth that it's up to them to teach their children to sleep well, but at the same time, they are fully aware that they have to respect their child's needs and temperament throughout the process. The main issue for authoritative parents who are sleep coaching is that, in general, they tend to second-guess themselves and their plan. If sleep coaching isn't going well for the first few days, authoritative parents may get concerned that they're trying the wrong method and may be tempted to change their plan too early and try a new method since their child's emotional needs are important to them. But then again, these same parents may get fed up when the new plan doesn't work either and decide to "get serious" and resort to a harsher sleep coaching method because they know that it's up to them to set limits for their child.

There are several other types of parenting philosophies, but these three present the broad parenting categories that my team and I see on a regular basis. Keep in mind that very few of us live out just ONE of these parenting philosophies. Most parents identify with a few different parenting philosophies and pick and choose what they see as the best of each of those philosophies. What's more, many parents will shift and tweak their parenting philosophies as their children grow to accommodate the child's (and, by extension, the entire family's) changing needs.

MAKE THE SLEEP SPACE SAFE AND COMFORTABLE

Whether your baby or toddler will be bed sharing, room sharing, or sleeping in a bassinet, crib, cot, Montessori bed, or toddler bed, you will want to make sure the sleep space is both safe and comfortable. This book will not go into great detail about safe sleep practices because the guidelines change over time and could become outdated within a short period of time. It is always a good idea to check with the manufacturer of any device to see whether or not it is safe and approved for sleep. To ensure that your baby's sleeping area is completely safe and that you are following safe sleep practices in your home, I recommend you consult with a healthcare provider.

In addition to safety, there are a few other things to consider in making your child's sleep space more comfortable. First, many parents tend to overdress or overheat their babies. It is natural to worry about your baby being too cold, but keep in mind that the ideal room temperature for sleep is between 68 and 70 degrees Fahrenheit (or 20 to 21 degrees Celsius). Any warmer than that is likely too warm. If you want to check that your baby is comfortable with the temperature, do a skin check; your baby's skin should be cool to the touch but not frigid. If your baby is warm or sweating, he or she is overdressed or the room is too warm, which tends to increase waking. Just like you and I may prefer different temperatures for sleep, babies will vary as to what's most comfortable for them. Some will be more sensitive to fluctuations than others, so don't get caught up on the "right" temperature so much as what's best for your child.

Aside from the temperature, consider making the sleep space more welcoming. While the sleep space should not be a playground (we do want to encourage sleeping after all), it should not seem like a jail, either. Consider safe objects such as mobiles or secured toys that play music, but stay away from unsafe things that may pose a hazard such as loose blankets and use alternatives (i.e. sleep sack). One or two items can make the sleep space a bit warmer and can also help when your child is spending nonsleep time in the space throughout the day, so it's not strictly used for sleep. In addition, blackout or room-darkening blinds, shades, or curtains can also help encourage longer naps once your baby is no longer confusing days and nights in the early days.

Lastly, consider introducing a transitional object. A transitional object (or lovey) is typically a blanket, stuffed animal, or something of that nature that your child can "love" while he or she goes to sleep. While you would not want to put anything loose in the sleep space when your child is too young, it takes time for attachment to occur, so you can start sooner rather than later. Holding it during feedings and other comforting moments can help encourage this attachment. Ask your child's medical provider when he or she can start sleeping with it.

ESTABLISH A CONSISTENT SLEEP ROUTINE

One of the first things you'll want to do prior to sleep coaching is to either create (if you don't have them in place already) or strengthen your child's pre-sleep routines. 'Pre-sleep' routines would include both the bedtime routine and the nap time routine.

A sleep routine is important because it's your child's cue that sleep is on the horizon and sets his or her expectations. They are also very useful when you are away from home and want to cue him or her to sleep elsewhere. A predictable sequence of events helps your child feel comfortable and secure in what's going to happen each night. Children thrive on routine. Routines are generally around 10 to 15 minutes long when your child is younger, and then get longer (15 minutes to as much as one hour long) as your child gets older. I know this seems odd; you wouldn't think they'd get longer as children get older, but toddlers tend to lollygag, want to look at every detail of the picture in the book, or add things onto the routine. While you want to stay a bit firm in your routine, expecting the length to be a bit longer is less frustrating for everyone.

A typical bedtime routine might include a diaper change and pajamas, a quiet game, nursing/bottle/sippy (for babies younger than one or two), teeth brushing, potty (if applicable), a book (or 2), singing and cuddling, and then lights out.

I purposely did not include a bath in my sample routine above for a few reasons:

⊘ Some parents simply don't have the time or desire to give their child a bath every single night. You might work full time and not get home until pretty close to bedtime.

⊘ Your child may have dry skin, and even plain water can dry out his or her skin more.

⊘ If your child is spirited, a bath can actually give your child a boost of energy instead of relax him or her.

Whatever your specific routine is, the individual steps are unimportant. It is only your **consistency** that makes your routines successful. Sometimes, all that's standing in the way of a child sleeping well is a good, consistent routine.

A nap routine is usually very similar to the bedtime routine but shorter (about 10 minutes). Again, the key is the consistency, not the specific steps.

Now, let me point out that while developing bedtime and nap time routines isn't rocket science, there are some common mistakes that many parents make when it comes to pre-sleep routines. In my work, I usually see parents make one or more of these five common mistakes….

1. The bedtime 'routine' is not routine! Remember, the key to a bedtime routine is to follow the same predictable pattern of events before bedtime. That is what puts the 'routine' in bedtime routine! If each day's bedtime looks

different, your routine is not a routine at all, and you are missing out on the benefits that a strong routine has to offer. Focus on creating a pattern of pre-bed activities, and then, make sure to follow it each night.

2. The bedtime routine starts too late each night. While many parents understand that the bedtime routine should contain predictable patterns of events, some miss a key element; the bedtime routine should happen at roughly the same time each night in relation to your baby's last nap. However, many families start the bedtime routine too late, pushing bedtime even later. Remember, it should take your baby roughly 10 minutes to fall asleep, so you need to lay him or her down ahead of time. Having your baby or toddler go to bed without being overtired is crucial to creating a healthy sleep schedule.

3. The bedtime routine has too much going on. If you are trying to cram eight different activities into your bedtime routine, you may be doing too much. Remember, babies and toddlers can quickly become overstimulated, so if the bedtime routine is packed full of action and requires you to transition between lots of different activities, your little one may actually become wound up instead of calm and relaxed. Instead, stick to a few simple activities at bedtime.

4. The bedtime routine is too long. We have already established that babies and toddlers can quickly become overstimulated; they also tend to become overtired very easily. So if your bedtime routine is too long, you can actually miss your child's ideal sleep window, which

means that by the end of the routine, your baby or toddler will be cranky and fussy instead of sleepy and relaxed. Try to keep the activities you do right before bed (reading books, singing lullabies, snuggling, etc.) relatively short, and be sure to watch your baby's sleep cues.

5. The routine ends when the baby is asleep. Remember, the goal in establishing a strong bedtime routine is to work towards your baby falling asleep independently. Therefore, it's key that the routine should end with your baby awake; if you inadvertently put your baby to sleep with your bedtime routine, then you're merely reinforcing sleep associations, which will set you back with sleep coaching.

ESTABLISH AN AGE-APPROPRIATE SCHEDULE

Another key step to work on prior to sleep coaching is tweaking your child's schedule as necessary. If sleep routines are helpful in signaling to your child that it's time to sleep, then your child's daily sleep and feeding schedule is downright critical to ensuring healthy, restorative sleep patterns! When you time your baby's sleep (naps, bedtime, and morning wake-up time) and feeding well, you are doing a lot to set your child up for success. Think about it this way: if your child has a tough math worksheet to finish, you have a role to play in helping your child finish it successfully. You can't do the math for your child, but you can give him or her a healthy snack, a quiet place to work, adequate supplies (like a sharpened pencil or a calculator), and plenty of encouragement and support. Doing those things is how you set your child up for success with homework. Similarly, timing up sleep and feedings and creating a sleep-friendly daily schedule is one way that you can set your child up for sleep success!

Ideal Bedtime

An early bedtime does not always happen until your baby is around three or four months old. At that point, ideally, bedtime should be between 6:00 and 8:00 p.m. Note that this is just an average; for two- to three-year-old toddlers who are still napping, a later bedtime may be necessary. In addition, cultural differences come into play with bedtime as well; many parents from Southern Europe, for example, prefer a much later bedtime. Be sure to account for your unique circumstances when planning a bedtime for your child.

For babies over four months old, typical bedtimes are often as early as between 6:00 and 7:00 p.m., depending on when the last nap ends. Many parents have been excited to see that their child is waking up at 5:00 a.m., and they simply make bedtime earlier. Their child then sleeps later in the morning. It is very counterintuitive, but it's true and it works. In addition, the baby is refreshed and rested and usually in a much better mood. Adequate sleep is instrumental in a child's development, and children are better able to learn new skills when they are well rested.

In my experience, one of the most misunderstood facts when it comes to a baby's sleep is the idea that you should keep your baby up longer to get more sleep out of him or her. This does not promote more sleep. In fact, many times, it creates less sleep!

It is very counterintuitive, but sometimes, the only thing standing in the way of a better night's sleep is an earlier bedtime. Although it is hard for many parents to accept, I promise this is true.

Obviously, this only rings true to an extent. You cannot put your child to bed at 5:00 p.m. and expect him or her to sleep until 7:00 a.m. the next morning. Although, during nap transitions (from four to three, three to two, or two to one), a baby will sometimes sleep extra long at night. My own son slept 13 hours straight during his transition to one nap and when he stopped napping altogether. I just would never expect that regularly.

The primary goal of the early bedtime is that your child is not overtired and will have a more restful sleep. Thus, it is important not to force bedtime to be later simply to achieve a later morning wake-up time. Not only does it not always work, but it sometimes has the opposite effect by making the baby wake up earlier in the morning and not sleep as restfully. An overtired baby will have more trouble falling asleep and, most importantly, staying asleep.

The problem with a bedtime that's too late and overtiredness is that when we are overtired (adults included), our bodies release hormones to fight fatigue. This makes it hard for us to settle down, relax, and sleep well. This is especially true for your baby.

The second part of the too-late-of-a-bedtime problem is that babies biologically (it's in their nature) tend to be early risers in the early days. The world is an exciting place, and they want to explore at the first sign of daylight! Don't worry. One day your child will be a teenager, and you will have to drag him or her out of bed! But, for now, this means that regardless of bedtime, you may not get to sleep in like you did before you had kids.

Use the following chart to determine when it's best to put your child to bed:

Age	Total Sleep	Avg. Wake Time*	Bed-time	Notes
Newborn	15-18 hours	Varies	N/A	Newborns need to eat frequently and will wake around the clock to feed, so a fixed bedtime is obsolete at this age. Watch your baby's sleep cues closely, and put him or her down for sleep at the first sign of tiredness.
1-4 Months	14-16 hours	Varies for 1-2 month olds; 3-4 month-olds average 1-2 hours	8-11 PM	Use a later bedtime for younger babies. By three or four months, you can gradually shift to using the earlier bedtime as your baby (hopefully) starts to sleep for one longer stretch at night.
4-8 Months	14-15 hours	2-3 hours	6-7:30 PM	Most babies are ready for a predictable schedule by about six months. Regular naps emerge at this time (four naps at first and then gradually moves to three naps). Use the earlier bedtime during the transition from four naps to three to ward off overtiredness.
8-10 Months	13-15 hours	3 hours	6-7 PM	Most babies are taking two naps at this age. This is also prime time for the eight-/nine-/10-month sleep regression! Use the earlier bedtime if the regression has your baby napping less or waking more at night and becoming overtired.
10-15 Months	12-14 hours	3-5 hours	6-7:30 PM	Stick with two naps, if possible; most babies aren't ready to transition to one nap until 15-18 months. If your baby goes through the 12-month nap regression, use the earlier bedtime to make up for lost nap sleep.
15 Months - 3 Years	12-14 hours	5 hours	6-8 PM	Your toddler will likely transition to needing just one nap by 18 months. That nap should be two to two and a half hours in length. Use the earlier bedtime during the transition from two naps to one and during the 18-month and 2-year sleep regressions to make up for any lost sleep. By 2 years of age, you should start using 7:00 p.m. as your earliest bedtime; the 6:00 p.m. bedtime is more appropriate for younger toddlers.
3-5 Years	10.75-11.25 hours	12+ hours if no longer napping	7-8:30 PM	Most children give up the afternoon nap at this stage. Substitute an afternoon rest time for the nap. Try to time bedtime so that you allow for roughly 12 hours of night sleep for children who are no longer napping. Use the later bedtime for children who are still transitioning away from the afternoon nap.

*Average Wake Time refers to the amount of time your baby or toddler is able to comfortably stay awake during the day between naps.

Fixed Points and How to Put Your Baby on a Schedule

One of the questions I hear pretty frequently from moms and dads who are working on creating sleep and feeding schedules is, "Where do I start?!" That's understandable; if you need to create a healthy sleep schedule from the ground up, it can feel overwhelming. Do you start with naps? With meals?

Neither, actually. You'll want to start with a fixed point and build from there. Fixed points are parts of your baby's daily routines that happen at approximately the same time each day. Note the 'approximately' there; these are not strictly clock based! However, a fixed point should happen at about the same time (in the same 30-45-minute window) from day to day.

A great way to start establishing fixed points in your child's day is to start with your child's morning wake-up time. The idea here is that you make sure your baby (or toddler) wakes up at approximately the same time each morning. If your baby or toddler has a consistent wake-up time, it will go a long way towards creating consistency in the rest of the day's activities. Keep in mind that as much as we'd love for our children to sleep in until 8:00 a.m. on the weekend, even if they need to be up at 6:00 a.m. during the week, this is not realistic for most children.

The next fixed point that many parents choose to work on is a consistent bedtime. Now, remember, if you have a newborn, "bedtime" will change a lot over the next few months. However, by the time your baby is about four or five months old, you can start aiming for a more consistent bedtime each day. As with the morning wake-up time, this fixed point works well for both babies and toddlers.

Nap time can also be a fixed point in your baby's schedule, specifically the timing of the first morning nap for younger babies (six months or younger) and the first two naps for older babies. Once you've got bedtime and the morning wake-up time down pretty well, you can start working on making the morning nap happen at about the same time each day, and then, you can add other fixed points like a second nap, if desired.

Meals can also become fixed points in your child's schedule *when your child is older and no longer needs feedings on demand*. For example, your toddler's meals can become fixed points each morning, afternoon, and evening, and then, you can fill in naps around those meals.

Here's the beauty of fixed points: you can start using them almost as soon as you bring your baby home from the hospital. Fixed points provide an incredibly gentle, scalable way to organize your baby's day. For newborns and young babies, just one or maybe two fixed points can be helpful. As your baby grows, you can begin strengthening those existing fixed points and adding in new ones. If you do this, eventually, you'll have a very consistent, predictable daily schedule carved out for your child, and the best part is that it will have happened gradually and gently over time.

How Rigid Should Your Schedule Be?

Depending on your personality, the word "schedule" either sounds like music to your ears or sends a shudder down your spine. And I get that; just as all babies are unique, all parents are unique, too! Some of us are more type-A and love predictable schedules and routines, but I know that many of you may be more go-with-the-flow parents and may really love spontaneity and flexibility in your daily plans.

It's no wonder, then, that "How rigid does my child's schedule have to be?" is a question I hear quite often in my line of work! The answer, really, is "it depends." And it does; it depends on your preferences, your child's personality and typical sleep patterns, and more. To really decide which is best for you and your family, however, you need more information. So, let's take a look at the benefits of both a rigid schedule and a more flexible schedule.

Benefits of a Rigid Schedule

The main benefit of a rigid baby sleep schedule is the fact that it's predictable. This can be really helpful to you as it allows you to plan things, like errands or play dates, with confidence, but it's also helpful to your baby as it helps him or her know what to expect every day, too. By prioritizing your baby's sleep and making sure he or she is in the crib at nap time and bedtime will make it that much more likely that your child will sleep well and will ensure your baby has the opportunity to nap longer. When you have a fairly rigid schedule in place, you are ensuring that your baby goes down for naps in his or her "sleep windows" and reinforcing the internal clock that directs sleep and wake cycles.

Benefits of a Flexible Schedule

What if your baby doesn't get sleepy at the same times every day? Or, what if your family life is such that your days have to be different from one to the next? A flexible baby sleep schedule allows you to have much more flexibility in your day. Your play date wants to meet at 10:00 instead of 11:00? No problem. That baby swim class is at 1:00 p.m. twice a week right when your baby's nap is? Not an issue! Grandma and grandpa come to visit for two hours, making bedtime an hour later? No sweat at all. Having a flexible sleep schedule is definitely appealing in many ways. It feels much less like your whole world revolves around your baby's sleep and schedule. That's for sure!

Is a Rigid or Flexible Sleep Schedule Right for Your Baby?

Unfortunately, what's convenient for us isn't always what works for our baby. While your personality will likely make one or the other seem more appealing, your baby's personality and sleep needs are important here, too. Simply put, your baby will make it a success or a failure, and sometimes, maybe it's somewhere in between leading to some good days and some bad days.

From a sleep perspective, it is usually best to keep a rigid sleep schedule (not necessarily feeding schedule) for highly inconsistent babies because it helps "set" their internal clock and biological rhythms. If you allow your inconsistent baby to drive the schedule, he or she is more likely to continue being even more inconsistent than what's "normal" for him or her.

For babies who are very sensitive to becoming overtired, which leads to less and less sleep, it's important to keep their sleep at a high priority. It doesn't necessarily mean keeping a rigid schedule by the clock, but it means making sure they are not awake too long before sleep. It means that swim class might have to wait until your child has changed his or her schedule.

For babies who can sometimes stay up longer and other times can't, having a rigid schedule where they are in the crib when they are not tired could lead to other sleep problems and frustration for your baby. Maybe your baby needs a more flexible schedule that is driven more by his or her sleep needs and cues.

The bottom line is that YOU will need to deal with the aftermath, if any, of any decision you make about scheduling. Everyone else who has an opinion doesn't have to deal with a cranky baby and doesn't have to get up with your baby at night; YOU do. When it came to my highly inconsistent son who was supremely oversensitive to being overtired (and still is but not AS much), I simply could not afford to let too many things disrupt his schedule or routine (especially since he did NOT sleep "on the go" AT ALL after he was a month old). At a minimum, it would set us off course for a week or so with night wakings and lots of crankiness. I tried it a couple of times, and to me, it just wasn't worth it. For others, maybe it would be. With my second son, I *finally* saw how on Earth people had more flexible schedules and could (gasp!) be out of the house sometimes during nap time! My second son was far more relaxed and adaptable than my first, so my family could enjoy occasional fun that pushed his nap back or forced his nap to end early; these occasional disruptions simply didn't affect my younger son the way they did my oldest.

Whether you have a rigid or flexible baby sleep schedule will be a personal decision based on your personality, your baby's personality, and what sleep problems it may or may not bring. Any "event" had to be "worth" the stress for us with our boys. Unfortunately, this meant that we missed several family picnics and other gatherings (which I'm sure we were criticized for), but I knew it would be a relatively short time in our lives.

So I can't answer for you whether a rigid sleep schedule or a flexible sleep schedule might be right for YOU, but I can tell you that I believe you need to do what's best for your child even if others criticize you or do not understand your motives.

What Should Your Schedule Look Like?

I hope, at this point, you're realizing that a healthy sleep and feed-ing schedule is key to ensuring that your baby learns to sleep well. Even the best sleep coaching plans will fail if you have problems with your daily schedule.

But with that said, what exactly does a healthy sleep and feed-ing schedule look like for your baby? After all, babies change at lightning speeds in that first year, and even toddlers will have change to their mealtime and sleep time patterns that seem to happen overnight.

In this section, we'll examine some general scheduling rules to follow, including how to time up your child's naps so that he or she gets enough rest and how to introduce a clock-based sched-ule in a way that's gentle and gradual and won't result in missed sleep for your child.

Two quick notes, though, before we start:

1. There are a lot of sample schedules that are arranged by age in the Appendix of this book; you can use these as starting points for creating your child's schedule.

2. One of the most popular scheduling tools my team offers is included in The Baby Sleep Site® app. It's a schedule gener-ator that allows you to enter your baby's age and typical morn-ing wake-up time, and then, it generates a customized schedule. The app is completely free to download and is available for both Apple® (www.babysleepsite.com/apple) and Android™ (www.babysleepsite.com/android) devices.

When used in combination, these scheduling resources (the schedule rules below, the sample schedules in the Appendix, and the custom schedule generator that's included in The Baby Sleep Site® app) should help you craft a schedule that's both age appropriate and sleep inducing.

One final word about scheduling: these guidelines and sample schedules are meant to be just that, guidelines and samples. As I always say to my clients, your mileage may vary! That is, your baby may need slightly more or less wake time between naps. Your baby may need smaller, more frequent feedings. Your child may need to hang on to night feedings a bit longer than average. There are so many unique factors to consider when creating a sleep schedule, and that's why I'm always quick to remind parents to trust their instincts and to check with their healthcare providers when necessary. You should absolutely feel free to tweak and adjust the guidelines and sample schedules I provide in this book to fit your unique child.

Alright, now on to the information that I'm sure many of you are eager to learn! Here are the steps I generally recommend for creating a healthy sleep schedule for babies who are older than four months. (Note: babies younger than this are simply not ready for a clock-based schedule.) Additionally, be advised that while some four- and five-month-old babies can manage a clock-based daily schedule, others can't and aren't ready for that until six or seven months. Use your judgment in determining if your baby is ready for a clock-based schedule, but avoid trying to force one too soon.

Okay, now on to the steps:

1. Start with your baby's average wake-up time.

Note the "average" here; your baby may not wake up at the exact same time every day because children, after all, are not robots! Instead, watch for about two weeks and note the average time your child wakes up, give or take half an hour. If your child doesn't have a usual wake-up time, use the wake-up time that you'd like your child to have.

2. Add the age-appropriate nap gap.

What's a 'nap gap?' It's simply the time between "sleeps." So think about the time between when your child wakes up and when he or she goes down for the first nap of the day; that's your child's nap gap. Now, for most children, their nap gaps are roughly the same between sleeps, so if your child has about an hour between waking up in the morning and going down for the first nap, you can plan for about an hour between the end of the first morning nap and the start of the next nap. Nap gaps do tend to lengthen a bit throughout the day, so a baby who needs to nap two hours after waking for the morning may need three hours between the final nap and bedtime.

As your child grows, nap gaps will gradually lengthen until the point where your child is ready to stop napping altogether (between ages three and five). The key, then, is to determine what kind of nap gap your child needs in order to be well rested. Here's a look at average nap gaps by age:

- ⊘ 0-2 months: 1 hour
- ⊘ 3-5 months: 1-2 hours
- ⊘ 6-8 months: 2-3 hours
- ⊘ 8-10 months: 2.5-3.5 hours
- ⊘ 11-15 months: 3-4 hours
- ⊘ 16-18 months: 5 hours
- ⊘ 19-24 months: 5-6 hours

⊘ 25+ months: 5.5-6.5 hours until your child is ready to stop napping (At that point, focus on nighttime sleep totals to determine if your child is getting enough sleep.)

You can see how the nap gap will drive your daily schedule. If you start with your child's morning wake-up time, you will use the nap gap to determine the timing of the day's naps.

3. Encourage a nap that is at least one hour long.

Now, speaking of naps, the next thing you want to do in your daily schedule is allow for a nap that's at least one hour long. Again, we are assuming that your baby is at least four to five months old; younger babies often have much shorter catnaps, which is perfectly normal. For babies four to five months old and older, we expect at least a one-hour nap one to two times per day, depending on age. The occasional catnap is fine; children often have catnaps when they're about to drop a nap and transition to fewer naps per day, when they're sick or teething, or if they happen to miss an earlier nap for some reason. Additionally, when your baby is firmly on a three-nap schedule, you will likely find that the third nap always remains a short catnap. But in general, if your child's naps are always shorter than an hour, there's a problem, and we'll need to focus on lengthening those naps until they're at least an hour.

As your child drops naps, you'll see that the length of each nap gets longer; this is why a toddler who takes only one afternoon nap may nap for two to three solid hours whereas a baby who is still taking two naps will probably nap for one to one and a half hours at a time and actually shouldn't nap for more than two hours.

4. Add the next age-appropriate nap gap based on when baby woke up from last nap.

When you know your child's age-appropriate nap gap and when you know the target length that each nap should be, you can turn all this out into a clock-based schedule. For example, if your child takes three naps a day and you want to aim for the first two naps to be at least one hour in length, combining that with the nap gap will give you very precise times for each nap. That's why it's best to plan the second (and possibly other) nap(s) and bedtime based on the nap gap since it allows for some flexibility to the schedule so that your baby is not too tired but tired enough to sleep well at naps and bedtime.

The beauty of this system, too, is that if your schedule gets off for some reason (i.e. if your baby has a nap that's too short or too long), you can easily correct the course by applying the nap gap to determine when the next nap (or when bedtime) should happen.

5. Repeat until bedtime, depending on age.

Now that you know how the nap gaps and the length of your child's naps work together, you can basically write out a detailed sleep schedule and then fill in meals around the naps. However, depending on your child's age, you may not actually want to lay out a specific time for every nap. Let me explain: the younger your child is, the less ironclad your child's daily schedule should be. What I mean by that is that for younger babies, it's usually best to use the fixed point approach I outlined earlier; that is, aim for a few fixed times each day but don't try to fix the time of EVERY nap and EVERY meal. Why? Simply because young babies usually can't stick to such a detailed, time-sensitive schedule.

As your child gets older, however, you can move more and more towards a schedule that's very specific and has every nap and every meal happening at a specific time.

Now, here's what to keep in mind: this is a start. Observe and re-evaluate how your baby is doing on the schedule. Schedule changes take one to two weeks to see the cumulative impact, so don't change your schedule too fast or give up on it after just two or three days. Tweak the schedule as necessary, but give the schedule some time to take hold. Once established, you can consider sticking more strictly to the clock if your baby isn't overly sensitive to overtiredness or schedule fluctuations.

> *Our daughter was sleeping well through the night; that actually wasn't our problem. Nap time was the issue, and I was beside myself with anguish over it. Fortunately, an age-appropriate schedule plus sleep coaching worked wonders. I worked on getting my daughter on a better schedule first and then worked with her on falling asleep without sleep associations. It worked! We even took a trip to California and back, and the napping routine remained fairly consistent. She falls asleep on her own now without fussing and is napping great.* **-Heather**

DETERMINE IF A NAP TRANSITION IS APPROACHING

Do you know what frustrates many parents? The fact that just when you work out a nice, predictable daytime sleep schedule, your child will get a little bit older and blow your perfectly crafted routine to pieces. Truth is, the first few years of a child's life are full of changes, and those changes add up to mean ever-shifting sleep patterns and schedules.

This is really apparent when you consider a child's typical nap schedule from birth to toddlerhood. If you've taken a look at the sample schedules in the Appendix, then you've seen that newborn babies take five or more naps each day; however, by 18 months, toddlers are taking one nap. That's a lot of change, and transitioning between all those nap schedules can be a huge headache for little ones and for their parents.

That's why, in this section, we'll take a look at exactly when common nap transitions happen, how to spot a nap transition approaching, and (most importantly) how to navigate the transition without making your child (and yourself) exhausted and frustrated.

When Do Nap Transitions Usually Happen?

Of course, there's no blueprint that'll let you know exactly when your baby or toddler is due for a nap transition. However, there's a general timeline that most babies and toddlers seem to follow, and that will be helpful in pinpointing when nap transitions are most likely to occur:

- ⊘ From one to four months, the number of naps your baby takes will be variable but will hover around four to five naps per day, depending on how long his or her naps are and how long he or she can stay up between naps.
- ⊘ By three or four months old, he or she will lean towards just four naps rather than five.
- ⊘ From five to eight months, most babies will have three

naps per day. They will start to resist the fourth nap no matter how tired they are. There are a few babies who will only have two naps at a very young age, but those naps are usually long.

- From nine to 15 or 18 months, your baby will nap two times a day on average. Although many people believe most babies can transition to one nap at 12 months, the average age is actually 15 to 18 months.

- From 18 months to four years, toddlers nap once a day. The age that a child transitions away from all napping varies a lot, ranging from two to five or more years old, but the average age is between three and four years old.

The early nap transitions (from five to four to three) usually happen quickly and aren't as problematic. It's the other nap transitions (from three to two to one to none) that tend to frustrate parents. For one thing, those nap transitions take longer as some children take months and months to transition from one nap to none, and they seem to affect children more noticeably. By far, the transitions that I get the most questions about from clients are the three to two transition and the two to one transition. In my experience, the two to one transition can be most difficult because you're dealing with a young toddler who's just beginning to discover that he or she has a mind of his or her own and is just beginning to realize that he or she can assert his or her will via these great little things called "tantrums".

How to Tell If a Nap Transition Is Approaching

How will your baby or toddler let you know that a nap transition is coming? Here are a few signs to look for:

⊘ Your baby or toddler begins consistently refusing a nap. Most parents find that their little one suddenly starts refusing a nap (usually an afternoon one) that, just yesterday, they agreed to without a problem. That tends to be the classic sign that a nap transition is approaching.

⊘ The timing of your baby's or toddler's naps begins to change; other parents discover that before a nap transition, the schedule generally goes crazy. Nap time goes from being predictable to being all over the place. This can interfere with nighttime sleep, too; if the afternoon nap doesn't happen until late afternoon or early evening, for example, it can interfere with bedtime.

⊘ The length of your baby's or toddler's naps begins to change. You may notice that one or more of your little one's naps are suddenly much shorter than normal. This can be a sign that your baby or toddler is getting ready to drop a nap.

Signs of an Approaching Nap Transition or Signs of a Sleep Regression?

Here's one thing to remember — not all nap craziness is a sign that a nap transition is coming. Refusing to nap is often a symptom of a sleep regression; in those cases, it shouldn't be treated as a sign that a nap transition is approaching.

For example, a baby who's in the throes of the eight-/nine-/10-month sleep regression may start to resist naps; however, this is not a sign that he or she should downshift from two naps to one. Most children aren't ready for one nap until 15 to 18 months. Similarly, an 18-month-old who suddenly starts refusing naps probably isn't giving up naps altogether; he or she is probably just going through the 18-month sleep regression.

How do you tell the difference? Wait a bit. Most regressions work themselves out within a week or two, but some can last for up to six weeks. If the napping issues haven't resolved themselves within a few weeks and if it's time for a nap transition to happen, then you can consider it a sign that your child is ready to drop a nap.

Making Baby and Toddler Nap Transitions Easier

How can you make your baby's or toddler's nap transitions less painful and easier to deal with? Here are a few ideas to consider:

- Use alternating nap schedules for a while. Nap transitions aren't an all-or-nothing process. During the nap transition itself (which can take weeks or even months), there's no harm in alternating nap schedules. If your baby is transitioning from three naps to two, for example, offer two naps for a few days and then switch back to three naps for a day or two. Going back and forth like this will ensure that your baby doesn't become overly exhausted during the nap transition and will help ease your child into the new routine. Of course, alternating like this tends to prolong the nap transition, and it won't work for every child. But it's a good approach for babies and toddlers who are especially sensitive to overtiredness.

- Make changes in small increments. Some children (especially those who are highly adaptable) won't bat an eye at big schedule changes. Others, though, have their worlds rocked by even small adjustments to the routine. If that sounds like your baby, then make the nap transition happen in small degrees. If your toddler is transitioning from two naps to one, for example, don't suddenly eliminate the morning nap altogether. Rather, push it back a bit (by even 10 or 15 minutes). Wait a few days, and then, push it back a little more. Sure, this approach takes awhile, but it's a gentle way to ease your toddler into the new schedule.

◎ Shift bedtime as necessary. When you're navigating a nap transition, everything else in the schedule is up for grabs, too. This can mean manipulating bedtime to account for the changing nap schedule. To be clear, we don't recommend pushing bedtime back; instead, we recommend waking your child up from a late afternoon or early evening nap that's going too long. We recommend an earlier bedtime on days when it seems necessary. For example, if your toddler is transitioning from one nap to none, an early bedtime might be in order on the days when he or she doesn't take a nap.

◎ Don't be afraid to wake your baby or toddler from a nap. It's rare that we recommend you wake up your child, but during a nap transition, you may need to wake your baby or toddler from a nap. For example, if an afternoon nap started later than normal and is going to extend into the "danger zone" (the point at which it starts to interfere with bedtime), by all means, end the nap. (Hint: typically, for children of all ages and in most situations, we recommend no napping after 6:00 p.m.) Your baby or toddler may need you to guide him or her through the nap transition to make sure that he or she is sleeping at appropriate times.

◎ Watch the morning wake-up time carefully. Nap transitions mess with sleep, plain and simple, and when your baby's or toddler's sleep is out of whack, it can lead to missed sleep, which in turn causes overtiredness. And what can overtiredness cause? Early waking. You'll want to watch for that during a nap transition. Generally, we consider anything before 6:00 a.m. early waking unless you WANT your child to be up for the day before that time. If your baby or toddler is waking too early, avoid getting them up for the day at their early waking time. Instead, treat that early rising like a night waking, and do what you can to keep them in bed and encourage sleep until at least 6:00 a.m. You can usually accomplish this by keeping the room dark and boring and by not engaging with your kiddo until it's time to wake up. By preventing an early wake up, you help preserve the schedule, which is key when you're trying to manage a nap transition. We'll share more on dealing with early morning waking later in this book.

DETERMINE IF YOU AND YOUR BABY ARE READY TO NIGHT WEAN

We've been talking a lot up to this point about daytime sleep and feeding schedules, but I know many of you reading this are, no doubt, dealing with some nighttime feeding as well. A question I hear often when working with parents on sleep coaching is, "Do I have to drop all my baby's night feedings now that I'm sleep coaching?" My answer is almost always no! In fact, I advise against it.

For starters, your baby may need some (or all) of those night feedings, so don't fall into the trap of assuming that all night feedings are problematic. Additionally, you generally don't want to work on night weaning and sleep coaching at the same time as it often results in "marathon" nights that are difficult to follow through with consistently. Instead, it's better to break your sleep coaching plan up into small pieces and tackle night weaning only after you've worked on other sleep coaching tasks first.

How Many Night Feedings Does Your Child Need?

The first step in dealing with your child's nighttime feedings is to determine how many night feedings your child actually needs. When you know, you can hold that information up against your child's unique needs and health concerns and get a good sense of when it might be time to night wean.

Now, what's tricky is that pediatricians all seem to disagree on when a baby can go all night without a feeding, and there's a lot of disagreement about just how many night feedings are necessary for babies of different ages as well! There is Ferber, who claims babies don't need to eat at night after three months old, and then there is Weissbluth, who says babies need one to two feedings up through nine months old. Who's right? They are both pediatricians with a lot of experience; your child's pediatrician may have an even different answer.

In most of my work with parents, I cannot, in good conscience, ever recommend purposely night weaning at three months old. I think that is extreme to think that all babies can do that, particularly breastfed babies. Moms who were exclusively breastfeeding and who night weaned their three-month-old babies would, no doubt, see a noticeable drop in milk supply. Now, some parents will tell you that their two- or three-month-old babies night weaned on their own, which is fine, but I would never recommend that you push your child to night wean at three months.

In general, I am not an extremist, and when it comes to hunger at night, I err on the side of caution. I know that it would be so much easier for us to not feed at night. However, keep in mind that plenty of adults can't go 12 hours without eating, so I am not sure why we expect our babies to. I am all for changing sleep associations and promoting healthy sleep for our babies, but I don't recommend night weaning until your baby is showing signs that he or she is ready and until it is age appropriate to do so. These two elements held together - signs that your baby is ready and your baby's age - are the keys to determining when it's time to night wean.

Signs That Your Baby Is Ready to Night Wean

Be on the lookout for these signs; they could be indications that your baby is ready to drop nighttime feedings:

1. Your baby is not eating as much during the day. If you find that your baby is not eating as much as usual during daylight hours but is still waking to eat one or more times during the night, that's a good indication that it may be time to drop (or at least reduce) nighttime feedings. Encourage your baby to eat more during the day; if he or she can get most or all of his or her calories in during the day, your child will be ready to wean away from eating at night.

2. Your baby is not eating much at night and treats nighttime feedings as play time. You may start to notice that even though your baby wakes at night and cries for you, he or she isn't very hungry. Your child might nurse a little

or drink a little of the bottle and then be wide awake and wanting to 'play.' In these cases, your baby is likely waking out of habit (or due to sleep associations) and not out of hunger. This may be a sign that the nighttime feedings are not really necessary anymore and that your child is ready to drop them.

3. Your baby has started solid foods at the appropriate time. (Disclaimer: there is a right time and a wrong time to start your baby on solid foods. In general, according to the American Academy of Pediatrics, it's best to wait until your baby is close to six months of age before starting solid foods.) Once your baby has started eating solid foods, it won't be too long before he or she is ready to wean from nighttime feedings. Your baby may continue to need one (or possibly two) night feedings after he or she starts solid food, but after a few months, you should be able to gradually wean from nighttime eating.

4. There is a wide variance in your baby's nighttime feeding. This one can be trickier to diagnose. But if you notice a lot of variation in when your baby wakes for night feedings, that can be a sign that it's time to night wean. For instance, if your baby wakes at 11:00 p.m. and 4:00 a.m. to eat one day, wakes at 3:00 a.m. the next day, and then wakes at 10:30 p.m. and not again until morning on the third day, that variance may mean it is time to start the night weaning process.

Keep in mind that none of these signs on their own mean that your baby is ready to night wean. For example, a three-month-old baby may have a few nights when there are big variances in the timing of night feedings, but that certainly does not mean that he or she is ready to stop eating at night! However, if you see two or three of these signs together and your baby is at an age when it would be appropriate to night wean, that is a good indication that you can begin the night weaning process.

> My baby never slept well, and I finally turned to a local 'sleep expert' in my city. She told me that my four-month-old breastfed baby should be sleeping 12 hours each night with no feedings. Well, I tried this for a few nights, but it was awful! Fortunately, I stopped trying to night wean my baby so early and, instead, really followed my instincts and my baby's signs. It's so refreshing to be reminded that I am capable of guiding this process (with my baby's help)!   **-Leah**

Night Feeding Averages by Age

Below are the number of feedings at night, at various ages, that are within "normal" range (in my experience) and don't throw up a red flag that there is more going on than just a feeding:

- Newborns to 3 months: feedings every 2-3 hours on demand
- 3-4 months: 2-3 feedings per night or every 3-6 hours on demand
- 5-6 months: 1-2 feedings
- 7-9 months: 1 or maybe 2 feedings
- 10-12 months: sometimes 1 feeding
- 12+ months: generally no feedings

Now, obviously, growth spurts are an exception to these totals; you should feed as needed during growth spurts. Growth spurts are generally over within a week, though, so if you notice a spike in night feedings around the time of a growth spurt, it should be over relatively quickly. And working moms who are separated from their babies for long periods of time may see slightly higher numbers.

Now, I know it can be tough to sort all of this information out, and when you apply your own child's unique sleeping and feeding patterns, it can be tough to figure out exactly when you should work on night weaning. So I'm going to give you a tip that I give to many of my clients: if you're not sure, I recommend at least an attempt at night weaning by eight to nine months of age. Why? Because, at some point, night feeding becomes a chicken-and-egg problem. A baby needs a certain amount of sustenance during the day, and if your child gets some at night, he or she won't eat more during the day. If your child doesn't eat more during the day, he or she needs it at night and so on…are you beginning to see the problem?

So, sometimes, a baby really does feel hungry at night, but it doesn't mean he or she can't go all night without a feeding. It simply means that your child needs to adjust how much he or she is eating during the day. The idea with attempting night weaning at eight to nine months is to gently help him or her do this.

Personally, I tried to night wean at around nine months, but with both my boys, they continued to eat at night up through one year. They did, however, sleep better after I nudged them in the right direction, so I was glad that I had at least tried. With the many parents I have worked with, most breastfed babies seem to night wean between nine and 12 months and formula-fed babies tend to night wean by six months.

One last note: if you're still unsure about night weaning or feel like you need more guidance, you can take my online night weaning quiz for extra help. You can find it here: www.babysleepsite. com/night-weaning-quiz

Night Weaning May Impact Breast Milk Supply

If you're not breastfeeding exclusively, this won't apply to you, but if you are exclusively breastfeeding and if you'd like to continue doing so even after your baby is night weaned, you'll want to be aware that night weaning may negatively impact your milk supply. In general, moms shouldn't go longer than five to 10 hours without breastfeeding, depending on the age of the baby.

DECIDE IF YOU REALLY NEED TO SLEEP COACH

Do you really have a sleeping problem? I have had quite a few emails telling me what they believe their baby "should" be doing based on age. Your three-month-old is "still" co-sleeping and everyone tells you she will be in your bed until she's 10 years old, so "should" you transition her to crib? You rock your baby to sleep and she sleeps for 12 hours and wakes for one night-time feeding, but everyone tells you that you "shouldn't" rock her to sleep. Not every "problem" truly is a problem. Our babies go through so many phases and changes these first few years. I promise that not all babies who are rocked to sleep will have sleep problems just like not all children will be in your bed until they are eight or 10 years old because you co-sleep now. I have worked with many six–month-, 10–month-, 18–month-, and 3-year-olds who are transitioning to their own sleep space. It is never too late to change sleep habits. Yes, sometimes it's harder, but sometimes, it's not. Find out what is working for you now, and don't be afraid to make your own "rules."

When you're struggling with your baby's or toddler's sleep and everyone around you either has "the answer" or the baby or toddler who is the perfect sleeper, it's easy to lose confidence and wonder if you're doing everything wrong. You might question your ability to parent. But what I tell my clients a lot is that sometimes you do EVERYTHING right and your baby just. won't. sleep. You can only do so much. You can lead a horse to water but can't make him drink is how the saying goes, and it is so true when it comes to your baby's sleep.

Your job is to provide a soothing sleep environment and to give the opportunity for sleep; unfortunately, the rest is up to your child. When my son, now older, tells me at bedtime, "I'm not tired" even though I know it isn't true, it is my job to set limits that lights are out at a certain time no matter what. Most of the time, he is asleep in a few minutes, and other nights, he might take 10 to 15 minutes while he listens to a CD playing. Either way, I've done my job. And when he was a baby, my job was to make sure we stuck to routine pretty regularly because of his temperament and to get him the sleep he needed because of the ramifications if we didn't. Sure, family members didn't understand why we had to skip the barbecue for his nap (among many other things), but his sleep and well being came first. We knew him best, AND we were the ones who had to get up at 10:00 p.m., 1:00 a.m., 3:00 a.m., etc. when he wasn't sleeping from being overtired. They weren't going to do it! There are many things to help promote sleep, of course, and that's what this is all about. But at some point, you do have to let go and realize that they are just going to do what they are going to do and that they will have good days and bad days just like we do.

All in all, YOU KNOW YOUR BABY BEST! You are the one who's with them day in and day out (even working parents like me). And you know what you can handle as a parent. We knew the result if we kept our son out too late, so we chose our special events very carefully. They would always set us back at least a week. Our second son was much more of a go-with-the-flow child, so I can definitely see how people do it. It just wasn't going to happen with our first son, and it's not because he was first. It's just his personality, temperament, and sleep needs. It's just how the cookie crumbles.

> *I worked for months to solve my daughter's sleep problems, and while I did make progress, it seems like just when we'd solve one issue, a new one would crop up. Well, once my daughter was a year old, I figured I could try night weaning as I could tell she really didn't need her 4:30 a.m. feeding anymore. It was a tough week of weaning her off that feeding, but the work was worth it; my daughter's now sleeping 11 hours straight each night! It's been great. What's more, I'm seeing now that night weaning has really helped my girl's sleep.... I think this may be the end of our sleep problems for a while!* **-Gina**

DETERMINE WHETHER OR NOT TO KEEP THE PACIFIER

Believe it or not, one of the key steps to take before you start sleep coaching is to determine whether or not you're going to keep the pacifier if your child uses one. Many families use pacifiers without issue. Especially in the first few months of your baby's life, the pacifier can be a great way to help soothe and calm your fussy infant. Your baby's innate sucking reflex is strong, and pacifiers can be a welcomed addition to your daily routines, giving breastfeeding mothers a break in some cases.

However, while some children can keep the pacifier as part of their daily routine, others need to be weaned from the pacifier either before or during sleep coaching because pacifiers can disrupt sleep. How can you tell whether or not your child needs to drop the pacifier? Here are some factors to consider. It is probably fine to keep the pacifier if...

- ...your baby can find and replace the pacifier (or learn to) when it falls out of his or her mouth all the time, every time and doesn't need you to help.
- ...your child uses the pacifier only for soothing when he or she is upset and it's not part of your child's sleep routines.
- ...your child sucks on the pacifier as part of the bedtime and nap time routines but does not need the pacifier to fall asleep or stay asleep.

However, you probably need to work on weaning your child away from the pacifier before or during sleep coaching if...

- ...your baby cannot replace the pacifier when it falls out and needs your help every time the pacifier needs replacing. In this case, it is no doubt unmanageable for you to replace the pacifier a dozen times each night.

- ⊘ ...your child cannot fall asleep or stay asleep without sucking on the pacifier, and it has become a sleep association.
- ⊘ ...the pacifier is causing you stress and frustration and is causing more problems than it's solving.

As for how to wean your child away from the pacifier, like anything else, you can just gradually fade out how long your child sucks on the pacifier at sleep times or how often your child uses the pacifier. For example, if your child is accustomed to falling asleep with the pacifier, you may want to start by sleep coaching during bedtime but giving him or her the pacifier the remainder of the night, and work your way up to all night without the pacifier. Keep in mind that day and night sleep are handled by two different parts of the brain, so you can stop using a pacifier at night but not during the day (or vice versa) in many cases. This allows you to gradually wean the pacifier rather than stop using it cold turkey, which can be hard to manage.

Another factor to consider is that toddlers often begin to feel emotionally attached to their pacifier as if it's their 'lovey' or favorite teddy bear. Therefore, I recommend to most families to stop using the pacifier before 18 months if possible. If that doesn't work, and your child is still using the pacifier at 18 months of age, then I usually recommend keeping the pacifier until he or she is old enough to stop napping, which will be around three to four years of age. Removing the pacifier before a child is done napping can prematurely inhibit napping. Of course, there are some pediatric dentists who will encourage you to remove the pacifier earlier. Every situation is different, but these are factors to consider if you keep the pacifier.

DETERMINE WHEN TO START SLEEP COACHING

Before you embark on sleep coaching, you'll want to take into account when your baby is "primed" for sleep coaching and when he or she is not. There are definitely seasons in your child's life when sleep coaching tends to go a little better as well as seasons when it tends to stall out or have lots of rough patches. Therefore, one of the ways to help sleep coaching go smoothly is to do it during one of your baby's ideal sleep coaching windows.

Your Baby's Ideal Sleep Coaching Windows

You can sleep coach your baby (or toddler) at any time, of course, but it may be a bit easier if you do it during one of these windows:

- The four- to seven-month window: This is best time to start for many families (although not all). Why? Because at this point, your baby is past the four-month sleep regression, so he or she is starting to develop more "adult" sleep patterns. Your baby is also much less mobile at this stage than he or she will be in a few more months, and that lack of mobility makes sleep coaching a bit easier. Finally, because your baby is still quite young at this point, any sleep associations he or she may have formed won't have had time to turn into strong habits. That means they'll be easier to change.

- The 11- to 16-month window: This isn't as ideal of a time to sleep coach as the four- to seven-month window, but if you skip that one, this is the next ideal window. Why? Because your baby is past the sleep regression that happens between eight and 10 months, and his or her sleep patterns should be back to normal. (Although if your baby has never been a great sleeper, his or her "normal" sleep patterns may be fairly crazy!) Remember, it's best to sleep coach when things are as normal as possible, so waiting until a sleep regression has passed is a good idea.

Less Ideal Times for Sleep Coaching

In general, it's best to avoid sleep coaching during a sleep regression. If possible, try to sleep coach before your little one is 18 months old; after 18 months, your toddler's growing sense of independence and willfulness might make sleep coaching tougher. But be careful: don't let this information paralyze you or make you put off or give up on sleep coaching! While sleep coaching may go a little more smoothly if you do it during one of these two windows, you can sleep coach at any time. You're the best judge of when it's time to start sleep coaching because you know your baby best!

A few more tips about exactly when to start sleep coaching:

First, I generally advise parents not to do formal sleep coaching (especially anything that involves crying) until the baby is at least four months of age. Some parents (particularly if they have a very challenging sleeper but have other kids to tend to) decide to start much earlier.. If you do decide to start early, don't be afraid to take a break if isn't going well and try again a few weeks later. I have worked with families who started sleep coaching at eight to 10 weeks old only to find it doesn't work and try again at 12 weeks with great success. If starting early, it's a good idea to close-ly monitor and reassess your child as necessary. Many parents start sleep coaching when the way their child falls asleep becomes a preference rather than a necessity. In other words, when a baby is six weeks old, parents can tell that their child needs their help falling asleep. Later on, they recognize that their child wants (not needs) their help, but their "help" only gets in the way of better sleep.

Second, it is never too early to start routines and set the stage for healthy sleep habits. For example, it does not hurt to try to put your baby down drowsy but awake from birth; even if your baby won't fall asleep this way, you can try it for one nap each day as a start to building healthy sleep habits. Also, I highly recommend not running to your baby at the slightest whimper. It is common for babies to resettle themselves, and when you race to soothe your baby too quickly, you may be inhibiting his or her ability to learn how to self soothe back to sleep.

The truth of the matter is that there is never a "perfect" time to start sleep coaching, meaning that there will always be a rea-son you can think of as to why you shouldn't. But that doesn't mean some regressions aren't harder than others. If a particular-ly challenging sleep regression starts during sleep coaching, the best thing to do is keep going, BUT recognize that progress could come in fits and starts and that sleep may not be perfect. Your baby is not a robot, so each day can be met with new challenges. The best way to get good at anything isn't to only "do" it when it's easy. To master it completely, you also need to do it when it's "hard." Of course, they are babies and may need your help with soothing and calming down, but if you ultimately follow through, you will be better off when the leap is over. This may mean you will have some good days and some bad and that's okay. It is certainly always an acceptable option to take a break for a few weeks, but just keep in mind that weeks can turn into months. So as long as you are happy with your journey and progress, that's all that matters. Just remember, there is not really a "perfect" time to start and there may always be challenges ahead of you, so choose a time when you can commit. Then, like Nike® says, "Just do it." The first step is often the hardest.

> *My son was nine months old when I finally decided to work on sleep. He'd been a decent sleeper until the four-month regression hit; after that, sleep went downhill. At the advice of our pediatrician, we tried a few different sleep coaching methods. Many nights, my husband and I were up checking on him every 10 minutes; we weren't getting any sleep and neither was my son! Finally, I couldn't take it anymore, so I stopped and went back to just holding my son all night long. I waited another month, did a ton of research and reading into sleep coaching, and then tried again using a different approach. And IT WORKED! It took a few weeks, but my son was eventually able to put himself to sleep without crying at bedtime, and he is now putting himself back to sleep when he wakes during the night!* **-Leann**

GATHER YOUR SUPPORT TEAM

Unfortunately, sleep coaching isn't always a quick process, and it's not easy for all families. As such, it is usually a good idea for you to gather a support team. The team may be small, including just you and your significant other. Or perhaps you want or need your best friend, aunt, or mother who is visiting for two weeks on your team. The primary reason to have a team is to help you through the process. Your sleep coaching team can...

- ⊘ make sure you know what your plan is
- ⊘ help you with the actual sleep coaching (for example, by letting you take a nap while the baby naps or by taking a sleep coaching shift while you take a break)
- ⊘ cheer you on if it's not going well yet
- ⊘ help you stick with it long enough to see results
- ⊘ help determine when it's time to re-evaluate or make some tweaks to your plan

While building a strong sleep coaching team is ideal, I know that you may not have anyone to add to your team. Maybe your significant other works long hours, or maybe your loved ones are just tired of hearing you talk about your baby's sleep (or lack of it) and aren't very supportive. I understand that; it happens! And in some cases, those around you are critical of the choices you make about your baby and wouldn't be great "team members" anyway. In these situations, some families find that hiring an "expert" in baby sleep is beneficial. Many families ask their pediatricians for advice, but in my experience, it's difficult to get detailed advice during a single visit and difficult to get answers to all your "what if" questions throughout the process.

There are professionals who can help with sleep coaching support and who will have the time and expertise to provide you with guidance about your baby's sleep. Sleep coaches, for instance, specialize in helping families throughout the process. Now, I know it might seem strange to hire a professional for what seems like such a natural thing as 'sleep.' But just like you might hire a personal trainer at the gym or go to a mechanic to change your oil, you may turn to an expert for help with your baby's sleep. It's not that you can't necessarily do it on your own, but it might take you 10 times longer or you might give up before you get anywhere. Let's use a personal trainer as an example. Maybe you are just too tired or busy to read all about what muscles to work out first or whether to do cardio and then lift weights or lift weights and then do cardio. Which is it? Or does it even matter? Each fitness book you read may give you a different approach to take, and that can be confusing and, not to mention, discouraging. Your personal trainer, on the other hand, can tell you what's right for you given your body type, goals, and food temptations. They can also cheer you on when you feel like giving up. It saves time and money, and best of all, it gets real results.

The same goes for sleep coaching; yes, you can work through it on your own, but you'll likely find that you have a ton of reading to do if you want to be as prepared as possible. And much of that literature will conflict. What's more, any sleep coaching advice you read won't be personalized for your situation. By hiring a coach, however, you're getting an expert who can put all the pieces together for you in a way that matches your goals. This can save you loads of time (and often money) and will get you the results you want.

Now, when it comes to hiring any professional, sleep coaches included, it is important you find a good match. Much like you wouldn't want to choose a personal trainer whose philosophy of exercise doesn't match yours (for instance, a trainer who expected you to work out for two hours every day when you've made it clear you only have 30 minutes), you don't want to hire a sleep consultant whose process may not match your parenting philosophy. Take some time to ask questions to make sure they're a good fit. In my survey of parents, the primary reasons for not hiring a sleep consultant were a fear of the baby crying and the cost. Learning more about your sleep consultant will resolve that first fear, and although the cost of hiring a consultant is sometimes out of reach, I have been told by many parents that skipping that pedicure, daily latte, or having the time to cook rather than eat out for a month or two was well worth the cost of hiring professional help!

In the end, whether your team consists of solely your significant other, several family members or friends, a professional sleep consultant, or any combination of the three, you will likely have a much smoother, enjoyable, and successful sleep coaching process if you have support to help you through it.

> *The first year of my son's life was very stressful due to many factors. I was in a foreign country away from my family, I suffered from PPD, I worked full-time from home, and I had a son that refused to sleep and/or go to sleep without lots of intervention. I (like many others) was exhausted and confused from all the literature out there on how to sleep train babies. There is WAY too much to read through and absolutely no way to determine what is best for your child than simply by trial and error. I decided to hire Nicole and her team to help me, and I'm so glad I did! They seemed to understand every*

nuance of our issues and came up with a plan for how to help our son learn to fall asleep on his own that involved very little crying. Sleep coaching was a commitment that I was determined to see through, but without knowing 'my team' was just an email away the whole time, I simply couldn't have done it. I had so many questions, and they were there to answer each and every one with helpful suggestions and supportive words. To be honest, Nicole felt like the mom I didn't have to help me through.   **-Rachel**

SUMMARY

Before you begin sleep coaching:

- ⊘ Get to know your baby's temperament and your own parenting style as both are key in selecting the best sleep coaching method and in creating a great sleep coaching plan.
- ⊘ Establish consistent bedtime and nap time routines.
- ⊘ Establish an age-appropriate daily schedule for your child. Use these basic steps to get started:
  - » Start by establishing a few fixed points in your baby's day. Bedtime is a great place to start.
  - » Figure out your baby's usual morning wake-up time, and time naps around that.
  - » To time naps, use age-appropriate "nap gaps."
  - » Work towards naps that are at least an hour long.

- Know how many naps your child needs and when naps usually happen:
  - » 1-3 months: 4-5 naps/day
  - » 3-4 months: 4 naps/day
  - » 5-8 months: 3 naps/day
  - » 9-15 months: 2 naps/day
  - » 15 months-3/4 years: 1 nap/day
- Know how many night feedings your baby may need. Most breastfed babies need one to three nighttime feedings through about nine months of age. Although, some babies will need approximately one feeding most nights through 12 months of age. Formula-fed babies may be able to night wean earlier.
- Know the signs that it may be time to night wean:
  - » Baby is not eating as much during the day and is eating more at night.
  - » Baby is not eating much during nighttime feedings and is treating them more as play time.
  - » Baby is eating one or more solid food meals per day.
  - » There is a wide variance in baby's nighttime feedings from one night to the next.
- Before you work on sleep coaching, decide if you should keep the pacifier. If your child relies on the pacifier to fall asleep and can't replace that pacifier when it falls out, you will likely want to wean away from the pacifier before/during sleep coaching.
- Before you work on sleep coaching, decide exactly when you'll start. Ideal times to sleep coach include four to seven months and 11-16 months.

CHAPTER 4:

SLEEP COACHING METHODS CAFETERIA STYLE

At this point in the book, we're finally ready to dive into the actual "meat" of sleep coaching, specifically how to sleep coach! Now, the goal of sleep coaching - helping your child sleep better and longer - is likely the same from one family to the next, but how parents accomplish that goal can look very different indeed. There are many ways you can sleep coach and teach your baby to fall asleep independently, sleep through the night, and nap longer and more consistently. During this journey, there will be times your baby may not like the changes you're making or is frustrated by learning something new. There are many specific strategies you may use in the process to settle and calm your baby. I will outline the most common methods we use when we work with families.

> " My first baby was pretty easy to sleep coach, and I just assumed that what I'd done for him would work for everyone else's babies. Well, fast forward to my second baby; I tried to do things the same way, and wow, my world was turned upside down! My second son had a different temperament, and nothing that worked with my oldest worked for my youngest. I had to take a very different route with sleep coaching. But I did learn the importance

of being flexible with how you parent your children; what works for one may not work at all for the next! **-Grace**

SLEEP COACHING METHODS FOR YOUR BABY

Substitution

The gentlest form of sleep coaching is simply substituting your baby's preferred method of falling asleep with something different. The idea is that your baby will get used to falling asleep in a new way, but since he or she preferred something else, your child has less incentive to wake in the middle of a sleep period and will ultimately learn to stay asleep. For example, if your baby likes being fed to sleep, you might start by rocking or patting your baby to sleep. Ideally, your baby will accept being pat or rocked and fall asleep, but since he or she isn't being fed to sleep, your child will possibly sleep in longer stretches. As you can probably imagine, the biggest potential problem with this method is your baby can become just as dependent on the new method of putting him or her to sleep, which doesn't help your child (or you) get longer stretches of sleep. However, it is a great first step in that for some babies, not being fed to sleep is a huge accomplishment, and that is progress no matter how small. As previously discussed, it's a step along the spectrum towards independent sleeping but doesn't rush you to the other end. The next method will take you the next step.

Progressive Fading Technique

The second gentlest sleep coaching method is simply "fading" out how much "work" you do versus your baby. Are you rocking your baby to sleep? Try reducing how much you're moving. The pace is up to you and your baby, but if you imagine you are rocking your baby at a level 7 out of 10, try spending one to two days rocking at a level 5 or 6, then one to two days at a level 3 or 4, and so on. See if your baby will fall asleep in your arms without any movement. If your baby starts fussing or crying, you can allow him or her to cry in your arms a bit, depending on your tolerance for crying, or you can rock/pat for 30 to 90 seconds to calm your child but NOT put him or her to sleep. Or you can experiment with something in between. How much your baby cries is, again, tied to his or her temperament. Learning to fall asleep without help is what he or she is learning to do. The ultimate goal is that your child falls asleep when you are not moving, feeding or otherwise reinforcing an unwanted sleep association. You do not want to be doing anything that needs to be repeated over and over again. Again, the pace is up to you. For some babies, they will "get it" within a few days while some families spend several weeks slowly fading out unwanted sleep associations.

Ideas on how to fade out sleep associations:

- Swaddling – Swaddle one arm out and then both arms, starting with just a short period of time and gradually lengthening.

- Rocking or Bouncing – Rock or bounce less and less over a period of a few days.

- Feeding – Try to unlatch from the nipple earlier and earlier once your baby is comfort feeding (but not before your baby has finished a full feeding).

- Pacifier – Try using the pacifier as part of the routine, but remove it when you finish the routine. Reuse it only to help calm your child, not to put him or her to sleep.

- ⊘ Holding – Try holding as part of the routine, but put baby down a bit earlier every night while he or she is still awake.
- ⊘ Co-sleeping / Bed Sharing – Snuggle as part of the routine, and then add a little more distance every day.
- ⊘ Patting - Pat all the way to sleep, and then move to patting less. Finally, move to just resting your hand on your baby.

Hands-On Approach

The next method is what I'd call very "hands on." You typically stay in the room with your baby the entire time, and you will help your baby fairly regularly. If I compare this with helping your baby learn to walk, this is you holding your baby's hand while he or she takes the first few steps. You are there every step of the way, helping your baby up and giving him or her moral support. The difference with this method, though, is that you recognize he or she will have frustrating moments. Your baby may fuss or cry because he or she can't do it. But just as we don't expect your baby to walk on the first try, we actually expect your baby to fail. Weird, I know, but failing eventually leads to success. And when your baby fails, you are there to help calm him or her down and reassure him or her, but you must ultimately recognize that you can't do it for your child just as much as you can't walk for him or her. So, how does this work in practice?

Imagine you are trying to stop holding your baby to sleep, so he or she will stop expecting to be held all night. Not only is this exhausting, but it can be dangerous if you are falling asleep while holding your child in a chair as you might drop him or her. The only way to "fade" out holding your child is to stop holding him or her. (I will talk more later on how you can break this into "baby steps" in regards to making your sleep plan.) But for the purpose of this example, imagine you are now having your child fall asleep in your bed if you're currently bed sharing or in a crib (in or out of your room, next to your bed, or wherever). Once you lay your child down, he or she might start playing, fussing, or crying. He or she may be frustrated or upset that you are no longer holding him or her. With this method, you will allow your child to do this and voice his or her frustrations. (Your child has a right to how he or she is feeling, and it's healthy to be able to express oneself.) You will let your child try to fall asleep this way just as he or she might try to take an independent step one day. After giving your child an opportunity to try to fall asleep (five to 10 minutes or as long you're comfortable depending on his or her level of upset), pick your child up, give him or her a hug, offer reassurance, calm him or her down, and then lay him or her down to try again. Your goal is to be supportive and understanding while still letting your child try, fail, and try again. Eventually, he or she will succeed and fall asleep. Not only that, but you and your child will both have a new level of confidence, which goes a long way. The key to this method is repetition, repetition, repetition, follow through, and consistency.

You may have heard about a method called "pick up, put down." This method is similar except we do not recommend you pick up your baby at the slightest noise or upset. We expect your child to be at least a little frustrated, but the goal is to help coach him or her through it and help him or her find success. We find many families are very successful with this method, and it is our most common method with which we start since it typically is a bit faster than the other methods but allows parents to be a part of the process. Keep in mind that the "best" method is not the most logical and is the one to which YOU will commit and follow through.

The Sit-In (or Guided Soothing) Method

Have you ever sat in on a college course or a meeting but didn't really participate? This method is when you sit on a chair or the floor near your baby and provide moral support but otherwise try not to interact very much. There are a variety of ways you can implement this method, but the typical method is to not pick up the baby if possible (or at least minimally). You let your baby try (and fail) just as before, but you are limiting the interaction to verbal support such as singing lullabies or shushing or occasionally patting. Your baby may fuss or cry a bit more with this method than the previous ones. But progress sometimes goes faster, and for some babies, it's less frustrating that you aren't "teasing" them by picking them up and putting them back down. With this method, you never leave the baby alone, but you are allowing him or her more opportunity for independent sleeping. If we imagine we're at the playground, this is like the first time you have your baby go down the slide without holding your hand. Of course, your baby is likely to be a bit more upset with you not rocking or feeding him or her to sleep than he or she will be if he or she falls on his or her bottom at the end of a slide.

To make even more progress with this method, you can move your sitting position every night or every few nights to add a bit more distance as your baby falls asleep. For some babies, moving a foot is a big deal while others won't be upset until you try to leave the room. The response varies a lot, depending on age and the baby or toddler. Again, the pace is ultimately up to you and your baby, and you can always slow down or speed up as you see fit.

The Give-Me-Space Technique (GMST)

Back at the playground, the give-me-space technique is more like you letting your child go play in a play house where you can't see him or her all the time, but you give him or her a little space to be independent, knowing you're right there and he or she can't leave without you seeing him or her. It gives your child a taste of independence without leaving him or her for long periods of time. It may seem like I'm listing these methods in order from least likely to make your child cry to most likely to make your child cry, but in my experience, some babies, ironically, cry less with this technique than the sit-in technique. Why? Some babies find it extremely frustrating seeing their mom or dad sitting there and not doing what they're "supposed" to be doing. In some ways, it "teases" them, and they end up even more frustrated. Unfortunately, though, we can't predict what your baby will do with any method, and the first few days are often the most difficult regardless of method chosen.

The give-me-space technique is also called "check and console," Ferberizing, or the Ferber method. But my team and I have added our own variations to all the different methods. There are many ways to achieve the same goal. First, you can give your baby space without leaving the room. Or you can leave the room for short periods and stay in the room for longer periods. The typical Ferber method says not to pick up your baby, but some babies only calm down when you pick them up. In the end, what works for YOUR baby will vary a lot from other babies. The amount of space you give your baby is up to you. Here is the way I recommend that you implement this method:

1. Do your bedtime routine, ending with your baby awake.

2. End the routine in a specific way that will be the same

every time. It could be a key phrase or phrases ("Night night. I love you. Time to sleep."), a certain song, etc.

3. Give your baby space (leave the room, sit on a chair across the room, lay on your bed if you're room sharing, etc.).

4. Decide ahead of time on how long you will let your baby try to fall asleep. The most common amount of time is three to five minutes to start and then increase to 10 to 15 minutes.

5. After your predetermined amount of time, go to your baby and help calm him or her. For some, this means a pat, and for others, it means pick him or her up, sway him or her, etc. Typically, you want your baby to "try to sleep" longer than you are soothing him or her, but it depends on the intensity of the baby.

6. After you've soothed your baby, lay him or her back down and let him or her try again.

7. Repeat steps three through six until your baby has fallen asleep or until your "sleep coaching cycle" is complete. A sleep coaching cycle is how long you've decided to sleep coach in one sitting, and most often, one cycle is about 45 to 60 minutes.

8. For older babies and toddlers, try increasing your soothing intervals every few days in order to give your child plenty of time to practice self soothing.

> *Like many parents out there with a new baby, I was sleep deprived and working full time. When my son turned four months old, I couldn't*

take the sleep deprivation anymore, and I decided to sleep coach. I used every method I could think of and read so many books...you name it, I bought it, read it, and tried it! However, I'm so glad I stuck with it because after a lot of trial and error, I found what worked for me and for my baby. My son is now eight months old and sleeps wonderfully; the sleep-deprived nights are a distant memory!   **-Jessica**

SLEEP COACHING METHODS FOR YOUR TODDLER

All of the methods above can be used with your toddler, but there are a few strategies that work better with toddlers than with babies, which are outlined below.

Fading with a Twist

When you have been co-sleeping or bed sharing for a lengthy amount of time, it can be a big step for a toddler to go from sleeping in your bed to sleeping alone in a room in his or her crib or bed. Not only are they alone, but it's not truly your child's bed because he or she is used to your bed. Sending your child to bed in his or her crib or bed is the equivalent of you going to sleep in a guest room or hotel. It won't feel like your child's own bed until he or she is used to it, which takes time. Therefore, sometimes, a very good step in transitioning from co-sleeping to another room or bed is to move an air mattress or something YOU can sleep on IN your toddler's room through the transition.

First, spend a few nights in his or her room on the air mattress together just to get used to the new room. Then, start bedtime with your child in his or her bed and you on the air mattress. Follow the fading method of soothing as previously stated. Again, the goal is to keep your child calm and relaxed but not help him or her fall asleep. Focus just on bedtime, and during night wakings, take him or her to bed with you to keep it manageable. Bedtime has the routine to set it apart, so you can remain consistent. Once bedtime is going smoother, you can start working on having him or her sleep in the crib or bed for the entire night while you are on the air mattress. The goal is that your presence is comforting and that he or she gets used to the new bed and can think of it as his or her own. After a few nights, start bedtime in your child's bed, and then, sleep in your bed in your own room and only return to the air mattress if absolutely necessary. One main key is that you don't want to move on to the next stage until things are going smoother. But at the same time, you don't want to stay on any stage so long that it's a new habit you'll need to break. I recommend two to four nights for each "step" of the plan you intend to take. Don't wait for a stage to go perfectly before you move on. If your child is still waking in the night at the end of the plan, you might graduate to the re-tuck strategy or the sit-in strategy and replace the mattress with a chair.

Silent Return to Bed

Since toddlers can often get out of their bed once they've transitioned out of a crib or cot, your baby may get out of bed during the sleep coaching process. That can be tricky! If he or she repeatedly gets out of bed, you should employ the "silent return to bed" approach. If your child gets up, put him or her back immediately. No talking. No interaction. Any positive or negative attention will often make it continue and possibly make it into a game. You may have to do many silent returns to bed the first couple of days, but it usually gets better after that as long as you follow through with him or her staying in bed and do not revert to old habits. Eventually, your child will get bored and go to sleep. Note that some children will play quietly in their rooms and then start to fall asleep on the floor. Most parents don't find this to be a problem. This new "trick" will get old, and the novelty will wear off after awhile.

Retuck

This method and "fading with a twist" are both methods that I have created based on experience with other parents and my own children. The "re-tuck" method is a way to reassure your toddler that you are close by, so you can check on him or her when he or she is asleep. This started when my son would keep calling us back over and over again for one last kiss or just because. I realized that he was looking for reassurance, nothing more, so as with many things, I built it into the routine. I recommend building any "stall" reasons into your routine. You would use this method if you "have" to stay with your toddler while he or she falls asleep. If that is not the case, you might need to adjust accordingly to solve whatever problem you are having.

The goal is that your toddler eventually falls asleep in his or her bed with you out of the room. Do your routine as always, including cuddle time for five minutes or so. After those five minutes are up, tell your child that "it's time to go to sleep." Then, put him or her in the crib or bed. Tell your child, "Lay down. Night, night. I love you," and rub his or her back for a minute or two and maybe sing a song. Then, you tell your child that you are going to go put on your pajamas (or go to the bathroom or whatever) and that you will be back in a few minutes, and then, do JUST THAT.

The idea is that you are reassuring your child that you aren't too far away and that you do check on him or her when he or she is asleep. It is important to establish the trust that you will actually go back, too. Do NOT say you are going to come back and don't. Violating trust will make the situation worse. Tell your child exactly what you are doing every step of the way, and if he or she is having some anxiety, you can even talk to him or her from the hallway or bathroom. Staying out of the room for even just 30 seconds at bedtime is a step towards building your child's confidence that you will always come back.

At first, use this method just at bedtime. For night wakings, do your normal routine to keep it manageable just in case bedtime takes awhile. You'll do the "retuck" and leave for five minutes the first couple of nights and then go back in and sit with your child until he or she falls asleep. Similar to the sit-in method, each night, you will move further from the crib or bed and closer to the door, and eventually, you'll sit in the doorway.

Now that your child is used to the new routine, start leaving before he or she is all the way asleep. You'll do the retuck, and then, when you go back in, you'll just kiss him or her good night and say, "See you in the morning." Also, start doing the retuck for night wakings, and only sit in the doorway if you have to go back. Work your way up to doing a short visit and leaving again.

Typically, less than a week later, your toddler will already be sleeping much better, but all children respond differently. Your child might temporarily lose quite a bit of sleep during this process. That is expected and definitely worth it in the long run.

Once you're sure that your toddler knows the "sleep rules" and what he or she is supposed to do, the goal is to work your way up to requiring your toddler to be quiet and stay in bed while you are gone for the "retuck." You will tell your child that if he or she is being loud, you won't come back in the room. If your child is crying and the five minutes are up, remind him or her from outside the door that Mommy (or Daddy) will come back in when he or she is quiet. If he or she gets out of bed, follow the silent return to bed method. The goal is to reinforce the behavior you want. It takes time, patience, consistency, and persistence on your part. I do not recommend requiring your child to be quiet until he or she KNOWS the routine. Once he or she has learned the routine, he or she should then learn all the rules.

The Open Door Policy

It's common for some toddlers to want their door open. My boys were around 14 months when I started to use the open door concept method. It was my instinct that told me that my 14-month-old didn't like it when I left the room, but it was adding insult to injury when I would shut the door behind me. I believe the reason they start to want their door open is so they don't feel "closed off" from the house, "cast away," or far away from you. It's another sort of separation anxiety. With my youngest son, I don't think he really knew he wanted the door open, but when I offered it, he decided he liked the idea.

If your toddler expresses interest in keeping the door open, you can actually use this to encourage a certain type of behavior. Think of this as your child earning a privilege by getting good grades. I can see how some might call it "bribing," but I think many of us, adults included, need some type of incentive to do something we'd prefer not to do. That seems like human nature.

Part of the "rules" when it comes to doors being open is that they have to be quiet and stay in bed (if they are at an age that they can get out). You might mention to your child that if he or she keeps the door open, he or she can see you putting away laundry or hear you doing the dishes (if your child actually can), so he or she knows you're nearby. Again, it might give him or her some reassurance that you aren't too far away. One method is to put three pieces of tape on the floor. If your child makes too much noise, cries, or gets out of bed, close the door to the first piece of tape and tell him or her the rules. Once your child gets to the third piece of tape, tell him or her that "since you are not being quiet (or staying in bed), I am going to close the door for a few minutes and then come back." Then, close the door (usually just 30 seconds to a minute works) and go back. Resettle your child and let him or her try again. They learn quickly to be quiet and stay in bed if they really do like that door open. Even if they can't talk, they can understand a lot. Try saying, "If you want the door open, you have to be quiet, or you will wake the cat (or dog)."

Cry It Out

There is one more method of sleep coaching for babies and toddlers that I purposely left for last, which is called "cry it out." This is the act of leaving and not coming back until your baby or toddler falls asleep or until morning depending on how you implement it. This is typically a "last resort" type of method and not a method I commonly recommend to the families I work with unless we have holistically looked at every other method and examined the child's daily schedule and have determined that it is the next course of action. There are some cases where nothing else works, and some families don't have the luxury of spending months and months sleep coaching. Think of the professions, including doctors, nurses, surgeons, and pilots, where life can literally depend on getting enough sleep and alertness. This method is difficult to implement for many families, and therefore, many families give up. As I've already illustrated earlier, there are a lot of ways in between putting your baby to sleep and letting him or her cry it out without you coming back until he or she is asleep. If you think you're at this point, please visit us at www.babysleep-site.com before you take this step, so we can help you make sure you've exhausted your options. After all, for a child who has an underlying schedule problem, for example, no amount of crying will make him or her sleep, and I've seen that mistake too many times to count.

> *After my daughter was born, it was a long five months of her waking up just about every two hours at night. I was at my wit's end. I had even resorted to co-sleeping, which worked in the beginning but became worse after a short time. She wouldn't nap more than 20 minutes or so and was very clingy. I thought about sleep coaching but didn't want to adhere to a strict cry-it-out routine. So I started off using gentler, more gradual methods, and it worked! It took some work and the help of Nicole's team of consultants, but within a few days, my daughter was sleeping in her crib and waking just once to feed and was napping better as well.* **-Michelle**

SUMMARY

◎ Sleep coaching methods for your **baby**, from gentlest to least gentle, include the following:

» Substitution: This is the gentlest possible method to use; it involves substituting one sleep association for another (i.e. substituting rocking for feeding to get your child to sleep). The theory is that the sleep association you've substituted will be easier to wean you child away from as the association isn't as strong.

» Progressive Fading Technique: This is another gentle method. Gradually fade out your child's sleep association by degrees until your child is going into the crib slightly awake.

» Hands-On Approach: Quite gentle, this method involves you staying right by your baby's bedside at sleep times. Lay your baby down slightly awake, but pick your child up if he or she becomes distressed.

» Guided Soothing: Sit in your child's room during sleep times, but avoid picking your child up if he or she becomes distressed; instead, soothe your child in other ways such as patting, rubbing, or shushing. Move your chair further and further from the bed each night until you are sitting right outside the open door; this gradually and gently moves you out of the room at sleep times and gets your baby used to the idea of falling asleep without you nearby.

» Give–Me-Space Technique: Put your baby to bed slightly awake, and leave the room. Then, if your child is fussing, go back into the room in intervals to soothe and offer comfort. At first, these intervals can be very short (several minutes in length), and then gradually, you can lengthen the intervals.

⊘ Sleep coaching methods for your **toddler**, from gentlest to least gentle, include the following:

» Fading with a Twist: This is a great method to use for transitioning your toddler from co-sleeping to sleeping in his or her own bed. To start, put your toddler in his or her own bed at bedtime, and sleep on an air mattress or sleeping bag right next to the bed. Then, gradually transition to leaving the room before your toddler falls asleep.

» Silent Return to Bed: This is a great technique for toddlers who are popping in and out of bed. When your toddler leaves his or her room, your goal is to silently return him or her to bed. If your child can't get a reaction out of you or interact with you, it's likely he or she will stop the "jack-in-the-box" behavior and stay in bed.

» Retuck: This is similar to the give-me-space technique we use with babies. Put your toddler in bed, and let him or her know that you'll be back to check on him or her in a few moments. The goal is for your child to get used to staying in bed. Once your child can stay in bed at bedtime, gradually lengthen the time you're out of the room until, ideally, your toddler falls asleep before you come in to check on him or her.

» Open Door Policy: This is a great incentive for toddlers who continue to get out of bed or break the sleep coaching "rules." Start out with a wide open door, but when your toddler gets out of bed or breaks one of your "rules," close the door a few inches. This provides an immediate consequence to any bad sleep behavior, and since many children see an open door as a reward, it reinforces good sleep behavior.

» Cry It Out: This works for both babies and toddlers, but in general, it's not a method we recommend. Full-blown cry it out means laying your baby down for bed and not going into the room again to offer comfort even if your baby is wailing. This is usually an emotional and difficult process for both children and parents alike, and there are better alternatives that work well for the majority of parents.

CHAPTER 5:

HOW TO BUILD A SLEEP PLAN THAT'S RIGHT FOR YOU

One of the most important pieces of sleep coaching is making a sleep plan. In my private practice, we create a Personalized Sleep Plan™ for almost all new clients. Many times, I've heard families say they just couldn't take it anymore and ripped off the bandage only to find themselves stressed, confused, and not getting any more sleep than before. Making a plan not only gives you a framework, but it makes you think through what you will do in different scenarios, keeps you accountable to see it through, and, most importantly, gives you confidence. People underestimate the important role your confidence plays in sleep coaching. If you don't have confidence, how will your baby?

There really isn't a "right" or "wrong" plan. The most logical plan isn't the one that will necessarily work. The best one is one that you can commit to. And it's just that: a plan. To be honest, babies don't always follow plans. And we can make the best plan known to man, but that doesn't mean it will go exactly the way it's supposed to. But in the end, your plan will give you a map of where to go next just like you're on a road trip. Sure, you might need to add pit stops when your baby gets sick, or maybe you need to make a detour when your baby starts rolling over in the midst of sleep coaching. The plan is often a living, breathing thing and can (and should) be modified as you go along your journey. That said, you don't want to keep changing your plan every day, either, because then there is no point to having a plan. Consistency is *very* important, so you don't send mixed and confusing messages to your child. We also need to give your baby time to adapt to your new sleep routine or approach. Many babies, and especially toddlers, will take several days to several weeks to embrace a new approach. The good thing is that it becomes their new "normal," and they won't expect anything different. Sometimes the longer you've had your current sleep habits, the more days you need to give your child to adjust. Just like you and I, it takes about 30 days to develop a new habit. Every child's plan will be unique. Even two different children in the same family, including twins sometimes, will have unique needs! So, how can you make a plan that makes sense for you?

As you go through these next few paragraphs, begin to jot down your thoughts and ideas. First, keep in mind that you may need to fade out several different sleep associations. Should you do all at once or one at a time? In general, I like keeping variables to a minimum so that you know *exactly* how your child is responding to each change. But some "baby steps" are unnecessary and will only lengthen the entire process, which can be exhausting. My general rule of thumb is to break "big" things apart. The following sleep associations are what I consider bigger accomplishments:

- ⊘ Feeding to sleep
- ⊘ Using a pacifier
- ⊘ Rocking/bouncing/driving to sleep
- ⊘ Transitioning to a new sleep space (crib, cot, or toddler bed)

Next, it's ideal for you to break down your goals into smaller ones. For example, it is too big of a goal to expect your 12-month-old to sleep in his or her own room and sleep through the night. That could be true, of course, but that's a high level or long-term, "big picture" goal. What are your smaller, short-term goals? Here's an example that shows you how to break this down:

I want my 12-month-old to:

1. not need to be rocked to sleep.

2. not need to be held to fall asleep.

3. stay asleep and not need me to rerock him or her every two hours at night.

4. sleep in his or her crib the entire night and not come to my bed.

5. not need night feedings.

6. not wake up at 5:00 a.m.

As you can see, there are quite a few things your baby may need to accomplish, and many times, there are more steps than this. In my experience, if we expect too much too fast, that is when many parents give up and are confused as to how to approach resolving their sleep problems.

Assuming you have nights and naps to work on, the next thing to decide is whether you will work on nights first or naps or both. In my experience, working on both is generally overwhelming for everyone, results in a lot of lost sleep, and leads to parents giving up. While it might seem logical and ideal to be consistent during the day and night, the best plan is the one that can be accomplished. For example, let's assume that all the bathrooms in my home need cleaning. Now, it might *make sense* for me to clean all the bathrooms in one sitting, but if I only have room in my busy schedule for a few 10-minute cleaning sessions, maybe it will be best for me to do one at a time when time allows. Sure, this means the work doesn't get done as quickly, and sure, I have to dirty my hands multiple times. The important part is that I get it done. Writing 'clean all the bathrooms' on my daily to-do list might be a lofty and noble goal, but if I just don't have the time to do all the cleaning at once, I'm essentially setting myself up to fail. It's so much better to break the big goal into smaller, incremental goals.

The same is true for sleep coaching. You could write up a plan that has you working on ALL your baby's sleep challenges at once, but for most families, this just isn't realistic. Too many times when a client comes to me, they did sleep coaching and "it didn't work;" for example, one of the reasons is that they night weaned at the same time. A hungry baby will be a LOT more difficult to settle, so it's better to help your child learn to sleep more independently before you expect him or her to stop eating at night. Or sometimes, we stop the eating at night and then work on independent sleeping if necessary. The order can be tailored to whatever makes sense for your situation. I would rarely night wean a six-month-old, but I might night wean a 2-year-old since eating at all in those older ages can reinforce the very waking you are trying to stop. If naps are the primary problem, we might start with naps and then move on to nights. Each family's situation is unique, and some parents *need* a baby to nap independently ASAP (i.e. parents who work from home).

What should be in your sleep plan?

- ⊘ Your goals
- ⊘ Sleep coaching method
- ⊘ Target sleep (and possibly feeding) schedule
- ⊘ Day-by-day plan

I have provided a few sample sleep plans at the end of this chapter that you can use to model your sleep plan. The appendix has a blank template for you to use.

> My daughter, Mina, slept poorly from birth, and by the time she was 11 months old, she was waking up to 16 times each night!!! She'd sometimes be up for two to four hours in the middle of the night, too, and her naps were so erratic. My daughter also has a few medical concerns, so needless to say, we had a challenging problem on our hands. However, by carefully drawing up a sleep plan that addressed all our needs and that gave us a step-by-step approach to tackling the problems, we were able to make a lot of progress using the gentle sleep coaching method that I felt comfortable with. Now, my daughter wakes only when she's teething or uncomfortable, and she has two long, consistent naps each day! The fact that she's sleeping well now means I can return to work, which is a huge milestone. **-Stephanie**

HOW LONG TO SLEEP COACH

When we sleep coach, we do it in what we call a "sleep coaching cycle." Reading the internet or books will sometimes make it seem like your baby will fall asleep in 10 to 20 minutes; if only that were true for every baby. I have read histories from some clients who say "sleep coaching didn't work for my baby," and they only worked on it for 20 to 30 minutes. Unfortunately, some babies will take longer than that. We typically decide how long to go in a stretch, take a break, and then try again. Your baby needs repetition and consistency. If after four or five nights you've had zero progress, you may need to re-evaluate the method or wait until your baby is older as he or she is possibly too young. For younger babies (five months and younger), I recommend a 20 to 30 minute sleep coaching cycle. After six months, I recommend 60 minutes. After 15 months old, you may want to consider 90 minutes or longer as toddlers can definitely be more persistent and really sink their teeth into old habits.

When it comes to sleep coaching at night, we generally repeat our sleep coaching cycle as many times as it takes until a baby falls asleep. Generally, it's two hours or less, and with our clients, I would estimate the average is 45 to 60 minutes. For persistent types, I'd say one and a half hours is the average, but all children are different. Sometimes when I read a description about a baby, I think he or she will take a long time, and then, he or she pleasantly surprises the parents. Other times, I think the baby sounds very adaptable and easy going only to find out that the baby took two hours to fall asleep. The bottom line is that you won't know until you take that first step, which is often the hardest. But I can tell you that a baby will surprise his or her parents much of the time, and I do hope yours surprises you! I can't tell you how many times I've gotten an email that says, "It wasn't as bad as I thought it was going to be," especially from those who swore their baby would take all night, which, in my experience, is *very* rare.

My best advice in regards to how long you should sleep coach is to do what feels right to you. Keep in mind that children that aren't as adaptable take longer to "warm up" to the idea about a new routine. I recommend that you try to commit to at least one to two hours, taking breaks if you or your baby needs it. Out of the 20,000+ clients our team has personally worked with, we've had ONE family go several hours and the next night was less than an hour, so it paid off. Most families are done in less than an hour.

But PLEASE do not give up after 20 minutes. However, if you do give up, just try again the next night. Even when a family doesn't do it the first night, sometimes the second night actually still improves. It's just like learning to walk. Just because he fell on his bottom 50 times today doesn't mean the next day won't be the day he successfully takes that first independent step.

WHERE TO START

The key to helping your baby sleep more soundly is to start putting your baby to bed "drowsy but awake." If you've been putting your child to sleep yourself, for example, by rocking or feeding, you need to begin weaning your child away from that sleep association, and instead, start to put him or her down for sleep at least slightly awake. But what does "drowsy but awake" actually mean? Does it mean eyes closed? Does it mean almost asleep? Does it simply mean relaxed?

In a perfect world, you'd soothe your baby to the point of being calm, relaxed, and eyes slightly closed. You'd lay your baby down, and he or she would reposition him or herself, flutter his or her eyes, briefly look at you leaving the room, and drift off into peaceful sleep. Of course, this doesn't usually happen at first! For example, your baby may be one who goes from wide awake to asleep without much of a "drowsy" state in between. In this case, your "drowsy but awake" would be somewhere in the calm state but not with closed eyes. Your child may appear wide awake yet content enough to not be moving around and crawling, walking, or playing.

Now, one question I hear frequently from parents who are just beginning sleep coaching is, "How long should I work on this whole 'drowsy but awake' thing, anyway?" In a perfect world, we'd get our babies drowsy and then lay them down awake every single time we put them down for sleep, but I know that for many families, especially when you're new to sleep coaching, this just isn't realistic. So while I think it's good to attempt drowsy but awake at bedtime and perhaps during one or two nap times, you don't need to worry about doing it perfectly at every sleep time.

First, if you are teaching your child a new routine, he or she is likely to perk up and wake up a bit anyway once you lay him or her down. You don't want to spend an hour working on getting your baby drowsy to only watch it come undone in a matter of seconds. Second, you don't want to strive for drowsy but awake so long that your baby becomes overtired since overtiredness will work against you. If you work for 30 minutes, pushing him or her past the comfortable awake time, your child is likely to upset quickly and resist the new routine even more. Third, if you work at drowsy but awake for a long time and finally DO get your little one calm and relaxed, keep in mind that you'll need to do it each time he or she wakes and cries, and few of us can keep up hours of working on drowsiness each day! In that case, you are really just dragging out the inevitable.

Ultimately, your goal is to create a consistent bedtime or nap time routine and stick to it. If you have an age-appropriate sleep schedule, your baby should be content at the end of your routine, and over the course of weeks, you should be able to have your baby less drowsy and more awake as he or she gets better and better at falling asleep. You probably won't see fast progress immediately, but if you stick with it, it'll get easier.

With all that said, here's my recommendation: spend up to 10 to 15 minutes getting your baby "drowsy but awake," and then, cut it off and lay him or her down. If your child isn't drowsy with your soothing methods, make sure you are trying to put him or her to sleep at the right time. Too tired might look like lots of crying OR hyper activity. Not tired enough might look like playful behavior and happy smiling rather than sleepiness.

In many ways, drowsy but awake is really the foundation of sleep coaching. So once you've established a healthy schedule, created a consistent bedtime and nap time routine, and laid the groundwork for sleep coaching, you can start by putting your baby down drowsy but awake for sleep times. We'll start with bedtime first and then move on to naps.

HOW TO WORK ON NIGHTS

Bedtime

I usually (but not always) recommend starting your sleep coaching by working on bedtime first. So to start out, you will work on putting your child to bed drowsy but awake. Remember, it is key that your baby goes into his or her sleeping area awake; after all, our goal in sleep coaching is to have your child learn to fall asleep without help! Keep in mind that this may take a lot of repetition at first. You can't expect your child to "get it" right away. Additionally, drowsy but awake is merely a starting point for your child; eventually, the goal is to have such a consistent routine in place that your child knows exactly when it's time to lie down and fall asleep. It is with the repetition on your part that your child will begin to accept this as the routine. Your child will learn to expect to be laid down AWAKE after feeding and will understand that it is then his or her "job" to close his or her eyes and go to sleep. Now, keep in mind that we absolutely cannot MAKE your child sleep. That will be up to him or her. However, even if your child is not consistent, you can be. Do the routine, and the rest will (eventually) be up to him or her. The key right now is to introduce drowsy but awake in a gentle way and then stick with it. Once you lay your child down, if he or she starts to play, this is okay; it's even a good thing as it indicates that he or she is comfortable in his or her sleep space. If he or she begins to cry, you will start using the sleep coaching method that fits you best to handle the crying (see Chapter 4).

When working on bedtime, the routine sets it apart, so if or when your child wakes later in the night, you'd take the path of least resistance and get him or her back to sleep by any means necessary even using the same sleep associations you are working to change. This is just for a few days to a week until you are ready to move on to the next step.

Nighttime Waking

After a few nights spent working on bedtime, begin working on the rest of the night. I recommend that you keep a reasonable number of feedings to start with, so you can be more confident that your child is not hungry. Your confidence will go a long way. But after any feedings, make sure you put him or her down awake (if possible) and continue with your sleep coaching. If it's impossible to keep your child awake, that's okay. Just do the best you can and work on any other night waking. After a few nights working on night waking, you can begin night weaning if applicable.

HOW TO NIGHT WEAN

The answer to the question of when a child can go all night without eating varies widely among the "experts" and pediatricians alike. Some will say once they double their birth weight while others will say one to two feedings up until nine months is normal. Some say they need to eat on demand every three to six hours until they are on three square solid meals per day. Many will say by six months, they can go all night without eating, and others say that they should be able to by three or four months.

Personally, I believe that babies vary and so will the answer to this question. Thus, it is up to *you*, who knows your baby best, and your pediatrician to determine whether your child needs to eat at night. It is important to note that it is not normal for a baby to need to eat every hour or two once they are at least three months old (or younger). If this is happening, it is likely that your baby has a sleep association with a bottle or nursing. Studies have shown that sleeping through the night has nothing to do with nutrition or solids but a developmental milestone, so please don't start solids only to lengthen sleep. It generally doesn't work. I typically err on the side of caution and say that a baby, particularly a breastfed one, needs to eat one to two times at night up through nine months or even a year. *My philosophy is to sleep coach to fix problems but not make a child go hungry if he or she can't comfortably go all night without nutrition.*

There are several methods to night wean your baby. Some people employ a "cold turkey" approach where they just decide to stop feeding at night. They may not go in at all, or they may check their baby but not feed him or her. Many babies usually stop eating in just a couple nights if they are ready.

An alternative and my recommended method would be to night wean slowly. Even if your baby doesn't "need" to eat at night, it doesn't mean your child isn't *used* to eating at night and is legitimately hungry. The idea is to slowly make your baby go longer between feedings and at the same time, eat less. So every night, you increase the time between feedings by 30 minutes while also decreasing how much he or she eats by one ounce if bottle fed or one minute if nursing. If you are unsure how long your child is nursing, just make an approximate guess of about eight to 10 minutes or start where you are comfortable. Whatever you choose, be consistent, and surprisingly, the details are actually unimportant. The key is simply: keep moving forward.

It is important to note that healthy babies WILL adjust and eat more during the day. Up until now, it's a chicken and egg problem because your child won't eat more during the day while getting some calories at night and won't stop eating at night if he or she doesn't eat more during the day. That's why a slower transition helps even it out with the least amount of tears. If your pediatrician has given you the okay to stop feeding at night, this is a good method to do so. The theory behind this method is that you "train" your body to get hungry at approximately the same time every day, which is similar to how you might get hungry for lunch at the same time every day. If you want to change what time you get hungry, you want to slowly adjust to a later or earlier time.

Below are a few examples of how to night wean, but keep in mind that there are a variety of ways to do so:

Example Night Weaning (Complete Night Weaning)

- ⊘ Current schedule: Two feedings at approximately 1:00 a.m. and 4:00 a.m. include two 4-oz. bottles or two eight-minute nursing sessions.

- ⊘ Night 1: Do not feed until 1:30 a.m. and 5:00 a.m. (you are increasing time between feedings) and decrease bottle to 3 oz. or nursing time to seven minutes.

- Night 2: Do not feed until 2:00 a.m. and 5:30 a.m. and decrease bottle to 2 oz. or nurse for six minutes.
- Night 3: Do not feed until 2:30 a.m. and 6:00 a.m. and decrease bottle to 1 oz. or nurse for five minutes.
- Night 4: Do not feed.

Example Night Weaning (Reduce to Just One Night Feeding)

- Current schedule: Two feedings at approximately 1:00 a.m. and 4:00 a.m. include two 4–oz. bottles or two eight-minute nursing sessions.
- Night 1: Do not feed until 1:30 a.m. (full feeding) and 5:00 a.m. (you are increasing time between feedings) and decrease only the second bottle to 3 oz. or nurse for seven minutes.
- Night 2: Do not feed until 2:00 a.m. (full feeding) and 5:30 a.m. and decrease second bottle to 2 oz. or nurse for six minutes.
- Night 3: Do not feed until 2:30 a.m. (full feeding) and 6:00 a.m. and decrease bottle to 1 oz. or nurse for five minutes.
- Night 4: Do not feed until 3:00 a.m. (full feeding) and do not feed a second time until it's time to get up.
- Make it a goal to get the one and only feeding to 3:00 or 4:00 a.m.

Example Night Weaning (Slower Method to Reduce to Just One Night Feeding)

- Current schedule: Two feedings at approximately 1:00 a.m. and 4:00 a.m. include two 4–oz. bottles or two eight-minute nursing sessions.

- ⊘ Night 1: Do not feed until 1:30 a.m. (full feeding) and 4:30 a.m. (maintain the 3-hour feeding gap) and decrease only the second bottle to 3 oz. or nurse for seven minutes.

- ⊘ Night 2: Do not feed until 2:00 a.m. (full feeding) and 5:00 a.m. and decrease second bottle to 2 oz. or nurse for six minutes.

- ⊘ Night 3: Do not feed until 2:30 a.m. (full feeding) and 5:30 a.m. and decrease bottle to 1 oz. or nurse for five minutes.

- ⊘ Night 4: Do not feed until 3:00 a.m. (full feeding) and do not feed a second time until it's time to get up.

- ⊘ Make it a goal to get the one and only feeding to 3:00 or 4:00 a.m.

HOW TO WORK ON NAPS

We'll tackle naps in a way that's similar to how we tackled nights, but we typically put a time limit on each attempt or sleep coaching cycle (30 minutes for five months and younger and 60 minutes for older babies and toddlers). For naps, you want to focus first on helping your baby learn to fall asleep at the beginning of the nap without any assistance from sleep associations. Although the sleep coaching method that works may be different during naps than it was for nights, we typically start with the method that worked at night. You can always decide to try a different method if things don't go well a few days later. Now, you may be thinking, "If I've already taught my child to fall asleep independently at bedtime and after night wakings, why do I have to do it *again* with naps?"

Great question! As I've mentioned already, the thing to remember is that night sleep and nap sleep are handled by two different parts of your baby's brain. So while all the work you've done to help your baby fall asleep independently at bedtime and minimize nighttime waking is great, it may or may not translate to naps. Bummer, I know!

While working on just the beginning of the nap, you will want to help your baby lengthen his or her nap "by any means necessary." Although this is somewhat inconsistent to our long-term goals, this preserves his or her sleep and keeps attempts more manageable. As long as this is temporary (a few days to a week only), your child can learn to take longer naps even if you start out helping him or her.

Making Naps Longer

Once your baby is falling asleep independently (within about 10 to 15 minutes) at the start of nap time, you can begin to work on lengthening the naps and helping your baby learn to fall BACK to sleep after he or she wakes in the middle of a nap. We do this by creating a "nap hour," during which your baby is to be in the crib whether or not he or she is asleep. Your baby's "nap hour" can vary in length, depending on age (shorter for younger babies and longer than an hour for toddlers). Also, keep in mind that there are some situations in which a catnap is expected (during a nap transition, for instance), so in some instances, you'll need to allow for a catnap during the day.

Now, I'll explain how the nap hour works. Let's say that your baby's "nap hour" is actually 60 minutes long. If you lay your baby down and he or she falls asleep in 10 minutes and then sleeps for 30 minutes, that means he or she has done 40 minutes of the 60-minute nap hour. Your child still has 20 more minutes to remain in the crib before the nap hour is up. During these 20 minutes, your goal is to teach him or her to fall BACK to sleep independently, using your method of choice (see Chapter 4), to finish out the nap hour. You would use the same sleep coaching methods and strategies here that you used for nighttime waking.

Why do we bother with the nap hour? Well, for starters, your baby likely wakes early from a nap for the same reason he or she wakes frequently at night: he or she is waking between sleep cycles and doesn't know how to get back to sleep. When you teach him or her how to fall BACK to sleep independently, you lay the ground work for lengthy, restorative naps. And that's something that virtually all children need in order to grow and thrive. Additionally, creating a "nap hour" helps your baby get a feel for how long naps should be and will help reinforce the desired daytime schedule that you're working towards.

HOW TO CREATE YOUR SLEEP PLAN

So how do you put all of this together? Here is a simple seven-step approach to make your very own sleep plan:

1. Determine your baby's average sleep needs. You may already know this based on your observations in the last few weeks or months, but if you don't, log your child's sleep for four to seven days and take the average. Knowing how much sleep your baby needs can help you set appropriate expectations for your child. If your child does not need 15 hours of sleep, for example, or will not sleep 12 hours at night even with your help, striving for anything close to that will likely leave you disappointed. Consider it a bonus if he or she begins to sleep more once you start sleep coaching, which happens quite often in my experience.

2. Break your goals into smaller goals or "phases." For example, you might break "sleeping through the night" into (a) going down for bedtime without being held, (b) waking up for just two night feedings, (c) waking up fewer than five times per night, and (d) waking up at 6:30 a.m. or later every day.

3. Decide on the sleep coaching method you'll start with. This doesn't mean you will necessarily end up succeeding with this method, but hopefully, you will succeed with your first choice!

4. Decide approximately how long you want the process to take. This doesn't mean your baby will agree, but set reasonable expectations. I recommend at least two to three weeks, which is realistic. You could be done faster, which would be another bonus!

5. Split up the goals you made in step #2 so that you're working on each small goal for a few days at a time. For example, on nights one through three, work on bedtime sleep coaching; nights four through six, work on having your baby go back to sleep on his or her own after each night feeding; and so on. Do your nights match up to the total amount of time you wanted the process to take? Are you being too optimistic? Are you taking too long in some phases? Make some adjustments.

6. Create a mantra that you will repeat to yourself when things get rough. Mine was something like, "Should I give up? No because then he would have gone through this all this time for nothing. My waffling is not fair to him. What is the alternative? To go back to how things were before sleep coaching? That isn't a solution. My child needs to learn how to sleep." Have this mantra handy for when the going gets rough.

7. Write all of this down and keep a journal, so you can see how far you've come in a short amount of time! One mistake I see parents make is not recognizing the successes no matter how small. Be proud of your baby for learning so much so quickly, and feel good that you helped him or her do that! Rome was not built in a day. It could take time, but you will get there.

After you have your plan, you may want to put it somewhere easy to see and "check off" as you go. Keep in mind that you may want to lengthen any given "phase," which is okay, but it really shouldn't take months and months to at least *improve* sleep. Will it be perfect? Depending on your baby and developmental milestones, it may not be. At any given time, you may need to settle for "good enough" until you can keep going, and that's okay, too. Also, remember your definition of "success" may look different than your friend's definition. Re-evaluate your plan every three to five days to see if you need to make any adjustments.

Having trouble getting started? Here are a few sample plans I've put together for you:

SAMPLE SLEEP PLANS

These sample sleep plans will give you some ideas for making your own sleep plan. Please note that this is not an exhaustive list and that there are a variety of ways to achieve the same goal. The pace (how many days this takes) will ultimately be up to you and your child's response to sleep coaching, but don't get so "stuck" in a phase that you aren't making any progress.

Sample 1: Resolving a rocking or feeding sleep association and reducing night feedings

Phase I: Work on bedtime, putting your baby in his or her desired sleep space to sleep. Help soothe him or her as much as needed just to get him or her used to falling asleep in the desired sleep space. Upon night waking, take the path of least resistance to limit sleep loss.

Phase II: Continue working on bedtime, but encourage more independence while falling asleep. Use the hands-on approach.

Phase III: Begin working on night waking, if necessary, using the hands-on approach.

Phase IV: Begin reducing nighttime feedings, if necessary.

Phase V: Continue being very consistent to solidify the new routine. If you want to work towards helping your child be more independent at sleep times, consider graduating to the sit-in method or the give-me-space technique.

Sample 2: Transition toddler to own sleep space

Realistically, in my experience, transitioning a toddler to his or her own sleep space takes about 30 days. It's a big change if your child has been sleeping in your bed all this time, and while "ripping off the band aid" works for some, it often includes a lot of crying and upset. In my opinion, a longer plan takes more patience but is often a more enjoyable experience.

Phase I: Work on bedtime, putting your toddler in the new sleep space to sleep. Help soothe him or her as much as needed just to get him or her used to falling asleep in the new sleep space.

Allow your toddler to sleep in the old sleep space for the rest of the night.

Phase II: Continue working on bedtime, but encourage more independence while falling asleep. Allow your toddler to sleep in the old sleep space for the rest of the night. Use the hands-on approach.

Phase III: Begin working on night waking using the hands-on approach so that your toddler will sleep in his or her own bed the entire night.

Phase IV: Sit in a chair that is placed a short distance from your toddler while he or she falls asleep in his or her bed at bedtime and throughout the night. Use the sit-in method.

Phase V: Start moving your sitting position closer to the door until you are sitting in the doorway or just outside the doorway where he or she can hear you but not see you while he or she falls asleep or falls back to sleep.

Phase VI: Continue following through and being consistent. Some days or nights may be better than others. If you want to work towards helping your child be more independent at sleep times, consider graduating to the give-me-space technique.

Sample 3: Stop using a pacifier and night wean

Phase I: Use the pacifier during the bedtime routine, but once you lay your baby down, remove the pacifier and let your baby fall asleep without it. Use your sleep coaching method of choice. Upon night waking, use the pacifier as you normally would to keep the process manageable just in case bedtime takes a long time the first few nights.

Phase II: Stop using the pacifier the entire night, but keep any current night feedings, if any. This will separate pacifier weaning from feeding, but be careful not to replace the pacifier with too many feedings.

Phase III: Night wean (see page 124 for details)

Sample 4: Naps

Phase I: Have your baby fall asleep in your arms without movement, feeding, or a pacifier (if you've chosen not to keep it).

Phase II: Work on having your baby fall asleep at nap time without his or her current sleep associations. If your baby takes a short nap, help him or her fall back to sleep for about 15 minutes. If your baby isn't asleep, get him or her up and end the nap.

Phase III: Implement the nap hour (see page 129 for details).

Still having trouble creating a plan or too tired to mess with it? We do have a "sleep plan generator" we call an Express Sleep Plan™ on babysleepsite.com if you need help creating one.

HOW YOUR PLAN MAY CHANGE AS YOUR CHILD GROWS

As I mentioned before, your plan can change over time. As your baby grows, your schedule will most definitely change and sleep challenges may vary. For example, when children are around two years old, we often see toddlers suddenly want their primary caretaker to stay in the room as they fall asleep even if they've been a great sleeper up to that point or since they were six months old. Your approach to that will be different than when you weaned your six-month-old from being rocked to sleep. In addition, a sleep coaching method that may have worked with a non-mobile baby may not work with your now strong 12-month-old who won't sit still in your lap or lay on your bed as he or she falls asleep. All this said, sometimes nothing changes. The same method could still work later. For example, if your now 14-month-old is recovering from a long illness, the methods you used when he or she was nine months old may still work.

SUMMARY

- ⊘ Follow these steps to make your sleep coaching plan:
  - » Identify your baby's sleep associations, and break big associations (like co-sleeping) into small baby steps.
  - » Identify your large sleep coaching goals (i.e. "I want my baby to sleep through the night"), and break this into smaller goals (i.e. "I want my baby to fall asleep in his or her crib at bedtime").
  - » Plan to start sleep coaching at bedtime, and then, move on to night wakings. Finally, work on naps (if necessary).
  - » Decide which sleep coaching method you'll use.
  - » Write out a day-by-day plan using your desired sleep coaching method. Be sure to allow for a reasonable timeline. Fourteen days is a good place to start; although, some sleep challenges may require more time, and gentle methods may take longer.
- ⊘ To sleep coach, do the following:
  - » Begin with bedtime. Work on laying your baby down drowsy but awake in his or her sleeping area.

» Once your baby is able to fall asleep independently at bedtime without much fuss, move on to night wakings. You'll want to put your baby back to bed drowsy but awake after night feedings and night wakings just like you did at bedtime.

» If night weaning is part of your plan, you can create fixed feeding times for the night, and plan to feed your baby at or after these times. Then, you'll gradually make these times later and later until you've phased out night feedings completely.

» When you've made progress with night wakings, move on to naps. Start by laying your baby down drowsy but awake at the start of nap time; when that's going well, move to lengthening the nap by creating a "nap hour."

> *As a first-time mom, boy was I surprised to learn that my daughter didn't just fall asleep when she was tired. We had a lot of challenges getting her to fall asleep and then staying asleep. For the first six months, she rarely napped for more than 20 minutes during the day. She was always overtired, and I felt like I could never go anywhere because I had to be home all day for her naps. At night, it would take about three hours to get her to bed. She would nurse, fall asleep, and then we would put her in her crib only for her to wake up and cry. So it would start all over again. She would even be crying while nursing or sucking our thumbs (she would never take a pacifier). At seven months, we had had enough.*

That's when we decided to sleep train using an actual sleep coaching plan. And it worked! Because we had a written-out, step-by-step plan, we were able to help my daughter learn to fall sleep unassisted. Now, she sleeps through the night and naps so much better. **-Sarah**

CHAPTER 6:

MOTIVATION (AND CONSISTENCY) IS HALF THE BATTLE

Here's something I tell all my clients: the right sleep coaching method (and the right sleep coaching plan) is one that works for both your baby *and* for you AND is one that you can commit to doing. Both of those elements matter. You can design the perfect sleep coaching plan that harmonizes with your philosophy and with your child's temperament, but if you can't actually stick to it, it's not the right plan. I can't emphasize this enough: consistency in sleep coaching is critical.

That said, consistency is tough to achieve for many families! And that's understandable. Some sleep coaching techniques require a lot of patience and a lot of time before they start to produce results. Other parents find it hard to stay consistent because of the way their babies or toddlers react to sleep coaching. But here's the thing: sleep coaching won't work unless you're consistent. This goes for other aspects of parenting too, doesn't it? For example, let's say you're trying to teach your baby not to touch electrical cords, which is a very wise thing to teach. Imagine if you spent three days strictly enforcing your new "don't touch electrical cords" rule only to give up on day four and not say a thing when your baby grabs the lamp cord with both hands and starts tugging. This is confusing for your baby; why was it wrong one day but fine the next? As a result of this mixed message, your child won't learn the "don't touch electrical cords" lesson nearly as quickly as he or she would if you'd been consistent in enforcing the rule.

The same is true for sleep coaching. For instance, let's say you've been rocking your baby to sleep for months now but want to wean him or her from that sleep association. For the first three days, you rock your baby for a few minutes before naps and bed, but then, put him or her in bed while he or she is drowsy but awake. This is a great start! But if you give up on day four and rock him or her straight to sleep for naps and bed, you're sending your baby a mixed message. This kind of inconsistency will set you back in your sleep coaching efforts and, unfortunately, often *increase* crying.

Why is consistency so important? Because people (both children and adults) need plenty of time and space to practice a new skill. In many ways, that's what sleeping through the night and napping well is for your baby or toddler, a new skill. Think about the times you've had to learn something new. You probably made lots of mistakes in the beginning and felt frustrated. But over time, you figured it out. Now, imagine if you were learning something new, and someone had stepped in and taken over just a few hours or days into your learning process and started doing it for you. It reminds me of a time in college when a friend of mine was learning to drive her new car. It had a manual transmission, and she had only ever driven an automatic. A well-meaning mutual friend took her out for a lesson, but after a few hours, he couldn't handle it anymore! She was grinding the gears and stalling out on hills. Finally, he made her pull over, so he could drive the car back to campus himself. In our sleep coaching analogy, my friend's driving instructor was like the parent who gets overwhelmed with sleep coaching and finally says, "I'll just take care of this myself." It's an understandable reaction as no one likes the sound of a fussy baby just as no one likes the sounds of grinding gears, but ultimately, in both scenarios, no one learned anything new. My friend couldn't learn to drive her new car unless she had the time and space to practice, and your baby can't learn to sleep through the night unless he or she has the same. So think about it this way: when you're consistent in your sleep coaching, you're giving your baby time and space to practice a new skill. The learning process may not be easy and may take longer than you'd like, but this is how learning often works.

> To be honest, it's been so long since sleep has been an 'issue' with my son! He's almost two and a half and is still a great sleeper. He averages about 11 hours a night and between two to three hours in the afternoon. It wasn't always that way, though. I was a first-time mom, and with a husband that is away at work all week, I went through so many days like a zombie at the beginning. After working on sleep coaching for awhile and having plenty of trial-and-error experiences, I have to say that the most important thing I learned was to BE CONSISTENT!! Consistency is so important in when you put them to sleep for bedtime and naps." **-Alana**

COMMON QUESTIONS DURING SLEEP COACHING

What about swaddling?

Swaddling can be an amazing way to soothe and comfort your young baby. It can also be a great way to help your baby fall asleep quickly and sleep longer with minimal waking. However, I often recommend that you wean your baby from the swaddle before you start any sleep coaching, especially because it can be a safety hazard if your baby rolls face down while swaddled. A huge part of sleep coaching is helping your baby learn to self soothe, and babies often need their hands free for self soothing. Additionally, swaddling tends to be a sleep association for younger babies, so it's something you'll want to wean away from before you work on sleep coaching. If your baby is heavily dependent on the swaddle and is six months or younger, you may want to wait two or three weeks and then attempt to wean away from the swaddle.

As for how to wean your baby from swaddling, I usually recommend that you start by leaving one arm unswaddled. Then, after a couple days, leave the other arm unswaddled, and just swaddle your baby's legs. (Alternatively, you can start with legs and then do arms if it's safe.) Then, your next step is to remove the swaddle completely. You can ease this transition by using a sleep sack or sleep bag as those tend to provide a snug, cozy feeling while still leaving the baby's arms free to move.

How long will it take to see success?

Oh, how I wish I could give you an exact answer on this! But how long it will take for you to see sleep coaching success is heavily dependent on a number of unique factors. For instance, if your child is slow to adapt, persistent, and intense, then sleep coaching will, no doubt, take longer than it would for an adaptable, easy-going child. Additionally, your own ability to stay consistent with your plan will determine how long it takes to start to see results.

In general, though, I find that low-cry sleep coaching techniques tend to take longer to produce noticeable results since the process is so gradual. The give-me-space technique, by contrast, generally goes a little faster. Of course, the pace of sleep coaching is dictated by you; you can make the fading method or the give-me-space technique (or any other method for that matter) move along as quickly or as slowly as you wish. But in general, gentler methods that are designed to be done gradually will likely take longer.

My recommendation to most families is to stick with your sleep coaching plan for a minimum of one to two weeks (two weeks, ideally). Why? Because the changes you are making to your child's schedule, sleep routines, and sleep habits have a cumulative effect, it may take you up to two weeks to see noticeable progress. You definitely don't want to start sleep coaching and then change tacks or give up after two or three days.

These same guidelines apply if you're thinking about changing up your sleep coaching method. If you're feeling like the sleep coaching approach you chose isn't working for your baby, I'd urge you to stick with your plan for at least a week (again, preferably two) before you scrap the plan and create a new one.

> *The main thing I've learned as a parent is that each child is different, and what worked for one kid may not work for yours. The sleep coaching methods that worked for my friends*

didn't work for me! It took time and trial and error for me to learn what worked for my baby, but we got there. You will, too; you and your baby will work it out together! **-Lindsay**

What if my baby is rolling over, sitting up, or pulling up?

Usually, when your baby learns a new physical skill, like rolling, sitting up or pulling to a standing position, you can bet that your baby will practice that new skill when he or she should be sleeping! In general, you may be okay with going in and rolling your baby over a couple times per night or laying him or her back down from a sitting or standing position, but you're probably not okay with doing it 10 times per night. I usually recommend you reposition your baby periodically in hopes that one of these times they are waiting, they will either learn to sleep on that side, learn to get down if they are pulling up, or learn not to pull up in the first place because it gets tiring. Note, however, that it's safest for babies to sleep on their backs, so if you have any concerns about your baby constantly rolling from his or her back to his or her stomach in the middle of the night, talk to your healthcare provider about how to proceed.

Do I sleep coach when my baby is sick?

You need to use your best judgment, but in general, I say not to sleep coach while your baby is sick. You know how you feel when you're sick, so your baby may need more comforting during this time. Having said that, when your baby is on the upswing and you are doing more harm than good "helping" him or her fall asleep, you may want to get back to sleep coaching to get more rest and get healthy again. You know your baby best, and you will be able to tell how he or she is feeling throughout the rest of the day to determine just how miserable he or she is.

Do I sleep coach when my baby is teething?

Some experts have said that teething does not disrupt sleep. I disagree. I believe some babies don't skip a beat when they get teeth, but I believe some definitely *are* affected. Since we can't feel what they feel, I err on the side of caution. I certainly don't remember what it felt like when teeth erupted through my gums for the first time! However, they teethe for what seems like a constant two years, and it's not good for either of you not to get enough sleep for two years! During rough teething patches, use appropriate teething remedies (best to ask your healthcare provider). Usually sleep disruptions only last a few days to a week. Any longer and you probably have a different sleep problem.

What do I do about traveling? Do I sleep coach while traveling?

Some people do sleep coach while traveling, but it usually depends on where you're going and for how long. If you are going camping for three days, it's unlikely you will be able to do much coaching because you would disturb your neighboring campers. If you are going to grandma's house for a month, you won't want to fall back into bad habits for so long. So you need to use your best judgment. Keep in mind that your child will be in a "foreign" place, so his or her schedule might be different, resulting in more overtiredness.

After traveling or being sick, how long will it take for my baby to start sleeping better again?

The good news is that, usually, previously sleep coached babies go back to sleeping well after just a couple of days (maybe longer for no-cry methods).

Will my baby sleep well from now on?

Not necessarily. I can tell you that it will probably be 10 times better, but depending on the child, sleep coaching is not always a cure-all. There could be ups and downs along the way as new milestones or sleep regressions (see Chapter 2) come up, as your child becomes much more aware of cause and effect, and as your child learns that he or she can sometimes get his or her way by crying.

What if I can't keep my baby awake during his or her feeding just before sleep times?

This is a very common question. Some families find that moving the feeding earlier in the routine is helpful, but it isn't always mandatory to improve sleep. However, when a baby can't help but fall asleep while feeding, it's usually a sign that the sleep time is too late. So start the entire process a bit sooner so that he or she takes about 10 minutes to fall asleep. Keep moving the sleep time earlier until he or she stays awake during the feeding.

SUMMARY

- ⊘ Consistency is key to seeing sleep coaching success! Stick with your plan for at least one week (two weeks is ideal). If you aren't seeing any progress by that point, you can adjust your plan.

- ⊘ These tips may help you see even greater sleep coaching success:

  » If your baby is still swaddled, plan to wean him or her from the swaddle before sleep coaching.

  » If your baby is constantly getting out of his or her sleeping position (by rolling over, sitting up, etc.), it's fine to reposition him or her a few times, but don't worry about doing it every time he or she moves.

  » If your baby gets sick during sleep coaching, pause your efforts until your baby is well.

  » If your baby begins teething in the middle of sleep coaching, plan to keep going, but offer extra comfort and plan to have two to three days during which you may not make much progress.

  » It's best not to travel during sleep coaching, so before you start, pick a stretch of time during which you'll have at least a few weeks of being home and having a normal schedule.

CONCLUSION

I sincerely hope that this book has been helpful to you and has given you the basics you need to get your baby started down the road to healthy sleep habits. No matter where you are in your sleep journey, remember that it's never too late - or too soon - to work towards promoting good sleep habits for your whole family!

We've covered a lot of ground in this book, but I hope that hasn't left you feeling overwhelmed. Yes, there's a lot of information here, but by no means do you have to internalize and apply all of it. I designed this book to give you choices and tools, so you could choose the tips and techniques that suit your family best.

I also want to offer you some encouragement. After years of working with sleep-deprived parents, I know that it's easy to feel like you're all alone in your sleep struggles. Maybe your spouse or partner isn't supportive of your desire to work on your baby's sleep. Maybe your friends and your family members all have babies who are great sleepers and who were sleeping through the night by the time they were eight weeks old! Maybe you're surrounded by well-meaning people who offer you conflicting advice about how to fix your baby's sleep. All that can add up to make you feel like you're so alone with your sleep struggles. Believe me,

I know this from experience; I felt so alone while I struggled with my oldest son's sleep!

Well, I'm here to tell you that you are NOT alone. The Baby Sleep Site® sees millions of visitors each year, and all of them are exhausted parents who are just like you and who want to solve their children's sleep challenges in a way that matches their parenting styles and their little one's temperament. Furthermore, I want to emphasize that there is hope and a light at the end of the tunnel. It can be so easy to feel like your baby might never sleep well and that the sleep problems you're facing are permanent. But this doesn't have to be true; you really can help your child learn to sleep in a way that your whole family can feel good about. The first step is often the hardest to take, but once you do, you'll most likely say, "Why didn't I do this sooner?"

Best of luck to you in your journey and happy sleeping!

FREE Resources For You!

This book isn't all The Baby Sleep Site® has to offer!

Visit www.babysleepsite.com and enjoy hundreds of free articles, 4 free e-books, a custom schedule generator, quizzes, and (most valuable of all) a large community of parents just like you!

Enjoy our most popular free e-Book, *5 Ways To Help Your Child Sleep Through The Night*, and get even more sleep coaching strategies + email tips on timely baby and toddler sleep topics delivered straight to your inbox each week.

Download your copy and sign up for our newsletter today!

Visit www.babysleepsite.com/baby-steps-free-ebook

APPENDIX A:

SLEEP PLAN TEMPLATE

Download at: http://www.babysleepsite.com/bookextras

MY PERSONAL SLEEP PLAN WORKBOOK

Background

Child's Name	
Age	
Medical Issues	
Temperament	
Current Day Sleep Total (Hours)	
Current Night Sleep Total minus Night Wakings (Hours)	
Average Total Sleep (Hours)	

Issues to Work On

Be very specific. For example, instead of writing "help my baby sleep all night," write "help my baby learn to fall asleep at bedtime without relying on a pacifier."

1.

2.

3.

4.

Goals

Short Term

In the next week, I'd like to see the following changes:

1.

2.

3.

Middle Term

In the next three to four weeks, I'd like to see the following changes:

4.

5.

6.

Long Term

In the next month or two, I'd like to see the following changes:

7.

8.

9.

Strategy

What strategy will you use? Again, be specific. Do not just say "use a no-cry method."

After my routine, I will lay my baby down awake, and then:

If/when he/she cries, I will:

_____

_____

_____

If he/she is hysterical, I will:

_____

_____

_____

If this process goes longer than _____ minutes, I will (circle one or more):

- ⊘ Take a _____-minute break and try again.

- ⊘ Have another loved one take a turn.

- ⊘ Try again tomorrow. (Note: Except for very young babies, children will learn quickly to resist "long enough" for you to give in, so use this option sparingly.)

- ⊘ _____

- ⊘ _____

- ⊘ _____

Your Day-By-Day Plan

Now, break your goals into phases (i.e. Bedtime, Night Wakings, Naps, Night Weaning). This breaks your goals into achievable chunks, so you can be successful. I typically recommend moving on to a new step roughly every three to five days for most babies. All babies are unique, and you may have special reasons to use a slower pace. These are just guidelines. Your plan may end up being a 10-day or a 45-day plan. I have left room for 30 days, which is usually the longest I go in personalized consultations. If you take too long in any one phase, you can quickly stall and have new habits to break.

First Phase:

Nights 1-3:

Nights 4-7:

Second Phase:

Nights 8-10:

Nights 11-14:

Third Phase:

Nights 15-18:

Nights 19-30:

Re-Evaluation Plans

All babies go through a unique journey. However, there are times when you feel like you are working on sleep too long, so you start to wonder if your plan is working.. This is when you may need to change your strategy or re-evaluate your plan. You must be realistic, though. While some babies are sleeping 12 hours per night three nights later, that is not always the case. This is where you set a realistic timeframe to re-evaluate. Give your baby enough time to learn but not so long that you are more sleep deprived than when you started. This can be an exhausting process.

If there is NO progress in _____ days, I will:
(No less than five days is recommended and up to 10)

_____

_____

_____

_____

If there is little progress in _____ days, I will:
(No less than five days is recommended and up to 10)

_____

_____

_____

_____

If there is progress and then we stall and are still working on this for _____ days, I will:
(No less than 14 days is recommended and up to 30)

_____

_____

_____

_____

When You Feel Like Giving Up

It helps to have something to rely on during the most difficult times. Repeat this any time you feel like giving up:

I will have:

- ⊘ Realistic Goals
- ⊘ Patience
- ⊘ Commitment
- ⊘ Consistency

I will not:

- ⊘ Compare my baby to books, friends' babies, or neighbors' kids
- ⊘ Compare my children to each other (if you have more than one)
- ⊘ Beat myself up if I stumble or fall
- ⊘ Give up. I will reach out for help before I give up.

Journal

It is a good idea to keep a journal, so you can reflect on your progress and remember how far you've come on your worst days. (Feel free to type this on your computer rather than write on paper.

Night 1:

Night 2:

Night _____ :

Night _____ :

Night _____ :

Night _____:

Night _____:

Night _____:

Night _____ :

Night _____ :

Night _____ :

Night _____ :

Night _____ :

Night _____ :

Night _____ :

Night _____ :

Night _____ :

SLEEP LOG TEMPLATE

Download at: http://www.babysleepsite.com/bookextras

Example

Day/ Date	Wake	Nap #1	Nap #2	Nap #3	Nap #4	Bed	Night Wakings	Feedings	Total Sleep
M 6/2	6:00 a.m.	9:00 a.m. 60 minutes	12:30 p.m. 60 minutes	4:00 p.m. 30 minutes		6:30 p.m.	0	2	14 hours
T 6/3	6:00 a.m.	9:00 a.m. 30 minutes	12:30 p.m. 45 minutes	4:15 p.m. 45 minutes		7:00 p.m.	0	2	13 hours
W 6/4	6:00 a.m.								

Average = 13.5 hours

Baby S.T.E.P.S. Method

Day/ Date	Wake	Nap #1	Nap #2	Nap #3	Nap #4	Bed	Night Wakings	Feedings	Total Sleep

Average = _____ hours

Day/ Date	Wake	Nap #1	Nap #2	Nap #3	Nap #4	Bed	Night Wakings	Feedings	Total Sleep

Average = ... hours

Day/ Date	Wake	Nap #1	Nap #2	Nap #3	Nap #4	Bed	Night Wakings	Feedings	Total Sleep

Average = _____ hours

APPENDIX C:

SAMPLE SCHEDULES BY AGE

All sample schedules reference daily nutritional goals. Please review these with your pediatrician!

FOUR MONTHS OLD

At this age, many four-month-olds are still waking one to three times to eat at night (or every three to six hours, variably). If it's more, you likely have a sleep association problem. Babies at this age can go two to three hours between feedings. My boys seemed to need to eat every two hours for a fairly long time (both were breastfed). Typically, formula-fed babies can go longer between feedings than breastfed babies, but all babies vary. In many ways, we want them to eat more during the day than at night anyway, so don't worry if they eat quite often.

Sample Schedule 1

This schedule assumes your baby is awake for one hour and 30 minutes before needing to sleep again. At this age, wake time should be one to two hours TOPS to prevent your baby from getting overtired. This also assumes your baby can go about two hours between feedings.

Time	Description	Notes
6:30 a.m.	Wake and Breast Milk or Formula	
8:00 a.m.	Nap	Usually 30-60 minutes

8:30 a.m.	Breast Milk or Formula	
10:00 a.m.	Nap	
10:45 a.m.	Breast Milk or Formula	
12:15 p.m.	Nap	Usually 30-45 minutes
12:45-1:00 p.m.	Breast Milk or Formula	
2:15 p.m.	Nap	Usually 30-45 minutes
2:45 p.m.	Breast Milk or Formula	
4:00 p.m.	Nap	30-minute catnap
4:45 p.m.	Breast Milk or Formula	
6:15 p.m.	Begin Bedtime Routine	
6:30 p.m.	Breast Milk or Formula and Bedtime	
6:45 p.m.	Goal Is to Be Asleep	
10:00 p.m.-12:00 a.m.	First Nighttime Feeding	Many babies can go 4-5 hours by this age but some can't.
1:00-3:00 a.m.	Second Feeding	Feeding should be 2-3+ hours later.
4:00-6:00 a.m.	Third Feeding	Feeding should be 2-3+ hours later.

Sample Schedule 2

This schedule assumes your baby is awake for one hour and 30 minutes before needing to sleep again. At this age, wake time should be one to two hours TOPS to prevent your baby from getting overtired. This also assumes your baby eats every three hours.

Time	Description	Notes
6:30 a.m.	Wake and Breast Milk or Formula	
8:00 a.m.	Nap	Usually 30-60 minutes
9:30 a.m.	Breast Milk or Formula	
10:15-10:30 a.m.	Nap	Usually 30-45 minutes
12:00 p.m.	Nap	Usually 30-45 minutes
12:30 p.m.	Breast Milk or Formula	
2:00 p.m.	Nap	Usually 30-45 minutes
3:30 p.m.	Breast Milk or Formula	
4:15 p.m.	Nap	30-minute catnap
5:45 p.m.	Begin Bedtime Routine	
6:15 p.m.	Breast Milk or Formula and Bedtime	
6:30 p.m.	Goal Is to Be Asleep	
10:00 p.m.-12:00 a.m.	First Nighttime Feeding	Many babies can go 4-5 hours by this age, but some can't.
1:00-3:00 a.m.	Second Feeding	Feeding should be 2-3+ hours later.
4:00-6:00 a.m.	Third Feeding	Feeding should be 2-3+ hours later.

FIVE MONTHS OLD

At this age, many five-month-olds wake one to three times to eat at night on average. If it's more, you likely have a sleep association problem or need to encourage eating more during the day.

Babies at this age often go two and a half to three hours between feedings. Typically, formula-fed babies can go longer between feedings than breastfed babies, but all babies vary. In many ways, we want them to eat more during the day than at night anyway, so don't worry about frequent feedings.

Sample Schedule 1

This schedule assumes your baby can stay up one hour and 30 minutes to two hours before needing to sleep again. At this age, wake time should be about two to three hours to prevent your baby from getting overtired. However, some five-month-olds aren't too different from four-month-olds and can't stay awake past two hours, so don't rush it. This also assumes your baby can go about two and a half hours between feedings.

Time	Description	Notes
6:30 a.m.	Wake and Breast Milk or Formula	
8:00 a.m.	Nap	Usually 60+ minutes
9:00 a.m.	Breast Milk or Formula	
11:00 a.m.	Nap	Usually 30-60 minutes
11:30 a.m.- 12:00 p.m.	Breast Milk or Formula	
1:30 p.m.	Breast Milk or Formula	
2:00 p.m.	Nap	Usually 30-45 minutes
3:45 - 4:15 p.m.	Breast Milk or Formula	
5:00 p.m.	Breast Milk or Formula	

Time	Description	Notes
6:30 p.m.	Begin Bedtime Routine	
6:45 p.m.	Breast Milk or Formula and Bedtime	
7:00 p.m.	Goal Is to Be Asleep	
12:00 p.m.	First Nighttime Feeding	Many babies can go 5+ hours by this age.
3:00 a.m.	Breast Milk or Formula	Second nighttime feeding should be 3+ hours after the first.

Sample Schedule 2

This schedule assumes your baby is awake for two hours before needing to sleep again. At this age, wake time should be two to three hours TOPS to prevent your baby from getting overtired. This also assumes your baby is hungry about every three hours.

Time	Description	Notes
6:30 a.m.	Wake and Breast Milk or Formula	
8:00 a.m.	Nap	Usually 60+ minutes
9:30 a.m.	Breast Milk or Formula	
11:30 a.m.	Nap	Usually 45-60 minutes
12:30 p.m.	Breast Milk or Formula	
3:00 p.m.	Nap	30-45–minute catnap
3:30 p.m.	Breast Milk or Formula	
5:30 p.m.	Possible Nap If Baby Hasn't Transitioned to Three Naps	Less than 30-minute catnap

173

Time	Description	Notes
6:00 p.m.	Breast Milk or Formula	
6:00-7:00 p.m.	Begin Bedtime Routine	
6:30-7:30 p.m.	Goal Is to Be Asleep	
11:30 p.m.-12:00 a.m.	First Nighttime Feeding	Many babies can sleep for 5+ hours at a time by this age.
3:00 a.m.	Second possible feeding	Second nighttime feeding should be about three hours after the first.

SIX MONTHS OLD

At this age, some six-month-olds can sleep all night without a feeding, but many need to eat one to two times per night. If it's more, you likely have a sleep association problem (aside from the six-month growth spurt that should only last a few days to a week).

Sample Schedule 1

This schedule assumes that your baby is still taking short naps, can stay up for two hours, and sleeps 12 hours at night (with night feedings).

Time	Description	Notes
7:00 a.m.	Wake and Breast Milk or Formula	
8:30 a.m.	Breakfast	
9:00 a.m.	Nap	Usually 30-60 minutes
10:00 a.m.	Breast Milk or Formula	
12:00 p.m.	Nap	Usually 30-45 minutes
1:00 p.m.	Breast Milk or Formula	

2:30 p.m.	Nap	Usually 30-45 minutes
4:00 p.m.	Breast Milk or Formula	
4:30-5:00 p.m.	Nap	30-minute catnap
5:30 p.m.	Breast Milk or Formula and Dinner	
6:30 p.m.	Begin Bedtime Routine	
6:45 p.m.	Breast Milk or Formula and Bedtime	
7:00 p.m.	Goal Is to Be Asleep	
12:00-2:00 a.m.	First (and Possibly Only) Nighttime Feeding	Feeding shouldn't need to be earlier than 12:00-3:00 a.m. (5+ hours after the last milk/formula feeding).
3:00-5:00 a.m.	Second Possible Feeding	Second nighttime feeding should be 3+ hours after the first.

Sample Schedule 2

This schedule assumes that your baby is still taking short naps, can stay up for two hours, and sleeps 11 hours at night.

Time	Description	Notes
6:00 a.m.	Wake and Breast Milk or Formula	
7:30 a.m.	Breakfast	
8:00 a.m.	Nap	Usually 30-45 minutes
9:00 a.m.	Breast Milk or Formula	
11:45 a.m.	Breast Milk or Formula	
12:00 p.m.	Nap	30-45 minutes

3:00 p.m.	Breast Milk or Formula	
4:00 p.m.	Catnap	30-45 minutes
5:00 p.m.	Breast Milk or Formula and Dinner	
6:30 p.m.	Begin Bedtime Routine	
6:45 p.m.	Breast Milk or Formula and Bedtime	
7:00 p.m.	Goal Is to Be Asleep	
12:00-3:00 a.m.	First (and Possibly Only) Nighttime Feeding	Feeding shouldn't be earlier than 12:00-3:00 a.m. (5+ hours from last milk/formula feeding).
3:00-5:00 a.m.	Second Possible Feeding	Second nighttime feeding should be 3+ hours after the first.

SEVEN MONTHS OLD

At this age, some seven-month-olds can sleep all night without a feeding, but many need one to two feedings at night. If it's more, you likely have a sleep association problem. At this age, most babies take three naps, but some babies only take two.

Sample Schedule 1

This schedule assumes that your baby is taking three naps, can go three hours between feedings, and sleeps 12 hours at night.

Time	Description	Notes
7:00 a.m.	Wake and Breast Milk or Formula	
8:15 a.m.	Breakfast	
9:00 a.m.	Nap	At least 1 hour

10:00 a.m.	Breast Milk or Formula	
12:30 p.m.	Breast Milk or Formula	
1:00 p.m.	Nap	At least 1 hour
3:00 p.m.	Breast Milk or Formula	
4:00 p.m.	Catnap	30-45 minutes
5:30 p.m.	Breast Milk or Formula and Dinner	
6:30 p.m.	Begin Bedtime Routine	
6:45 p.m.	Breast Milk or Formula and Bedtime	
7:00 p.m.	Goal Is to Be Asleep	
12:00-3:00 a.m.	First (and Possibly Only) Nighttime Feeding	Feeding shouldn't be earlier than 12:00-3:00 a.m. (5+ hours from last milk/formula feeding).
3:00-5:00 a.m.	Second Possible Feeding	Second nighttime feeding should be 3+ hours after the first.

Sample Schedule 2

This schedule assumes that your baby is taking three naps, can go three hours between feedings, and sleeps 11 ½ hours at night

Time	Description	Notes
6:30 a.m.	Wake	
7:30 a.m.	Breast Milk or Formula	
8:30 a.m.	Breakfast	
9:30 a.m.	Nap	At least 1 hour
10:30 a.m.	Breast Milk or Formula	

12:00 p.m.	Lunch	
1:30 p.m.	Breast Milk or Formula	
2:00 p.m.	Nap	At least 1 hour
4:30 p.m.	Breast Milk or Formula	
6:00 p.m.	Dinner	
6:30 p.m.	Begin Bedtime Routine	
6:45 p.m.	Breast Milk or Formula and Bedtime	
7:00 p.m.	Goal Is to Be Asleep	
12:00-3:00 a.m.	First (and Possibly Only) Nighttime Feeding	Feeding shouldn't be earlier than 12:00-3:00 a.m. (5+ hours from last milk/formula feeding).
3:00-5:00 a.m.	Second Possible Feeding	Second nighttime feeding should be 3+ hours after the first.

EIGHT MONTHS OLD

At this age, many eight-month-olds can sleep all night without a feeding, but some are still waking one to two times to eat at night (mostly just one, which you might need to encourage). If it's more, you likely have a sleep association problem. At this age, many babies are still taking three naps, but some babies are on the verge of transitioning to just two if they haven't already. This is a common age for nap issues, specifically fighting naps.

Sample Schedule 1

This schedule assumes that your baby is taking three naps, can go up to three hours between feedings, and sleeps 12 hours at night.

Time	Description	Notes
6:30 a.m.	Wake, Breast Milk or Formula, and Breakfast	
8:45 a.m.	Breast Milk or Formula	
9:00 a.m.	Nap	At least 1 hour
11:45 a.m.	Breast Milk or Formula and lunch	
1:00 p.m.	Nap	At least 1 hour
2:45 p.m.	Breast Milk or Formula	
4:00 p.m.	Nap	30-45-minute catnap
5:00 p.m.	Breast Milk or Formula and Dinner	
6:00 p.m.	Begin Bedtime Routine	
6:15 p.m.	Breast Milk or Formula and Bedtime	
6:30 p.m.	Goal to be Asleep	
2:00-5:00 a.m.	(Possible) Nighttime Feeding	

Sample Schedule 2

This schedule assumes that your baby is taking two naps, can go three and a half to four hours between feedings, and sleeps 11 ½ hours at night.

Time	Description	Notes
6:30 a.m.	Wake, Breast Milk or Formula, and Breakfast	
9:30 a.m.	Nap	At least 1 hour
10:30 a.m.	Breast Milk or Formula	

12:00 p.m.	Possible Breast Milk or Formula (Offer Prior to Lunch)	
1:30 p.m.	Nap	At least 1 hour
2:30 p.m.	Breast Milk or Formula	
5:30 p.m.	Breast Milk or Formula and Dinner	
6:30 p.m.	Begin Bedtime Routine	
6:45 p.m.	Breast Milk or Formula and Bedtime	
7:00 p.m.	Goal Is to Be Asleep	
2:00-5:00 a.m.	(Possible) Nighttime Feeding	

NINE MONTHS OLD

At this age, many nine-month-olds can sleep all night without a feeding. Some babies do need a very early morning feeding up through a year, but I typically recommend at least an attempt at night weaning. At this age, most babies have transitioned to two naps.

Sample Schedule 1

This schedule assumes that your baby is taking two naps and sleeps 12 hours at night.

Time	Description	Notes
6:30 a.m.	Wake, Breast Milk or Formula, and Breakfast	
9:00 a.m.	Breast Milk or Formula	
9:30 a.m.	Nap	At least 1 hour
12:00 p.m.	Breast Milk or Formula and Lunch	

1:30 p.m.	Nap	At least 1 hour
2:45 p.m.	Breast Milk or Formula	
5:30 p.m.	Breast Milk or Formula and Dinner	
6:00 p.m.	Begin Bedtime Routine	
6:15 p.m.	Breast Milk or Formula and Bedtime	
6:30 p.m.	Goal Is to Be Asleep	
4:30 a.m.	(Possible) Nighttime Feeding	

*Keep in mind that moms who breastfeed and work may need to keep two nighttime feedings through the first year to avoid a drop in milk supply.

Sample Schedule 2

This schedule assumes that your baby is taking two naps and sleeps 11 hours at night.

Time	Description	Notes
7:00 a.m.	Wake, Breast Milk or Formula, and Breakfast	
9:00 a.m.	Breast Milk or Formula	
10:00 a.m.	Nap	At least 1 hour
11:00 a.m.	Breast Milk or Formula	
12:30 p.m.	Lunch	
1:45 p.m.	Breast Milk or Formula	
2:00 p.m.	Nap	At least 1 hour
4:45 p.m.	Breast Milk or Formula	

5:30 p.m.	Dinner
7:15 p.m.	Begin Bedtime Routine
7:45 p.m.	Breast Milk or Formula and Bedtime
8:00 p.m.	Goal Is to Be Asleep
5:00 a.m.	(Possible) Nighttime Feeding

10 MONTHS OLD

At this age, most 10-month-olds can sleep all night without a feeding. Some babies do need one very early morning feeding up through a year, but I typically recommend at least an attempt at night weaning. At this age, babies are taking two naps. A small number of babies will transition to one nap at this age, but I typically recommend keeping two naps as long as possible.

Schedules at nine and 10 months don't vary that much except that your baby will likely have an easier time staying up until the next nap. I have provided additional schedules down below for a variety.

Sample Schedule 1

This schedule assumes that your baby is taking two naps and sleeps 12 hours at night.

Time	Description	Notes
7:15 a.m.	Wake, Breast Milk or Formula, and Breakfast	
10:15 a.m.	Nap	At least 1 hour
11:15 a.m.	Breast Milk or Formula and Lunch	

2:15 p.m.	Nap	At least 1 hour
3:15 p.m.	Breast Milk or Formula	
6:00 p.m.	Possible Breast Milk or Formula and Dinner	
6:45 p.m.	Begin Bedtime Routine	
7:00 p.m.	Breast Milk or Formula and Bedtime	
7:15 p.m.	Goal Is to Be Asleep	

*This schedule assumes no night feedings, but one night feeding is considered normal and healthy for some 10-month-old babies.

Sample Schedule 2

This schedule assumes that your baby is taking two naps and sleeps 11 hours at night.

Time	Description	Notes
7:00 a.m.	Wake and Breast Milk or Formula	
9:00 a.m.	Breakfast	
10:00 a.m.	Nap	At least 1 hour
11:00 a.m.	Breast Milk or Formula	
12:30 p.m.	Lunch	
2:45 p.m.	Breast Milk or Formula	
3:00 p.m.	Nap	At least 1 hour
5:30 p.m.	Breast Milk or Formula	
6:30 p.m.	Dinner	

7:15 p.m.	Begin Bedtime Routine
7:45 p.m.	Breast Milk or Formula and Bedtime
8:00 p.m.	Goal Is to Be Asleep

*This schedule assumes no night feedings, but one night feeding is considered normal and healthy for some 10-month-old babies.

11 MONTHS OLD

At this age, most 11-month-olds can sleep all night without a feeding. Some babies do need one very early morning feeding up through a year, but I typically recommend at least an attempt at night weaning. At this age, babies are taking two naps, but some will start to transition to one nap in this month. I typically recommend keeping two naps as long as possible. At this age, you might need to do a little more nap management to keep two naps by making sure morning naps end early enough to make room for an afternoon nap.

Sample Schedule 1

This schedule assumes that your baby is taking two naps and sleeps 12 hours at night.

Time	Description	Notes
7:45 a.m.	Breast Milk or Formula and Breakfast	
10:45 a.m.	Nap	At least 1 hour
11:45 a.m.	Breast Milk or Formula and Lunch	
2:45 p.m.	Breast Milk or Formula	
3:00 p.m.	Nap	At least 1 hour
6:00 p.m.	Breast Milk or Formula and Dinner	

7:15 p.m.	Begin Bedtime Routine
7:30 p.m.	Bedtime
7:45 p.m.	Goal Is to Be Asleep

*This schedule assumes no night feedings, but one night feeding is considered normal and healthy for some 11-month-old babies.

Sample Schedule 2

This schedule assumes that your baby is taking two naps and sleeps 11 hours at night.

Time	Description	Notes
6:00 a.m.	Wake and Breast Milk or Formula	
8:00 a.m.	Possible Breast Milk or Formula and Breakfast	
9:00 a.m.	Nap	At least 1 hour
10:30 a.m.	Breast Milk or Formula	
11:30 a.m.	Lunch	
1:30 p.m.	Breast Milk or Formula	
2:00 p.m.	Nap	At least 1 hour
4:30 p.m.	Breast Milk or Formula	
5:30 p.m.	Dinner	
6:15 p.m.	Begin Bedtime Routine	
6:45 p.m.	Breast Milk or Formula and Bedtime	
7:00 p.m.	Goal Is to Be Asleep	

*This schedule assumes no night feedings, but one night feeding is considered normal and healthy for some 11-month-old babies.

12 - 18 MONTHS OLD

Welcome to toddlerhood! At this age, most 12-18 month-olds should be able to sleep all night without a feeding. At this age, toddlers are often still taking two naps, but some will start to take just one nap. The average age to transition to one nap is 15- to 18 months old. I typically recommend keeping two naps as long as possible. At this age, you might need to do a little more nap management to keep two naps by making sure morning naps end early enough to make room for an afternoon nap. And you might need to wake your toddler up by a certain time in the afternoon to keep an early enough bedtime to prevent night waking or an early wake-up time in the morning.

> ⊘ *NOTE - The schedules below assume your child is taking just one nap per day; however, many 12- to 15-month-olds still need two naps per day to be fully rested. If your 12- to 15-month-old is still taking two naps per day, use the 11-month schedules for another month or two.*

Sample Schedule 1

This schedule assumes that your toddler is taking one nap and sleeps 12 hours at night.

Time	Description	Notes
7:00 a.m.	Wake	
7:00 a.m.	Milk* and Breakfast	
9:00 a.m.	Snack	
11:30 a.m.	Milk and lunch	
12:00 p.m.	Nap	1 ½ to 2+ hours (some nap as long as 3 hours)

5:00 p.m.	Milk and Dinner	
6:30 p.m.	Begin Bedtime Routine and Offer Bedtime Snack and Possibly Milk	
6:45 p.m.	Bedtime and Lights Out	
7:00 p.m.	Goal Is to Be Asleep	

*In this case, milk includes human milk, infant or toddler formula, and full-fat animal milk. Be sure to speak to your baby's doctor before offering plant-based milks or low-fat milks since plant-based milks do not have the same nutritional content as traditional milks. Also, the brain is still growing at a fast rate and needs the sugar and fat in full-fat milk to grow properly. Talk to your baby's doctor about the appropriate amount of milk at this age. Many doctors may recommend limiting milks other than human milk to no more than 16 to 20 ounces per day.

*This schedule assumes no night feedings, but one night feeding is considered normal and healthy for some 12-month-old babies.

Sample Schedule 2

This schedule assumes that your baby is taking one nap and sleeps 11 hours at night.

Time	Description	Notes
6:00 a.m.	Wake and Milk	
6:15 a.m.	Breakfast	
9:00 a.m.	Snack	
11:30 a.m.	Lunch and Milk	
12:00 p.m.	Nap	1 ½ to 2+ hours (some nap as long as 3 hours)
2:30 p.m.	Snack	
5:00 p.m.	Dinner and Milk	
6:15 p.m.	Begin Bedtime Routine and Offer Bedtime Snack and Possibly Milk	

6:45 p.m.	Bedtime and Lights Out
7:00 p.m.	Goal Is to Be Asleep

*This schedule assumes no night feedings, but one night feeding is considered normal and healthy for some 12-month-old babies.

CASE STUDIES

CASE STUDY: FOUR-MONTH-OLD BABY STRUGGLING WITH FOUR-MONTH SLEEP REGRESSION AND SWADDLING AND PACIFIER SLEEP ASSOCIATIONS

This case study reflects a Baby Sleep Site® client's sleep coaching experience. This case study has been written with the client's permission. Names have been changed to protect privacy.

The Problem

Nadia and Brad came to us when their daughter, Abigail, was four and a half months old. Abigail was struggling with both nighttime waking and napping. Nadia reported that Abigail had been taking naps that were at least 45 minutes long, but now, she was waking after 30 minutes of napping on the dot and needed to be held to sleep in order to sleep any longer.

Nights were also tough. Abigail would have a longer stretch of sleep (about three hours) at the beginning of the night but would wake every two hours for the rest of the night. Nadia swaddled Abigail and used a pacifier and white noise in order to help Abigail fall asleep. They would also pat and shush Abigail to help encourage sleep. Nadia reported that while they made sure Abigail fell asleep in her crib at the beginning of the night, by the end of the night, Nadia would often bring Abigail into her bed to help everyone get a little more sleep.

Nadia let Liz, her sleep consultant, know that she and Brad had done a little sleep coaching previously; they had helped Abigail learn to soothe herself to sleep using the pacifier. However, after temporarily moving in with Nadia's parents while they waited to move into a new home, Abigail regressed and returned to needing Nadia and Brad to put her to sleep.

Current Schedule

- ⊘ 5:30 a.m. Abigail wakes up. Nadia picks her up, and they go back to sleep together.
- ⊘ 7:15 a.m. – Abigail wakes up for the day.
- ⊘ 7:30 a.m. – Breastfeeding
- ⊘ 9:15 – 10 a.m. – Abigail naps in the crib or swing.
- ⊘ 10:10 – 11:10 a.m. – Abigail wakes but isn't ready to get up, so Nadia puts her back to sleep and holds her for an additional hour.
- ⊘ 11:00 a.m. – Breastfeed and Rice Cereal
- ⊘ 12:50 – 1:35 p.m. – Abigail naps in the crib.
- ⊘ 1:40 – 2:25 p.m. – Abigail wakes from her nap but is fussy, so Nadia puts her back to sleep and holds her for an additional 45 minutes.
- ⊘ 2:30 p.m. – Breastfeeding
- ⊘ 4:10 p.m. – Abigail naps in her crib.
- ⊘ 4:45 - 5:15 p.m. – Abigail wakes from her nap but is fussy, so Nadia puts her back to sleep and holds her for an additional 30 minutes.
- ⊘ 6 p.m. – Breastfeeding
- ⊘ 7:10 p.m. – Bath
- ⊘ 7:30 p.m. – Breastfeeding
- ⊘ 8:00 p.m. – Nadia swaddles Abigail, puts on some white noise, and puts Abigail down to sleep in her crib.

- 11:00 p.m. – Abigail wakes. Nadia gives her a pacifier, and she goes back to sleep.
- 1:15 a.m. — Abigail wakes. Nadia gives her a pacifier, and she goes back to sleep.
- 2:45 a.m. – Abigail wakes. Nadia feeds her, and she goes back to sleep. Abigail then sleeps until 6:15 a.m.

Parent Goals

- Abigail wakes at night only when she's hungry and needs to be fed.
- Abigail learns to fall asleep in her crib on her own without needing to be held.
- Abigail learns to nap on her own without needing to be held.
- Abigail takes longer, more restorative naps.
- Abigail drops her nighttime feeding when she's ready and sleeps 10 to 12 hours.

Additional Information

Abigail is a spirited child, according to Nadia and Brad. She is generally happy, but when she is overtired, she quickly becomes unhappy and very fussy. Nadia also reported that Abigail is a very restless sleeper and tends to move around a lot (kicking her legs, changing positions, etc.) when she sleeps. Finally, Nadia noted that she felt a little reluctant to take away the pacifier since Abigail depended so heavily on it for soothing and comfort. However, she also reported that she and Brad were ready to get some sleep and that they were willing to do whatever Liz suggested in order to make that happen!

The Proposed Solution

After reviewing Nadia and Brad's Family Sleep History form, Liz indicated to Nadia that it was likely that Abigail had gone through the four-month sleep regression, and that's what accounted for the change in her sleeping patterns (particularly the change in her napping habits). Liz assured Nadia and Brad that this was completely normal and that lots of families face the same problem.

Liz also pointed out that Nadia and Brad would need to work towards breaking Abigail's pacifier association in order to help her learn how to self soothe.

From there, Liz made specific day-by-day recomendations as to how to solve Abigail's sleep problems and to achieve the family's sleep goals.

Step 1: Work on bedtime first, and then, work on night wakings.

Phase I: Liz indicated that these would likely be the toughest nights for the whole family. She instructed Nadia and Brad to swaddle Abigail with one arm out (so that Abigail could suck on her fingers or hands to self soothe) and to then do what they needed to do to help Abigail become drowsy. At that point, Nadia and Brad were to put Abigail in her crib drowsy but awake and without her pacifier. Liz indicated that Abigail would likely protest this change in routine. Therefore, some crying was expected, but she encouraged Nadia and Brad to use the fading method, which consisted of comforting Abigail as best they could while still leaving her in the crib and then gradually 'fading out' their presence. Because Abigail was young and because Nadia and Brad understandably wanted to limit crying, this approach was a good choice. Finally, Liz explained that for these first three nights, Nadia and Brad should handle all night wakings the way they normally would — with a full swaddle and pacifier.

Phase II: At this point, Liz instructed Nadia and Brad to begin doing the modified swaddle and to eliminate the pacifier for all nighttime wakings. Liz also encouraged Nadia to make sure that Abigail didn't breastfeed before midnight, and she recommended that Nadia and Brad make sure that Abigail was put back in her crib awake so that she could practice putting herself to sleep. Liz pointed out that for nonfeeding night wakings, Nadia and Brad should soothe and settle Abigail the same way they did at bedtime using the fading method, which is done by doing a modified swaddle, putting her back into her crib drowsy but awake, and then slowly fading out their presence. Liz also recommended that Nadia consider sleeping in Abigail's room during these nights on an air mattress on the floor as a way to make the process easier and to ease Abigail away from the middle-of-the-night co-sleeping that had been happening.

When to Night-Wean: Liz recommended that Nadia consider night weaning Abigail at around seven or eight months (or sooner if Nadia felt ready). When Nadia felt ready to night wean, Liz explained that she should gradually move Abigail's nighttime feedings back by about 30 minutes or so each night. In addition, Nadia should try to gradually shorten the length of Abigail's nighttime feedings. Then, when the 'night feeding' had reached the point to where it was happening around 6:00 a.m., Liz recommended that Nadia stop feeding and focus on making it the first morning feeding of the day.

Step 2: Work on Naps

Liz pointed out that she recommends working on nights first and waiting to work on naps until nighttime sleep has somewhat improved. This helps ward off overtiredness, and it helps families break down the big tasks of improving sleep into smaller, more manageable steps.

Phase I: Liz instructed Nadia to first focus on helping Abigail learn how to fall asleep in her crib on her own at nap time. Liz pointed out that Nadia could use the techniques she had been using for nights. She could lay Abigail down in her crib drowsy but awake with one arm out of the swaddle and no pacifier. Then, she could soothe Abigail when she became fussy by shushing and patting.

Phase II: Liz informed Nadia that, at this point, she could start to work on lengthening the naps themselves. By this point, Liz stated that Abigail would likely be falling asleep more easily in her crib at nap time, so the focus could shift to lengthening the naps themselves. Liz instructed Nadia to work on lengthening Abigail's naps by using the same methods she had employed in helping Abigail learn to fall asleep on her own. So if Abigail woke up early from a nap, Nadia should leave her in her crib but should shush and pat her for comfort. Liz added that if Abigail's naps hadn't improved by day 14, she and Nadia should tweak the plan together.

Recommended Nap Schedule for Abigail

Four-Nap Schedule:

- 7:00 a.m. – Abigail wakes up for the day.
- 8:30 a.m. – Abigail naps for 30 to 60 minutes.
- 11:00 - 11:30 a.m. – Abigail naps for 30 to 45 minutes.
- 2:00 p.m. – Abigail naps for 30 to 45 minutes.
- 4:30 p.m. – Abigail catnaps for 30 minutes.
- 5:45 - 6:45 p.m. – Nadia and Brad begin the bedtime routine (note: use the earlier 5:45 time if Abigail skipped a daytime nap).

- 6:00 - 7:00 p.m. – Bedtime and lights out
- 6:15 - 7:15 p.m. – The goal is for Abigail to be asleep at this time.

Three-Nap Schedule (only if Abigail is consistently resisting the fourth nap):

- 7:00 a.m. – Abigail wakes up for the day.
- 9:00 a.m. – Abigail naps for 1+ hour.
- 12:00 p.m. – Abigail naps for 1+ hour.
- 3:30 - 4:00 p.m. – Abigail naps for 30 to 45 minutes.
- 6:30 p.m. – Nadia and Brad begin the bedtime routine.
- 6:45 p.m. – Bedtime and lights out
- 7:00 p.m. – The goal is for Abigail to be asleep at this time.

What Happened

Within three weeks of starting the plan, Nadia reported that Abigail had become a pro at putting herself to sleep at night! In fact, Nadia said, "There are times when she puts herself to sleep faster than I could put myself to sleep!" Nadia indicated that because Abigail had made such progress in falling asleep on her own at bedtime, she and Brad had moved on to working on nighttime wakings and were seeing progress there as well. Nadia indicated that there had been a few nights when Abigail slept from 7:00 p.m. to 3:00 a.m., woke up to feed, and then went right back to sleep on her own! Liz let Nadia know that this was, indeed, fantastic progress! (A side note: Nadia also mentioned that she'd skipped the step of swaddling Abigail with one arm out as it had seemed to frustrate Abigail more than anything.)

Once nights had improved, Nadia moved to working on naps. Unfortunately, this proved to be much tougher. While putting

Abigail down for a nap every one and a half hours during the day was helping ward off overtiredness and fussiness (a technique that Liz had suggested), Nadia reported that Abigail was still taking short, 30-minute catnaps throughout the day. She wasn't having any luck with lengthening those naps.

Liz pointed out to Nadia that Abigail was right on the cusp of being to the point where her naps might naturally lengthen. By five or six months, many babies gradually begin taking longer, one–hour naps, but before that point, they aren't able to do so. She encouraged Nadia to stick to it, and it paid off! A few days later, Nadia wrote in to let Liz know that Abigail was beginning to take a longer, one-hour nap each day. (Sometimes, the nap was as long as an hour and a half!)

At this point, everyone got busy with the Christmas season, so Nadia didn't write in again until early January. When she did, she let Liz know that while nights were pretty much perfect (waking just once each night around 3:00 or 4:00 a.m. to feed and then going back to sleep on her own without any fuss), naps were a different story. While Nadia and Brad had seen some good progress with naps for a few weeks right around Christmas, Abigail had regressed and was back to taking lots of short, 30-minute naps and fussing quite a bit at nap time.

Liz indicated that some of the fussiness could be due to tummy trouble as a result of the increased solids Abigail was eating. (Abigail was about six and a half months old by this point.) Liz recommended that Nadia and Brad focus on giving her 'P' foods (prunes, peaches, etc.) to help improve digestion.

Liz also let Nadia know that it was likely time for an adjusted nap schedule now that Abigail was older. Liz made the following suggestions:

- 6:30 - 7:00 a.m. – Abigail wakes for the day.

- 8:30 - 9:00 a.m. – Abigail naps for 1+ hour.

- 12:00 - 12:30 p.m. – Abigail naps for 1+ hour.

- 4:00 p.m. – Abigail catnaps for 30 to 45 minutes.

- 6:30 p.m. – Nadia and Brad begin the bedtime routine.

- 6:45 p.m. – Bedtime and lights out

- 7:00 p.m. – The goal is for Abigail to be asleep by this time.

Liz also recommended that Nadia base Abigail's naps on her wake times using the following guidelines:

- No morning naps before 8:00 a.m.

- No early afternoon naps before 12:00 p.m.

- No late afternoon naps before 3:00 p.m.

- No bedtimes before 6:00 p.m.

- Limit total daytime sleep to three hours.

The Result

With Liz's help, Nadia and Brad have been able to help Abigail learn to fall asleep on her own and to put herself back to sleep after her one nighttime feeding. While naps have proven harder to conquer than nights, Nadia and Brad have been able to help Abigail learn to fall asleep on her own for naps and are working on lengthening her naps. They are seeing good progress in that department; Nadia reports that now, 90 percent of the time, Abigail's first and second naps of the day are at least an hour long. The third nap is between 30 and 45 minutes.

At the time of this case study's publication, Liz had recommended that Nadia consider night weaning Abigail. (Abigail is now seven months old.) This is due to some fussiness on Abigail's part during her nighttime wakings. Nadia reports that after the second night of night weaning, Abigail slept all night long and didn't wake to eat until 5:30 a.m.!

Key Takeaways

- ⊘ It is generally best to work on nights before working on naps (although not always as this is dependent on unique factors). This can help make sleep coaching much more manageable, and it also ensures that the baby doesn't become overtired.

- ⊘ While you are working on breaking nighttime associations, like the pacifier, it's okay to continue using those associations during naps. This won't cause confusion since nap sleep and night sleep are controlled by different parts of the brain.

- ⊘ Before about five or six months of age, most babies are not capable of taking long, one-hour naps. Before this point, 30 to 45 minute naps are considered adequate as long as the baby seems rested and happy.

- ⊘ Nap needs change significantly in the first year of a baby's life, and this is one of the things that makes naps so challenging. Just when you get naps down, the nap needs change, and it's time for a new nap schedule!

CASE STUDY: EIGHT-MONTH-OLD BABY STRUGGLING WITH EIGHT-MONTH SLEEP REGRESSION, BREASTFEEDING SLEEP ASSOCIATIONS, NAPPING PROBLEMS, AND MEDICAL ISSUES

This case study reflects a Baby Sleep Site® client's sleep coaching experience. This case study has been written with the client's permission. Names have been changed to protect privacy.

The Problem

When Carrie and Ben came to us for sleep help, their son Elliot was eight months old, and their son Andrew was four years old. Carrie reported that Elliot had been a decent sleeper as a newborn but that he had gradually regressed to waking up frequently at night and needed to nap either in his swing or in his infant chair. Eventually, the infant chair was no longer an option for naps after Elliot (described as a fearless little guy) was able to escape the chair's restraints! It was tough, though, because at this time, Elliot refused to lie flat in his crib and preferred to sleep upright in his swing or chair. This, no doubt, had something to do with his silent reflux (explained later).

Needless to say, after eight months of sleeplessness, Carrie was exhausted and in need of a break. She let her sleep consultant, Amy, know that she had already tried a modified cry-it-out method with Elliot but that it hadn't gone well. Rather than 'crying himself out,' Elliot's crying just intensified the longer it went on! Carrie also indicated that Elliot was diagnosed with silent reflux early on and that he had eczema. However, she indicated that both of these were under control, yet Elliot's sleep challenges continued. Therefore, Carrie knew that while these factors contributed to Elliot's sleeping challenges, they were not solely to blame.

Carrie and Ben also let Amy know that they needed a custom schedule that fit their lifestyle. Ben worked as a retail pharmacist, so he was home late many evenings. Carrie worked two days a week and was often late getting home on those nights, too. Carrie and Ben requested a schedule that allowed for later bedtimes and wake-up times to accommodate their family's work schedules. Carrie also specified that she needed a bedtime routine that was short and manageable enough that she could do it on her own during the nights when Ben worked late.

Current Schedule

- 8:30 a.m. — Elliot wakes and feeds. (Carrie reported that big brother Andrew usually went into Elliot's room at this time and found him awake.)
- 10:00 – 10:30 a.m. — Elliot has a morning nap in his swing.
- 12:00 p.m. — Elliot has lunch and nurses.
- 3:00 p.m. — Elliot attempts a nap and has a short nursing. (Carrie reported that the afternoon nap was hit or miss.)
- 5:30 p.m. – Elliot eats dinner and nurses.
- 6:00 p.m. – Elliot takes a catnap.
- 7:30/8:00 p.m. — Carrie and Ben begin the bedtime routine; Elliot has a final nursing and goes to bed.

*Elliot wakes approximately twice each night to feed and needs to be nursed back to sleep.

Parent Goals – SHORT TERM

- Less anxiety for the whole family at bedtime and nap time. (Carrie reported that she didn't want to invest two hours trying to get Elliot to take a one-hour nap or spend hours getting her boys to sleep at night.)

- ⊘ No more bedtime or nap time tears for Elliot OR Carrie!
- ⊘ Customized schedule that works with Carrie's and Ben's work schedules.

Parent Goals – LONG TERM

- ⊘ Elliot consistently sleeps through the night – all night long!
- ⊘ Elliot is put down to sleep awake and can put himself to sleep.
- ⊘ Elliot will nap consistently during the day, allowing Carrie to organize her days while ensuring that Elliot is well rested.
- ⊘ Elliot and Andrew are both asleep by 9:30 p.m. so that Carrie and Ben can enjoy some downtime together.
- ⊘ A bedtime routine that Carrie can handle on her own for when Ben works late and Carrie has to do the bedtime routine solo.

Additional Information

Carrie shared that Elliot is typically a super happy baby, but when he gets upset, watch out! She also shared that Elliot is fearless and is an on-the-move baby who is constantly crawling and trying to keep up with and emulate big brother Andrew. Carrie and Ben joke that Elliot has FOMO, the Fear Of Missing Out!

Carrie also shared that she and Ben felt they needed more downtime together to keep their marriage a priority instead of having to spend every moment in the evening helping their boys fall asleep and dealing with Elliot's night wakings.

Finally, Carrie shared that she was having some 'mom guilt' surrounding Elliot's sleeping issues and that some people around her were subtly making her feel like it was her fault that Elliot wasn't sleeping. This was (understandably) discouraging to Carrie.

The Proposed Solution

After reviewing Carrie and Ben's Family Sleep History form, Amy indicated to Carrie that it was likely that Elliot was experiencing the sleep regression that happens around eight, nine, or 10 months, which is a time when babies are becoming more mobile and are, therefore, sleeping less. Amy also suggested that Carrie and Ben may want to consider introducing a lovey to Elliot to help him self soothe at night and during nap time. Finally, Amy identified Elliot's sleep associations; she pointed out that Elliot needed to nurse to sleep and that he relied on the motion of his swing to put him to sleep for at least one of his naps.

Step 1: Work on Bedtime First

Amy indicated that the first step was to work on how Elliot fell asleep at night. She explained that Elliot needed to learn to fall asleep at bedtime without help from Carrie (in the form of nursing, rocking, holding, etc.). Amy instructed Carrie to lay Elliot down in his crib drowsy but awake at bedtime; Elliot was to be awake enough to know that he was being put into the crib so that he could learn and get used to the new bedtime process. Amy indicated that this would not be easy at first; Elliot would certainly show resistance and want to be fed to sleep. However, Amy explained that if Carrie was persistent, Elliot would eventually learn how to fall asleep without help and would, in fact, expect to be laid down awake at bedtime. Amy also pointed out that it was fine if Elliot 'played' a bit after going down awake into the crib.

Amy explained that if, at any point, Elliot began to fuss, Carrie should pat and shush him gently just enough to calm him but not enough to put him to sleep. She explained that if Elliot got too upset, it was fine to pick him up, resettle him, and then lay him back down to fall asleep. Amy indicated that while it was okay to occasionally nurse Elliot to help settle him, Carrie should try rubbing or patting him first, and if she did nurse, she should ensure that Elliot didn't fall asleep during the nursing.

Amy pointed out to Carrie that this was different than the cry-it-out sleep coaching she had tried up to this point because Carrie was to stay in the room with Elliot at bedtime as he fell asleep and then gradually move farther and farther away from his crib and towards the door as the sleep coaching progressed. Amy explained that this gentle method was a great way to 'show' Elliot what he needed to do at bedtime instead of leaving him to figure it out for himself.

Amy indicated that this was step one: teach Elliot the new bedtime routine and get him used to falling asleep without help. For this reason, Amy explained it was important that Carrie and Ben stay 100% committed to the process. However, she also pointed out that if the process felt overwhelming at any point, Carrie could take a break every 45 to 60 minutes by taking Elliot out of the crib, leaving the bedroom, and doing something else for 20 minutes or so. Upon returning to Elliot's room, Carrie would do a miniature bedtime routine and try again.

Amy explained that Carrie and Ben should continue to focus only on bedtime and getting Elliot to fall asleep on his own until the point where he was falling asleep within five to 10 minutes of being laid down at bedtime. At that point, Amy explained that Carrie and Ben could consider bedtime 'done' and move on to dealing with Elliot's night wakings.

Step 2: Work on Night Wakings

Amy explained that while Carrie and Ben were focusing on bedtime, they should continue to do what they had always done during Elliot's night wakings – nurse him to sleep.

Once the bedtime step was done, however, Amy instructed Carrie and Ben to start working on night wakings. Specifically, Amy told Carrie to start waiting about five to 10 minutes after Elliot woke up before going into his room. Amy indicated that, over time, Elliot would likely learn how to resettle himself in that amount of time after waking at night, and that would eliminate any unnecessary night wakings.

Now, in terms of nighttime feedings, Amy indicated that Carrie and Ben should plan feeding Elliot once or twice per night. She suggested that Carrie time the first night feeding for midnight or later and the second nighttime feeding at least three hours after the first (sometime between 3:00 a.m. and 5:00 a.m.). Amy indicated that if Elliot woke up before midnight, Carrie should work with him to help him fall back to sleep until midnight, and then, feed him at his next night waking. Finally, Amy also explained to Carrie that if Elliot did not wake around midnight to feed, Carrie should let him sleep until he naturally woke up on his own.

Amy instructed Carrie to lay Elliot down drowsy but awake after his night feedings, following the same rules she had been using at bedtime.

Finally, Amy explained to Carrie and Ben that the period between 4:00 a.m. and 6:00 a.m. is usually the lightest period of sleep throughout the whole night and that it often takes a different skill to go back to sleep during that window of time. She also reminded Carrie and Ben that any wakings during that window of time should be considered night wakings, not Elliot's morning wake-up time.

Day-by-Day Plan for Nights

⊘ **Mini Step #1** (ideally about 2 to 3 nights to lessen crying): Carrie worked on putting Elliot in his crib drowsy but awake. Carrie had the option to pat and comfort Elliot all the way to sleep to help him stay calm and to lessen his crying.

⊘ **Phase I:** Carrie and Ben worked on bedtime with Elliot using the strategies outlined in the bedtime section. Carrie nursed Elliot but removes the breast before he was asleep. Amy indicated that Elliot would likely protest the change in the routine and fuss and that Carrie should reassure him with her presence without necessarily trying to eliminate ALL crying. Amy also indicated that during nights one through three, Carrie should continue to do what she had been doing during any night wakings (nursing to sleep) to keep the sleep coaching manageable. Finally, Amy explained that the first three nights would likely be the toughest for Carrie and Ben.

⊘ **Phase II:** Carrie worked on the entire night so that Elliot was going back to sleep on his own after each night waking, and she ensured that Elliot was awake after each feeding so that he could practice falling asleep on his own. Amy noted that for nonfeeding night wakings, Carrie should soothe and resettle Elliot the same way she had been doing at bedtime. Amy indicated that the first few nights would be tough, but Carrie should see definite improvement by night seven.

⊘ **Phase III:** Carrie worked on getting Elliot down to one feeding (eventually, no feedings). To do this, Amy instructed Carrie to start moving the time of Elliot's night feeds back by 30 minutes per night. So instead of the first feeding happening at midnight, it would happen at 12:30 a.m., and the second feeding would happen between 3:30 and 5:30 a.m. Amy also encouraged Carrie to keep the second feeding short to discourage it. Using these two strategies, Carrie would eventually be able to eliminate the second feeding by merging it with the first morning feeding. During any nonfeeding night wakings, Carrie should soothe and re-settle Elliot but allow him to fall asleep on his own as she had been doing up to this point. Amy indicated that once Carrie was down to one night feeding at 3:00 or 4:00 a.m., she should stick with that feeding for one to two weeks to let her breast milk supply adjust. Amy also explained that at this point, Carrie should use her instincts to determine whether or not Elliot was ready to completely night wean or whether he needed the night feeding for a few more months.

Step 3: Work on Naps

Amy urged Carrie and Ben to wait until night sleep had improved before working on naps. She pointed out that night sleep didn't necessarily need to be perfect but that it should have noticeably improved prior to working on naps.

Day-by-Day Plan for Naps

⊘ **Phase I (or Weekends 1 & 2):** Using the strategies they used for bedtime and night wakings, Carrie and Ben were to put Elliot in his crib at each nap time instead of in his swing and focus on helping Elliot learn to fall asleep. Amy explained that if Elliot woke early from a nap, Carrie should redo the nap time routine and then put him back in his swing for the remainder of his nap if he seemed overtired.

⊘ **Phase II:** Carrie and Ben work on lengthening Elliot's naps by having him spend the whole nap hour in his crib. If Elliot woke up early from a nap (i.e. before the one-hour mark), Carrie and Ben were to encourage him to fall back to sleep on his own in his crib, using the strategies used at bedtime and for night wakings.

Recommended Daily Nap Schedule for Elliot

⊘ 8:00 a.m. — Elliot wakes for the day.

⊘ 11:00 a.m. — Elliot goes down for his morning nap (1-2 hours in length).

⊘ 3:00 p.m. — Elliot goes down for his afternoon nap (1-2 hours in length).

⊘ 7:30 p.m. — Carrie begins the bedtime routine.

⊘ 7:45 p.m. — Bedtime and lights out

⊘ 8:00 p.m. — The goal is for Elliot to be asleep by this time.

What Happened

Carrie and Ben were excited about and impressed with the plan right away, but while they were eager to implement it, they decided to wait a few days until Ben's work schedule allowed him to be home to help. Carrie did, however, try to work on naps right way, but she quickly discovered that it wasn't a good plan. She tried to put Elliot down without nursing for his afternoon nap, but he fussed big time and only got about 30 minutes of sleep and was completely overtired at bedtime. Carrie decided to hold off on trying anything else until she could implement the plan as written with Ben the following Wednesday.

Upon implementing the first step of the day-by-day plan, Carrie discovered right away that staying in the room with Elliot while he was trying to fall asleep at bedtime simply wouldn't work. She let Amy know that her presence was upsetting Elliot more than it was helping and that if she stayed in the room and rubbed his back, he simply screamed. Amy replied and advised that instead of sitting next to the crib, Carrie could leave the room and check back at short intervals (i.e. every 10 minutes), offering comfort for a few minutes and then leaving again. This 'check and console' approach proved to work much better.

The next time Carrie emailed Amy was six days after she had started implementing the plan at home with Elliot. She reported that they had seen HUGE improvements in night sleep in those six days. Carrie indicated that it took about an hour and a half for Elliot to finally fall asleep in his crib at bedtime the first night (and she described those 90 minutes as torturous). It took him progressively less and less time to fall asleep each night until, finally, on the night she wrote her email, Elliot was able to go down for bed at 7:45 p.m. and fall asleep completely on his own without making a peep!

She also reported that naps have improved; aside from occasionally falling asleep in the car, Elliot was falling asleep in his crib without help at each nap time. However, Carrie also indicated that the nap schedule was tough to stick to and that Elliot's nap sleep was more erratic and interrupted than his night sleep.

Amy wrote a follow-up e-mail in which she congratulated Carrie on her fantastic progress and gave her some tips on how to manage naps. Primarily, she suggested that if Elliot's afternoon nap seemed too short and if he was overtired at bedtime, Carrie could try incorporating a mini nap later in the afternoon. (But she noted that all naps should be over and done with by 5:30 p.m., so it doesn't interfere with bedtime).

Carrie's next report to Amy was great as well; she indicated that the improvements in Elliot's sleep had changed her and Ben's lives and that they no longer dreaded the evenings. She reported that Elliot was sleeping in his crib for naps and at night, was following a semi-predictable nap schedule, and crying very little (and often not at all) at night. She did tell Amy that night wakings were still happening about 35 percent of the time and asked what she could do to eliminate those night wakings. She pointed out that the timing of the night wakings was erratic. She also mentioned that while Elliot woke up from his morning nap happy, he usually woke up from his afternoon nap crying and fussy.

Amy responded by celebrating with Carrie and then offering some ideas about the night wakings. Amy indicated that the erratic timing of the night wakings was likely a sign that it was time to night wean Elliot. Amy created a night weaning game plan for Carrie. Carrie was to pick a time (Amy suggested 3:30 a.m.) and plan that if Elliot woke up before that time, she would not nurse him but would help him resettle and go back to sleep. If he woke up after that time, however, she would nurse him. Each night, she was to move the time back by 30 minutes. This would gradually increase the 'no nursing' window of time and decrease the nursing window of time until Elliot was finally night weaned.

Regarding the fussy afternoon nap wakings, Amy pointed out that Elliot was getting the two to three recommended hours of nap sleep, so the fussiness likely wasn't a sign that he needed more sleep. Amy suggested that Carrie wait five to 10 minutes after Elliot woke up before going into his room to get him up from the afternoon nap. She explained that this would provide time for Elliot to either fall back asleep (if he did need more sleep) or to wake up to the point where he was less fussy.

The Result

With Amy's help, Carrie and Ben have been able to radically change Elliot's sleeping habits. Elliot went from waking several times each night and needing to be nursed back to sleep to waking just once per night for a feeding (and being able to fall back to sleep on his own in his crib without help)! Elliot went from having to nap in his swing in the morning and from having a hit-or-miss second nap to taking two reasonably long naps in his crib and falling asleep at nap time on his own without any help from Carrie or Ben. According to Carrie, she and Ben have their sanity back!

Key Takeaways

- ⊘ It is generally best to work on nights before working on naps (although not always as this is dependent on unique factors). This can help make sleep coaching much more manageable, and it also ensures that the baby doesn't become overtired.

- ⊘ While you are working on breaking nighttime associations, like the nursing to sleep, it's okay to continue using those associations during naps. This, generally, does not cause confusion since nap sleep and night sleep are controlled by different parts of the brain.

- ⊘ When a baby is down to one night feeding, if the timing of that night feeding is erratic AND IF that baby is older than six or seven months old, it may be a sign that it is time to night wean.

CASE STUDY: SHIFTING CHILD'S SCHEDULE (EIGHT-MONTH-OLD WAKING TOO EARLY)

This case study reflects a Baby Sleep Site® client's sleep coaching experience. This case study has been written with the client's permission. Names have been changed to protect privacy.

The Problem

Heather won a free consultation in a Baby Sleep Site® Mother's Day giveaway. At that time, her eight-month-old son, Brian, had many sleeping problems, including naps that were too short (none longer than 30 minutes) and several more night wakings than usual for a baby his age. With advice about how to tweak their schedule and respond to Brian's intense personality, Heather and her husband were able to work on their baby's sleep so that many of their problems improved significantly. After a couple of months, the remaining problem was that Brian woke up too early at 5:00 a.m. The sleep-training books Heather consulted had suggested that she should just leave Brian in his crib until 6:00 a.m., and he would eventually learn to sleep until that time. She tried it for over a month, and his wake-up time stayed exactly the same except that Brian cried many tears as he waited until 6:00 a.m., which was horrible for Heather and her husband to endure. Heather was unwilling to continue leaving her baby in his crib to cry, but she also desperately wanted him to sleep past 5:00 a.m. She was balancing being a new parent, a graduate student, and a college instructor, and every moment of sleep was precious to her. She turned to The Baby Sleep Site® for help.

Current Schedule

- ⊘ 5:00 a.m. – Wake
- ⊘ 8:00 a.m. – Nap (falls asleep by 8:15 a.m.)

- ⊘ 1:00 p.m. – Nap (falls asleep by 1:15 p.m.)
- ⊘ 6:00 p.m. - Bedtime

Parent Goals

- ⊘ Have Brian wake later than 5:00 a.m.!

The Proposed Solution

Nicole, Heather's sleep consultant, informed Heather that, in a sense, Brian's sleeping problem wasn't a problem at all. Some babies sleep 12 hours each night, but others sleep 11 (and the minimum is 10). Since Brian was going to sleep at 6:00 p.m. and waking up alert and happy at 5:00 a.m. (and not able to fall back asleep even when left in his crib), Nicole determined he was getting enough sleep. To help him sleep later, though, she devised a plan to shift his entire schedule forward.

Here was the big-picture plan that they would tweak along the way:

- ⊘ Day 1: 5:00 a.m. - Wake, 8:15 a.m. - Nap, 1:15 p.m. - Nap, 6:00 p.m. - Bed
- ⊘ Day 2: Repeat Day 1
- ⊘ Day 3: 5:00 a.m. - Wake, 8:30 a.m. - Nap, 1:30 p.m. - Nap, 6:15 p.m. - Bed
- ⊘ Day 4: Repeat Day 3
- ⊘ Day 5: 5:15 a.m. - Wake, 8:45 a.m. - Nap, 1:45 p.m. - Nap, 6:15 p.m. - Bed
- ⊘ Day 6: Repeat Day 5
- ⊘ Day 7: 5:15 a.m. - Wake, 9:00 a.m. - Nap, 2:00 p.m. - Nap, 6:30 p.m. - Bed
- ⊘ Day 8: 5:30 a.m. - Wake, 9:15 a.m. - Nap, 2:15 p.m. - Nap, 6:30 p.m. - Bed

- ⊘ Day 9: Repeat day 8
- ⊘ Day 10: 5:30 a.m. - Wake, 9:30 a.m. - Nap, 2:30 p.m. - Nap, 6:45 p.m. - Bed
- ⊘ Day 11: 5:30 a.m. - Wake, 9:45 a.m. - Nap, 2:45 p.m. - Nap, 6:45 p.m. - Bed
- ⊘ Day 12: 5:45 a.m. - Wake, 10:00 a.m. - Nap, 3:00 p.m. - Nap, 7:00 p.m. - Bed
- ⊘ Day 13: 6:00 a.m. - Wake, 10:00 a.m. - Nap, 3:00 p.m. - Nap, 7:00 p.m. - Bed

Nicole indicated that the key to making this kind of change is to do it slowly and incrementally. And for it to work, the entire schedule has to be shifted forward, not just the bedtime. So after learning from Heather what time Brian's naps were and how he handled being overtired, Nicole created a schedule that shifted his naps and bedtime forward in 15-minute increments over a two-week period. The plan was to change his schedule so that he went to bed at 7:00 p.m. instead of 6:00 p.m. and woke up for the day at 6:00 a.m. instead of 5:00 a.m. Because Heather reported that Brian was usually very cranky by the time he reached his 6:00 p.m. bedtime and because their current naps were on the early side, Nicole decided to have them shift the naps forward by two hours rather than one hour, so Brian would be less overtired by the time he reached bedtime.

Nicole also gave Heather several pieces of advice. She warned Heather that there may be cranky days, and that one particularly sensitive baby she had worked with never made the switch even after working on a schedule change for a month. She also indicated that it was important not to let Brian make up lost sleep during the day; since his naps had been exactly one hour before working on the switch, she was to wake him up if he ever slept beyond that point. Heather planned to check in every day or two to update Nicole so that they could tweak the schedule as they went, depending on how Brian responded to it.

What Happened

The first day went well with Brian managing to stay awake until the later times. He was only noticeably crankier during the 15 minutes when Heather and her husband tried keep him up until his new, later nap times. After the first day, he also slept in until 5:15 a.m., which seemed like a good sign.

Soon after, though, there were signs that Brian was getting overtired as his nap and bed times started to become later, but he continued to wake up at his normal 5:00 a.m. time. By the second day, his naps had shrunk down to 35 to 45 minutes. Nicole encouraged Heather that this was normal and expected and that she should continue to hang in there. On the fourth day, Heather had to wake Brian up from his nap because he went past an hour, an action that she said felt "tragic" to her considering how hard they had worked as a family to get Brian to take any nap longer than 30 minutes. She knew it was for a good cause, though.

The first sign of real progress occurred on the fifth day. Heather ecstatically wrote Nicole to tell her that Brian had slept until the unprecedented time of 5:38 a.m. Things seemed to be on a good track in spite of the fact that Brian was having an increasingly hard time making it to his later and later nap times.

That night, however, was difficult. Brian woke up at a time that he didn't traditionally nurse, and instead of crying for a little while and putting himself back to sleep (which was what he usually did if he woke up around that time), he alternated between crying hard and fussing for quite some time. Heather checked on him to make sure he was okay, and he was fine; it seemed to her that he was just awake and didn't know how to fall back asleep. Because she didn't want him to lose too much sleep in the night (he'd been up by that time almost an hour), she finally nursed him to help him fall back asleep. Then, he woke up for the day at 4:45 a.m.

Seeing this behavior as a sign that Brian was extremely over-tired, Nicole suggested that Heather take a breather for a day or two. She still encouraged her not to go backwards, though, in terms of the schedule; she recommended following the previous day's schedule instead of pushing him forward any more that day. She also suggested letting Brian sleep an hour and fifteen minutes if he chose to for his naps rather than waking him up after an hour.

He was cranky that day, but Heather was nearly able to keep to the previous day's schedule. The next day, she reported that Brian slept in until 5:43 a.m. (each minute counts). She even noticed that Brian woke up at 5:00 a.m. and then put himself back to sleep, which is something she called "miraculous."

The family moved forward without incident for another couple of days with Brian generally doing well with the time changes but just getting cranky about 15 minutes before his designated nap times. Then, they experienced another rough night. Brian woke up at 4:15 a.m., thinking he was up for the day, and he was unable to put himself back to sleep. Heather finally went to him after he cried for an hour. Again, the family stuck to the previous day's schedule, and Nicole encouraged Heather to try to let Brian stay in his crib until as close to 6:00 a.m. as possible if he woke up early again.

That day, which was the ninth day of the project, was the worst day that the family experienced since they had started the sched-ule shift. After waking up way too early, Brian took two very short naps that day (30 minutes and 15 minutes). Since he was so overtired, Brian was unsurprisingly very irritable, and Heather was discouraged that Brian's internal clock hadn't yet made the switch. Nicole encouraged her to, again, stick to the previous day's times and to persevere as things would improve after Brian made it past this hump.

The next day was better than expected in terms of naps, and while Brian still woke up as though he was up for the day at 5:00 a.m., he did finally fall back asleep again at 5:45 a.m. for about 15 minutes. Nicole asserted that this was progress, especially because Brian traditionally would not fall back asleep once he thought he was awake for the day. She was right! In an e-mail full of exclamation marks, Heather reported the next morning that Brian's naps the previous day were each an hour long, and that morning, he had slept in until 5:46 a.m. Heather reported that he was also "so happy and full of the dickens" that morning. From Nicole's perspective, he had made it over the hump, and she celebrated by sending Heather an e-mail containing an excited "Woohoo!"

After about two weeks, Brian was sleeping in most days until about 5:30 a.m., was much less overtired at bedtime, and was taking two solid one-hour naps. Heather was happy to say the least. But then he did something that was truly extraordinary; he slept through the night for the first time in his little life. Heather was truly thrilled.

Nicole's summer vacation coincided with the family hitting the two-week mark, so they planned to connect again a week later. On the same day, Heather and her family also went to a weekend family reunion. Traveling had upset Brian's schedule in the past, and in this case, it was no exception. While they were gone, he woke up in the morning at times between 4:45 and 5:20 a.m., and since they were staying with other family members, Heather and her husband didn't feel comfortable leaving him in his crib to likely disrupt the sleep of others. So when they returned home, Brian was off track, waking up each day between 5:00 and 5:30 a.m.

By the time Nicole returned from vacation, things had gotten better. Brian was sleeping in until closer to 6:00 a.m., but Heather was nervous. The family was leaving in several days for a trip to Canada, which would involve a time zone switch and nine days away from home. Since Brian's nighttime sleep had been disrupted by just a weekend away, they didn't know what the trip would hold.

The Result

After the trip, Heather was enthusiastically able to say that the shift had been successful. Brian adjusted to the time difference in Canada right away, and he slept beautifully at night. (Only one day did he wake up about 30 minutes too early.) He did start to get overtired as the week wore on, and some of his naps became too short. All things considered, Heather thought he had been a wonderful trooper. In fact, on the trip, Heather and her family shared a cabin with another family whose baby was just a month older, and Brian slept better on the trip than the other baby. This fact just reinforced for Heather how far they had come. She wrote, "I felt, for the first time, that I had a 'normal' baby in terms of sleep. I can't believe how much better my quality of life is, and I know it's due to your help."

Now that several weeks have passed since that trip, the new schedule has had time to solidify. Brian's nap times have inched backward by about half an hour, which Nicole indicated might happen. (He now has three and a half to four hours of wakefulness between each sleeping time and is not overtired at bedtime, so these new times seem to fit him well.) He also continues to sleep through the night, which is an added bonus!

Key Takeaways

- Shift schedules in small increments; it can take up to two weeks, depending on how far forward you are going.

- Shift the entire schedule, including naps and meals, if necessary, not just bedtime.

- Do not let your child make up his or her sleep in the daytime as he or she will shift sleep from day to night and vice versa.

- If your child starts getting too cranky, take a breather, but try not to go backwards. Keep moving forward. We expect your child to get overtired, but it is temporary.

- Sometimes, less time between nap and bedtime can help avoid overtiredness at bedtime, resulting in better sleep even though it's the same amount in 24 hours.

CASE STUDY: TRANSITIONING FROM CO-SLEEPING (17-MONTH-OLD TODDLER)

This case study reflects a Baby Sleep Site® client's sleep coaching experience. This case study has been written with the client's permission. Names have been changed to protect privacy.

The Problem

Samantha and Susan came to The Baby Sleep Site® for help when their daughter, Julie, was 17 months old. Even though Julie was well into toddlerhood, she was still waking several times each night and was sharing a bed with one of her parents all night long. Samantha and Susan were understandably exhausted and wanted to help Julie learn to fall asleep on her own in her own crib and sleep through the night.

Samantha let Nicole, her consultant, know that she and Susan had, in fact, tried what she called "Ferberish" sleep coaching (a sort of check-and-console approach she had come up with) twice before with Julie, but the crying just made it too hard to stay consistent. Samantha reported that each time, they seemed to make progress at first, but then, Julie would cry and grow increasingly upset; at that point, Samantha and Susan stopped the sleep coaching.

Samantha and Susan let Nicole know that while they had grown more comfortable with some tears and crying from Julie as she had gotten older, they wanted to aim for minimal-crying methods. They also pointed out that they suspected Julie was going to be unhappy about the changes that sleep coaching would bring, and they were anxious about that.

Current Schedule

Samantha and Susan work full-time outside the home, so Julie is in childcare from 8:00 a.m. to 5:00 p.m. where she takes one nap each day.

Her evening schedule looks like this:

- ⊘ 6:00 p.m. – Dinner
- ⊘ 6:30 p.m. – Books, a bit of time spent watching an educational video, brush teeth, bath, and pajamas
- ⊘ 7:00 p.m. – Nursing and rocking in rocking chair
- ⊘ 7:30 p.m. – Asleep

Parent Goals
- ⊘ Julie will learn to fall asleep on her own.
- ⊘ Julie will sleep in longer stretches and, eventually, sleep through the night.
- ⊘ Julie will transition to her crib.
- ⊘ Julie will wake later in the morning.

Additional Information

Samantha shared that Julie is vivacious and outgoing but is also strong willed and had recently begun having strong opinions (totally age appropriate, of course) and reacts strongly when she doesn't get her way.

The Proposed Solution

After reviewing Samantha and Susan's written sleep history, Nicole indicated that it was likely that Julie was experiencing the sleep regression that happens around 18 months, which is a time when toddlers are going through renewed separation anxiety and are also becoming more persistent and independent, all of which can combine to ruin sleep. Nicole also suggested that even though Samantha and Susan had tried introducing a lovey to Julie before without success, they should try again as part of a renewed effort to help Julie self soothe. Finally, Nicole identified Julie's sleep associations; she pointed out that Julie likely had a sleep association with nursing and that the pacifier that Julie sometimes used may have been causing more problems than Samantha and Susan realized.

Step 1: Work On Bedtime First

The first step was to work on how Julie fell asleep at night. Nicole explained that Julie needed to learn to fall asleep at bedtime without help from Samantha or Susan (in the form of nursing, rocking, holding, etc.). She instructed Samantha and Susan to lay Julie down in the shared bed drowsy but awake at bedtime. Julie was to be awake enough to know that she was being put in bed so that she could learn and get used to the new bedtime process. The key at this point was to teach Julie to fall asleep independently without help in the shared bed first; once that was set, they would work on transitioning Julie out of the shared bed and into her own crib.

Nicole explained that if, at any point, Julie began to fuss, Samantha and/or Susan should pat and shush her gently just enough to calm her but not enough to put her to sleep. She explained that if Julie got too upset, it was fine to pick her up, resettle her, and then lay her back down to fall asleep. Nicole indicated that while it was okay to occasionally nurse Julie to help her settle, Samantha and Susan should try rubbing or patting her first, and if she did nurse, they should ensure that Julie didn't fall asleep during the nursing.

Nicole pointed out to Samantha that this was different than the Ferberish sleep coaching she had tried up to this point because Samantha and Susan were to stay in the room with Julie at bedtime as she fell asleep and then gradually work up to the point where they were able to leave the room before Julie fell asleep.

Finally, Nicole indicated that Samantha and Susan could work on bedtime while still co-sleeping at first to make the process go more smoothly for everyone. Eventually, however, once Julie had learned how to fall asleep independently in the shared bed, the goal would be for Julie to start falling asleep independently at bedtime in her own crib.

Step 2: Work on Night Wakings

Nicole explained that while Samantha and Susan were focusing on bedtime, they should continue to do what they had always done during Julie's night wakings – offer her a pacifier, cuddle her, nurse, etc.

Once the bedtime step was done, however, Nicole instructed Samantha and Susan to start working on night wakings. Specifically, she told Samantha and Susan to start waiting about five to 10 minutes after Julie woke up before offering the breast or pacifier, even while bed sharing. Nicole indicated that, over time, Julie would likely learn how to resettle herself in that amount of time after waking at night, and that would eliminate any unnecessary night wakings.

Finally, Nicole explained to Samantha and Susan that the period between 4:00 a.m. and 6:00 a.m. is usually the lightest period of sleep throughout the whole night and that it often takes a different skill to go back to sleep during that window of time. She also reminded them that any wakings during that window of time should be considered night wakings, not Julie's morning wake-up time. Since one of our goals was to help Julie sleep a bit later each morning, it was crucial that they didn't treat any wakings during this time as Julie's "up for the day" time.

Day-by-Day Plan for Nights

⊘ **Mini Step #1** (about 2 to 3 nights): Samantha and Susan teach Julie to fall asleep in their arms without nursing or rocking to sleep for two to three days, and then, move on to the next step.

⊘ **Phase I:** Next, Samantha and Susan work on bedtime with Julie using the strategy above in the shared bed. They could nurse her, but Nicole urged them to remove the breast before Julie was asleep. This way, she wouldn't fall asleep while nursing (which would inadvertently reinforce the nurse-to-sleep association).

⊘ **Phase II:** Samantha and Susan work on the entire night – night wakings and all – in the shared bed. For night wakings, Samantha and Susan resettle Julie the same way they did at bedtime. Nicole did note that a child who is in bed with parents or even in the same room may wake much more frequently, so if this stage was just too difficult, Samantha and Susan should move on to the next phase even if this one is not going well.

⊘ **Phase III** (or when ready): Samantha and Susan work on bedtime in Julie's crib using the same methods. Nicole explained that the goal was for Julie to associate her own crib as hers; otherwise, Samantha and Susan's bed would become her bed, and then asking her to sleep in her crib would be the equivalent of asking her to sleep in a hotel. She also let Samantha and Susan know that they could pat or rub her back ALL the way to sleep in this step to help Julie stay calm and solely focus on having her get used to the crib. Samantha and Susan were to do this for two to three more days and then work on the steps below, focusing on putting Julie down drowsy but awake in the crib. Upon night waking, Samantha and Susan could bring Julie back into their bed and follow 'Phase II' if needed.

⊘ Phase IV: Samantha and Susan work on the entire night in her crib. Nicole warned Samantha and Susan that these may be some long nights at first, but if they could get through three nights, things would be MUCH better by the fourth. She also let Samantha and Susan know that they could lie down on an air mattress or a cushion next to the crib, as Julie fell asleep. This sometimes eases the transition and keeps it more manageable.

Recommended Daily Nap Schedule for Julie

⊘ 6:30 - 7:00 a.m. — Julie wakes for the day.

⊘ 11:30 a.m. – 2:30 p.m. — Julie goes down for her nap at daycare; nap is ideally two to three hours long.

⊘ 6:00 - 6:30 p.m. — Samantha and Susan begin the bedtime routine.

⊘ 6:15 - 6:45 p.m. — Bedtime and lights out

⊘ 6:30 - 7:00 p.m. — The goal is for Julie to be asleep by this time.

What Happened

Right from the start, Samantha and Susan reported that bedtime went great! There was very little crying on Julie's part, which Samantha and Susan were thrilled about. But night wakings were tough at first; after starting sleep coaching, Julie actually started waking MORE often at night (from one to two times to three to four times). For the most part, Samantha and Susan were able to comfort Julie without putting her back to sleep. They worked with her on putting the pacifier in her hand, and then, she would put it into her own mouth. Samantha and Susan expressed concerns about the increased night wakings and asked Nicole for guidance.

Nicole explained that sometimes night wakings do increase as a result of the changes to the "norm." She also pointed out that Samantha and Susan may want to get rid of Julie's pacifier as it may have been causing her to wake more frequently.

Samantha and Susan continued to work and, eventually, made the transition to putting Julie to bed in her own crib, and they let Nicole know that it went GREAT! Samantha and Susan did spend a few nights in her room sleeping on couch cushions; at first, when Julie woke up at night, Samantha or Susan would reach through the crib bars and hold her hand to reassure her. They reported that Julie did stand up and cry for a bit, but within a few minutes, she would calm down, lie down, and go back to sleep.

And here was their most exciting news: Samantha and Susan reported that within three or four days of transitioning Julie to her crib, she began sleeping through the night! This was obviously huge progress as she had been waking several times per night up to that point.

Key Takeaways

⊘ If you're transitioning away from co-sleeping AND if your little one has sleep associations that you want to work on, it's usually best to focus on overcoming the sleep associations first while your child is still sleeping in bed with you. Then, once your little one has made progress in learning to fall asleep alone, you can begin putting your baby or toddler to bed in a separate sleep space (crib or bed) at bedtime and work on the transition that way.

⊘ The intermediate step of working on night wakings while still sharing a bed ('Phase II') CAN work for some families, but other times, it ends up being an exercise in frustration. Since a child tends to wake more frequently when near the parents, this can become a real Catch-22 in that you're trying to minimize night wakings while sleeping in an arrangement that tends to increase them!

⊘ The pace is ultimately up to you. You can speed up or slow down based on how it's going and how your baby or toddler is responding. This is not a race after all, and if you feel like you are starting to stall, move on to the next phase.

Made in the
USA
Columbia, SC